COMPANY LAW

MADHU TYAGI
ARUN KUMAR

Published by
ATLANTIC PUBLISHERS AND DISTRIBUTORS
B-2, Vishal Enclave, Opp. Rajouri Garden, New Delhi-110027
Phones : 25413460, 25429987, 25466842

Sales Office
7/22, Ansari Road, Darya Ganj, New Delhi-110002
Phones : 23273880, 23285873, 23280451
Fax : 91-11-23285873
web : www.atlanticbooks.com
e-mail : info@atlanticbooks.com

Typeset at
APD Computer Graphics, Delhi
Printed in India at
Nice Printing Press, Delhi

Preface

A statute is a law established by the act of legislative power—an Act of the legislature. Statutes may be codifying, declaratory, remedial, amending, consolidating and penal. Company law, a branch of Civil Law, is both consolidating and amending. The law should be according to time and place. The Act has been amended many times since its passage. A complete new Comprehensive Bill relating to companies is pending before the Parliament.

The provisions of the Companies Act, 1956 relate to both principles of law and procedures to be followed by companies including the format of important documents and forms.

The book is primarily based on the Companies Act, 1956. The language is simple and lucid and many examples have been given in each topic. The book is intended for B.Com., M.Com., LL.B., M.B.A., C.S. and C.A. students. Questions drawn from different examinations papers have been given at the end of each Chapter. All the amendments made upto the year 2002 have been incorporated in the book. Main provisions of the pending Companies Bill before the Parliament have also been given.

The publishers, M/s Atlantic Publishers and Distributors, deserve the credit and thanks for publishing the book in an attractive style.

Suggestions, if any, for the improvement of the book in the next edition are cordially invited from the readers.

MADHU TYAGI
ARUN KUMAR

CONTENTS

1

History of Company Legislation

HISTORY OF ENGLISH COMPANY LAW

Classification of Period

1. From middle ages (1000 A.D.) till the passing of the Bubbles Act in 1720.

2. From 1720 to 1825 the repeal of the Bubbles Act.

3. From 1825 till to date.

1. From Middle Ages until the Passing of the Bubbles Act in 1720. In medieval days two types of partnerships were recognised in England known as merchant guilds and were of two types : (i) Commanda and (ii) Societas. In the former, a financier used to provide a trade with money in return for a share in the profits of business. The liability of the financier remained limited to the extent of money lent. In the latter, the liability of all partners was unlimited.

Regulated Companies

Though the formation of companies by Royal Charter started in the 14th century, but incorporation of Companies could become popular in 16th century. Royal Charters were granted with a view to acquire monopoly or trade. East India Company was one of such regulated companies established by a Charter in 1600. These Companies were known as Regulated Companies. Each member traded with his own stock and on his own account subject to obeying the rules of the Company. The liability of each member was distinct from that of the Company and the other members. Members started to operate on a joint account with a joint stock. The Companies came to be known as joint stock Companies.

Formation of Companies

Until the end of 16th century, most of the companies were formed as partnerships, by agreements under seal. It was provided for the division of the undertaking into shares which were transferable by the original partners. The liability of members was unlimited. Perceptivity, legal entity, common seal, majority rule and transferability of shares were secured for the partnership.

Powerful monopolistic domestic companies came into existence in England in the middle of 17th century. By the end of 17th century, Companies had started inviting public to subscribe to their share capital. Share dealings had become common. Two types of companies were popular in those days (i) Regulated and (ii) Joint Stock.

2. From 1720 to 1825 : Passing of the Bubbles Act in 1720. First 20 years of the 18th century in England noticed boom in the floatation of companies leading to the South Sea Bubble. Some of these companies either did not care to obtain charters or carried on business under obsolete charters. A company known as South Sea Company decided to acquire practically the whole of the National Debt by buying out the holders or exchanging their holdings for the company's stock, believing that the possession of an interest bearing loan owned by the State would be a good security for raising large amounts of money from the public to expand its trade. Sanctioning of the South Sea Company's Scheme by the Government led to the gambling mania, speculative promotions and rash speculation in security prices. In 1719, Bubble Act, was passed to regulate the working of the companies. It prohibited the formation of joint stock companies except by Royal Charter or an Act of Parliament. It proved inadequate and ineffective because of its vagueness. Companies formed before 24th June 1718 were left out and exempted from the provisions of the Act.

A large number of companies failed. The public confidence was completely shattered. This retarded the growth and development of incorporated companies. A large number of companies could not survive to obtain charters due to the difficulties in the incorporation of the company, only a few regulated chartered companies and some unincorporated companies could survive.

The Bubble Act became a dead letter after 1750. It was difficult for unincorporated companies to sue or be sued. The ownership of the companies was frequently changing. The partners of such unincorporated bodies suffered from the risk of unlimited liability. The personal liability of the members was largely illusory. There was no check on the activities of dishonest promoters.

Repeal of the Bubble Act, 1825

At the beginning of the 19th century the pressing needs of war and the growth of railways led to an outbreak of company promotions and a large scale speculation in security prices. In 1825 the Bubble Act was repealed by the Government. The Board of Trade was made responsible for guiding the development of company legislation in England.

3. From 1825 till Today : Passing of the First Companies Act, 1844. The Trading Companies Act 1834 was passed to confer to letters of patent for some Trading privileges of incorporation except limited liability to the companies without actually granting them a Charter. The Chartered Companies Act of 1837 provided for limited liability of the members to a specified amount per share by an express provision in the letters of patent. In 1844 the first Joint Stock Companies Act of England was passed. It provided for incorporation of the business associations by registration. Most of the associations took the form of partnerships, unincorporated joint stock companies and companies incorporated by statute or Royal Charter.

Lord Gladstone is called the father of Company Law. The first Companies Act was passed in 1844 because of his efforts. New Companies with more than 25 members were required to get registered. This Act prohibited the formation of large unregistered companies. The liabilities of members remained unlimited.

Companies Clauses Consolidation Act, 1847

It gave legal status to companies and cheapened and shortened the statutory recognition of companies. The freedom from personal liability was still denied to the members of the company. It was made clear that the bankruptcy of the company did not necessarily mean the bankruptcy of its members.

The following three types of business Organisation came to exist after passing the first Companies Act :

(i) Unincorporated private partnerships of not more than 25 persons with unlimited liability.

(ii) Chartered and statutory companies with limited liability or no liability and

(iii) Registered companies with unlimited liability.

In 1855, limited liability was granted to certain companies which satisfied certain conditions. A new and more comprehensive Joint Stock Companies Act was passed in 1856 with 116 sections. It replaced Deed of Settlement by Memorandum of Association and Articles of Association. It also provided for greater control on the working of the companies. In 1857, it was also made applicable to Insurance Companies. It was replaced by New Companies Act of 1862 which contained 212 sections and introduced guarantee companies for the first time.

Limited Partnership Act, 1907

From time to time the Companies Act had been reviewed. After the World War II, some important trends were noticed in the history of growth of the company legislation. The control of shareholders in the management has been declining while the state control over company affairs has been increasing. Mergers have been frequent. This has been responsible for the increasing concentration of economic power. In 1908, the whole existing law was consolidated and after amending statutes in 1929 and 1948, the Companies Act of these years repealed the existing law. The Companies Act 1948 was amended by Companies Acts of 1967, 1976, 1980, 1981 and 1983. In 1985, the Companies Act 1985 was passed which consolidated the then existing law relating to

Companies. Companies Act 1989 has made some amendments relating to pre-incorporation contracts, doctrine of ultravires, buy-back of shares and position of directors.

HISTORY OF THE INDIAN COMPANIES ACT

The Companies Act contains laws relating to companies in India. It provides the guidelines for the management, administration and control of companies in India. Companies Act in India has been based upon companies Act of Great Britain. It has been drafted so as to accommodate the Indian circumstances and the socio-capitalist pattern of Indian economy to the best possible extent.

Indian Companies Act has passed through various stages of developments and amendments. These may be enumerated as follows :

1. Joint Stock Companies Act, 1850. In 1844, a Joint Stock Companies Act was passed. It was the first Companies Act of the world. On its basis a Joint Stock Companies Act was passed in India in 1850, the first Companies Act of this country. Its main provisions were as under :

(i) It provided for the registration of companies.

(ii) High Courts of Bombay, Calcutta and Madras were empowered to register the companies.

(iii) Shareholders were allowed to transfer their shares.

(iv) The liability of the shareholders of the companies registered under this Act was unlimited.

2. Joint Stock Companies Act, 1857. In 1857, the Joint Stock Companies Act, 1850 was replaced by passing a new Act, Joint Stock Companies Act, 1857. It has a very important place in the history of Indian Companies Act. It provided for the first time for the limited liability of the shareholders. Banking Companies and Insurance Companies were not allowed to be registered under the provision of limited liability. These could be registered only under the provision of unlimited liability of shareholders. For all other types of companies, the liability of shareholders was limited to the value of shares purchased by them.

3. Joint Stock Companies Act, 1860. After three years, in 1860, Joint Stock Companies Act, 1857 was replaced by this Act, based upon the British Companies Act, 1856. It allowed Banking Companies and Insurance Companies also to be registered with the provision of limited liability. Thus after this Act all the companies were allowed to be registered with the provision of limited liability.

4. Joint Stock Companies Act, 1866. It was based upon the British Companies Act, 1862. It incorporated all the rules and regulations of all the previous Companies Acts.

5. Joint Stock Companies Act, 1882. It was based upon the British Companies Act, 1880. It enlarged the Companies Act, 1866. Later on following three other Acts were also passed so that the drawbacks of this Act may be removed :

(i) Companies Memorandum of Association Act, 1895.

(ii) Companies Branch Register Act, 1900 and

(iii) Companies Amendments Act, 1910.

6. Indian Companies Act, 1913. Based upon the British Companies Act, 1908, this Act remained in force for 43 years *i.e.* from 1913 to 1956. However, some amendments were passed to this Act in 1936, 1937, 1939, 1940, 1941, 1942, 1943, 1944, 1945, 1946 and 1951.

COMPANIES ACT, 1956

Based upon H.C. Bhaba Committee recommendations, Companies Act, 1956 was passed. It came into force since 1st April 1956. It is one the largest Act of the country. It contains 658 sections and 12 schedules. 13 schedules have also been added to it after the Amendment Act, 1974. It is based upon the British Companies Act, 1948.

Salient Features

This Act has the following salient features :

1. It provides broad coverage of rules regarding the promotion and incorporation of companies.
2. It provides broad outlines to the appointment, remuneration, rights, duties and liabilities of Directors, Managing Directors, Managing Agents and Auditors etc.
3. It provides detailed rules regarding the maintenance of books of accounts, their publication and audit.
4. It provides detailed extensive rules for the control of mismanagement of companies.
5. It provides broad outlines to protect the interests of shareholders.
6. It empowers the Central Government to intervene into the affairs of any company.

Important Amendments

In order to accommodate the changing trends of the times in trade, commerce and social values the following amendments have been passed to the present Companies Act :

1. The Companies (Amendment) Act, 1960. Passed in 1960, this amendment, based on Sastri Committee, imposes some restrictions upon the management and managerial remuneration of private companies. It widely amended 218 Sections.

2. The Companies (Amendment) Act, 1962. Passed only after two years of the first amendment, this amendment relates to the contributions by the companies to political parties and National Defence Fund.

3. The Companies (Amendment) Act, 1963. Passed in 1963, only one year after the last amendment, this amendment is very important. A 'Company Tribunal' and a 'Company Law Board' were established. Various powers were decentralised from the Central Government to the Company Law Board in order to have a more practical and effective control. It provides for the control on the excess capital issue and mismanagement of companies.

4. The Companies (Amendment) Act, 1964. It provided temporary protection to employees during investigations by an inspector pendency of proceedings before the Court, in certain cases under sec. 635B.

5. The Companies (Amendment) Act, 1965. This amendment checks some *malafide* practices going on in the administration of the companies and provides the rules for the proper management of the funds of companies.

6. The Companies (Amendment) Act, 1966. It deals with the sanction of loan to companies under one and the same management and contains some amendments to the provisions of transfer of shares. The Companies (Second Amendment) Act, 1966 amended section 108 so as to exempt production of a proper instrument of transfer where share are deposited by way of security for payment of loans and advances or performance of any obligation.

7. The Companies Tribunal (Abolition) Act, 1967. By this amendment, the Companies Tribunal, set up by the third amendment in 1963 was abolished. However, Company Law Board continued.

8. The Companies (Amendment) Act, 1969. Passed in 1969, it restricted the donations to political parties and the appointment of managing agent, secretary and treasurer. Since 3rd April, 1970, no company can appoint any of these personnels.

9. The Companies (Amendment) Act, 1971. It entitled the Board of Directors of companies to donate upto Rs. 25,000 or upto 5% of Profits in National Defence Fund and any other recognised fund. If donation exceeds this limit, it was to be passed by the general meeting of the company.

10. The Companies (Amendment) Act, 1972. It empowered Central Government to nominate directors upto any number if it is of the view that there is mismanagement in the affairs of company.

11. The Companies (Amendment) Act, 1974. This most important amendment ever passed in the history of Indian Companies Act came into force since Ist February 1975. Its main provisions are as under :

(i) Section 2(18)A. The word Group has been re-defined and individual organisations, partnership firms and incorporated institutes have been included in 'Group'.

(ii) Section 4(A). Specialised Financial Institutions have been assumed as the Public Financial Institutions.

(iii) Section 10(E). Number of members of Company Law Board has been increased from 5 to 9.

(iv) Section 17, 18 and 19. Company Law Board has been empowered to approve the alterations in the Object Clause and Registered Office Clause of the Memorandum of Association. Previously, this right was exercised by the Central Government.

(v) Section 43(A). If the average turnover of a Private Limited Company exceeds Rs. one crore in a year, it will be treated as Public Limited Company.

(vi) Company Law Board has been empowered to allow the issue of share by a company at discount. Rules regarding the allotment of the shares and debentures, being listed in a recognised stock exchange, of such companies have been amended.

(vii) Section 108(A) to 108(H). Some new rules have been introduced regarding the transfer of shares.

(viii) Section 141. Company Law Board has been empowered to allow the changes in the register of charges. Company Law Board has also been empowered to allow the extension of time for such changes as per requirement.

(ix) Section 180. Company Law Board, has now been empowered to call any other meeting of the company, other than the Annual General Meeting.

(x) Section 204(A). Former managing agents, secretaries and treasurers cannot be appointed in the company at any designation for a period exceeding 5 years.

(xi) Section 205. Any company can declare the dividend only when the sufficient amount has been transferred to the Reserve Account of the company.

(xii) Section 205(A). Any dividend, not distributed within 42 days from the date of its declaration, will have to be transferred to the Specific Reserve Account.

(xiii) Section 205(B). Shareholders entitled to get the dividend can present their demand of the payment of dividend before the Central Government of India.

(xiv) Section 209(A). Registrars and Inspectors, appointed by the Central Government of India for company, will have the rights equivalent to Income Tax Officers.

(xv) Section 217. The company will have to produce the list of all its employees getting Rs. 36,000 per annum or more.

(xvi) Section 224. A person cannot be appointed the auditor for more than 20 companies at one time and the auditor will have to inform the Registrar of Companies within 7 days of his re-appointment in the company.

(xvii) Section 224(A). An Auditor for the companies whose 15% paid up capital is with the Public Financial Institutions, will have to be appointed by a special resolution.

(xviii) Section 233(B). Audit of Cost Accounts of the companies will be done only by Cost Accountants who are qualified for this according to Cost and Works Accountants Act, 1959.

(xix) Central Government is fully authorised to make rules for the appointment and re-appointment of Directors, Managing Directors and Managers.

(xx) Section 383(A). A company whose paid up share capital is Rs. 25 lakhs or more, will have to appoint a full-time Company Secretary.

(xxi) Section 637(AA). Central Government is empowered to fix the maximum limit of managerial remuneration for the companies.

12. Other Minor Amendments Passed after 1974. After 10th Amendment of 1974, following minor changes have been introduced from time to time :

(i) In 1977, The Companies (Amendment) Act empowered central government to grant time extension of repayment of deposits (Sec. 58A), to file three copies of balance sheet and P&L A/C even if annual general meeting has not been held, ceiling of donation upto Rs. 50,000 [Sec. 293 (1) (c)] and power of Company Law Board of an execution Court (Sec. 634A).

(ii) In 1978. Public Corporations were made entitled to convert their loans or debentures into their shares.

(iii) On 9th November 1978. Revised guidelines have been issued for managerial remuneration.

(iv) Since 4th January 1979. Vertical form of the balance sheet of companies has also been recognised.

(v) On 4th October 1979. Certain clarifications have been made regarding subscription by companies to political parties.

(vi) In 1980. Revised rules have been framed and issued for the public deposits to be accepted by companies.

(vii) In 1985, the amendment was made in Sec. 293A by which the blanket ban on political contributions by Companies was lifted, right of appeal in case of assessment of compensation in an amalgamation scheme (Sec. 396) and dues of workmen have been equated of every secured creditor (Sec. 529A).

(viii) On 4th June 1986. Companies have been banned to convert their loans and debentures into their shares.

13. The Companies (Amendment) Act, 1988. An amendment in the Companies Act, it was brought after gaining a long experience from 1956 and then the recommendations made by the Sachar Committee. On 12th May, 1988, this Bill was adopted by the Lok Sabha. The President of India assented to this Bill on 5th June, 1988. The salient features of the amendment are as follows :

(i) An Independent Company Law Board will be set up to exercise such judicial and quasi-judicial functions as are presently being exercised either by the court or the central government and are proposed to be transferred to that board.

(ii) Offences punishable with fine.

(iii) Section 269(2). No appointment of a person as managing director or whole time director or manager in a public company or a private company which is a subsidiary of a public company, shall be made except with the prior approval of the central government. However, no such approval is required where the appointment is made in accordance with the conditions specified in Schedule XIII and a return in the prescribed form is filed within 90 days from the date of such appointment.

(iv) Section 43A. A Private Company becomes a Public Company (known as Deemed Public Company) :

(a) Where at least 25% of the paid up share capital of the private company is held by one or more bodies corporate (Bodies Corporate means public companies or private companies which have become public companies by virtue of Section 43-A). In computing this percentage, no account is taken of the shares of the private company held by a banking company on trust or as executors.

(b) Section 43-A (I-A). Where the average annual turnover of the private company at any time is Rs. 5 crores (Rs. 10 crores with effect from 18th September, 1990) for three consecutive financial years, the private company becomes a public company after three months from the last day of relevant period during which the company had the average annual turnover.

(c) Section 43-A (I-B). Where the private company holds at least 25% of the paid up share capital of public company, having a share capital.

In cases (a) and (c), the private company becomes a public company on and from the date on which the aforesaid percentage is first held.

(d) Section 43-A (I-C). Where the private company invites (by way of invitation by advertisement), accepts or renews deposits from the public, such, private company shall be a public company and thereupon all the provisions of Sec. 43-A shall apply thereto.

(v) De-linking of the rates of depreciation specified under Income-Tax Act and laying down the rates of depreciation in the Companies Act itself to reflect the true and fair view of the state of affairs of the company.

(vi) The Company Law Board will take care of the interests of the investors. It will intervene against non-repayment of public deposits and compulsory redemption of preference shares in certain cases. It will require companies to disclose reasons for refusal to register transfer of shares. It will protect the rights of the transferee pending mutation of his name in the register of members and also compulsory listing of all public issues.

(vii) The Company Law Board will reduce unnecessary cost or burden by requiring companies to attach only an abridged form of prospectus to the application form and only an abridged version of balance sheet and auditors report to the members and also to hold a poll in general meeting only at the instance of the shareholders having some minimum stake in the company. The companies will be asked to file full Annual Return only once in five years.

(viii) These are a few provisions for disclosure of information relating to conservation of energy, technology absorption, foreign exchange earnings and outgo as well as particulars of employees having some minimum stake in the company and drawing remuneration in excess of that drawn by managerial personnel.

(ix) These are provisions to plug loopholes and remove same lacunae which had come to surface in the working of the Act, and to streamline some of the existing provisions for better working and administration of an Act.

The amendments have started operating from 15th June, 1988.

14. The Companies (Amendment) Act, 1996. This amending Act has dispersed with the requirement of seeking confirmation of Company Law Board for alteration of the object clause of the memorandum of association (Sec. 17) and the period of redemption of redeemable preference shares to a maximum of 20 years from 10 years (Sec. 80).

15. The Companies (Amendment) Act, 1999. This amending Act has amended Sections 4A, 58A, 78, 80, 82, 205A, 205B, 211, 217, 227, 370, 372 and 642. It added new sections 77A, 77AA, 77B, 79B, 109A, 109B, 205C, 210A, 372A. Some of the new sections are given below :

(i) Facilities for Nomination. By an amendment of S. 58-A and by introducing Sections 109-A and 109-B, depositors in companies, shareholders and debenture holders have been given the right to nominate any person at any time in whom the interest in the security will be vested on the death of the depositor or security holder. Section 109-B enables the nominee to register himself as a shareholder on the death of the nominator or transfer the securities in question.

(ii) Buy-back of shares (S. 77-A). By introducing S. 77-A, companies have been given the right to purchase their own shares under a buy-back scheme. Earlier to this amendment, one of the basic norms of Company Law was that subject only to a few modifications stated in S. 77, no company was permitted to purchase its own shares. A buy-back scheme has to observe the requirements of the section and SEBI or Central Government Guidelines.

(iii) Sweat Equity Shares (S. 79-A). Persons working as directors or employees with companies have been given this privileged position that the company can issue them shares at a discount or for consideration other than cash, for example, for providing intellectual property, know-how etc. Such shares have been given the name sweat equity shares.

(iv) Investor Education and Protection Fund (S. 205-C). A fund is to be created under the name of Investor Education and Protection Fund for propagation of knowledge as to matters of investment. In addition to other sources of fund supply as specified in the section, one channel of cash flow to the fund is the amount accumulating in the *Unpaid Dividend Accounts* of companies. Before the Amendment Ordinance, this money remained with the company for three years and then it was transferred to the Central Government's General Revenue Account. Now the amount would remain in the company's Unpaid Dividend Account *for seven years* and, thereafter, it would be transferred to the Investor Education and Protection Fund.

(v) National Advisory Committee on Accounting Standards (S. 210-A). A National Advisory Committee is going to be constituted for formulating and laying down standards of accounting and auditing practices and accounting policies. The committee will play the advisory role to the Central Government. The standards would have to be followed and the auditors would have to certify on that fact. The companies would have to state reasons for not following the standards. (For details *see* under the section).

(vi) Inter-corporate loans and investments (S. 372-A). Sections 370 and 372 which dealt with inter-corporate loans and *investments have been abrogated.* They have been replaced by a single section, namely, S. 372-A. The requirement of Central Government permission has been dispensed with. The control mechanism henceforth will be wholly internal. The Board of Directors may, of their own decision, *go up to 60%.* Beyond this a *special resolution* of the shareholders would be needed. Guarantees can be provided by the company with the authority of the Board resolutions. (For details *see* under S. 372-A).

16. Companies (Amendment) Act, 2002. The Government introduced a comprehensive Companies Bill, 1997 in Rajya Sabha on 14-8-1997 and the same was referred to Standing Committee of Parliament for examination and report thereon. The process of examination, however, is not yet over and is still to take some more time. The passing of this Bill is thus likely to be delayed further. It is however considered desirable by the Government that some more important changes in the Companies Act, 1956 are brought out in order to provide immediately certain measures for good corporate governance and for protection of investors. These measures are as follows :

(i) to provide a minimum paid-up capital of Rs. 1 lakh for private companies and Rs. 5 lakh for public companies;

(ii) to delete provisions relating to deemed public companies;

(iii) to reduce the period for disbursing dividend/interim dividend to shareholders from 42 days to 30 days;

(iv) to request the companies to inform Company Law Board within sixty days if the company fails to make repayment of deposits on maturity to small deposit holders and the Company Law Board would be enabled to consider these defaults reported by companies and make an order within thirty days which the company shall be bound to comply with. A company which fails to report or comply with the order of the Company Law Board shall be punishable for imprisonment which may extend to three years and shall also be liable to fine or a fine of not less than Rs. 500 per day during which such default continues;

(v) to provide that the Securities and Exchange Board of India be entrusted with powers with regard to all matters relating to public issues and transfers including power to prosecute defaulting companies and their directors;

(vi) to include a Directors' Responsibility Statement in the Board's report to highlight the accountability of directors in good corporate governance;

(vii) to provide that public listed companies with paid-up capital of Rs. 5 crores or more shall be required to set up an Audit Committee of the Board of Directors as a measure for better corporate governance;

(viii) to require companies with paid-up capital of Rs. 10 lakh or more and which do not have whole-time Secretary in their employment to submit a Secretarial Compliance Certificate from Company Secretary in whole-time practice;

(ix) to delete the provisions for appointment of public trustee by Central Government with a view to enabling the Trust to directly exercise the voting power;

(x) to provide that any offer of shares or debentures to more than 50 persons shall be treated as public issue with suitable modification in the case of public financial institutions and non-banking financial companies;

(xi) to prescribe voting through postal ballot in case of only important items with effect from such date as may be notified by the Government to ensure good corporate governance;

(xii) to empower Regional Director to allow change of registered office of companies from jurisdiction of one Registrar of Companies to another Registrar of Companies within the same State;

(xiii) to empower the Comptroller and Auditor-General of Indian to appoint the auditors in respect of Government Companies and also to provide that shareholders of such companies will fix their remuneration in annual general meeting;

(xiv) to provide that in case of a public company which does not file annual account and annual returns continuously for three years, the directors of such company will be debarred from becoming the director of other public companies for five years. Similarly, in case of any public company which fails to repay its depositors on maturity of deposit amount/debentures, dividend and interest on deposits/debentures on due dates, the whole-time directors of defaulting companies as on such date will be debarred from becoming a director of any other public company for a period of five years;

(xv) to provide that for purpose of managerial remuneration, the amount of depreciation will be the same as provided in Profit and Loss Account of the Company;

(xvi) to provide that no person can hold office of director in more than fifteen companies at a time;

(xvii) to provide for appointment of one director as a nominee of small share-holders who constitute a minimum of 1000 in number and having shares of not more than Rs. 20,000 with effect from the date to be specified and subject to such other conditions as may be prescribed by the Central Government;

(xviii) to provide penal provisions for increased fine for offences under the Act;

(xix) to provide that a shareholder of the company be disqualified for appointment as auditor of the company;

(xx) to delete the provisions relating to managing agents, secretaries and treasures as they have become redundant after abolition of the system of managing agent, secretaries and treasurers;

(xxi) to provide that private limited companies shall be excluded in reckoning the number of companies which an auditor can audit.

It is expected that the above amendments in a short Bill will ensure better corporate governance, transparency in working of companies and also ensure more effective enforcement by enhancing the penalty/punishment for contravention so as to ensure better compliance of the provisions of the Companies Act, 1956.

Following sections have been omitted by the Companies (Amendment) Act 2000—Sec. 88, 204A, 248, 249, 261, 298, 324 to 369 (except 349, 350 and 355), 375, 377 to 383, 618.

INSTRUMENT OF SOCIALISM

Indian Company Law has passed through various stages of developments. New Acts were passed and implemented, the present Indian Company Law is the seventh Companies Act passed in 1950. It followed the recommendations of 'Companies Acts Enquiry Committee' set up by the Central Government, under the Chairmanship of Shri H.C. Bhabha. It was implemented on 1st April, 1956. It was formulated in the light of the new policies and targets of the Indian Government which decided to achieve self-dependence through rapid industrialisation of the country. Since Ist April, 1951 India adopted the path of planned economic developments through Five Year Plans. This required the rapid growth of Industries, Trade and Commerce in the country as India decided to go on socialistic pattern of society. This Act provided various incentives for the establishments of companies, and for the maximum investments in the companies form of organisations. It also leads the company management in the manner that it may achieve the goal of socialism. The main features of this Act in the direction of socialism are as follows :

1. Encouraging the establishment of Government Companies so that healthy competition may be created.

2. Imposing a restriction upon the maximum managerial remuneration to be 11% of the profits so as to curb the exploitation of companies funds.

3. Introducing the democratic pattern in the management of companies.

4. Containing many laws to protect the interests of minorities.

5. Empowering all the shareholders of the company to get the copy of all the relevant documents of the company and to get all the information regarding the management of the company.

6. Eliminating the system of managing agents, secretaries and treasurers.

THREE-TIER ADMINISTRATION

Under the Companies Act, 1956 the Company Law Administration had a three-tier set up as follows :

(i) Department of Company Law Administration (which is now known as Department of Company Affairs);

(ii) Regional Directors for four Regional Offices;

(iii) Registrar of Companies for each State.

In addition, there were official Liquidators attached to each High Court in the States. The Central Government also set up an Advisory Commission to advise it on certain matters as required by Section 410 of this Act.

Under the Companies (Amendment) Act, 1963 a Board of Company Law Administration, popularly known as the Company Law Board (CLB) was established. A Companies Tribunal was set up to take speedy action in cases of cheating, fraud, and misfeasance, malpractices and irregularities in company management. However in 1967 the Companies Tribunal was abolished. Under the Act, the Central Government was empowered to appoint a Public Trustee by notification in the Official Gazette to discharge the functions and exercise the rights and powers conferred on him by or under the Act. It deleted the Sections 410 to 415 of the Act dealing with Advisory Commission. A new Section 410 was enacted providing for the appointment of an Advisory Committee. Under the Companies (Amendment) Act, 2002 National Company Law Tribunal has been constituted to highest judicial authority for company matters.

PRESENT COMPANY LAW ADMINISTRATION

At present the Company Law Administration has following powers to deal with companies :

1. The Central Government (Government of India).

2. The Board of Company Law Administration. The Administrative set up of the Board of Company Law Administration consists of :

(i) The Central Office;

(ii) The Regional Offices headed by Regional Directors;

(iii) The Registrar of Companies.

3. The Public Trustee.

4. The Official Liquidators.

5. The Advisory Committee.

COMPANY LAW BOARD

Powers of Law Board

Department of Company Affairs deals on behalf of the supreme authority the Central Government. The Board of Company Law Administration (popularly known as Company Law Board) exercises the powers of the Companies (Amendment) Act, 1988 and any other powers if delegated to the Company Law Board by the Central

Government. It exercises such judicial and quasi-judicial functions as are presently being exercised either by the court or the Central Government and are proposed to be transferred to that Board.

Members of Law Board

According to Section 10-E(2), the Company Law Board shall consist of such number of members, not exceeding nine as the Central Government deems fit to be appointed by notification in the Official Gazette. The limit of members of the board was raised from five to nine by the Companies which have been transferred to it. The members of the Company Law Board shall possess such qualifications and experience as explained in Section 10-E (2-A).

Order of the Law Board

The Company (Amendment) Act, 1988 explains and directs that the orders of the Company Law Board be obeyed in a manner as if these were the orders of a court.

Administration of the Law Board

The Company Law Board has the following 3-tier Administration System :

1. The Central Office at New Delhi.
2. Four Regional Offices headed by Regional Directors at Mumbai, Calcutta, Chennai and Kanpur.
3. Registrars of Companies in every state.

1. The Central Office. It deals with the interpretation of the Act and offers the advice.

2. The Regional Directors. These function under the control and supervision of the Company Law Board. They can exercise only the powers and functions delegated to them by the Company Law Board.

3. The Registrars. These are the field officers who occupy the lowest tier in the organisation set up of the Company Law Board. However, appointment of a Registrar of the Companies in every State as a full time Officer will be made by the Central Government. A Registrar of Companies deals directly with the companies registered or intended to be registered within his jurisdiction.

Public Trustee

In 1963 the position of Public Trustee was created to protect the interests of the shareholders and debenture holders. The appointment of Public Trustee will be made by the Government of India to safeguard the interests of the shareholders and debenture holders and to prevent the use of voting rights attached to such shares by trusts in the personal interest of the donors.

Official Liquidators

An Official Liquidator is appointed by the Central Government. He is attached to each High Court for the purpose of winding up of companies by the Court. He is partly under the control of the High Court and partly under the Company Law Board.

Advisory Committee

The Companies (Amendment) Act, 1965 deleted Sections 410 to 415 and substituted a New Section 410 for the purpose of advising the Central Government and Company Law Board on matters arising out of the administration of the Companies Act, 1956, as may be referred to it by the Central Government or by the Company Law Board. The Central Government is not bound to constitute an Advisory Committee. Neither the Central Government nor the Company Law Board is bound to accept the advice of the Advisory Committee. While giving his judgement in the case of "Goail Khaitan *Vs.* State A.I.R. (1969). Honourable Justice remarked about this act that this act has been formulated with a view to check the financial irregularities and to eliminate the disturbing elements in the establishment of a welfare state, along with other objects. Various provisions of this Act are the active and aware watchman for serious criminals and help in checking the serious offences.

To conclude, the Indian Companies Act, 1956 and amendments made time to time provide for the provisions for the maximum utilisation of companies funds and natural resources, for the quality products and services to the nation; for the best possible protection to investors; and for the rapid industrialisation of the country. It helps the country in achieving the object of the establishment of a socialistic pattern of society.

THE COMPANIES BILL, 1997

The Government introduced a comprehensive Companies Bill, 1997 in Rajya Sabha on 14th August, 1997. The Bill was referred to Standing Committee of Parliament for examination and report thereon. The process of examination, however, is not yet over and is still to take some more time. The passing of this Bill is thus likely to be delayed further. It was, however, considered desirable, by the Government that some more important changes in the Companies Apt, 1956 are brought out in order to provide immediately certain measures for good corporate governance and for protection of investors. These measures are as follows :

1. Minimum Capital Requirement for Private and Public Companies

The Bill proposes to provide a minimum paid-up capital of Rs. 1 lakh for private companies and Rs. 5 lakhs for public companies (Section affected 3).

2. Deemed Public Limited Companies to go

The Bill proposes to delete provisions relating to deemed public companies (Section 43-A to be deleted).

3. Disbursement of Dividend within 30 days

The Bill proposes to reduce the period for disbursing dividend/ interim dividend to shareholders from 42 days to 30 days (Section affected 205-A).

The Bill also proposes to substitute a new Section for Section 207. The substituted Section 207 is as follows :

"Section 207. Penalty for failure to distribute dividends within thirty days. Where a dividend has been declared by a company but has not been paid, or the warrant in respect thereof has not been posted, within thirty days from the date of declaration, to any shareholder entitled to the payment of the dividend, every director of the company shall, if he is knowingly a party to the default, be punishable with simple imprisonment for a term which may extend to three years and shall also be liable to a fine of one thousand rupees for every day during which such default continues and the company shall be liable to pay simple interest at the rate of eighteen per cent per annum during the period for which such default continues :

Provided that no offence shall be deemed to have been committed within the meaning of the foregoing provisions in the following cases, namely :

(a) where the dividend could not be paid by reason of the operation of any law;

(b) where a shareholder has given directions to the company regarding the payment of the dividend and those directions cannot be complied with;

(c) where there is a dispute regarding the right to receive the dividend;

(d) where the dividend has been lawfully adjusted by the company against any sum due to it from the shareholder; or

(e) where, for any other reason, the failure to pay the dividend or to post the warrant within the period aforesaid was not due to any default on the part of the company."

4. Company Law Board to be informed of Default in Repayment of Deposits

The Bill proposes to require a company to inform the Company Law Board within Sixty days if the company fails to make repayment of deposits on maturity to small deposit-holders. The Company Law Board would thus be enabled to consider these defaults reported by the company and make an order within thirty days which the company shall be bound to comply with. Whoever fails to report or comply with the order of the Company Law Board shall be punishable for imprisonment which may extend to three years and shall also be liable to fine of not less than Rs. 500 per day during which such default continues (New Sections 58-AA and 58-AAA inserted).

"58-AA. Small depositors. (1) Every company, which accepts deposits from small depositors, shall intimate to the Company Law Board any default made by it in repayment of any such deposits or part thereof or any interest thereupon.

(2) The intimation under sub-section (1) shall, —

(a) be given within sixty days from the date of default;

(b) include particulars in respect of the names and addresses of each small depositor, the principal sum of deposits due to them and interest accrued thereupon.

(3) Where a company has made a default in repayment of any deposit or part thereof or any interest thereupon to a small depositor, the Company Law Board on receipt of intimation under sub-section (1), shall —

(a) exercise, on its own motion, powers conferred upon it by subsection (9) of section 58-A;

(b) pass an appropriate order within a period of thirty days from the date of receipt of intimation under sub-section (1) :

Provided that the Board may pass order after expiry of the period : of thirty days, after giving the small depositors an opportunity of being heard

Provided further that it shall not be necessary for a small depositor to be present at the hearing of the proceeding under this sub-section.

(4) No company shall, at any time, accept further deposits from small depositors, unless each small depositor, whose deposit has matured, had been paid the amount of the deposit and the interest accrued thereupon :

Provided that nothing contained in this sub-section shall apply to —

(a) any deposit which has been renewed by the small depositor voluntarily; or

(b) any depositor, whose repayment has become impracticable due to the death of the small depositor or whose repayment has been stayed by a competent court or authority.

(5) Every company, which has on any occasion made a default in the repayment of a deposit or part thereof or any interest thereupon

to a small depositor, shall state, in every future advertisement and application form inviting deposits from the public, the total number of small depositors and amount due to them in respect of which such default has been made.

(6) Where any interest accrued on deposits of the small depositors has been waived, the fact of such waiver shall be mentioned by the company in every advertisement and application form inviting deposits issued after such waiver.

(7) Where a company had accepted deposits from small depositors and subsequent to such acceptance of deposits, obtains funds by taking a loan for the purposes of its working capital from any bank, it shall first utilise the funds so obtained for the repayment of any deposit or any part thereof or any interest to the small depositor before applying such funds for any other purpose.

(8) Every application form, issued by a company to a small depositor for accepting deposits from him, shall contain a statement to the effect that the applicant had been apprised of :

(a) every past default by the company in the repayment of deposit or interest thereon, if any, such default has occurred and

(b) the waiver of interest under sub-section (6), if any, and reasons therefore.

(9) Whoever knowingly fails to comply with the provisions of this section or comply with any order of the Company Law Board shall be punishable with imprisonment which may extend to three, years and shall also be liable to fine for not less than five hundred rupees for every day during which such non compliance continues.

(10) If a company or any other person contravenes any provision of this section, every person, who at the time the contravention was committed, was a director of the company, as well as the company, shall be deemed to be guilty of the offence and shall be liable to be proceeded against and punished accordingly.

(11) The provisions of section 58-A shall, as far as may be, apply to the deposits made by a small depositor under this section.

Explanation : For the purposes of this section, "a small depositor" means a depositor who has invested in a financial year a sum not exceeding twenty thousand rupees in a company.

58-AAA. *Default in acceptance or refund of deposits to be cognizable :* Notwithstanding anything contained in Sections 621 and 624, every offence connected with or arising out of acceptance, of deposits under Section 58-A or Section 58-AA shall be cognizable offence under the Code of Criminal Procedure, 1973 (2 of 1974).

5. Public Issues and Transfers

The Bill provides that the Securities and Exchange Board of India be entrusted with powers with regard to all matters relating to public issues and transfers including power to prosecute defaulting companies and their directors (New Section 55-A inserted).

55-A. *Powers of Securities and Exchange Board of India :* The provisions contained in Sections 55 to 58, 59 to 81 (including Sections 68-A, 77A, 80-A), 108, 109, 110, 112, 113, 116, 117, 118, 119, 120, 121, 122, 205, 205-A, 206, 206-A, 207, 209 and 211 shall, —

(a) in case of listed public companies;

(b) in case of those public companies which purport to be listed, be administered by the Securities and Exchange of India and

(c) in any other case, be administered by the Central Government.

6. Directors' Responsibility Statement

The Bill proposes to include a Directors' Responsibility Statement in the Board's report to highlight the accountability of directors in good corporate governance [Sub-Section 2-AA inserted in Section 217].

"(2-AA). The Board's report shall also include a Directors' Responsibility Statement, indicating therein, —

(i) that in the preparation of the annual accounts, the applicable accounting standards had been followed along with proper explanation relating to material departures;

(ii) that the directors had selected such accounting policies and applied them consistently and made judgments and estimates that are reasonable and prudent so as to give a true and fair view of the state of affairs of the company at the end of the financial year and of the profit or loss of the company for that period;

(iii) that the directors had taken proper and sufficient care for the maintenance of adequate accounting records in accordance with the provisions of this Act for safeguarding the assets of the company and for preventing and detecting fraud and other irregularities

(iv) that the directors had prepared the annual accounts on a going concern basis."

7. Constitution of Audit Committee

Public listed companies with paid-up capital of Rs. 5 crore or more shall now be required to set up an Audit Committee of the Board of Directors as a measure for better corporate governance. For this purpose new Section 292-A has been inserted.

"292-A. *Audit Committee :* (1) Every public company having paid-up capital of not less than five crore of rupees shall constitute a committee of the Board known as Audit Committee which shall consist of not less than three directors and such number of other directors as the Board may determine of which two-thirds the total number of members shall be directors, other than managing or whole-time directors.

(2) Every Audit Committee constituted under sub-section I shall act in accordance with terms of reference to be specified in writing by the Board.

(3) The members of the Audit Committee shall elect a chairman from amongst themselves.

(4) The annual report of the company shall disclose the composition of the Audit Committee.

(5) The auditors, the internal auditor, if any, and the director-in-charge of finance shall attend and participate at meetings of the Audit Committee but shall not have the right to vote.

(6) The Audit Committee shall have discussions with the auditors periodically about internal control systems, the scope of audit including the observations of the auditors and review the half-yearly and annual financial statements before submission to the Board and also ensure compliance of internal control systems.

(7) The Audit Committee shall have authority to investigate into any matter in relation to the items specified in this section or referred to it by the Board and for this purpose, shall have full access to information contained in the records of the company and external professional advice, if necessary.

(8) The recommendations of the Audit Committee on any matter relating to financial management, including the audit report, shall be binding on the Board.

(9) The chairman of the Audit Committee shall attend the annual general meetings of the company to provide any clarification on matters relating to audit.

(10) If a default is made in complying with the provisions of this section, the company, and every officer who is in default, shall be punishable with imprisonment for a term which may extend to one year, or with fine which may extend to fifty thousand rupees, or with both."

8. Secretarial Compliance Certificate

The companies with paid-up capital of Rs. 10 lakh or more and which do not have a whole-time secretary in their employment shall be required to submit a Secretarial Compliance Certificate from a company secretary in whole-time practice. For this purpose the following Proviso has been inserted in Sub-section (1) of Section 383-A.

"Provided that every company not required to employ a whole-time secretary under Sub-section (1) and having a paid-up share capital of ten lakh rupees or more shall file with the Registrar a certificate from a secretary in whole-time practice in such form and within such time and subject to such conditions as may be prescribed, as to whether the company has complied with all provisions of this Act or not."

9. Public Trustees to go

The Bill proposes to delete the provisions for appointment of public trustees by Central Government with a view to enabling trusts to directly exercise the voting power (Sections 153-A, 153-B, 187-B, 187-C to be deleted).

10. Offer of Shares or Debentures to more than 50 Persons to be treated as Public Offer

The Bill provides that any offer of shares or debentures to more than 50 persons shall be treated as public issue with suitable modification in the case of public financial institutions and non-banking financial companies [Proviso to Section 67 (3) inserted].

11. Passing of Resolutions by Postal Ballot

The Bill prescribes voting through postal ballot in case of only important items with effect from such date as may be notified by the Central Government to ensure good corporate governance (New Section 192-A inserted).

"192-A. *Passing of resolutions by postal ballot* : (1) Notwithstanding anything contained in the foregoing provisions of this Act, a listed public company may, and in the case of resolutions relating to such business as the Central Government may, by notification, declare to be conducted only by postal ballot, shall, get any resolution passed by means of a postal ballot, instead of transacting the business in general meeting of the company.

(2) Where a company decides to pass any resolution by resorting to postal ballot, it shall send a notice to all the shareholders, alongwith a draft resolution explaining the reasons therefore, and requesting them to send their assent or dissent in writing on a postal ballot within a period of thirty days from the date of posting of the letter.

(3) The notice shall be sent by registered post acknowledgement due, or by any other method as may be prescribed by the Central Government in this behalf, and shall include with the notice, a postage prepaid envelope for facilitating the communication of the assent or dissent of the shareholder to the resolution within the said period.

(4) If a resolution is assented to by a majority of the shareholders by means of postal ballot, it shall be deemed to have been duly passed at a general meeting convened in that behalf.

(5) If a shareholder sends under Sub-section (2), his assent or dissent in writing on a postal ballot and thereafter any person fraudulently defaces or destroys the ballot paper or declaration of identity of the shareholder, such person shall be punishable with

imprisonment for a term which may extend to six months or with fine or with both.

(6) If a default is made in complying with Sub-sections (1) to (4), the company and every officer of the company, who is in default shall be punishable with fine which may extend to fifty thousand rupees in respect of each such default."

12. Change of Registered Office within a State

The Bill empowers Regional Direct or to allow change of registered office of companies from jurisdiction of one Registrar of Companies to another Registrar of Companies within the same State [New Section 17-A inserted].

"17-A. *Change of registered office within a State :* No company shall change the place of its registered office from one place to another within a State unless it is confirmed by the Regional Director."

13. The Comptroller and Auditor-General of India to appoint Auditors in Government Companies

The Bill empowers the Comptroller and Auditor-General of India to appoint auditors is respect of Government companies and also to provide that shareholders of such companies will fix their remuneration in annual general meeting [Section 224 to be amended].

14. Bar on Appointment of Defaulting Directors

The Bill provides that in case of a public company which does not file annual accounts and annual returns continuously for last three years, the directors of such companies will be debarred from becoming directors of other public companies for five years. Similarly, in case of any public company which fails to repay its depositors on maturity of deposit amount/debentures, dividend and interest on deposits/ debentures on due dates, the whole-time directors of defaulting companies as on such date will be debarred from becoming a director of any other public company for a period of five years [Clause (g) inserted in Section 274 (1)].

"(g) such person is already a director of a public company which, —

(A) has not filed the annual accounts and annual returns for any continuous three financial years commencing on and after the first day of April, 1999; or

(B) has failed to repay its deposit or interest thereon on due date or redeem its debentures on due date or pay dividend and such failure continues for one year or more :

Provided that such person shall not be eligible to be appointed, as a director of any other public company for a period of five years from the date on which such public company in which he is a director failed to file annual accounts and annual returns under sub-clause (A) or has failed to repay its deposits or interest or redeem its debentures on due date or pay dividend referred to in clause (B)."

15. Quantum of Depreciation

The Bill provides that for purpose of managerial remuneration, the amount of depreciation will be the same as provided in Profit and Loss Account of the company (Section 349 to be amended).

16. Number of Directorships

The Bill provides that no person can hold office of director in more than 15 companies (reduced from 20 to 15) at a time (Sections affected 275, 276, 277, 279).

17. Nominee Director of Small Shareholders

The Bill proposes to provide for appointment of one director as a nominee of small shareholders who constitute a minimum of 1,000 in number and have shares of not more than Rs. 20,000 with effect from the date to be specified and subject to such other conditions as may be prescribed by the Central Government [Proviso to Section 252 (1) to be inserted].

"Provided that a public company having, —

(a) a paid-up capital of five crore rupees or more;

(b) one thousand or more small shareholders, shall have at least one director elected by such small shareholders in the manner as may be prescribed.

Explanation : For the purposes of this sub-section, "small shareholder" means a shareholder holding shares of nominal value of twenty thousand rupees or less in a public company to which this section applies."

18. Enhancement of Fine

The Bill makes penal provisions more stringent. The quantum of fine has been increased 10 times. The Sections affected are 11, 22, 25, 39, 40, 49, 56, 58-A, 59, 60, 63, 68 to 70 72, 73, 75 to 77, 79, 80, 80-A, 84, 89, 95, 97, 107, 108-J, 111, 113, 115, 118, 127, 133, 137, 142 to 144, 146 to 152, 154, 157, 158, 162, 163, 165, 168, 176, 188, 192, 193, 196, 197, 202, 203, 205-A, 207, 209, 209-A, 210 to 212, 217 to 219, 221, 223, 224, 232, 233, 233-A, 233-B, 234, 240, 250, 269, 272, 283, 286, 294, 295, 299, 300 to 305, 307, 308, 320, 322, 371, 374, 391, 393 to 395, 404, 407, 416, 420, 423, 425, 454, 481, 485, 488, 493, 495 to 497, 500, 501, 508, 509, 513, 514, 516, 542, 547, 550, 551, 559, 598, 606, 615, 621-A, 629-A, 630, 631, 642.

19. Restriction on Appointment of a Shareholder as Auditor

The Bill seeks to provide that a shareholder of a company shall be disqualified for appointment as auditor of the company.

20. Deletion of Provisions Relations to Managing Agents and Secretaries and Treasurers

The Bill proposes to delete the provisions relating to managing agents and secretaries and treasurers as they have become redundant after abolition of the system of managing agents and secretaries and treasurers. The Sections affected/deleted are :

4, 16, 54, 77, 89, 159, 160, 165, 173, 197-A, 198, 199, 201, 202, 204, 204-A (deleted), 209, 211, 212, 215, 220, 221, 226, 239, 234-A, 239, 240, 240-A, 241 to 243, 245, 247, 248(d), 249(d), 251, 261 (deleted), 283, 292, 294, 295, 298 (deleted), 302, 305 to 309, 314, 318, 323, 324, 324A, 325, 325-A, 326 to 348, 351 to 354, 383 (deleted), 388-E, 393, 398, 402, 405, 407, 409, 416, 427, 469, 491, 513, 543, 560, 568, 583, 618 (deleted), 627, 640-B.

21. Exclusion of Private Companies for audit

The Bill provides that private limited companies shall be excluded in reckoning the number of companies which an auditor can audit (Section 224).

The above amendments will ensure better corporate governance, transparency in working of companies and also more effective enforcement by enhancing the penalty/punishment for contraventions so as to ensure better compliance of the provisions of the Companies Act, 1956.

QUESTIONS

1. Write an essay on "The history of the Indian Companies Act."
2. Give the brief history of Company Law in India.
3. "Indian Companies Act has passed through various stages of developments and amendments." Explain the statement.
4. Discuss the important stages of the history of the Indian Company Law.
5. Is the Indian Company Law an instrument of socialism? Discuss the nature of Indian Company Law in the light of objectives for which it was framed.
6. What are the significant provision of the Company Second Amendment Bill 1999?

2

NATURE OF COMPANIES

Literally, the term company means a group of persons associated for any common object such as business, charity, sports etc. It is an association of persons.

DEFINITION OF COMPANY

(A) Definitions given by Well-known Authors

(i) *Kimball and Kimball.* "A Corporation (Company) is by nature, an artificial person created or authorised by the legal statue for some specific purpose.

(ii) *Prof L.H. Haney.* "A Company is an artificial person created by law having a separate entity with a perpetual succession and a common seal."

(iii) *Dr. W.R. Spriegal.* "The Corporation (Company) is a creature of state and possesses an entity distinct from the persons owing its stock or other securities."

(B) Definitions given by Well-Known Justices

(i) *Lord Lindley.* "By a company is meant an association of many persons who contribute money or moneys worth to a common stock and employ it for a common purpose. The common stock so contributed denoted in money and in the capital of the company. The persons who contribute it or to whom it belongs are members. The proportion of capital to which each member is entitled is his share."

(ii) *Lord Selborne.* "The company is mere abstraction of law."

(iii) *Lord Macnaughten.* "The company is at law a different person altogether from the subscribers to the memorandum of association."

(iv) *Lord Justice James.* "Company means an association of persons united for a common purpose."

(v) *Justice Hidayatullah.* "An incorporated company has a separate existence and the law recognizes in as a legal person distinct from its members."

(vi) *Justice Charlesworth.* "A company is an artificial person incorporated for certain specified object."

(vii) *Chief Justice Marshall.* "A corporation (Joint Stock Company) is an artificial being, invisible, intangible and existing only in the contemplation of law. Being a mere creation of law, it possesses only the properties which the charter of its creation confers upon it either expressly or as incidental to its very existence."

To conclude, a company may be defined as an incorporated association, an artificial legal person, having an independent legal entity, with a perpetual succession, a common seal, and carrying limited liability.

DEFINITION UNDER COMPANIES ACT

"The Companies Act under Section 3(i) defines company as : A Company means a company formed and registered under this Act, or an existing company" as defined in clause (ii).

As per above section the term 'company' in general parlance means an association of a certain number of persons formed for the purpose of a common interest. Thus, the company is a legal person as distinct from its members. However, this distinction is possible only if the company is incorporated, otherwise it is not regarded in law as separate from its members.

JOINT STOCK COMPANY

Definition

Section 566 of the Companies Act, 1956, defines joint stock company as :

(1) For the purposes of this part so far as it relates to the registration of companies as companies limited by shares, a joint stock company means a company having a permanent paid-up or nominal share capital of fixed amount divided into shares, also of fixed amount, or held and transferable as stock, or divided and held partly in the one way and partly other, and formed on the principle of having for its members the holders of those shares or that stock, and no other persons.

(2) Such a Company, when registered with limited liability under this Act, shall be deemed to be a company limited by shares.

Lord Justice Lindley defines the company as follows :

"A company is a voluntary association or an organisation of many persons who contribute money or moneys worth to a common stock and employ it in some trade or business and who share the profit and loss arising therefrom. The common stock so contributed in denoted in money and is the capital of the company. The persons who contribute it or to whom it belongs are members of the company. The proportion of capital to which each member is entitled to is his share. The shares are of fixed value and the whole capital of the company is divided into the equal number of shares. The shares are generally transferable although, under certain circumstances, the right to transfer may be restricted."

Common characteristics of Joint Stock Companies :

(1) A company possess permanent paid-up or nominal share capital of fixed amount.

(2) The capital divided into shares of fixed amount.

(3) The capital may be divided partly in shares and partly in stocks.

(4) Persons who hold these shares or stocks are called members of the company.

(5) The shares or stocks are transferable.

(6) The company must be registered under the Companies Act with limited liability.

Prof. Haney has provided a more comprehensive and widely accepted definition of the company which incorporates the main essential features of the company. He says, *"A company is an incorporated association which is an artificial person created by law having a separate entity with a perpetual succession and a common seal."*

MAIN FEATURES OF A COMPANY

(1) **Incorporated Association.** The company is an incorporated association, an association of persons of more than ten in banking business and more than twenty in any other type of business. It must be compulsorily registered or incorporated under the Companies Act. An association which is not registered cannot be called a body corporate and the liability of the members of such an association is unlimited.

(2) **Artificial Legal Person.** The company is an artificial person in law. It does not exist physically but it does exist legally. It is considered as a single person in law as distinct from the members of the company who are called the shareholders. J. Hidayatallah observes that "unlike an unincorporated company which has no separate existence and which the law does not distinguish from its members, an incorporated company has a separate existence and the law recognises it as a legal person distinct from its members. This new legal personality emerges from the moment of incorporation." Therefore, a company can enter into contracts, acquire and dispose of property in its own name as any individual can do. The actions of its members do not bind the company nor the actions of the company bind the members. But in case of a partnership, the actions of a partner bind the firm because of firm does not have a separate existence as distinct from its partners. Thus, company can do all such acts as any other person who is competent to contract. It can sue and can be sued. Legal proceedings may be instituted between the company and its members.

(3) **Common Seal.** A company has a common seal as required by

Section 34(2) of the Act. Recognised as an artificial person without physical existence, it cannot by itself put its signature. This is done by means of common seal regarded as the signature of the company. As the seal of a company is affixed to a document, it is said to be authenticated. After the seal is affixed two directors and the secretary sign the documents. Now, the document is considered as the will of the company. The seal is in the custody of the board of directors or any responsible official. It is affixed whenever the documents are to be signed by the company. In England the possession and use of common seal has been dispensed with in 1989.

(4) Perpetual Succession. A company has perpetual succession. It continues to exist and its life is permanent unless it is wound-up under certain circumstances. As a company has a separate legal entity, its existence is not affected by death, insolvency, lunacy or retirement of its members or the board of directors members may come and members may go but the company can go on for ever. If a private company has two members, who are directors of the company also, die in an accident, the company will still exist. The perpetuity of existence marks out the joint stock company from other forms of business organisations.

(5) Limited Liability. The liability of every member of a public limited company is limited to the extent of the total amount of the shares he has purchased. The shareholder of a limited company is free of his liability the moment his share is fully paid-up. Hence his private property cannot be seized in the event of winding-up the company for the payment of its debts.

(6) Transferability of Shares. Shares of a public limited company are freely transferable to any person as per the choice of a shareholder. Formal approval of the company may be necessary to regularise the transfer. Where the proposed transferee is of bad character or of very bad financial position and the shares to be transferred are only partly paid, the company may put certain restrictions on the right of the shareholder concerned. But, generally no shareholder can be prohibited from transferring his shares and if any provision is made to this effect, it will be in contravention of the Companies Act.

(7) Separate Property. Shareholders are not, in the eyes of law, part owners of the property of the company. He does not have insurable interest or legal and equitable interest therein. A company can sue and be sued.

CONSEQUENCES OF NON-REGISTRATION

(1) No Legal Existence

(i) No legal contract can be entered into.

(ii) Neither the association nor its members can sue any outsider for getting the dues from him.

(iii) Members themselves cannot sue each other in respect of any matter pertaining to the association.

(iv) The association being not recognised by law cannot be dissolved under Court order.

(2) Unlimited Liability. Under Section 11 (4) any member of such unrecognised association will be personally liable for all the liabilities of such association, *i.e.*, his liabilities will be unlimited and even his personal property can be attached for paying the debts of the association. His liabilities being unlimited, the creditors of the association can sue him.

(3) Fine. Section 11(5) of the Act makes every member of such illegal association liable to pay a fine which may extend to Rs. 10,000.

(4) Other Provisions

(i) Illegal association is liable to pay income-tax.

(ii) A member can claim back his subscription provided it is not used by the association.

(iii) It remains illegal till it gets registered even though the member or members are brought below 20.

(iv) It is liable for all acts done prior to its registration.

(v) A member cannot sue for partition or dissolution of illegal association.

Section 11 does not apply to (a) Stock Exchange (b) association not for profit making (c) Joint Hindu family business.

Partnership Firm *Vs.* Joint Stock Company

(1) Legal Entity. A company formed under the Companies Act is a distinct legal entity having a separate existence of its own as distinct from the members constituting it. A partnership 'firm' has no separate legal existence apart from its members. A company on incorporation attains the status of an artificial person, with a perpetual succession and a common seal, but a partnership does not.

(2) Members. A company may consist of any number of members not less than seven if it is a public company and not less than two or more than 50 if it is a private company. A partnership cannot have more than 20 persons in general business and more than ten in banking business.

(3) Transfer. A partner cannot transfer his share in the partnership firm without the consent of all other partners. On the other hand one of the main features of the company is the transferability of its share capital.

(4) Dissolution. Unless otherwise provided for by the partnership agreement, a partnership is dissolved by the death of a partner. On the other hand, the death of a shareholder will not affect the existence of a company.

(5) The Agent. The actions of a partner bind the firm and other partners. A shareholder's actions cannot bind the company.

(6) Property. The property of a company belongs to the *legal person* called the *company* and not to the shareholders as such. In the case of partnership, property belongs to the partners collectively.

(7) Liability. A partner is liable for the debts of the firm both jointly and severally. The liability of a shareholder of a limited company is restricted to the amount due and unpaid on the shares held by him. He cannot be held liable for the debts of the company.

(8) Participation. All partners are entitled to take part in the management of the partnership business. Shareholders have only very restricted rights to interfere in the management of the affairs of the company which is usually managed by a board of directors.

(9) Disabilities imposed by Law. There are some disabilities imposed by law on limited companies which do not occur in the case of partnerships *e.g.*, a company cannot buy its own shares; it cannot alter its share capital except under certain conditions. The partners, however, can by mutual consent vary the terms of partnership and can also buy the share of other partners.

ADVANTAGES OF COMPANY

1. Perpetual Succession. As a company is created by law it can be dissolved only by law, if required. It is not affected by the existence of its members. It is not affected by the death, lunacy or insolvency of its members. It goes on even if all the members die. "Members may come, members may go but the company goes on for ever."

2. Adequate Finance. A company collect its finance by the issue of shares to a large number of persons. It can collect any amount it requires. Bank and other financial institutions also grant the easy loans and advances to company.

3. Limited Liability of Members. As member's liability is limited, company is a very attractive form of Organisation. Members can be held responsible only upto the value of shares they have purchased.

4. Transferability of Shares. Investors like to invest in the company because its shares are easily transferable. They can withdraw their investment whenever they like by selling their shares.

5. Democratic Set-up. Company is managed in a democratic manner by the representatives elected by its members. Directors have to manage and administer the company according to the rules framed by the shareholders.

6. Efficient Management. The company is managed by the representatives of its owners, who, of course, can be the experts in their fields.

7. Scope for Expansion. A company can easily be expanded whenever required as it can collect required money easily, its expansion never suffers due to lack of funds.

8. Necessary for Giant Projects. Projects and plans requiring huge amount of capital and skill can be implemented through a company form of organisation because all other forms of organisation suffer from the drawback of limited capital and skill.

9. Incentives for Small Savings. A company encourages the small savings of the country because the nominal value of its share is very small, say Rs. 10 or Rs. 100. These can be purchased by most of persons. Thus, every citizen of the country may contribute towards the economic growth of the country.

10. Helpful in the Industrial Development. Company organisation helps in promoting the industrial development of the country by making the establishment of big companies possible.

DISADVANTAGES OF A COMPANY

1. Legal Formalities. At the time of incorporation of company has to undergo numerous difficult legal formalities. This is also true for the routine management, administration and winding up. So, it is difficult to establish, manage and dissolve a company.

2. Ownership and Management are Divorced. A great drawback of the company is the divorce between ownership and management. It is not managed by those who own it and it is not owned by those who manage it.

3. Slack in Management. Separation of ownership and management creates problems in the management of a company. Due to possible differences between director and shareholders on various points often the decisions are imposed by majority on minority.

4. Exploitation of Shareholders Interests. As a company is managed by a Board of Directors they may exploit the company resources in their interest and not in the interest of shareholders.

5. Fraud by Promoters. Sometimes the promoters of a company cheat the shareholders by making fraudulent sales and purchases in their own interests.

6. Delay in Decisions. In taking any decision a company has to undergo a pre-decided procedure. This causes unnecessary delay in the decision making process and the company sometimes misses the golden opportunity.

7. Speculation in Securities. As Companies shares and debentures are dealt by the brokers working in stock exchanges, it may lead to speculation in the value of securities.

8. Lack of Secrecy. A company has to publish its accounts, directors report and auditors report which deprives it of the secrecy.

9. Lack of Direct Motivation. As its ownership and management are separate, company form of organisation suffers from the lack of direct motivation.

10. Disadvantages of Large Scale. As a company is generally established for carrying on big business plans and projects, it carries with it all the disadvantages of large scale trade or production.

PRINCIPLE OF CORPORATE/COMPANY VEIL

A Company is an artificial person created by law having an independent entity, with a perpetual succession, a common seal and carrying limited liability. Though it is an artificial person, it has got the rights and duties like a natural person. It can sue and can be sued. Its existence is different from that of its members. If it sues, it is not considered to be a suit by its members. If it is sued, it cannot be considered to be a suit upon its members. A company can be created by law, and can be dissolved only by the law.

Solomon *Vs.* Solomon and Co. Ltd.

A company's separate existence from its members was judicially recognised by the House of Lords in a very famous case of Solomon Vs. Solomon and Co. Ltd., 1897.

Mr. Solomon was carrying on a prosperous business as a leather merchant. He sold his business for the sum of £ 30,000 to Solomon & Co. Ltd. which had only seven members : Mr. Solomon himself, his wife, his daughter and his four sons. The purchase consideration was paid by the company to Mr. Solomon by : (i) allotment of 20,000 fully paid up shares of the company of £ 1 each and (ii) £ 10,000 in the form of debentures of the company. These debentures were secured by a floating charge over all the assets of the company. Remaining six members of the company, the members of his family subscribed only one share each of the value of £ I and the amount was paid for in cash. Mr. Solomon was the Managing Director of the company and he had complete control over the company.

One year after its establishment the company became insolvent and the winding up process was started. The statement of affairs of the company was as under — Assets : £ 6,000; Liability : Solomon as debenture holder — £ 10,000 and unsecured creditors £7,000. Thus, the assets were only £ 6,000 against its liabilities £ 17,000 running short of its liabilities by £ 11,000.

The unsecured creditors claimed priority over debenture holder (Mr. Solomon) on the ground that Mr. Solomon and Solomon and Co. Ltd., were practically one and the same and that a person cannot owe to himself, so Mr. Solomon had no priority. They further argued that the company was merely an 'alias' for Mr. Solomon. It was being carried on solely by him, for him. It was a total fraud and, hence, Mr. Solomon should indemnify the company against its unsecured trade creditors.

The House of Lords held that the existence of a company is entirely different from the existence of its members and as a rule, secured creditors must be given priority in payment in comparison to unsecured creditors.

Lord Macnaughten, a learned Justice in this case, observed, "The company is at law, a different person altogether from subscribers to the memorandum; and though it may be that after incorporation the business is precisely the same as it was before and the same persons are managers, and the same hands receive the profits, the company is not in law the agent of the subscribers as members liable, in any shape or form, except to the extent and in the manner provided by the Act."

The case of Solomon proved it beyond doubt and controversy, that the company is different from its members and there is a veil between the company and its members. Courts will generally, not pierce this veil. Lifting the corporate veil means that the company and members behind the company are not treated separate entity but one and same. The court may lift the veil under two ways :

(a) under Judicial Interpretation

(b) under Statutory Provisions

Exceptions. The various cases in which corporate veil has been lifted are as follows :

UNDER JUDICIAL INTERPRETATION

The Supreme Court has upheld the application of this doctrine in many cases *e.g.,* Cotton Corporation of India Ltd. *Vs.* G.C. Odusumathd (1999) and state of U.P. *Vs.* Renu Sagar Power Co. (1991).

1. *Protection of Revenue :* The Courts may ignore the corporate entity of a company where it is used for tax evasion [Juggilal *Vs.* Commr. of Income-tax, A.I.R. (1969) S.C. 9821. Tax planning may be legitimate provided it is within the framework of law. Colourable devices cannot be part of tax planning.

Sir Dinshaw Maneckjee Petit, Re, A.I.R. (1927) Bom. 371. D, an assessee, who was receiving huge dividend and interest income, transferred his investments to 4 private companies formed for the purpose of reducing his tax liability. These companies transferred the income to D as a pretended loan. Held, the companies were formed by D purely and simply as a means of avoiding tax obligation and the companies were nothing more than the assessee himself. They did no business but were created simply as legal entities to ostensibly receive the dividends and interest and to hand them over to D as pretended loans.

2. *Prevention of Fraud or Improper Conduct :* The legal personality of a company may also be disregarded in the interest of justice where the machinery of incorporation has been used for some fraudulent purpose like defrauding creditors or defeating or circumventing law.

Jones *Vs. Lipman*, (1962) All E.R. 442. L agreed to sell a certain land to J. He subsequently changed his mind and to avoid the specific performance of the contract, he sold it to a company which was formed specifically for the purpose. The company bad L and a clerk of his solicitors as the only members. J brought an action for the specific performance against L and the company. The Court looked to the reality of the situation, ignored the transfer, and ordered that the company should convey the land to J.

3. *Determination of Character of a Company whether it is Enemy* : A company may assume an enemy character when persons in *de facto* control of its affairs are residents in an enemy country. In such a case, the Court may examine the character of persons in real control of the company, and declare the company to be an enemy company.

Daimler Co. Ltd. *Vs.* Continental Tyre & Rubber Co. Ltd., (1916) 2 A.C. 307. A company was incorporated in England for the purpose of selling in England tyres made in Germany by a German company which held the bulk of shares in the English company. The holders of the remaining shares, except one, and all the directors were Germans, resident in Germany. During the First World War, the English company commenced an action for recovery of a trade debt. Held, the company was an alien company and the payment of debt to it would amount to trading with the enemy and, therefore, the company was not allowed to proceed with the action.

4. *Where the company is a sham :* The Courts also lift the veil where a company is a mere cloak or sham (hoax). The following case illustrates the point :

Gilford Motor Co. Ltd. *Vs.* Horne, (1933) Ch. 935 C.A. Horne, a former employee of a company, was subject to a covenant not to solicit its customers. He formed a company to carry on a business which, if he had done so personally, would have been a breach of the covenant. An injunction was granted both against him and the company to restrain them from carrying on the business. The company was described in this judgment as "a device, a stratagem", and as "a mere cloak or sham for the purpose of enabling the defendant to commit a breach of his covenant against solicitation."

5. *Company Avoiding Legal Obligations* : Where the use of an incorporated company is being made to avoid legal obligations, the Court may disregard the legal personality of the company and proceed on the assumption as if no company existed.

6. *Company Acting as Agent or Trustee of the Shareholders* : Where a company is acting as agent for its shareholders, the shareholders will be liable for the acts of the company. It is a question of fact in each case whether the company is acting as agent for its shareholders. There may be an express agreement to this effect or an agreement may be implied from the circumstances of each particular case.

7. *Avoidance of Welfare Legislation :* Avoidance of welfare legislation is as common as avoidance of taxation and the approach of the Courts in considering problems arising out of such avoidance is generally the same as avoidance of taxation. It is the duty of the Courts in every case where ingenuity is expended to avoid welfare legislation to get behind the smoke screen and discover the true state of affairs.

8. *Protecting Public Policy :* The Courts invariably lift the corporate veil to protect the public policy and prevent transactions contrary to public policy. Thus where there is a conflict with public policy, the Courts ignore the form and take into account the substance [Connors *Vs.* Connors Ltd., (1940) 4 All E.R, 174].

9. To determine the technical character of the company (New Horizons Ltd. *Vs.* Union of India (1995).

10. To punish for contempt of court.

11. In case of illegal or improper purpose and economic offences.

Statutory exceptions. 1. Number of members below statutory minimum (Section 45). If a company carries on business for more than 6 months after the number of its members has been reduced below 7 in case of a public company or 2 in case of a private company, every person who knows this fact and is a member during the time that the company so carries on business after the six months, is severally liable for the whole of the debts of the company contracted during that time, *i.e.*, after six months. It may be noted that in such a case the continuing members (*i.e.*, those who continue to be members after six months) :

(a) can be sued and not those who have withdrawn from the membership;

(b) shall be liable only if they are aware of the fact of the number falling below the statutory minimum.

2. Misrepresentation in prospectus (Section 62 and 63).

3. *Failure to Refund Application Money* [Section 69 (5)]. The directors of a company are jointly and severally liable to repay the application money with interest if the company fails to refund the application money of those applicants who have not been allotted shares, within 130 days of the date of issue of the prospectus.

4. Failure to deliver share certificate within time (Section 113).

5. *Misdescription of Company's Name* [Section 147 (4)]. Where an officer or agent of a company does any act or enters into a contract without fully or properly mentioning the company's name and the address of its registered office, he shall be personally liable. Thus where a bill of exchange, *hundi* or promissory note is signed by an officer of a company or any other person on its behalf, without mentioning this fact that he is signing on behalf of the company, he is personally liable to the holder of the instrument unless the company has already paid the amount.

6. *Fraudulent Trading* (Section 542). Sometimes in the course of the winding up of a company it may appear that some business of the company has been carried on with intent to defraud creditors of the company, or any other person or for any fraudulent purpose. In such a case, the Court may declare that any persons who were knowingly parties to the carrying on of the business in this way are personally liable without any limitation of liability for all or any of the debts or other liabilities of the company as the Court may direct. The Court may do so on the application of the Official liquidator, or the liquidator or any creditor or contributory of the company.

7. *Holding and Subsidiary Companies :* In the eyes of the law, the holding company and its subsidiaries (for definition of holding and subsidiary companies, refer to Chapter 2) are separate legal entities. But in the following two cases, a subsidiary company may lose its separate identity to a certain extent :

(1) Where at the end of its financial year, a company has subsidiaries, it must lay before its members in general meeting not only its own accounts, but also a set of group accounts showing the profit or loss earned or suffered by the holding company and its subsidiaries collectively, and their collective state of affairs at the end of the year (Section 212).

(2) The Court may, on the facts of a case treat a subsidiary company as merely a branch or department of one large undertaking owned by the holding company [Free Wheel (India) Ltd *Vs.* Ved Mitra, supra].

8. For investigation of ownership of company (Section 247) or investigation in the affairs of the company (Section 239).

DIFFERENCES BETWEEN A COMPANY AND A PARTNERSHIP

Partnership is the relation between persons who have agreed to share the profits of a business carried on by all or any of them acting for all. Persons who have entered into partnership with one another are called individually partners and collectively a firm (Section 4 of the Indian Partnership Act, 1932). Following are the differences between a company and partnership :

1. *Regulating Act :* A company is regulated by the Companies Act, 1956, while a partnership is governed by the Indian Partnership Act, 1932

2. *Mode of Creation :* A company comes into existence after registration under the Companies Act, 1956. Registration is not compulsory in the case of a partnership.

3. *Legal Status :* A company has a legal personality distinct from that of its members. A firm is not a person in the eyes of the law; it is made up of the several persons who compose it [Solomon *Vs.* Solomon, (1897) A.C. 22]. From the above it follows :

(a) The members of a company are not personally liable for its contracts, debts or for wrongs done by it, while the members of a partnership firm are.

(b) The property and rights of a partnership are vested in its members, so that on a change in its membership its assets must be transferred to the new partners; the property and rights of a company arc vested in it, so that it is never necessary to transfer its assets when there is a change in its membership.

(c) The property of a company belongs to the company and not to its individual members or shareholders whereas the property of a partnership firm is the joint property of the partners who are collectively entitled to it. So long as the company continues to exist, the members or the shareholders composing the company cannot be said to have any interest, legal or equitable, in the property of the company.

4. *Liability of Members :* The liability of the members of a company (except an unlimited company) to contribute towards satisfaction of the company's debts and liabilities is limited, whereas partners are liable without limit to contribute towards payment of the partnership debts and liabilities. In the case of the partnership firm, the partners are jointly and severally liable to the creditors of the firm. A creditor obtaining judgment against the firm can proceed against and attach the private property of any of the partners in the firm. But the creditor of a company is the creditor not of shareholders but of the company. He cannot proceed against and attach the private property of the shareholders, who are not directly liable to him. He can do so only against the property of the company.

5. *Management :* The affairs of a company are managed by its directors or managing director or manager, and its members have no right to take part in the management. On the other hand, every member of a partnership firm may take part in its management unless the partnership agreement provides otherwise. Even if the agreement provides otherwise, each partner still has ostensible authority to bind the partnership by contracting as its agent and may render it liable for torts committed by him.

6. *Transferability of Interest :* Shares in a company are freely transferable unless its Articles otherwise provide. When shares are transferred, the transferee becomes a member of the company and succeeds to all the rights of the transferer. A partner cannot transfer his share without the consent of the other partners. He may assign his share in the partnership, provided the partnership agreement does not provide otherwise; but the assignee merely becomes entitled to the financial benefits in respect of the share, and he does not become a partner unless other partners of the firm agree.

7. *Authority of Members* : Each partner is an agent of the partnership

firm to make contracts and incur liabilities so long as he acts in the ordinary course of the firm's business. On the other hand, a shareholder is not an agent of the company and has no such power to bind the company his acts [Baird's Case, (1870) Ch. App. 725].

8. *Powers :* A partnership firm can do anything which the partners agree to do and there is no limit to its activities a company's powers are limited to those allowed by the objects clause in its Memorandum of Association.

9. *Restrictions on Powers :* In a partnership, restrictions on the powers of a particular partner contained in the partnership agreement will not avail against outsiders, but those in the Articles of Association of a company are effective as against the public because it is a public document and anyone can inspect it to find out what is in it.

10. *Insolvency of firm and Winding up of Company :* The insolvency of a partnership firm means insolvency of all the partners, whereas the winding up of an insolvent company does not make the members insolvent.

11. *Debts :* If a company owes a debt to any of its members he can claim payment out of its assets when it is wound up rateably with its other creditors, whereas a partner who is owed money by his firm cannot prove against the firm's assets in competition with its other creditors.

12. *Dissolution :* Unless a partnership is entered into for a fixed period, it may be dissolved at any time by any partner, and the partnership will automatically be dissolved by the death or insolvency of a partner. A company has a perpetual succession. No personal circumstance affecting a member, such as death, insolvency or unsoundness of mind, will affect its existence. It comes to an end only when it is wound up according to the provisions of the Companies Act, 1956.

13. *Number of Members :* (a) Minimum. The minimum number of partners in a firm is 2 whereas the minimum number of members in a private company is 2 and in case of a public company 7.

(b) *Maximum :* The maximum number of partners in a firm carrying on banking business can be 10 and in any other business 20. The maximum number of members in a private company is 50 : there is no limit to the maximum number in case of a public company.

14. *Maintenance of Books :* A company is bound by law to maintain books of account and have its accounts audited annually by qualified auditors. There is no such statutory provision in the case of a partnership firm.

QUESTIONS

1. "A joint stock company is an artificial person created by law with a perpetual succession and a common seal." Do you agree with this definition of a company?

2. Discuss the notion of corporate personality in the light of the decision given in Salomon *Vs.* Salomon & Co. Ltd.
3. What is a corporate veil? When is it pierced?
4. "The doctrine of legal personality as applied to a company has produced astonishing effects and has been applied with few exceptions." Discuss.
5. "A company is a legal entity distinct from its members." In what cases do the Courts ignore this principle?
6. Define a company. Distinguish it from a partnership.
7. Write short notes on : (a) Lifting the corporate veil. (b) Perpetual succession. (c) Separate legal entity. (d) Corporate veil.

PRACTICAL PROBLEMS

1. 5 persons are the only members of a private company. All of them go in a boat on a pleasure trip into the open sea. The boat capsizes and all the 5 die being drowned. Does the private company cease to exist?
   [**Hint.** No. The company has a perpetual succession].
2. A husband and wife, who were the only 2 members of a private limited company, are shot dead by dacoits. Does the company also die with them?
   [**Hint.** No. The company has a perpetual succession].
3. During the war all the members of a private company, while in general meeting, were killed by a bomb. Does the company cease to exist because all the members died? State reasons.
   [**Hint.** No. The company has a perpetual succession].
4. The number of members in a public company became reduced to 6 on l0th November 1998. The company incurs trade debts on 11th November 1998. 2nd April 1999, 17th May, 1999 and 10th June 1999. How far are the remaining 6 members liable for the debts?
   [**Hint.** They are personally and severally liable for debts contracted on 17th May and 10th June, 1999 (Section 45)].
5. X and Y sold a certain business to Z and agreed not to compete with him for a certain period. After some time they organised a private limited company becoming the principal shareholders and directors and started a similar business. What right is available to Z and the company?
   [**Hint.** Z may have the company enjoined from competing with him].

3

Classification of Companies

Companies may be classified as follows on the basis of modes of incorporation; extent of the liability of the members; number of members; basis of ownership; extent of public participation; and the basis of nationality.

1. Classification on the Basis of Incorporation

On the basis of incorporation the companies may be classified as (1) Incorporated Companies and (2) Un-incorporated Companies.

1. Incorporated Companies. An Incorporated company also known as a Registered Company, means a company registered under the Indian Companies Act. Incorporated Companies may be classified as follows :

(i) *Companies Incorporated by Royal Charter :* This system of formation of companies under a Royal Charter was in the practices under the British Govt. The East India Company, for example, was incorporated by the Royal Charter granted by the King or Queen of British. Such a company was regulated and controlled by its charter. Now-a-days this is not in practice.

(ii) *Companies Incorporated by Special Act of Parliament :* Companies incorporated by a Special Act of Parliament or State Legislature, are formed for the fulfilment of some special objects at the National level. These companies also known as Corporation include The Reserve Bank of India, State Bank of India, etc.

(iii) *Companies Incorporated under Indian Companies Act :* All the companies in India formed under the Indian Companies Act, 1956 are regulated and controlled by their memorandum of association and articles of association.

2. Un-incorporated Companies. A group of persons which is not registered under Indian Companies Act is known as Un-incorporated company. It may be a big partnership Organisation or a large groups of persons but not a company. The liability of its members is unlimited as they are not different from its entity. Such type of company has been restricted under section 11 of Indian Companies Act, 1956.

II. Classification on the Basis of Liability

Companies may be classified on the basis of Liability as follows :

(1) Limited Liability Companies and

(2) Unlimited Liability Companies.

1. Limited Liability Companies. In this type of companies, by using the word 'LIMITED' with their name, the liability of members is limited. Such companies may again be of following two types :

(i) *Companies Limited by Shares :* According to Section 12(2)(a) of the Companies Act, "a company having the liability of its members limited by the memorandum of association to the amount, if any unpaid on the shares respectively held by them is termed as a company limited by shares." Such a company **is** commonly known as Limited Liability Company as the liability of the members is limited up to the face value of the shares held. Most of the companies established in India are limited by shares.

(ii) *Companies Limited by Guarantee :* Section 12(2)(b) of the Indian Companies Act states that "A company having the liability of its members limited by its memorandum to such amount as the members respectively thereby undertake to contribute to the assets of the company in the event of its being wound up in this Act termed" a company limited by guarantee. Therefore, the liability of the members of such a company remains limited to the amount they agree to contribute to the company, if the need may be. This amount of guarantee cannot be demanded from the members until company is wound up, therefore, this amount is known as 'Reserve Capital'. Generally, such companies are formed without share capital for non trading purposes, *e.g.*, for the promotion of art, science, trade, and culture etc.

2. Unlimited Companies. Section 12(2)(c) of the Companies Act states that a company not having any limit on the liability of its members, is called unlimited liability company as the liability of members may go up to the personal property of the members and every member of such a company is liable to contribute any amount in proportion to his interest in the company towards the liabilities of the company. This liability of a member can be enforced only at the time of the winding up.

III. Classification on the Basis of Number of Members

Companies may be classified as follows on the basis of number of members : (1) Public Company and (2) Private Company.

1. Public Company. A public company is one which is registered under the Indian Companies Act, 1956 or an existing company having 7 or more members. Section 3 (i) (iv) of the Companies Act lays down that public company means a company which :[1]

1. Substituted by the Companies (Amendment) Act, 2000, w.e.f. 13.12.2000

(a) is not a private company;

(b) has a minimum paid-up capital of five lakh rupees or such higher paid-up capital, as may be presented;

(c) is a private company which is a subsidiary of a company which is not a private company.

A public company must have minimum 7 members. There is no restriction with regard to maximum number of members of a public company. It may be equal to the number of shares offered by the company.

2. Private Company. Section 3(i)(iii) of the Companies Act defines

(i) "private company" [*means a company which has a minimum paid-up capital of one lakh rupees or such higher paid-up capital as may be prescribed, and by its articles*, :][2]

(a) restricts the right to transfer its shares, if any;

(b) limits the number of its members to fifty not including—

(i) persons who are the employment of the company; and

(ii) persons who, having been formerly in the employment of the company, were members of the company while in that employment and have continued to be members after the employment ceased; and

(c) prohibits any invitation to the public to subscribe for any shares in, or debentures of, the company;

(d) *prohibits any invitation or acceptance of deposits from persons other than its members, directors or their relatives* :

Provided that where two or more persons hold one or more shares in a company jointly, they shall, for the purpose of this definition be treated as a single member.

According to Section 3 of Companies Act :

(i) Every private company, existing on the commencement of the Companies (Amendment) Act, 2000, with a paid-up capital of less than one lakh rupees, shall, within a period of two years from such commencement, enhance its paid-up capital to one lakh rupees.

(ii) Every public company, existing on the commencement of the Companies (Amendment) Act, 2000, with a paid-up capital of less than five lakh rupees, shall, within a period of two years from such commencement, enhance its paid-up capital to five lakh rupees.

(iii) Where a private company or a public company fails to enhance its paid-up capital in the manner specified in sub-section (3)

2. Substituted by the Companies (Amendment) Act, 2000, w.e.f. 13.12.2000

or sub-section (4), such company shall be deemed to be a defunct company within the meaning of section 560 and its name shall be struck off from the register by the Registrar.

(iv) A company registered under section 25 before or after the commencement of Companies (Amendment) Act, 2000 shall not be required to have minimum paid-up capital specified in this section.

IV. Classification on the Basis of Ownership

On the basis of ownership, companies may be classified as (1) Government Company and (2) Non-Government Company.

1. Government Company. Section 617 of Indian Companies Act defines a Government or State Government Company as, "any company of which not less than 51 per cent of the (paid-up share capital) is held by the Central Government or by any State Governments [and includes a company which is a subsidiary of a Government Company as thus defined]." Government companies function in the same manner as other companies. All the provisions of Companies Act apply to these companies. However, the central government may exempt any company from the application of the provisions of the act except Section 619 and 619(a) which are specifically meant for government companies.

2. Non-government Company. A Non-government company is that which is not a government company but company owned by the private entrepreneurs. Most of the companies in India are of this type.

V. Classification on the Basis of Independence

On the basis of independence, companies may be classified as (1) Subsidiary Company and (2) Holding company.

1. "Holding Company" and "Subsidiary". (1) For the purposes of this Act, a company shall, subject to the provisions of sub-section (3), be deemed to be a subsidiary of another if, but only if,—

(a) that other controls the composition of its Board of directors; or

[(b) that other—

(i) where the first-mentioned company is an existing company in respect of which the holders of preference shares issued before the commencement of this Act have the same voting rights in all respects as the holders of equity shares, exercises or controls more than half of the total voting power of such company;

(ii) where the first-mentioned company is any other company, holds more than half in nominal value of its equity share capital; or]

(c) the first-mentioned company is a subsidiary of any company which is that other's subsidiary.

For example, if company 'A' holds more than half of the equity share capital of company 'B' the company 'B' will be a subsidiary of company 'A'. Again, if company 'B' holds more than half of the equity share capital of company 'C' the company 'C' will be the subsidiary of both the companies 'A' and 'B'.

2. Holding Company. Section 4 of the Act states that a company may be termed as Holding Company if it has any company as its subsidiary.

VI. Classification on the Basis of Nationality

On the basis of nationality companies may be classified as : (1) Inland Companies and (2) Foreign Companies.

1. Inland Companies. An Inland Company is that which is formed, regulated and controlled by any of the Companies Act of India.

2. Foreign Companies. Section 591 of the Indian Companies Act, 1956 states that a Foreign Company is one which is incorporated outside India, but is doing its business in India. However, Foreign Company may also do its business outside India as well.

Application of sections 592 to 602 to foreign companies. [(1) Sections 592 to 602, both inclusive, shall apply to all foreign companies, that to say, companies falling under the following two classes, namely :—

(a) companies incorporated outside Indian which, after the commencement of this Act, establish a place of business within India; and

(b) companies incorporated outside India which have, before the commencement of this Act, established a place of business within India and continue to have an established place of business within India at the commencement of this Act.

[(2) Notwithstanding anything contained in sub-section (1), where not less than fifty per cent, of the paid-up share capital (whether equity or preference or partly equity and partly preference) of a company incorporated outside Indian and having an established place of business in India, is held by one or more citizens of Indian or by one or more bodies corporate incorporated in India, or by one or more citizens of India and one or more bodies corporate incorporated in India, whether singly or in the aggregate, such company shall comply with such of the provisions of this Act as may be prescribed with regard to the business carried on by it in India, as if it were a company incorporated in India.]

Distinctions Between Public Company and Private Company

Basis of Difference	Public Company	Private Company
1. Minimum Number of Members and Capital	7 members. 5 Lakh	2 members. 1 Lakh
2. Maximum Number of Members.	No restriction with regard to maximum number of members.	The number of members should not exceed 50, excluding past and present employees of the company.
3. Invitation to Public.	It can invite public to subscribe its shares and debentures.	It cannot invite the public to do so.
4. Transfer of shares.	The shares can be easily transferred.	The shares cannot be transferred.
5. Commencement of Business.	It cannot commence its business unless it gets the certificate of the commencement of business.	It can commence its business immediately after it gets the certificate of incorporation.
6. Statutory Meeting the Statutory Report.	It has to call a Statutory Meeting for where it has submit a Statutory Report	There is no need to call the Statutory Meeting and to submit the Statutory Report.
7. Allotment of Shares.	It cannot allot its shares unless it has called minimum subscription and has received atleast 5 per cent of the nominal amount of the shares in cash on application.	It can allot its shares immediately after incorporation.
8. Issue of Prospectus.	It has to issue a prospectus or submit a statement in lieu of prospectus.	It has to submit neither a prospectus nor a statement in lieu of prospectus.
9. Use of Word.	It has to use the word 'Limited' with its name.	It has to use the word 'Private Limited' with its name.
10. Number of Directors.	It must have a minimum of three directors.	It should have a minimum of two directors.
11. Loan to Directors.	It cannot sanction any loan to its directors unless it is permitted by the Central Government.	It can sanction loan to its directors without permission from the Central Government.
12. Retirement of Directors by Rotation.	Its Directors have to retire by rotation compulsorily.	It is not necessary for the Directors to retire by rotation.
13. Submission of Documents.	It has to submit the list of Directors, their consent and the contract entered into by the Company with them.	It has not to submit any such documents.

Basis of Difference	Public Company	Private Company
14. Signature on the Memorandum.	Its memorandum must be signed by at least 7 persons.	Its memorandum should be signed by 2 persons only.
15. Issue of Share Warrant.	It can issue share warrants only if the shares are fully paid.	It cannot issue share warrants.
16. Articles of Association.	It is not bound to have its own articles of association. If a Public Schedule 'A' applies to it company does not have its articles.	It is bound to have its own articles of association.
17. Vote by Directors.	Its Directors cannot vote on a proposal in which they are interested.	Its Directors can vote on such proposals also.
18. Increase in the Number of Directors.	It cannot increase number of its Directors without the permission of the Central Government.	It can increase the number of its Directors without such permission.
19. Accounts for Public Inspection.	Its Accounts must be open to public for inspection.	It is not bound to offer its Accounts for public inspection.
20. Investment in the same group of companies.	It cannot invest in the same group of companies.	It can do so.
21. Restriction on Managerial Remuneration.	It cannot pay more than 11 per cent of its net profits by way of managerial remuneration.	There is no such restriction with regard to payment of managerial remuneration.

ONE MAN COMPANY

Though a company must be established in accordance with the provisions of Indian Companies Act, 1956, however, in some cases only one man holds practically the whole of shares of a company and takes few more dummy members to meet the legal requirements. Such a company is known as one man company. For example, a private company should have minimum two members. A person may take all of its shares except one which may be given to any of its family members. Similarly, in case of a public company, it must have minimum 7 members. A person may take all of its shares and only a few shares may be allotted to the rest 6 members, usually from his family. Such a company is perfectly in order in the eyes of law and cannot be refused to be registered under the Act, because it fulfils all the legal requirements. But practically the company is owned by only one member and, therefore it is called one man company. The best example is Solomon and Co. Limited.

PRIVATE COMPANY

Definition

Section 3(i)(iii) of the Indian Companies Act, 1956 (as amended by Companies (Amendment) Act, 2000) defines a Private Company which has a minimum paid-up capital of one lakh rupees or such higher paid-up capital as may be prescribed and by its articles :

(a) restricts the right to transfer its shares; if any

(b) limits the number of its members to 50, excluding its past and present employees;

(c) prohibits any invitation to the public to subscribe for its shares and debentures; and

(d) prohibits any invitation or acceptance of deposits from persons other than its members, directors or their relatives.

Registration

A private company can be registered with minimum number of two members and cannot have more than 50 members. The number 50 does not include its past and present employees, and joint shareholders of the company are counted as one person. A private company cannot issue the prospectus to invite public to subscribe for its shares and debentures. It has no right to allow free transfer of its shares.

Special Privileges or Exemptions

1. Minimum Number of Members[Section 12]. It can be registered with only two members while a public company must have atleast 7 members.

2. Allotment of Shares [Section 69]. It can make the final allotment of its shares without collecting the minimum subscription. There is no restriction over the allotment of shares by a private company.

3. No Need to file Prospectus or Statement in Lieu of Prospectus [Section 70]. It cannot and need not file any prospectus or statement in lieu of prospectus before making the allotment.

4. No Restriction on Right Issue [Section 81]. It is not bound to offer its new issue of share capital to its existing shareholders. It means that a private company can issue its further issues to new members also.

5. No Need to get the Certificate of Commencement of Business [Section 149]. It can start its business immediately after getting the certificate of incorporation. A private company need not wait to get the certificate of commencement of business like a public company.

6. No Need to call Statutory Meeting [Section 165 (10)]. It is not bound to call the statutory meeting like a public company and therefore it is not bound to file a statutory report also.

7. Exemption as to the Rules of Division of Shares and Voting [Section 80]. It is not bound to follow the division of share and voting by the shareholders.

8. No Restriction regarding Managerial Remuneration [Section 198]. It is free to decide the managerial remuneration while a public company cannot distribute more than 11 per cent of its net profit to its managerial personnel.

9. No Restriction of Quorum [Section 147 (1)]. It can proceed at its meeting only if the two members are present while in a public company there must be atleast 5 members for the quorum.

10. Exemption regarding Transfer of Shares [Section 111]. It cannot allow free transfer of its shares and in this regard it may cancel or refuse any application for the transfer of its shares. The shareholders are not allowed to apply to the central government or court against such refusal.

11. Exemption regarding Certain Sections [Section 171 to 186]. It can by its articles, exempt itself from the application of Section 171 to section 186 of the Indian Companies Act, 1956.

12. Exemption regarding Financial Statement [Section 220 (1)]. It is not bound to file three copies of its profit and loss account and balance sheet with the Registrar. It is not bound to open its accounts for the public inspection.

13. Number of Directors [Section 252 (2)]. The minimum number of directors for it is two while for a public company it is three.

14. Exemption [Section 259]. It need to take the permission of central government for increasing the number of directors while a public company cannot increase the number of its directors unless it gets the permission of central government to do so.

15. Exemption regarding Directors [Section 255]. The directors are not required to be retired by rotation like a public company.

16. Exemption regarding Appointment of Directors [Section 263]. It can appoint two or more directors by a single resolution. It need not pass a separate resolution for the appointment of every director.

17. Exemption regarding Appointment of Director other than the Retiring One [Section 264]. If it appoints a director other than the retiring one, the newly appointed director need not file his written consent with the Registrar of Companies.

18. No Restriction on the Appointment of Director [Section 266]. Restriction regarding the appointment and the advertisement for appointment of directors are not applicable to it.

19. Exemption regarding Appointment of Managing Director [Section 269]. It can appoint the managing director or full time director without getting the permission from Central Government.

20. Exemption regarding Loan to Director [Section 295]. It can finance its directors while a public company can not do so.

21. Exemption regarding Right of Directors [Section 293]. There is no restriction regarding the powers and rights of directors in a private company.

22. Exemption regarding Vote by Directors [Section 300]. Its directors can participate in the discussion and can also vote on the proposal in which they themselves are interested.

23. No Restriction Upon Increase in the Remuneration of Directors [Section 310 & 311]. It is not bound to get the permission of central government to increase the remuneration of its directors while a public company can not do so, without getting the permission from the central government.

24. No Restriction Upon Appointment of a Managing Director [Section 316]. It is empowered to appoint any person as its managing director even if he is already working as a managing director in one or more companies.

25. No Restriction Upon Appointment of Managing Director for Long period [Section 317]. It can appoint its managing director for a period of more than 5 years while a public company cannot do so.

26. No Interference by Central Government regarding Board of Directors. Central Government is not empowered to interfere with regard to the change in composition of board of directors even if such a change is against the interest of the company.

PRIVATE COMPANY TREATED AS PUBLIC COMPANY

(1) If a private company violates any of the three conditions specified in Section 3(l)(iii) of the Indian Companies Act, 1956, its privileges and exemptions will cease and it will be treated as a public company. However, the Registrar of Companies may exempt from the application of this provision, if he is satisfied with the reason furnished by it for violation of such conditions such penalty as applicable to public company may be imposed if a petition by the company is made such conversion is called 'conversion by default.'

(2) The Companies (Amendment) Act 2000 has made Section 43A, introduced in 1960, inoperative. (Under Section 43A, a private company was "deemed public company" on the basis of turnover or share holdings). Now under Section 3(1)(iii) if a private company accepts deposits from public shall become a public company. These private companies which were regarded as "deemed public companies" have to apply, if they want again private company status to the Registrar.

(3) A private company may, of its own choice become a public company by passing a special resolution and by increasing the number of members and directors if they are less than 7 or 3 respectively. It has to issue a prospectus or a statement in lieu of prospectus is to be

filed with the Registrar, within 30 days, as per details required by Schedule II (Section 44).

PUBLIC COMPANY

Definition

1. Section 3(l)(i) of Indian Companies Act, 1956. "Company" means a company established under this Act or an existing company.

2. Section 3(l)(ii) of Indian Companies Act, 1956. "An existing company" means a company formed and registered under any of the former Company Acts.

3. Professor Haney. "A Company is an incorporated Organisation, which is an artificial person created by law, having separate entity, with a perpetual succession and a common seal."

Thus, a company is an incorporated organisation having an independent legal entity, with a perpetual succession, a common seal, carrying limited liability and its shares can be transferred easily.

CONVERSION OF A PUBLIC COMPANY INTO A PRIVATE COMPANY

Though the Indian Companies Act is silent about the rules regarding conversion of a public company into private company, Section 31 of the Companies Act lays down the following procedure for such conversion :

1. Change in Articles of Association. If a public company makes alteration in its articles of association by passing a special resolution to that effect it becomes a private company. In this case, company must provide for the fulfilment of three basic conditions as specified in Section 3(l)(iii) for a private company.

2. Permission of Central Government. In order to become a private company, a public company must compulsorily get the permission from central government for such changes, so that the central government may be convinced that the proposed change will not cause any harm to any group or any person.

3. Filing a Copy of Changed Articles of Association with the Registrar. After getting the permission of central government the company must file a copy of amended articles of association with the Registrar of Companies within 30 days. Filing of the amended articles of association of the company is compulsory to enable the registrar to make necessary changes in his record. After being satisfied the registrar issues a fresh certificate of incorporation to the company.

4. Reduction of Number of Shareholders. A company will have to reduce the number of its shareholders to 50. It will have to restrict the transfer of its shares and will have to add the world "Pvt. Ltd." with its name.

CONVERSION OF A PRIVATE COMPANY INTO A PUBLIC COMPANY

In order to convert itself into a private company a public company will have to follow the following procedure under Section 43 and 44 of Indian Companies Act, 1956 :

1. Violation of the Basic Conditions. If a private company violates any of the three conditions under Section 3(l)(iii) it will automatically be converted into a public company. However, if the Registrar of Companies is satisfied with the reasons furnished by a company for the violation of basic conditions, he may allow it to continue as a private company.

2. Changing the Articles of Association. A private company may pass a resolution to the effect that articles of association are changed in the manner that it may become a public company. In this case the restriction of Section 3(l) (iii) of Companies Act will not apply on the company and it will be deemed to be a public company since the date of passing such resolution.

3. Filing of the Prospectus or Statement in Lieu of Prospectus with the Registrar. If a private company passes a resolution to convert itself into a public company, it will have to file the prospectus or the statement in lieu of prospectus with the Registrar of Companies within 30 days of the changes in articles of association.

4. Changing the Name and Capital Clause. In order to convert into a public company, a private company will have to call a meeting of its shareholders at a notice of 21 days and will have to change the name clause. The word Private will be eliminated. The capital clause will be changed to a great extent. The total share capital will be divided into a number of shares and the shares will be allowed to be transferred freely.

5. Changing the Number of Directors and Members. To be converted into a public company, a private company will have to change the number of its directors and members, as required for the public company. It should have the minimum of 7 members and the minimum of 3 directors.

6. Provision of Penalty. If the company does not comply with the above requirements and procedure, every officer of the company liable for the mistake will have to pay a penalty upto Rs. 5000 per day.

7. Procedure. When a private company seeks to covert itself into a public company, to directors' draft resolution to that effect and call an extraordinary meeting of its shareholders, to pass this resolution. The private company is converted into a public company on the day when the resolution is passed as a special resolution. The directors of the private company will have to submit a declaration with the Registrar of Companies that all the requirements for the conversion of company into a public company have been duly complied with. The Registrar scrutinises the declaration. If he is satisfied, he registers the relevant information and makes the necessary changes in the memorandum of association and articles of association of the company. He also issues a fresh certificate of incorporation to the company. With this is completed the procedure of the conversion of a private company into a public company.

[(2A) *Where a public company referred to in sub-section (2) becomes a private company on or after the commencement of the Companies (Amendment) Act, 2000, such company shall inform the Registrar that it has become a private company and thereupon the Registrar shall substitute the words "private company" for the words "public company" in the name of the company upon the register and shall also make the necessary alterations in the certificate of incorporation issued to the company and in its memorandum of association within four weeks from the date of application made by the company.*]

FOREIGN COMPANY

A Foreign Company means a company incorporated outside India under the law of the country of incorporation and carrying on business in India.

Definition of Foreign Company

Section 591 of the Indian Companies Act, 1956 defines a foreign company as a company :

(i) Which is incorporated outside India and established the place of its business in India after the enactment of this act and
(ii) Which is incorporated outside India and which established its place of business in India before the enactment of this act and has maintained its place of business in India, even after the enactment of this act.

Documents to be submitted for Registration

Section 592 of Indian Companies Act, 1956 states that a foreign company has to furnish the following documents to the Registrar of Companies within 30 days of the establishment of its business in India :

(i) A certified copy of charter, memorandum of association, articles of association, and the statutes. All these documents must be in English. If any instrument is not in English language a certified translation thereof should be filed.
(ii) Full address of the registered office of the company.
(iii) List of directors and secretary of the company. Such a list should give their name in full, their registered address, their nationality of origin and the particulars of other directorships or secretary-ships held by them.

(iv) Name and address of persons who are residing in India and are authorised to accept the certificates and notices on behalf of the company.

(v) The full address of the office of the company in India which is to be treated as place of its business in India.

Information of Changes in Documents

1. Section 593 of Indian Companies Act. It states that if any change or alteration takes place in any of the above documents or information filed by foreign company with the Registrar of Companies under Section 592, such change or alteration must be informed to the registrar within the time allotted for it so that he may make the necessary changes in the relevant documents well in time.

2. Section 601 of the Act. It states that if the charter, memorandum of association or articles of association or registered office are changed by any reason, such a change should be informed to the Registrar till 31st January next of the year in which such change takes place.

Obligations regarding Accounts

Section 594 of the Indian Companies Act imposes following obligations on a foreign company regarding its accounts :

(i) Every foreign company, unless exempted by central government, is required to file with the registrar every year 3 copies of its balance sheet and profit and loss account.

(ii) Besides, 3 copies in the prescribed form of all the places of its business in India should also be sent to the registrar every year.

(iii) If any of the above documents are not in English language, the certified translation thereof should be submitted.

Its Name and Country of Incorporation

1. Name. Every foreign company has to specify the name of country of incorporation in its prospectus. The commercial letters, bills, notices and all other publications of the foreign company should bear its name and the name of country of incorporation in English language.

2. Section 595. If the liability of the members of foreign company is limited, the information of this limited liability must be specified on every statement, commercial letter, bill, notice, advertisement etc., of the company in English.

Procedure to Communicate

Section 596 of the Indian Companies Act states that communication of any message or letter is taken to be completed in case of a foreign company only when it has been communicated to the right person at the right address of the company. The address must be similar as has been given to the registrar.

Office where Documents are to be Delivered

Section 571 of the Companies Act, requires that any document which any foreign country is required to deliver to the Registrar of the Companies, should be delivered by the company to the registrar in his office at New Delhi and also to the registrar of the state in which the particular place of business of the company is situated.

Penalty for Foreign Company

If a foreign company fails to comply with any of the above requirements, the company and every office of the company which is in default shall be punishable with a fine which may be up to Rs. 10,000 and if the fault continues, and additional fine which may be up to Rs. 1000 per day, during the period in which default continues, may be imposed.

Section 599 of the Companies Act states that even if any foreign company is guilty of the above faults, it does not make any difference regarding the validity of any contract entered into by the company. The company may be sued for any contract entered into it but the company cannot file any suit for such contracts till it obeys the above provisions fully and completely.

Related Provisions of Indian Companies Act

1. The Provisions of Section 124 to 145. Those relating to the registration of changes will also apply to foreign companies.

2. The Provision of Section 118. Those relating to the rights of members or debenture holders will also apply to foreign companies.

3. Section 600 of the Companies Act. Those relating to the maintenance of books of account at the particular place of business of company will also apply to a foreign company.

4. The Provision of Section 159. Those relating to the filing of written consent with the registrar shall also apply to a foreign company.

5. The Provision of Section 209a. Those relating to inspection of books of accounts to the power of central government.

6. Section 233. Those relating to the power of central government to order for special audit.

7. Section 234 to 246 and 600. Those relating to the power of registrar shall also apply to a foreign company.

GOVERNMENT COMPANY

Section 617 of Indian Companies Act, 1956 defines a Government Company as "Any company in which not less than 51 per cent of the (paid-up share capital) is held by the Central Government or by any State Government or Governments or partly by the Central Government and partly by one or more State Governments [and includes a company which is a subsidiary of a government company as thus defined."]

Special Provisions

Following are the special provisions regarding Government Company in Indian Companies Act, 1956 :

1. Restriction on the Appointment of Managing Agent [Section 618]. It states that no government company **can** appoint the managing agents.

2. Audit of Accounts. Following rules are applied for the audit of government companies :

(i) Section 619 (2). The auditor of a government company shall be appointed or re-appointed by central government on the advice of Controller and Auditor General of India.

(ii) The auditor so appointed or re-appointed can not hold appointment as a auditor in more than 20 companies at one time, of which not more than 10 companies should have the paid up share capital of Rs. 25 lakhs or more.

(iii) The Auditor General can direct the auditor of government company relating to the conduct of audit and performance of his duties.

(iv) Section 619 (3). The auditor so appointed can hold the supplementary test audit of the companies accounts and for this purpose he can appoint the required persons also.

(v) Section 619 (4 & 5). The auditor of a government company has to submit a copy of his report to the Comptroller and Auditor General who can comment upon the report. These comments of the Auditor General shall be placed before the annual General meeting of the company along with the audit report.

Thus, the provisions of section 224 to section 233 of the act relating to the Audit of general company do not apply to the government company.

3. Annual Report. Following are special provisions relating to annual report of government companies :

(i) Section 619 A (1). If the central government is a member of a government company, it will prepare annual report on the work and affairs of the company within three months of the annual general meeting. This annual report is to be laid before both the houses of Parliament together with a copy of auditor's report along with a copy of comment made by Comptroller and Auditor General of India.

(ii) Section 619 A (2). Where a state government or state governments are also a member of government company, in addition to the central government, the state government or governments shall place a copy of the annual report, as prepared by the central government, along with a copy of auditor's report and copy of the comments on Auditor's report before the house or both houses of the state legislature or legislatures, as the case and need may be.

(iii) Section 619 A(3). When the central government is not a member of government companies and only state government or more than one state governments are the members of government company, every member state government shall prepare a report on the working and affairs of the company on the same lines as before, and they will lay it before the house or both the houses of the state legislature along with a copy of auditor's report and a copy of comments thereupon.

4. Power to modify Companies Act in Relation to Government Companies (Section 620). Indian Company Act, 1956 states that a government company should be registered under the Companies Act, as it may be a public company or a private company.

The central government may, by notification in the official gazette order that either the provisions of Indian Companies Act shall not apply or shall apply to government companies or shall apply with such modifications as may be specified in the notification. But such a notification shall be effective only if it is approved by the Parliament. If the Parliament does not approve this notification, it cannot be effective. If there is no such notification, government companies are governed by the Companies Act in the same manner as other companies are governed.

5. Depository Receipts (Section 605A). One of the ways to raise finance in international financial markets is by offering depository receipts *e.g.* Global depository receipt, American depository receipt and Indian depository receipt. If a foreign company wants to raise funds in India (even it does not have place of business in India) it may offer I.D.R. to raise funds. Indian companies offer G.D.R. and A.D.R. A prospectus is to be issued, failing which is fine upto Rs. 50,000 or imprisonment upto six months or both.

HOLDING COMPANY *Vs.* SUBSIDIARY COMPANY

1. Difference of Definition. When a company is in a position to control the management of author company, the former is called a holding company and the latter is called a subsidiary company.

(i) Section 4(4) of the Indian Companies Act, 1956. It defines holding company as, "A company shall be deemed to be holding company of another if that other company is its subsidiary."

(ii) Section 4(l) of the Indian Companies Act, 1956. It defines a subsidiary company as "a company shall be deemed to be subsidiary of another if,

(a) that other company controls the majority composition of its board of directors with the sole object of management; or

(b) that other company holds more than half in the nominal value of its equity share capital; or

(c) in the case of an existing company (having registered under the earlier act) if the holders of preference shares have the same voting right as the holders of equity shares, that other company holds more than half of its total voting power; or

(d) it is a subsidiary of any other company of which that other company is a subsidiary."

2. Difference of Circumstances. The above definition makes it clear that the terms holding company and subsidiary company are established by the circumstances. There is no holding company as such because a company can be a holding company only if there is one or more subsidiary companies for it. Similarly, there can be no subsidiary company if there is no holding company. Therefore, it is a question of circumstances of the company and not of the incorporation of the company. If, for example, a company 'A' is in a position to control the composition of the board of directors of company 'B', or it has more than half in the nominal value of the equity share capital of company 'B', the company 'B' will be subsidiary and the company 'A' will be a holding company.

3. Exceptions. If company 'A' is a holding company and company 'B' is its subsidiary, and company 'C' is the subsidiary of company 'B', company 'C' will automatically be subsidiary of company 'A' also, though it has no direct contact with that company. The very interesting fact to note is that an investment company whose business is to acquire and hold the shares, debentures or stock or any other securities of other companies cannot be a holding company, only on the basis that it has acquired more than 50 per cent shares of another company.

4. Foreign Company. It is also to remember that a private company which is a subsidiary of a foreign company shall be deemed to be a subsidiary of a public company because in this case foreign company would have been considered as a public company. The Indian Companies Act considered all Indian private company which is a subsidiary of a foreign company equal to a private company which is a subsidiary of an Indian public company.

5. Trustee. If the shares of one company are held by another company as a trustee and that company is in a position to appoint the majority of directors of that company, even then, the former company will not be a holding company, a lender company has acquired more than 50 per cent shares of the borrower company merely as a security for transaction entered in the ordinary course of business, does not empower the lending company to be the holding company.

6. Lender. If the company must hold either the majority of the equity share capital or must in order to be called a holding company possess the power to appoint the majority of directors in another company with the sole object of controlling the management of another company. It cannot be called a holding company if the object of holding is either as a security for a loan or a fiduciary capacity or only as investment.

INVESTMENT COMPANIES

Under Section 372 (10) an investment company is a company whose principal business is the acquisition of shares, stock, debentures or other securities. The investment company is expected to hold the securities for a reasonable time. It is different from public financial institutions. Under Section 4A the central government specifies which are public financial institutions. Examples are G.I.C.I; N.H.B; U.T.I; LIC and I.D.B.I etc.

PROHIBITION OF LARGE PARTNERSHIPS

Illegal Association

Under Section 11 a company, association or partnership consisting of more than 10 persons for the purpose of carrying on banking business and of more than 20 persons for the purpose of carrying on any other business with the object of earning profits can be legally formed only when it is registered under the Companies Act, 1956, or is formed in pursuance of some other Indian law or is a Joint Hindu Family carrying on business as such. If the number of members in an association or partnership exceeds this statutory limit and it is not registered under the Companies Act, it is an *illegal association* and has no legal existence.

An association of more than 20 persons which exists not for acquisition of gain but for some other purpose such as the promotion of art, charity, religion, science, etc., does not require registration. Thus there are two exceptions where registration law does not apply

(a) In case of H.U.F.

(b) an association formed not for earning profit.

Consequences of illegal association. The consequences of an illegal association are as follows :

1. *Personal liability :* Every member of an illegal association is personally liable for all liabilities incurred in the business and is punishable with fine which may extend to Rs. 10,000 under Section 11(5).

2. *Contracts :* (a) An illegal association cannot enter into any contract nor can it sue any member or outsider, not even if the company is subsequently registered.

(b) It cannot sue or be sued for debts due to it or from it in carrying on its business for it cannot contract debts, or enter into any contract.

(c) No member of the association can sue any other member in respect of any matter connected with the association.

(d) The members cannot either individually or collectively bring an action to enforce any contract which they may have purported to make on behalf of the association, or to recover any debt given to the association.

3. Such association can not avail any of the income tax exemption.

4. *Winding up* : An illegal association cannot be wound up under the Companies Act either at the instance of a creditor, or a member or the association itself. The Court will do nothing in relation to it that will amount to its recognition. In fact, the Court does not even entertain a petition for its winding up, for if it did, it would be indirectly according recognition to the illegal association.

Penalty for improper use of words "Limited" and "Private Limited". If any person or persons trade or carry on business under any name or title of which the word, "Limited" or the words "Private Limited", or any contraction or imitation thereof is or are the last word or words, that person or each of these persons shall, unless duly incorporated with limited liability, or unless duly incorporated as a private company with limited liability, as the case may be, be punishable with fine which may extend to [*five hundred rupees*] for every day upon which that name has been used.

QUESTIONS

1. What is a private company? How much capital is needed to register it?
2. Describe briefly the procedure for effecting the conversion of a private company into a public company. How does a private company differ from a public company?
3. 'Not only does the Legislature recognise the private company, it may be said to bestow its benedictions upon it." Comment, indicating the advantages to be derived from the conversion of a trading firm into a private company.
4. Explain what is meant by a 'holding company' and a 'subsidiary company'. Give examples.
5. How can a limited company be formed without the word 'Limited' or the words 'Private Limited' as the last word/words in its name?
6. What is a Government Company? State its special features. How far is it governed by the Companies Act, 1956?
7. What is a foreign company? What are the provisions of the Companies Act, 1956 relating to foreign companies?
8. Write a note on 'one-man company".
9. State the law regarding compulsory registration of an association formed for the purpose of carrying on business. What are the

legal consequences where an association which must be registered under the Companies Act, 1956 is not registered?

PRACTICAL PROBLEMS

1. X, a trader, carried on business under the name of X & Co. Ltd., without being registered as a company with limited liability. Discuss the consequences of the act of X.
[**Hint.** Refer to Sections 11 and 631].
2. An association of 12 members starts a banking business without being registered. 4 members retire and thereafter a suit is instituted by one of the continuing members for the partition of assets of the business. Is the suit valid?
[**Hint.** No (Section 11)].
3. 35 per cent of the paid-up capital of a private company is held by a public company. Does the private company become a public company? Give reasons for your answer.
[**Hint.** Yes (Badri Prasad *Vs.* Nagarmal).
4. X & Co. and Y & Co. are 2 firms registered under the Indian Partnership Act, 1932, each consisting of 12 partners. The firms desire to carry on business jointly as partners under the name XY & Co. Does XY & Co. require registration and, if so, under what provisions of the Companies Act?
[**Hint.** Yes (Section 11)].
5. A joint Hindu family consisting of a father and 5 major sons and another family consisting of a father, 5 major sons and 1 minor son carried on banking business, as owners thereof. Does the organisation require registration under the Companies Act, 1956?
[**Hint.** Yes (Section 11)].

4

FORMATION OF PUBLIC COMPANIES

Incorporating a Company

Under Section 12 any seven or more (two or more in case of private company) persons in case of a public company may, by subscribing their names to the memorandum can get a company registered, with or without limited liability.

In order to get the company incorporated the promoter will have to prepare and file with the Registrar of Companies the following documents :

(1) Memorandum of Association.

(2) Articles of Association.

(3) List of persons who have consented to act as directors.

(4) Consent of directors in writing to act as such.

(5) Director's undertaking to take up and pay for qualification shares, if any.

(6) Agreement to appoint Managing Director.

(7) Statutory declaration by an advocate of the Supreme Court or a High Court or by an attorney (may be a Chartered Accountant or Company Secretary or any one of them) or a responsible officer of the company that all requirements of the Companies Act, 1956, and the rules thereunder have been complied with in respect of registration and other matters pertaining thereto.

(8) Notice of registered address within 30 days of incorporation or commencement of business.

The necessary stamp duty, registration fees, and the filing fees will be paid along with the above documents. If the Registrar is satisfied on all matters, he will issue a "Certificate of Incorporation", after which the company is said to have been incorporated or registered.

(1) MEMORANDUM OF ASSOCIATION

Definition

1. Section 2(28) of the Companies Act, 1956. Memorandum means the memorandum of association of a company as originally framed or as altered from time to time in pursuance of any previous companies law or of this Act.

Legally speaking, memorandum means the memorandum of association of' a company as originally framed or as altered according to the procedure laid down by the Act. No company can be registered without the memorandum of association.

2. Lord Cairns. "The memorandum of association of a company is its charter and defines the limitation of powers of a company. The memorandum contains the fundamental conditions upon which alone the company is allowed to be incorporated".

3. Lord Macmillan. "The purpose of the memorandum is to enable the shareholders, creditors and those who deal with the company, to know what is its permitted range of enterprise."

4. Charles Worth. "The memorandum of association is the company's charter and defined the limitations of its powers. Its purpose is to enable shareholders, creditors and those who deal with the company, to know what is its permitted range of enterprise. It is the document which informs all persons dealing with the company, what the company is formed to do, what capital it has to do with and what its nationality is. It regulates the company's external affairs, while the articles of association regulate its internal affairs".

From the above definitions, it may be concluded that the memorandum is the most important document. It has been variously described as its foundation, charter and the constitution without which a company cannot be incorporated.

Importance of Memorandum

(1) Charter. Memorandum of Association of a company is its charter which defines the limitation on the powers of the company established under the Act.

(2) Conditions of Incorporation. The Memorandum contains the fundamental conditions upon which alone the company is allowed to be incorporated.

(3) Most Important Document. The Memorandum of Association is the most important document with regard to its constitution.

(4) Foundation. It is the foundation on which the whole superstructure of the company is built-up.

(5) Two-fold Purpose. Its first is that the prospective investor knows within what field his money is to be risked. Secondly, outsiders also know the nature of the activities the company is authorised to carry on and accordingly their rights against the company in times of breach of contracts. Thus, however great the need may be the company cannot depart from the provisions contained in the memorandum. It can exercise only such powers as are either expressly stated or implied. If it does not, it would be *ultra vires* of the company and therefore wholly void and cannot be enforced by law.

(6) Basis of Existence. The memorandum is the basis of the company on which its existence depends. It sets out written goals round which the company's activities revolve. The Act lays down special procedure for alteration of contents of memorandum.

(7) Unalterable Document. The Companies Act, 1956, lays down under Section 16(1), *A company shall not alter the conditions contained in its memorandum except in the cases, in the mode, and to the extent, for which express provision is made in this Act.*

Therefore, the memorandum must be drafted with extreme care. It must be wide enough to ensure that the activities in which the company engages are fairly and justly authorised by it. Its objects must be legal and very clearly defined. The expressions such as "the company is allowed to do all such business and things as may be incidental or conducive to the attainment of the above object or any of them" are vague and inadequate. A specific enumeration of the principal objects must be given.

Subscriber Persons (Section 12 of the Act)

(1) Number of Persons. At least seven persons should subscribe to the memorandum where a public company is to be formed and at least two persons should subscribe to the memorandum where a private company is to be formed.

(2) Limit to Numbers. There is no upper limit placed on the number of members in the case of a public company while in a private company there cannot be more than 50 members excluding its employees who are also shareholders.

(3) Number below the Limit. When the number of members falls below seven in the case of a public company and below two in the case of a private company, the proper course for the company is to wind-up its business compulsorily. If, however, the company carries on business when its number of members falls below the statutory limits (seven) as laid down in the Act, for a period of more than six months while the number is so reduced every person who is a member during such period and is aware of the fact that the number of members has fallen below the statutory minimum, he will personally be liable for the debts of the company contracted during such period. (Section 45).

(4) Lawful Purpose. The persons who subscribe to the memorandum to form themselves into an association should do so for a 'lawful purpose' and or a lawful business.

(5) Consent to Combine. By subscribing to the memorandum, the members declare that they have really consented to combine together to form a company.

(6) No Necessary Benefit. A subscriber to the memorandum of association need not be beneficially interested in the shares to which he has subscribed.

(7) Agent. An agent may sign a memorandum on behalf of a subscriber if he is authorised by a power of attorney to do so.

(8) Foreigners. Even if all the subscribers are foreigners the company will still be an Indian company, if registered in India.

(9) Not less than One Share. No subscriber of the memorandum shall take less than one share.

(10) Quoting Shares. Each subscriber of the memorandum shall write opposite to his name the number of shares he has taken.

Memorandum in Different Types of Companies

(1) Company Limited by Guarantee. It will adopt the form given in Table C, Schedule I of the Act. The contents will be : Name of the company with the word Limited, the place of a Registered Office, objects, limited liability clause and finally the undertaking by the members that in the event of a company being wound-up and the assets and property of the company being not enough to meet the liabilities of the company, everyone of them will contribute such amount not exceeding the specified amount towards the deficiency.

(2) Unlimited Company. Its Memorandum shall state : the name of the company, its registered office and objects, share capital and the fact that the liability of members is unlimited.

(3) Co. Limited by Shares. Among other things it shall state the name of the company with the word *Limited*, its registered office and objects, followed by the limited liability clause, share capital and its division thereof into shares of fixed amounts.

Minimum Clauses

Though there is no restriction in law as regards the clauses which a Memorandum may contain. Section 13 of the Act prescribes the minimum without which a company cannot be registered. These are : (1) the name clause, (2) domicile or situation clause, (3) objects clause, (4) liability clause, (5) capital clause and lastly (6) the association clause.

Clauses of Memorandum and their Alteration

1. Name Clause. (i) *Limited in the Last :* It sets out the name by which the company proposes to be registered. The Act lays down certain conditions before a company can choose its name. The word "Limited" must appear as the last word in its name. This gives distinct notice to all persons dealing with the company, that the liability of its members is limited.

(ii) *Not Undesirable :* The name must not be, in the opinion of the Central Government, "undesirable" (Section 20). The word "undesirable" means that the name of a company must not contain words like "Government", "Municipality" which imply patronage of such bodies except with the express permission of the Government. The promoters can make an application in Form No. 1A to State Company Registrar to ascertain if the proposed name is undesirable.

(iii) *Different from Others :* No company can trade with a name identical or similar to that of an already existing company (Section 22). Similarly, the name of a company which is in the course of liquidation cannot be taken unless consent of such a company is obtained in the manner required by the Registrar.

(iv) *Announcement :* The sign board denoting the name of the company must be painted, letters must be legible and must be placed on the outside of the premises where its business is carried on. Language used should be the one which is in general use in that locality. Its name must be engraved legibly on its seal, on letter-heads, notices, advertisements, bills of exchange, endorsement, etc. (Section 147). If a company fails to comply with this provision, it shall be punishable with fine which may come to five hundred rupees. If an officer of a company uses the seal of the company or issues any business letter, or bill head, or signs on behalf of the company any bill of exchange, hundi or promissory note, shall be punishable with a fine of Rs. 5000.

(v) (a) *Alteration of Name Clause :* According to Section 22, if a company is unintentionally registered under a name identical or similar to that of another company such a company can change its name by passing an ordinary resolution with the previous consent of the Central Government. If the Central Government within 12 months of the commencement of this Act or within 12 months of its first registration or within 12 months of its registration by a new name, whichever is later, directs a company to change its name, it must do so within a period of three months from the date of such direction by passing an ordinary resolution and with, the previous permission of the Central Government. Failure to comply with this provision will render every officer who is in default punishable with fine up to Rs. 1000 for every day of default or from the date of commencement of its business whichever is earlier (Section 22).

(b) A company may, also by passing a special resolution, and with the approval of the Central Government in writing, change its name (Section 21). The change will be complete only when the secretary informs of it to the registrar of companies who shall enter the new name on the register in place of the old one and also shall issue a certificate of incorporation altered according to the need of the case. The change of name of the company will not affect the rights of the company against outsiders and *vice versa.* (Section 23)

(c) *Addition or Deletion of the Word Private :* Under Section 21 of the Companies (Amendment) Act of 1965 no approval of Central

Government is necessary where the only change in the name of the company is the addition or deletion of the word "Private" from the name of company when the company is converted from a public company into a private company or from a private company into a public company in accordance with the provisions of this Act. The form of resolution seeking change in the name will be as follows :

Resolved that the name of the company be changed from "The Johnson Trading Company" to "The Johnson and Johnson Trading Company Ltd." and that the Secretary be and he is hereby authorised to communicate this chance to the Central Government in order to obtain their consent to such alteration and that on receipt of such consent, the Secretary should take necessary steps to bring about changes in the seal, letterheads, name, etc.

2. Domicile Clause. It states the place or the State where the registered office of the company is situated (Section 13). As the company is regarded as an artificial person having no physical existence hence the place of its registered office must be communicated to the Registrar of companies so that the books of accounts, minutes and other documents maintained by the company at its registered office may be inspected by the authorities, members or other persons without trouble. The Registrar should also know the place of registered office of the company to send notices and other communication to the company. This clause determines the legal jurisdiction of the company. It ascertains its domicile and nationality.

The actual and full address of the registered office of the company must be communicated to the Registrar within 30 days from the date of its incorporation, or from the day on which it begins to carry on business whichever is earlier. From the day it commences business the company shall have a registered office to which all communication or notices may be addressed (Section 146). Every change in the place of registered office must be communicated to the Registrar for record within 30 days from the date of change [Section 146(20)].

Procedure for Alteration of a Domicile Clause

(i) *From One State to Another State :* By passing a special resolution a company may transfer its registered office from one State to another. It will have to obtain a confirmation order from the Company Law Board after the special resolution has been passed. Before confirming the alteration the Company Law Board must satisfy itself that sufficient notice has been given to every creditor of the company whose interest might be affected. Further, the Board is required to serve a notice of the application for confirmation of the alteration on the Registrar who shall appear before the Board and state his objections or suggestions, if any, regarding the confirmation of alteration. The Board may pass the confirmation order on such terms and conditions as it thinks fit. The company must file the certified copy of the confirmation order together with the printed copy of the altered memorandum with the Registrar of each State within 3 months from the date of the Board order, or within such further time as the Board may order. The registrar of each State shall register and certify the same within one month from the date of filing the documents. He shall send all documents relating to the company registered, recorded or filed in his office to the registrar of the other State where the office is to be shifted. The company must give notice of its new place of registered office within 30 days to the registrar of the State where the office is shifted. It must alter suitably every copy of the memorandum issued thereafter.

If the documents as explained above are not filed with registrar within the required time, the alteration and the confirmation order of the Company Law Board will become inoperative under the Act (Sections 17, 18, 19, 146).

(ii) *From One Place to Another Place in the Same State* : In this case the company has first to pass a special resolution. A printed or type written copy of the resolution must be filed with the registrar within 30 days of the resolution. After the office is shifted to the new place, the company must give notice of its new place of its registered office within 30 days (Sections 17, 146).

(iii) *From One Locality to Another Locality in the Same City* : In this case, no general body resolution is necessary. A resolution by the board of directors to this effect is sufficient. However, the registrar should be notified of this new place of registered office within 30 days of its removal. A public notice is generally given by the company for the information of the shareholders and the general public (Section 146).

If default is made in complying with the above mentioned requirements, the company and every officer of the company who is in default shall be punishable with fine which may extend to fifty rupees, for every day during which the default continues.

3. Objects Clause. It defines the objects of the company. It lays down the objects for which the company is formed. It determines the extent of the power and authority which the company can exercise in order to achieve its objects. It states affirmatively the gambit and extent of the power which, by law, are given to the company. The company cannot go beyond these objects. Objects and power must be stated in a clear and unambiguous manner so that a reader can identify the field of industry of that company. The objects must not be illegal, contrary to the public policy or against the Companies Act, 1956. The company must not carry an activity which goes beyond the memorandum, otherwise such act will be *ultra vires.* The activity carried on should not be wholly outside the objects of the company. But if a company, authorised by its objects to engage in the business of manufacturing chemicals, spends money in scientific research for the attainment of that object, such activity is a part of the main objects of the company. Therefore, the objects clause is often closed with the words as "to do all such other things as the company may deem expedient". This clause does not give the company limitless powers. Its validity should be construed along with the main objects of the company.

Alteration of Objects Clause

It can be done for any one of the causes enumerated in Section 17, namely :

(i) to carry on its business more economically or efficiently;
(ii) to attain its main purpose by new or improved means;
(iii) to enlarge or change the local area of its operation;
(iv) to carry on business which, under existing circumstances, may conveniently be combined with the business of the company;
(v) to restrict or abandon any of the objects specified in the memorandum;
(vi) to sell or dispose of the whole or part of the undertakings of the company and
(vii) to amalgamate with any company or body of persons.

The question whether a particular activity of the company falls within the sphere of any of the clauses stated above may be decided by the Company Law Board. The company must pass a special resolution to bring about the alteration of the objects clause. The company, should make an application to the Company Law Board to obtain a confirmation order. Before passing the confirmation order the Company Law Board must get itself satisfied that proper and sufficient notice has been given to every creditor and debenture-holder of the company and to all such parties whose interests are likely to be affected by the proposed alteration and that they have no objection to such alteration. If any creditor or debenture-holder objects to the alteration, then the Company Law Board must be satisfied that the claims of such creditors are settled or otherwise secured. The Companies (Amendment) Act, 1974, requires that the Company Law Board shall cause notice of the petition for confirmation of the alteration to be served on the Registrar, who shall also be given a reasonable opportunity to appear before the Company Law Board and state his objections, if any, with regard to the alteration. The Company Law Board should also be satisfied that the proposed alteration is fair and just and is in the interest of the company as a whole.

The Company Law Board may pass the confirmation order on such terms and conditions as it deems fit. It may allow the alteration only in part or refuse the alteration if it thinks that the main object of the company will be defeated. It may adjourn the proceedings order that an arrangement may be made to its satisfaction for the purchase of the interests of dissentient members. It may give such directions and make such orders as it thinks fit for facilitating or carrying into effect any such arrangement; provided that no part of the company may be expended in any such purchase.

The company must file the certified copy of the confirmation order together with the printed copy of the altered memorandum with the registrar within 3 months from the date of the order of the C.L.B. or within such extended time as the C.L.B. may grant. The registrar will register the alteration and issue a certificate of registration within one month from the date of filing the documents, which are to be submitted within three months of the order. The certificate of registration will be deemed to be conclusive proof that all the legal requirements regarding the alteration, have been properly fulfilled. If the documents are not filed with the registrar within required time the alteration and the confirmation order of the C.L.B. will become inoperative under the Act unless the C.L.B. revives the same on proper application made within a further period of one month (Section 19).

Procedure for Alteration

(i) The company should pass special resolution effecting the alteration.

(ii) A printed or type-written copy of the resolution should be filed with Registrar.

(iii) The C.L.B. must be petitioned to confirm the alteration.

(iv) A certified copy of the C.L.B's order confirming the alteration together with a printed copy of the altered memorandum should be filed with the Registrar within 3 months of the Company Law Board's order.

(v) The Registrar must register and issue a certificate of registration within one month of the filing of the documents. The alteration will become effective only after registration.

4. Liability Clause. The company clearly states in this clause that the liability of its members is limited to the extent of the face value of the shares taken by its members. In the case of a company limited by shares the liability of a member ceases as soon as the full amount of the shares he has undertaken is paid. The liability of directors of a limited company can, however, be made unlimited. But a notice in writing has to be given to them that their liability is unlimited. Under Section 45, however, if the number of members falls below seven in the case of a public company and the business of the company is carried on for more than 6 months thereafter, then every person who knowingly continues to be a member of the company after the period of six months is personally liable to all the debts of the company contracted thereafter *i.e.*, his liability becomes unlimited.

A company registered with unlimited liability need not mention the "Liability Clause" in its Memorandum of Association. Shareholders of a company with unlimited liability can get their liability limited by passing a special resolution and obtaining the requisite sanction of the Court. A copy of the special resolution so passed should be filed with the Registrar within 30 days of its passing and the copy of the Court's confirmation order within three (3) months of the order passed. The alteration becomes effective on the date of registration by the Registrar.

5. Capital Clause. In its the company states the amount of share capital with which it is to be incorporated and the division thereof into shares of fixed amount. If there are different classes of shares, then the capital should be shown under these different classes with their respective denominations. The Companies Act, 1956, has allowed only two classes of shares : equity or ordinary shares and preference shares. The amount of registration charges depends on the amount of authorised or registered capital with which a company is to be registered. The amount of capital mentioned under the capital clause of the memorandum is called Authorised, Nominal or Registered Capital of the Company.

Alteration of Capital Clause

Under Section 94, a company can alter its capital by :

(i) Increasing its share capital;

(ii) Consolidating its share capital into shares of higher denomination;

(iii) Sub-dividing its share capital into shares of lower denomination;

(iv) Converting its fully paid-up shares into stock;

(v) Cancelling the unissued capital and

(vi) Reducing its share capital under Section 100.

A company can bring about the first five alterations noted above by passing an ordinary or special resolution as provided in the articles of association. If no provision is made in the articles of the company, then the company must first change the articles by passing a special resolution. The company can alter the capital as provided under Section 94 by merely passing a resolution and no confirmation by the Company Law Board is necessary. The company can also reduce the capital under Section 100.

6. Association Clause. Those who have agreed to subscribe to the memorandum must signify their agreement to associate and to form a company. The clause runs in some such form : "We, the several persons whose names and addresses are subscribed, are desirous of being formed into a company in pursuance of this Memorandum of Association and we agree to take the number of shares in the capital of the company shown against our names". Each subscriber to the memorandum shall take at least one share.

Subscription to the Memorandum

The signatures of the various subscribers, at least seven in the case of public company and two in the case of a private company to the memorandum must be put in the presence of one witness who shall attest the same. The subscriber as well as the witness must also add their respective addresses, designations and occupations, if any.

Thus, the company cannot alter the conditions of the memorandum except in cases, and in the manner and to the extent for which express provision is made in the Companies Act, 1956. The word "conditions" refers to the provisions set out in Section 13 or any other specific provision of the Act required to be set in the memorandum. Other provisions contained in the memorandum relating to the appointment of a managing director, managing agents are not to be regarded as "conditions". They can be altered in the same way as the Articles. Section 13 refers to the "clauses" of memorandum which have been explained above in detail.

The memorandum must be printed, divided into paragraphs and serially numbered. Necessary filing fees and registration charges have to be paid to the Registrar of Companies. A copy of the memorandum is to be submitted to him.

(2) ARTICLES OF ASSOCIATION

Meaning of Articles

Section 2(2) of the Act states :

"Articles" means the articles of association of a company as originally framed or as altered from time to time in pursuance of any previous companies law or of this Act.

In legal language, "Articles" means the articles of association of a company as originally framed or altered from time to time in pursuance of any previous Companies Law or of the Companies Act, 1956. The articles of association are the rules and regulations of a company framed for the purpose of managing its internal affairs. Whereas the memorandum gives objects of the company, defines and formulates the principal conditions of the company's incorporation, the articles merely set out the composition and mode by which the company desires to attain those objects.

Characteristics of Articles

(i) The articles of a company are subordinate to Memorandum of Association.

(ii) It is controlled by Memorandum of Association.

(iii) Articles are only internal regulations over which members of the company have full control and may alter them as they think fit.

(iv) Articles of Association may be used to explain any ambiguity in the Memorandum of Association.

Importance of Articles

The significance of the articles of association has been aptly brought out by Lord Cairns in the case of Ashobury Carriage Co. *Vs.* Richie where he says : "The articles play a part subsidiary to the memorandum of association. They accept the memorandum as the charter of incorporation of the company, and so accepting it, the articles proceed to define the duties, the rights and the powers of the governing body as between themselves and the company at large, and the mode and form in which the business of the company is to be carried and the mode and form in which changes in the internal regulations of the company may from time-to-time be made".

Contents of the Articles

(1) The business of a company,
(2) The amount of capital issued;
(3) The classes of shares into which capital is divided;
(4) The rights of each class of the shareholders;
(5) Rules as to making of calls;
(6) Company's lien on shares;
(7) Transfer of shares;
(8) Method of holding meetings;
(9) Voting at meetings, quorum, poll, proxy;
(10) Number, appointment and powers of directors;
(11) Declaration of dividends;
(12) Keeping of register of members;
(13) Annual amount and audit, etc.

Section 26 of the Companies Act, 1956, provides that the company limited by shares may register the articles of association along with its memorandum signed by the subscribers of the memorandum prescribing regulations for the company. The registration of the articles is not compulsory in the case of a public company. Where the company proposes not to have its own articles, then all provisions of 'Table A' of the First Schedule of the Companies Act, 1956, will be applicable to it. However, the preparation of Articles is compulsory for :

(i) Companies limited by guarantee,
(ii) Unlimited companies and
(iii) Private companies limited by shares.

Form of Articles

Those have been given in 'Table C', Schedule I of the Act.

(1) Private Company. The articles should refer to restrictions of transfer of shares, invitation to public subscription and total number of members.

(2) Unlimited Company. The articles should state the number of members with which the company is to be registered and if the company has a share capital should be stated.

(3) Company Limited by Guarantee. The articles should state the number of members with which the company is to be registered.

The articles must be printed and divided into paragraphs, serially numbered and signed by every subscriber to the memorandum with his address, description and occupation. The signature must be witnessed by at least one person and his description, occupation and address should also be mentioned. It must be properly stamped as required under the Indian Stamp Act (Section 30).

A public limited company may or may not file its articles of association with the Registrar. However, unlimited companies, companies limited by guarantee and private companies must register their articles of association along with the memorandum.

By its articles the company gets wide powers to control its affairs and its relation with its members. The articles must not contain provisions contrary to the Act, or to the provisions of its memorandum.

Alteration of Articles

According to Section 31, the articles can be amended by passing a special resolution subject to the provisions of the Act and to the conditions contained in the memorandum. Thus, the company can alter or add to its articles. Such alteration or addition shall be valid as is originally contained in the articles.

Statutory Conditions of Alteration

(i) *Special Resolution :* Alteration can be made by passing a special resolution only.

(ii) *Legal :* The alteration must not be inconsistent with or beyond the provisions of the memorandum or illegal or against the provisions of the Act.

(iii) *Conversion :* The alteration cannot be made which has the effect of concerting a public company into a private company unless it has been approved by the Central Government and further that unless the company has filed a printed copy of the articles as altered with the Registrar within one month of the date of the receipt of the order of approval (Section 31).

(iv) *Liability :* The alteration must not increase the liability of a member without his written consent to take more shares than he had held prior to the alteration (Section 38).

(v) *Alteration by the Court :* The Court has power to alter the memorandum and the articles of association of the company on an application made by any member of the company praying for redress on the grounds of "oppression" or "mismanagement" under Sections 397 and 398 in any way it thinks fit. When the Court has ordered the amendment of the memorandum or the articles, then the company cannot alter the memorandum or the articles which is inconsistent with the Court's order (Section 404).

(i) *Bona fide :* The alteration must be made *bona fide* and for the benefit of the company as a whole. The principle was brought out in the case of Side Bottom *Vs.* Kershaw Leese & Co. (1920).

(ii) *Fraud on Minority :* The alteration should not constitute a fraud on the minority by the majority. This principle is illustrated by the case of Menier *Vs.* Hooper's Telegraph Co. (1874).

(iii) *Unalterable :* The alteration must not make the articles unalterable as it is regarded bad in law

Specimen Resolution for the Alteration of Articles

"Resolved that the articles of the Company be altered by deleting Article 144 thereof and by substituting, in the place of the said Article, the following Article :

"Article 144 : The Directors shall provide for the safe custody of the seal and the seal shall never be used except by the authority of the Directors or a Committee of the Directors previously given and two Directors (or persons acting on behalf of the Directors under Registered Power of Attorney) at least or one Director (or person acting on behalf of the Director under registered Power of the Attorney) and the Secretary (or some other person appointed by the Board for the purpose) shall sign every instrument to which the seal is affixed. Provided, nevertheless, that any instrument bearing the seal of the company and issued for a valuable consideration shall be binding on the company notwithstanding any irregularities touching the authority of the Directors to issue the same."

Miscellaneous Provisions of Alteration

The Companies Act expressly provides that notwithstanding anything to the contrary contained in the memorandum or the articles of a company, the provisions of the Act shall have effect and anything contained in the memorandum or the article which is repugnant to the provisions of the Act shall be void (Section 9).

Every company will send to a member within seven days of his requisition and on payment of rupee one a copy of (i) the memorandum, (ii) the articles, (iii) agreement, if any, entered into or proposed to be entered into, by the company with any person appointed or to be appointed as its managing agent or as its treasurers and secretaries and (iv) every other agreement and every resolution required to be registered under Section 39.

In default of the above provisions the company and every officer who is a party to the default are liable to be punished for each offence with a fine not exceeding Rs. 500 (Section 39).

When the memorandum or the articles of association are altered, such alteration should be incorporated in every copy of the memorandum and the articles and they should be issued in accordance with the alteration. Failure to comply with this provision will make the company and every officer who is in default liable to fine to the extent of Rs. 100 for every copy so issued. (Section 40)

Articles *Vs.* Memorandum

(1) Powers. Whereas the memorandum is regarded as the constitution of the company and governs the relations of the company with the outsiders, the articles governs the internal relation of the company with its members.

(2) Functions. The memorandum defines the objects of the company and, the sphere of its activities and the company cannot exceed the powers conferred by the memorandum. The articles, however, define the ways and means by which the objects as set out in the memorandum can be achieved.

(3) *Ultra Vires.* Any action undertaken by the company beyond the scope of its memorandum is *ultra vires,* but if any thing is *ultra vires* of the articles, it does not necessarily mean *ultra vires* of the memorandum.

(4) Relationship. Thus, the articles of association is the subservient document to the memorandum of association.

Doctrine of Constructive Notice of Memorandum and Articles

After the registration of the Memorandum and Articles of Association with the Registrar, both these documents become public documents and thus can be inspected by any one on payment of the prescribed fees. This may be in any medium as specified in Section 610A *e.g.* microfilms, facsimile copies and computer printouts. Because of this, every person dealing with the company is expected to have read and understood the contents of these documents before making any contract with the company and if he does not do so, he will have to bear its consequences. Thus, a person dealing with the company is supposed to have read the so-called public documents like memorandum, Articles and other regulations and understood the same. Such a presumption is called the "Constructive Notice of Memorandum and Articles" or the "Doctrine of Constructive Notice". Its effects are as follow :

(i) *Ultra Vires Acts :* As every person dealing with the company is presumed to have knowledge of the contents of memorandum and thereof if an act is *ultra vires* the company, he cannot claim relief on the ground that he was unaware of the fact that the act is beyond the memorandum.

(ii) *Acts beyond the Authority of Directors :* As lack of authority of the directors or other agents of the company is evident from public documents like articles and other regulations, the person dealing with the company will be presumed to have the notice of the lack of authority and therefore he cannot hold the company bound by the directors or other agents.

(iii) *Inconsistent Agreements :* A person dealing with the company is presumed to have the notice of the contents of articles and he cannot make a contract with the company which purports to override any rights created by the articles.

The Doctrine of Indoor Management

A person dealing with the company can presume that the company is supposed to do all internal matters as per Companies Act and he can hold the company liable if any internal formalities are found invalid. This rule as per Lord Hathierly is called "Doctrine of Indoor Management" and was first laid down in Royal British Bank *Vs.* Turquand.

However, such a person will not be protected under the following circumstances :

(1) Where he has been served with notice to the effect of internal irregularity.

(2) *Forgery* : Where he is found to have relied upon a forged document.

(3) *Negligence* : Where he has failed to make proper enquiries which would have enabled him to know the irregularities, despite so suspicious circumstances as to invite further enquiry.

(4) Knowledge. Where ontsider has knowledge of irregularity or has no knowledge of articles.

(5) Where the question is to the very existence of agency.

The Doctrine of *Ultra Vires*

Being an artificial person, having no conscience of its own the company cannot act by itself and hence cannot protect its own interests. So far as the protection of interests of shareholders and creditors of the company is concerned the *Doctrine of Ultra Vires* is very important. It restricts the misuse of corporate funds in unauthorised and illegal activities. All activities and transactions which are beyond the objects of the company would be *ultra vires* the company and shall be entirely void. The company cannot ratify such acts afterwards even if all the shareholders consent to ratify them. All actions against the memorandum, or the Companies Act or other law in force will be *ultra vires.* All the *ultra vires* acts will not bind the company. If the directors do any act which is *ultra vires* the company, they can be held personally liable to the company. A person who borrows money which is *ultra vires* the company can be sued by the company to recover the amount so lent. If, however, an act is *ultra vires* the articles of association, the same can be ratified by the shareholders afterwards. The company can even alter the articles and adopt new articles. Similarly an act which is *ultra vires* the directors can also be ratified. It is only where an act is *ultra vires* the company that it becomes wholly void and cannot be ratified and validated in any event.

The doctrine was first applied in England in 1875 in the case of Ashbury Railway Carriage and Iron Co. Ltd. *Vs.* Riche. The word 'ultra' means beyond and 'vires' means powers. A company may do an act which is necessary for or incidental to the attainment of its objects or which is otherwise authorised by the Act. If it is not so the act will be *ultra vires* the memorandum. However, because of its some complications resulting in occasional injustice, English Companies Act 1985 has abolished this doctrine. A company will now be liable to a person acting in good faith for every act decided by directors. The validity of an act done by a company shall not be called in question on the ground of lack of capacity by reason of anything in the Company's memorandum.

In India the doctrine was affirmed by Supreme Court in case of A. Lakshmana Swami Mudaliar *Vs.* Life Insurance Corporation of India in 1963 and still is valid. The effects of *ultra vires* transaction may be following :

1. Injunction. Any member can get an injunction to restrain a company from proceeding to any *ultra vires* act.

2. Personal liability of Directors. If the funds of a company are diverted for ultra vires acts, the directors are personally liable.

3. Breach of warranty of authority. Directors, as agents of the company, will be personally liable to outsider for any loss caused by *ultra vires* act of the company.

4. Property Acquired. Any *ultra vires* property acquired from company's funds will rest in the company, though wrongly acquired.

5. An *ultra vires* contract cannot became *ultra vires* by reason of estopple lapse of time, ratification or decay because it is void *ab initio*.

(3) LIST OF PERSONS WHO HAVE CONSENTED TO ACT AS DIRECTORS

There should be at least three persons as directors in the case of public company and at least two directors in the case of a private company. The list contains the full names, addresses, description and occupation of each person and is signed by the secretary or any other responsible officer of the company. A specimen form is given at the end of the chapter.

(4) CONSENT OF DIRECTORS TO ACT AS SUCH

Alongwith the list of directors, their consent in writing that they agree to act as directors of the company must be submitted from each director.

(5) DIRECTORS' UNDERTAKING, TO TAKE UP AND PAY FOR QUALIFICATION SHARES

In this document the directors declare that they will take up and pay for the qualification shares fixed by the company. The Act now lays down that the nominal value of qualification shares shall not be more than Rs. 5,000 [Section 270(3)].

(6) AGREEMENT TO APPOINT MANAGING DIRECTOR

The Companies (Amendment) Act, 1988 has inserted a new Sub-section (C) to Section 33(1) which states, "the agreement if any, which the company proposes to enter into with any individual for appointment as its managing or whole-time director or manager".

According to this Sub-section, a copy of the agreement which the company proposes to enter into with any person for appointment of managing director or whole-time director or manager is required to be filed alongwith memorandum and articles of association at the time of registration of the company. After incorporation, copies of the agreement or resolution relating to the appointment of managing director is to be filed with the Registrar within thirty days of executing the agreement or passing the resolution under Section 192(4)(C).

(7) STATUTORY DECLARATION BY THE SECRETARY OR AN ADVOCATE

A statutory declaration by the secretary or the attorney or a responsible officer of the company that all the legal provisions of the Companies Act and the rules thereunder have been properly complied with in respect of registration of the company must also be filed with the Registrar.

All the documents referred to above have to be delivered to the Registrar. And after having duly scrutinised them and found to be correct and in order, the Registrar will register them and issue a Certificate of Incorporation if he is satisfied that all the provisions of the Act have been properly complied with by the company and the prescribed fees have been paid. After the issue of Certificate of Incorporation, the company is said to have been incorporated or registered.

EFFECTS OF INCORPORATION

(1) Conclusive Evidence. The Certificate of Incorporation is *conclusive evidence* that all the requirements of the Act in respect of registration and of matters precedent and incidental thereto have been complied with and that the company is duly registered under the Act, and the Court will not entertain any complaint about the original registration being defective.

(2) Legal Person. The company becomes a *legal person* or entity, quite distinct from the members composing it. A creditor of the company can proceed only against the company. The liability of the company is not the liability of the individual shareholders.

(3) Corporate Body. From the date of its incorporation, members become a body corporate by the name of the company mentioned in the memorandum. It is capable of exercising all functions through the Board of Directors. It has a perpetual succession and a common seal.

(4) Public Document. The Memorandum and Articles of Association are public documents. After paying necessary fees the outsiders can inspect these documents at the Registrar's office.

(5) Member's Right. A member has the right to demand a copy of these documents from the company. Which, in its turn, must supply them within seven days of the request, by charging necessary fees for this purpose, otherwise penalty is imposed by the Act for the failure to supply copies of these documents.

After receiving the Certificate of Incorporation, the promoters will proceed to the next stage in the formation of public companies, namely, raising of share capital for starting the business of the company. For this purpose, they will issue another important document called "Prospectus".

QUESTIONS

1. State the provisions of the Companies Act relating to restrictions on the alteration of Articles of Association.
2. "The M/A of a company is its charter and it defines the limitations on the powers of the company established under the Act". Support this statement.
3. Compare and contrast Memorandum of Association and Articles of Association. Mention the restrictions of the alteration of Articles. Draft a Resolution.
4. (a) Enumerate the provisions of the Companies Act, 1956, relating the name of a company.
5. Define a company and describe in brief the steps to be taken in connection with the incorporation of a public limited company.
6. In what way may a company alter its share capital by ordinary resolution? State in every case the circumstances in which a company might desire to effect such alterations.
7. (a) "Memorandum of Association is a fundamental and unalterable character of a company". Comment.
   (b) Set out the steps to be followed by a company which desires to alter the objects clauses of its Memorandum of Association.

5

FORMATION OF PRIVATE COMPANIES

As a form of business organisation the private limited companies found its home first in England. With the development and advance of trade, transport and industries, proprietary concerns and partnership firms were not found suitable to collect adequate amount of capital to run the business. Some businessmen experienced difficulties in the formation and management of public companies on a large-scale. Other businessmen carrying business in medium or small-scale felt handicapped by the risk of unlimited liability. These two factors led to the midway form of business organisation or a via-media known as private limited company.

Comparison of Partnership Firms and Private Companies

(1) Attachment of Personal Property. If the business assets of a partnership firm are not sufficient to pay out the liabilities, then the private and personal property of the partners can be attached to pay the creditors. However, as in the case of a private limited company the liability of its members is limited to their contribution to the share capital, their personal properly cannot be attached.

(2) Legal Status. A private limited company is an incorporated organisation considered as a legal person in law and invested with separate legal existence from its members. But a partnership firm is not recognised in the eyes of law as distinct and separate from the partners. Therefore, partners are individually and severally liable for the debts of the firm.

(3) Individual Contract. While partner cannot enter into a contract with his firm, a member of the private limited company can do so.

(4) Termination of Membership. A partnership shall be terminated on lunacy or insolvency of a partner, on the death or retirement of a partner or on the dissolution of the firm. A private limited company has perpetual membership.

Comparison of Private Companies and Public Companies

(1) Number of Promoters. While two or more persons can form private company, seven persons are required to form a public company.

(2) Legal Requirements. There are very few legal requirements in the case of formation of a private company as compared with those of a public company.

The procedure of forming a public company is very complicated and elaborate. A private company can start its business after obtaining the "certificate of incorporation". It also enjoys several privileges over a public company granted under the Act.

(3) Secrecy. A private company can keep its business secrets undisclosed to the outside public, while they are open for inspection to any member of the public in the case of a pubic company.

Thus, the advantages which private companies enjoy over those of public companies weigh against their disadvantages. The above mentioned merits led to the growth and popularity of private companies in recent years.

DEFINITION OF A PRIVATE COMPANY

Section 3(iii) of the Companies Act, 1956, defines, a private company as a company which by its article :

"(a) restricts the rights to transfer its shares (if any);

(b) limits the number of its members to fifty not including —

  (i) persons in the employment of the company and

  (ii) persons who, having been formerly in the employment of the company, were members of the company while in that employment and have continued to be members after the employment has ceased and

(c) prohibits invitation to the public to subscribe for any shares or debentures of the company :

(d) prohibits any initiation or acceptance of deposits from persons other than its members, directors or their relatives.

Provided that where two or more persons hold one or more shares in a company jointly, they shall, for the purpose of definition, be treated as a single member".

Thus, employees of the company either present or past can purchase shares and may retain control over their masters. Small employers can purchase a larger number of shares from a number of persons, concentrating thereby the capital in the hands of a few individuals.

STAGES OF FORMATION OF A PRIVATE COMPANY

1. The promotion stage. It is similar to that of a public company; the only difference being that the stage is shorter than that of public company. A person can conceive an idea and form a private limited concern by inviting another person, or convert his existing partnership business into a private company.

2. Incorporation. Two persons are enough to form a private company by following the relevant provisions of the Act in that behalf. The promoter proceeds with the drafting of and filing the following with the Registrar :

(1) Memorandum of Association.
(2) Articles of Association.
(3) Notice of situation of the registered office.
(4) Declaration by the attorney or secretary or manager of the company that all the requirements regarding registration have been complied with.

1. MEMORANDUM OF ASSOCIATION

The memorandum of association of a private company shall contain the same clauses as those which are contained in the memorandum of a public company. However, the exception is as regards "Name Clause". The name of a private company must contain the words "Private Ltd." as its last words. A subscriber to the memorandum must take at least one share. The subscription to the memorandum can be done by two persons. Even a minor, a married woman or a bankrupt can become a subscriber to the memorandum of association. He need not be independent or unconnected person. The form of memorandum shall follow any of the forms B, C, D and E of Scheme I of Companies Act, 1956. As in the case of a public company, memorandum must be printed, divided into paragraphs and signed and attested. Rules and formalities for alteration of memorandum of association are the same as in the case of a public company.

2. ARTICLES OF ASSOCIATION

A private company must register its articles along with the memorandum. These articles must expressly contain provisions restricting :

(i) membership to 50;
(ii) issue of share capital to the public and
(iii) the right of members to transfer shares. A private limited company can adopt all or any of the regulations of Table A subject to the exceptions given in it or may frame its own articles. Otherwise private companies may adopt Tables C, D, E as far as possible. The formalities with regard to signature and attestation of articles are the same in both cases. The same is true as regards the alteration of articles.

3. NOTICE OF THE SITUATION OF REGISTERED OFFICE

This notice is sent to the Registrar along with the copies of the memorandum and articles. Declaration is filed with the Registrar of joint-stock companies by a secretary, manager or attorney that legal requirements precedent to incorporation have been complied with.

After close scrutiny the Registrar will issue a certificate of incorporation to the company. From that date the company is incorporated and the same effects will follow as those of a public company. A private company can start its business after getting the certificate of incorporation without waiting for a certificate to commence business as is necessary in the case of a public company.

Restrictions

(A) Restrictions on a Private Company

(1) It must contain the words "Private Ltd." as the last words of its name.

(2) Registration of articles is compulsory.

(3) The right of members to transfer shares is restricted.

(4) It cannot invite the public to subscribe to its share capital by issuing a prospectus.

(5) The total number of members must not exceed fifty. Since, however, past and present employees holding shares are not counted as members, the share capital can be collected on a large-scale and membership can exceed fifty.

(6) At least two directors are required. No body corporate, association or firm can be appointed as a director of the company.

(7) It can not appoint a managing director (an individual) for more than five years at a time.

(8) It must file annual returns incorporating therein information as to the membership in details.

(9) It must appoint qualified auditors as in the case of a public company.

(10) It must send to the Registrar three copies each of balance sheet and that of profit and loss account.

(11) It must circulate among its members and debenture-holders copies of balance sheet and profit and loss account together with auditor's report.

(12) It cannot issue share warrants.

(B) Restrictions put on Private Companies which are Subsidiaries of a Public Company

(1) It must have at least three directors.

(2) Two-thirds of the total number of directors must retire by rotation.

(3) Increase in number of directors requires sanction from the Central Government.

(4) Any firm or body corporate or association cannot be employed or appointed as its manager.

Privileges

(A) Privileges of All Private Companies

(1) Two members are enough for incorporation.

(2) It can proceed to allot shares without waiting for the receipt of minimum subscription amount. It need not file with the Registrar a prospectus or a statement in lieu of prospectus.

(3) It can start business immediately after obtaining the certificate of incorporation; it need not obtain the trading certificate.

(4) It need not hold statutory meeting or file with the Registrar a statutory report.

(5) Restrictions imposed on public companies regarding further issue of capital do not apply to a private company.

(6) It need have only two directors while a public company must have three directors on its board.

(7) Its directors are not required to file their consent in writing, their willingness to act as directors. Similarly they need not file the undertaking as regards the qualification share that they will take up such shares and will pay for them.

(8) Quorum required to hold general meeting is two members only while in the case of a public company the quorum required is five members.

(9) It need not maintain the index of members.

(B) Privileges of Independent Private Companies

(1) It can appoint a firm of body corporate to office or place of profit.

(2) It need not file with the Registrar consent of proposed directors to act as directors.

(3) Additional grounds for disqualification of directors may be provided by articles.

(4) In calculating the number of companies of which a person may be a director, a private company, which is neither a subsidiary, nor a holding company of a public company shall be excluded.

(5) A director who has reached the age of 75 years need not vacate his office.

(6) Birth-date of a director need not be entered on Directors' Register.

(7) Provisions relating to share qualification of a director do not apply.

(8) Any amount may be paid as remuneration to a director, even the amount exceeding eleven per cent of net profit.

(9) No notice is necessary for the election of a director in case of a person who is not a retiring director.

(10) A separate resolution for electing every director is not necessary.

(11) A director interested in any contract which is made with the company may take part in its discussion and tender his vote.

(12) Provisions relating to the restrictions on powers of the Board and restrictions on companies regarding granting of loans to director do not apply.

(13) The Central Government cannot prevent a change from taking place in the ownership of shares held.

(14) It can give a loan for the purchase of its own shares or the shares of its holding companies.

(15) All the directors may be appointed for life and the requirements of retirement by rotation do not apply.

(16) Number of directors can be increased beyond the limit laid down in the articles of association without the consent of the Central Government.

(17) Approval of the Central Government for the appointment or reappointment of a managing director or a whole-time director is not required.

(18) Inter-investment of funds in the companies under the same management is allowed. (Section 370)

(19) It is permitted to purchase shares or debentures of other companies in the same group (Section 372).

(20) It can issue deferred shares with disproportional voting rights (Section 90).

QUESTIONS

1. Define a Private Company and explain stages of its formation.
2. Describe the restrictions and privileges of a Private Company.
3. Compare and contrast Private and Public Company.

PRACTICAL PROBLEMS

1. A promoter signed a circular inviting subscriptions for shares in a company which stated that about one-third of the capital had already been subscribed in the U.S.A. In fact, a third of the capital had been subscribed but not in cash. The promoter, however, believed honestly that the statement was true. P subscribed on the faith of the circular and the company became insolvent after some time. P sued the promoter for fraud. Decide. [**Hint.** P can rescind the contract to take shares and can also recover damages from the promoter (Ross *Vs.* Estates Investments Co.)].

2. A company issued a prospectus containing mis-statements on which action could be taken against the company. A person purchased shares in the market relying on the prospectus and filed a suit against the company for damages for the mis-statements. Will he succeed?
[**Hint.** No (Peek *Vs.* Gurney)).
3. Prem Paul applied for 100 shares in a company in a fictitious name. The shares were allotted in the fictitious name. Did he incur any liability under the Companies Act, 1956?
[**Hint.** Yes. He shall be punishable with imprisonment for a term which may extend to 5 years {Section 68-A (1)}].
4. An allottee of shares in a company brought action against a director in respect of false statements in a prospectus. The director contended that the statements were prepared by the promoters and he had relied on them. Is the director liable under the circumstances?
[**Hint.** Yes (Adams *Vs.* Thrift)].
5. A. an allottee of shares in a company, came to know of the misrepresentations in the prospectus on the basis of which he had not applied for share, but he did not care to take any action for 5 months after coming to know of the misrepresentations. Can he be precluded from obtaining relief?
[**Hint.** Yes (Christineville Rubber Estates Ltd., Re (1911) W.N. 116)].
6. A company altered the objects clause of its Memorandum of Association according to the procedure laid down by law. *i.e.,* by passing a special resolution. A copy of the resolution was filed with the Registrar 4 months after the passing of the resolution. Can the Registrar register the alteration?
[**Hint.** No. Section 18].
7. A company carrying on business in jute is empowered by the objects clause of its Memorandum of Association to do any other business connected with jute. By a resolution passed unanimously the company resolved to alter the objects clause to include the power to carry on additional business in rubber. Is this alteration covered by Section 17?
[**Hint.** No].
8. A company was started with the object of building 'a hall with shops'. The building was destroyed by fire and the company wanted to alter the objects clause in the Memorandum by substituting the words 'a hall with shops' with the words 'shops, dwelling houses and warehouses for letting purposes.' Is this alteration covered by Section 17?
[**Hint.** Yes].
9. A company put up telephone wires in a certain area. There was no power in the Memorandum to put up wires there. The defendants

cut them down. Can the company sue for the damage done to the wires?
[**Hint.** Yes (National Telephone Co. *Vs.* St. Peter Port Constables)].

10. The Memorandum of Association of a company formed to improve and encourage the breeding of poultry contained a provision that no remuneration should be paid to the members of the governing body of the company. But the company owing to its increase in the business passed a special resolution providing for equitable remuneration to such members for services rendered. Is this alteration of the Memorandum covered by Section 17?
[**Hint.** Yes (*Scientific Poultry Breeders' Assn. Ltd.*, Re)].

6

COMPANY PROMOTERS

The term promoter is a term of business and not of law. It has not been defined anywhere in the Act, but a number of judicial decisions have attempted to explain it. The idea of carrying on a business which can be profitably undertaken is conceived either by a person or by a group of persons called promoters. After the idea is conceived, the promoters make detailed investigations to find out the weaknesses and strong points of the idea, to determine the amount of capital required and to estimate the operating expenses and probable income. A promoter may be an individual, a firm, an association of persons or even a company.

DEFINITION OF PROMOTER

1. *L. J. Brown.* "The term promoter is a term not of law but of business, usefully summing up in a single word a number of business operations familiar to the commercial world by which a company is generally brought into existence."

2. *Justice C. Cockburn.* "Promoter is one who undertakes to form a company with reference to a given object and to set it going, and who takes the necessary steps to accomplish that purpose."

3. *Palmer.* "Company Promoter is a person who originates a scheme for the formation of the company, has the memorandum and the articles prepared, executed and registered, and finds the first directors, settles the terms of preliminary contracts and prospectus (if any) and makes arrangement for advertising and circulating the prospectus and placing the capital."

4. *G. Tiruvengadachariar Vs. Velu Mudaliar.* A person cannot be held as promoter merely because he has signed at the foot of the Memorandum or that he has provided money for the payment of formation expenses.

5. *Lord J. Lindley.* "The word promoter has no very definite meaning. As used in connection with companies, the promoter involves the idea of exertion for the purpose of getting up and starting a company, or what is called floating it and also the idea of some duty towards the company imposed by, or arising from the position which the so called promoter assumes towards it."

Thus, the promoter is usually an industrial expert who performs all the preliminary actions necessary to bring a company into existence. He does every thing required to convert the idea into a business concern. He may be an individual, a firm, an association of persons or even a company, depending upon the circumstances of the case.

TYPES OF PROMOTERS

(1) **Accidental Promoters.** Sometimes some idea strikes to the mind of some persons accidentally and they try to convert it into reality. These are known as accidental promoters. Such promoters do not take the promotion as their profession, they try to bring a business concern into existence for their own settlement or for their family.

(2) **Professional Promoters.** These promoters take the promotion as their profession and a means of their livelihood. They perform the work of promotion for various business undertakings. They may be an individual, a partnership firm, an association of persons, and even a company.

(3) **Financial Promoters.** Some promoters who undertake the promotion of a company, complete the promotional activities and then purchase the entire share capital of the company promoted. Thus they provide financial certainty and assurance to the company. Later on, they sell shares at some profit. As they provide and offer the financial services, they are known as financial promoters.

FUNCTIONS AND ROLE OF COMPANY PROMOTERS

1. To get the idea of the formation of a company.
2. To analyse the idea.
3. To consult experts of the field regarding the feasibility of the idea.
4. To search out the persons who may agree to be the first directors of the company and to sign the memorandum of association.
5. To decide the name, the place of registered office, the place of office, the objects of company, the amount of capital and its composition.
6. To prepare and enter into contracts with underwriters.
7. To select and decide the bankers, auditors, brokers and legal experts.
8. To prepare the memorandum of associations and articles of associations and prospectus.
9. To file the necessary documents with the Registrar of Companies.
10. To get the certificate of incorporation.
11. To get the permission and to arrange for the issue of capital.
12. If the company has to purchase a going concern business, to finalise the purchase of such business.

13. To enter into contracts with the vendors, underwriters, brokers and managing agents.
14. To collect the amount on the issue of share capital.
15. To get the certificate of commencement of business.
16. To pay the preliminary expenses.
17. To appoint the requisite personnel for the whole process.

To sum up, a promoter performs all activities right from the idea in his mind to the commencement of business by the company. He gets the company established and after the establishment of company, he comes out of the picture and lets the company go on with its business.

REMUNERATION OF PROMOTERS

(1) Cash Payment. To pay in cash is the very first and the traditional method of making the payment for the services of promoters.

(2) Shares and Debentures. Another method for making the payment to promoters is to allot them the shares and debentures of the company, promoted by them.

(3) Commission. Promoters may be paid for their services by way of commission in the net profits of the company for a certain period.

(4) Appointment at Suitable Post. A very common method for payment for the services of promoters is to accommodate them in the company at any suitable post according to their qualifications and experience. This can be possible only in private companies and not in public companies.

In the absence of an agreement with the company after its incorporation, a promoter cannot file a suit in any court of law for the recovery of his remuneration because he has acted for a person who has not taken the birth so far, and no person can enter into a contract before his birth. Thus, a promoter can be paid only if he has entered into contract with the company. A private company, comes into real existence after getting the certificate of incorporation. The promoters must have a contract in their pocket after the incorporation of company. But in case of a public company, the real existence of company is possible only after the certificate of commencement of business. Under Section 149(4) of the Indian Companies Act, a public company is not liable even for the contracts entered into after its incorporation. It is bound to pay the promoter's remuneration only after it gets the certificate of commencement of business.

RELATIONSHIP OF PROMOTERS WITH THE COMPANY

(1) Fiduciary Relations. A promoter has the fiduciary relations with the company. He must perform all his duties with utmost good faith. These relations of a promoter with the company continue till the company comes into existence.

(2) Liable for All the Functions regarding Formation of a Company. As the promoter is the founder of a company, he is personally liable for all the functions regarding the formation of company. He enters into the preliminary contracts with brokers, underwriters, bankers etc.

(3) No place in the Company. Promoter performs all the functions of the company. He brings the company into existence. But, legally, he has no place in the company because the company is managed by the board of directors and is owned by the shareholders.

LEGAL POSITION OF THE PROMOTER

Lord Lindley has mentioned following five facts regarding the legal position of promoters :

(1) Fiduciary Relations. The promoter has fiduciary relations with the company and with all those persons to whom he inspires to become the shareholders of the company. Thus, the promoter should not get any undisclosed profit from the company. If he gets any such profits, he must refund it to the company. He cannot and should not sell any of his personal property to the company at a profit. If does so, he should disclose all the relevant facts to the company.

(2) Liable for Contracts. The directors of the company can compel the promoters to follow up all the contracts entered into by them as promoters. Therefore, a promoter cannot keep himself away from the contracts he made.

(3) Promoters are not Personally Liable. The promoters cannot be held personally liable for any loss caused to the company by their acts, provided they have performed their duties in utmost good faith and with due care and honesty.

(4) To breach the Contract entered into on Misrepresentation. If it is proved that one party of the contract has induced the other party of the contract on the basis of misrepresentation, the other party may breach such a contract.

(5) No Termination of Contracts on the Change of Parties. If the parties of the contract are changed, the contract cannot be terminated even if it was a voidable contract.

Because there is no company yet in existence the promoter is neither a trustee nor an agent of the company. The correct way to describe his legal position is that he stands in a fiduciary position towards the company about to be formed. Lord Cairns has correctly stated the position of promoter in Erlanger *Vs.* New Sombrero Phosphate Co. as follows : "The promoters of a company stand undoubtedly in a fiduciary position. They have in their hands the creation and moulding of the company. They have the power of defining how and when and in what shape and under what supervision, it shall start into existence and begin to act as a trading corporation."

Following two important results follow :

(i) *A Promoter cannot be allowed to make Any Secret Profits* : If it is found that in any particular transaction of the company, the promoter obtained a secret profit for himself, he is bound to refund the same to the company. The following example illustrates this provision :

The old 'Olympia' Co. was in difficulties and the debentures were worth very little. A syndicate consisting of X, Y and Z purchased Olympia for $ 1,10,000 and sold it to a new company which they promoted for $ 1,80,000. Consequently the debentures were paid in full out of $ 1,40,000 and the syndicate made a profit of $ 20,000 on debentures. X, Y and Z became directors of the new company they disclosed their profit of $ 20,000. It was held that there was no sufficient disclosure and X, Y and Z must pay $ 20,000 to the company.

(ii) *The Promoter is not allowed to derive a Profit from the Sale of his Own Property to the Company unless All Material Facts are disclosed.* If the promoter contracts to sell his own property to the company without making a full disclosure, the company may either repudiate/ rescind the sale or affirm the contract and recover the profit made out of it by the promoter.

The following examples will illustrate this provision :

1. Erlanger *Vs.* New Sombrero Phosphate Co. (1878) 3 A.C. 1218. A syndicate of which E was the head purchased an island containing mines of phosphate for $ 55,000. Ethen formed a company to buy this island. A contract was made between X a nominee of the syndicate and the company for its purchase at $ 1,10,000. The details of the sale were not disclosed to the shareholders or contract of sale. It was held that as there had been no disclosure by the promoters of the profit they were making, the company was entitled to rescind the contract.

2. Erlanger *Vs.* New Sombrero Phosphate Co. (1878) 3 A.C. 1218. A promoter who wishes to sell his own property to the company must make a full disclosure of his interest. The disclosure may be made (i) to an independent board of directors, or (ii) in the articles of association of the company, or (iii) in the prospectus, or (iv) to the existing and intended shareholder directly. Lord Cairns observed :

"I do not say that an owner of property may not promote and form a joint stock company and then sell his property to it but I do say if he does he is bound to take care that he sells it to the company through the medium of a board of directors who can and do exercise an independent and intelligent judgement on the transaction."

If the promoter fails to discharge the obligation demanded of his fiduciary position the company may rescind the contract or may in the alternative choose to take advantage of the contract and sue the promoter for damages for breach of his duty to the company. Secret profits on the sale of property can be recovered from a promoter only when the property was bought and sold to the company while he was acting as a promoter.

RIGHTS OF PROMOTER

1. Right of Indemnity. Where more than one person act as the promoters of the company, one promoter can claim against another promoter for the compensation and damages paid by him. Promoters are severally and jointly liable for any untrue statement given in the prospectus and for the secret profits.

2. Right to receive the Legitimate Preliminary Expenses. The promoter is entitled to receive the legitimate preliminary expense which he has incurred in the process of formation of company such as cost of advertisement, fee of solicitor and surveyors. The right to receive the preliminary expenses is not a contractual right. It depends upon the discretion of the directors. The expenses claim should be supported by vouchers.

3. Right to receive the Remuneration. A promoter has no right against the company for his remuneration unless there is a contract to that effect. In some cases, articles of association of the company provide for the directors paying a specified amount to the promoters for their services but this does not give the promoters any contractual right to sue the company. This is simply an authority vested in the directors of the company.

However, the promoters are usually the directors, so in practice the promoters receive their remuneration which may be paid in any of the following ways :

(i) *Commission of Purchase :* A commission may be paid to the promoter on the purchase price of the business or property taken over by the company through him.

(ii) *Lump Sum Amount :* The promoters may be granted by the company a *lump sum* amount.

(iii) *Shares :* Promoters may be given fully or partly paid shares in consideration of their service rendered.

(iv) *Commission on Shares :* A promoter may be given a commission at a fixed rate on the shares sold.

(v) *Sale of Property :* A promoter may purchase the business or other property and sell the same to the company at an inflated price after disclosing this fact.

(vi) *Unissued Shares :* A promoter may take an option to subscribe within a fixed period for a certain portion of the company's unissued shares at par.

Whatever be the nature of remuneration, it must be disclosed in the prospectus if paid within the preceding 2 years from the date of prospectus.

DUTIES OF PROMOTER

1. To disclose Secret Profit. A promoter should not make any secret profit. If he has made any secret profit, it is his duty to disclose all the money secretly obtained by way of profit. He is empowered to deduct the reasonable expenses incurred by him.

2. To disclose all Material Facts. A promoter must disclose the material facts. If he contracts to sell the company, a property without making a full disclosure, and the property was acquired by him at a time, when he stood in a fiduciary position towards the company, the company may either repudiate the sale or affirm the contract and recover the profit made out of it by the promoters.

3. To make Good to the Company What He has Obtained as a Trustee. A promoter stands in fiduciary position towards the company. It is his duty to make good to the company what he has obtained as trustee and not what he may get at any time [Lord Dunldin in Jubilee Cotton Mills Ltd. Lewis (19-24].

4. To disclose Private Arrangements. The promoter should disclose all the private arrangement resulting in giving him profit by the promotion of the company.

5. To stand in Fiduciary Position to the Future Allottees. The promoters stand in a fiduciary position towards the company. It does not mean that they stand in such a relation only to the company or to the signatories of memorandum of association, they will also stand in this relation to the future allottees of the shares.

LIABILITIES OF PROMOTER

1. Liability to account in Profit. As a promoter stands in a fiduciary position to the company, he is liable to account to the company for all secret profits made by him without full disclosure to the company. If the promoter fails to disclose the profit the company may adopt any one of the following courses :

(i) The company can sue the promoter for an amount of profit and recover the same with interest.

(ii) The company can rescind the contract and can recover the money paid.

2. Liability for Mis-Statement in the Prospectus. (i) Section 61(1). It makes the promoter liable to pay compensation to every person who subscribes for any shares or debentures on the faith of the prospectus for any loss or damage sustained by reason of any untrue statement included in it.

(ii) Section 62. It provides certain grounds on which a promoter can avoid his liability.

(iii) Section 63. It provides for criminal liability for mis-statements in the prospectus and a promoter may also become liable under this section.

The promoter may be imprisoned for a term which may be extended to 2 years or may be punished with the fine upto Rs. fifty thousand for untrue statement in the prospectus.

3. Personal Liability. The promoter is personally liable for all contracts made by him on behalf of the company until the contracts have been discharged or the company takes over the liability of the promoter. The death of a promoter does not relieve him from liabilities.

4. Liability at the Time of Winding up of the Company. (i) Section 543. During the course of winding up of the company, on an application made by the official liquidator, the court may make a promoter liable for misfeasance or breach of trust.

(ii) Section 478. Where fraud has been alleged by the liquidator against a promoter the court may order for his public examination.

PRELIMINARY CONTRACTS/PRE-INCORPORATION CONTRACTS

Meaning

Preliminary contracts are those contracts which are made by the promoters with the different parties on behalf of the company yet to be incorporated. Such contracts are generally entered into by promoters to acquire some property or right for and on behalf of the company to be formed.

The promoters enter into preliminary contracts, generally as agents or trustees of the company. Such contracts are not legally binding on the company because two consenting parties are necessary to a contract whereas the company is a non entity before incorporation.

Limitations of Preliminary Contracts

As the company has no legal existence until it is incorporated, it therefore, follows :

1. That when the Company is Registered, It is not bound by the Preliminary Contract. The following examples will illustrate it.

A solicitor prepared the memorandum and articles of association and paid the necessary registration fees on the instruction of persons who later became directors. He claimed his fees and expenses on the liquidation of the company. It was held that the company was not liable to pay the solicitors costs though it had taken the benefit of his work.

Here Lord Justice Williams observed the following :

"There is no binding authority for the proposition that a company, because it has taken the benefit of work done under a contract entered into before the formation of the company can be made liable in equity under that contractor."

2. That the Company when Registered cannot ratify the Agreement. The company was not a principal with contractual capacity at the time of contract. A contract can be ratified only when it is made by an agent for a principal who is in existence and who is competent to contract at the time when the contract is made.

3. That if the Agent undertook any Liability under the Agreement, He would be Personally Liable notwithstanding that He is described in the Agreement as an agent and, that the Company may have attempted to ratify the Agreement. The following example will illustrate it :

An agreement was made between K and B, B was acting on behalf of the proposed hotel company. Wine supplied under the contract was used by the company which had 'ratified' the agreement after incorporation. The company went into liquidation before paying the debt. It was held that B was personally liable and no ratification could release him from his liability. [*Kelner* Vs. *Baxter* (1866) L.R. 2 C.P. 174].

4. The Company cannot enforce the Preliminary Agreement. This is clear by the following example :

N company agreed with Mrs. C an agent of a syndicate before its incorporation that N company would grant a mining lease to the syndicate. The syndicate was incorporated as P company. P company discovered coal whereupon N company refused to grant the lease. The Privy Council held that there was no binding contract between N company and the P company as the later was not in existence when the contract was signed. [*Natal Land and Colonisation Company Vs. Pauline Colliery & Development Syndicate Ltd.* (I 904) A.C. 1201.

The preliminary contracts made by promoters generally provide that if the company adopts the agreement the promoter's liability shall cease. If the company does not adopt the agreement within a certain time either party may rescind the contract. In such a case promoter's liability would cease after the lapse of fixed time.

Important Exception

A company not bound by the preliminary contracts is subject to an important exception which is laid down in section 15 and 19 of the Specific Relief Act, 1963. These provide that "where the promoters of a company have before its incorporation, entered into contracts for the purposes of the company and such contracts are warranted by terms of incorporation, specific performance may be obtained by or against the company if the company has accepted the contract after its incorporation and has communicated such acceptance to the other party." Warranted by the terms of incorporation means within the scope of the company's objectives as stated in the memorandum. The following example will illustrate it :

The promoters of an ice manufacturing company entered into a contract with M for purchase of the manufacturing machinery for the company. The company on its incorporation adopted the contract and sent the communication of acceptance to M. It, was held that the contract was for the purpose of the company and as such the company could sue or be sued upon it. [Imperial Ice Manufacturing Co. Ltd. *Vs.* Manchershaw I.L.R (1889) 13 Bom. 4151.

It is ONLY the Company which is allowed under S.R. Act to adopt and enforce its pre-incorporation claims against third parties. Section 19 of the Act also allows the other party to enforce the contract against the company if it had adopted the same after incorporation and contracted is warranted by the terms of the incorporation.

PRELIMINARY *VS.* PROVISIONAL CONTRACTS

Difference in Definitions

Preliminary contracts are those agreements or contracts entered into between different parties on behalf of or for the benefit of the company prior to its incorporation. According to Section 149(4) of the Companies Act, contracts made by the company after incorporation but before the commencement of business with other parties are known as provisional contracts.

The points of differentiation between preliminary contracts and provisional contracts are listed in the following table :

S. No.	Basis of Difference	Preliminary Contracts	Provisional Contracts
1	2	3	4
1.	Nature	Those contracts entered into between different parties on behalf or for the benefit of the company prior to its incorporation.	Contract made by, the company after incorporation but before the commencement of business with other parties.
2.	Binding	Not binding on the company.	Not binding on the company pany till such certificate has been obtained.
3.	Existence	At the time of contracts the company is not in existence.	At the time of contracts the company is a separate legal entity.
4.	Liability	The promoters are personally liable.	The authorities signing on behalf of company are not personally liable.
5.	Ratifications	These may be ratified by the company and converted into a new contract based on the conditions of an old contract.	There is no question of ratification or acceptance.

QUESTIONS

1. Define the term promoter. What are their functions? Discuss their rights and liabilities.

2. Who is a company promoter? Discuss the work of a company promoter and his relationship with the company. What are the rights and liabilities of the promoter and how is he remunerated by the company for his work.
3. 'The services of a promoter are quite extraordinary'. Explain this statement with reference to the functions of a promoter. Discuss his legal relationship with the company he manages.
4. "A promoter is not a trustee or an agent for the company but stands in a liabilities position towards it." Comment. Discuss the rights, duties and liabilities of a promoter.
5. Write a short note on preliminary contracts.
6. Distinguish between preliminary contracts and provisional contracts.

PRACTICAL PROBLEMS

1. The promoters of a company, before its incorporation, enter into an agreement with P to buy a plot of land on behalf of the company. After incorporation the company refuses to buy the said plot of land. Has P any remedy either against the promoters or against the company?
[**Hint.** P has no remedy against the company. The promoters are personally liable on the contract].
2. 6 of the 7 signatures to the Memorandum of Association of a company were forged. The Memorandum was duly presented, registered and a certificate of incorporation was issued. Can the existence of the company be subsequently attacked on the ground that the registration was void. Decide.
[**Hint.** No (Section 35, Rule in Peel's Case)].
3. The Memorandum of Association of a company was presented to the Registrar of Companies for registration and the Registrar issued the certificate of incorporation. The company after complying with all the prescribed legal formalities started a business. The company contends that the nature of the business cannot be gone into as the certificate of incorporation is conclusive. Discuss.
[**Hint.** The company's contention is untenable and the nature of the business can be gone into].
4. The Memorandum of Association of a company was signed by 2 adult members and by a guardian of the other 5 minor members, the guardian signing separately for each minor member. The Registrar registered the company and issued under his hand a certificate of incorporation. The plaintiff contended that —
(a) conditions of registration were not duly complied with, and
(b) there were no 7 subscribers to the Memorandum.
Will the Court uphold his contention?
[**Hint.** No (Peel's Case)].

5. The Express Newspapers (Pvt.) Ltd., leading publishers of newspapers and weeklies, sold its undertaking to a new company, Andhra Prabha (Pvt.) Ltd., consequent upon the Government adopting certain recommendations of the Wage Board for improvement in the terms of service and salaries of the working journalists. Shall the registration of the company be declared void on the plea that new company was formed for the purpose of evading the new obligations imposed by the Wage Board? [**Hint.** No (T. V. Krishna *Vs.* Andhra Prabha (Pvt.) Ltd., (1902) 2 Ch 809)].

7

Organisation of Public Companies

Prospectus

After the company is incorporated, its affairs will be taken over by the board of directors. The promoters are the first directors of the company which they help to promote. The secretary who is generally appointed in the pre-incorporation stage continues to play his role and comes into more prominence than he was before incorporation and his work considerably increases. The directors are the persons named in the articles; otherwise the subscribers to the memorandum are deemed to be the first directors of the company. These directors elect one among them as the chairman of the board of directors. Now the board of directors proceed to organise the company and take the following steps :

1. Appointments. Appointment of various expert agencies such as bankers, solicitors, auditors and brokers.

2. Underwriting. Entering into underwriting contracts and determining the terms and conditions in order to secure minimum subscription.

3. Ratification. Ratification of preliminary contracts entered into by the promoters on behalf of the company.

4. Listing. Preparation for listing of shares and debentures on the stock exchanges.

5. Prospectus. Drafting the prospectus and finally issuing the prospectus to the public.

(1) Appointment of Expert Agencies. The board of directors first appoint solicitors, bankers, brokers, auditors, etc. The promoters generally make the various appointments mentioned above and the Board confirms their appointments. The naming of such expert agencies is compulsory under the Companies Act, 1956. Every public company is required to deposit application moneys with a scheduled bank. They can be removed after the expiry of their period of appointment. If the promoters have not appointed a secretary at the time of promotion, the Board selects some person for this post and enters into a contract with him on behalf of the company. If he is already appointed, the contract, which is entered into by the promoters with the Secretary on behalf of the company, is now ratified and a new contract on the old lines is entered into with him.

(2) Preliminary Contracts. These are entered into by the promoters on behalf of the company for purchasing property and assets necessary for the purpose. In order to bind the company, the promoters get confirmed such contracts from the board of directors who do so on behalf of the company.

(3) Underwriting Contracts. There is an agreement between the underwriters and the promoters of the company and the agreement is called "the underwriting agreement". It is a contract between the promoters and the underwriters by which the latter undertake in consideration of a stipulated commission called the underwriting commission to take up shares or a portion thereof which may not be subscribed by the public. Underwriters may be individuals, institutions like banks, insurance companies or investment syndicates, who undertake to purchase and pay for the shares of a company, if the public do not purchase the shares when issued. The underwriting commission is paid at a fixed percentage on the issue price of shares. The underwriting agreement is entered into by the promoters to ensure the financial safety of the flotations of the company. The underwriter insures the capital issue and guarantees the minimum subscription fixed by the board of directors. Shares of Public limited company cannot be allotted unless the minimum subscription amount is collected. If they fail to raise minimum subscription the directors of the company are expected to refund the application money and wind up the affairs of the company.

Individual brokers, banks or investment companies may enter into a simple underwriting agreement under which the company will sell shares directly to the public and if the whole issue is sold, underwriters will collect their underwriting commission. If the shares are not fully subscribed by the public, the underwriters will take up the unsold shares and will pay for them. They may later on dispose them of as they like. On the other hand, they may themselves undertake to sell the shares. The company is indifferent whether the shares are sold fully or partly. When a large number of shares are issued, some underwriters may form themselves into a temporary syndicate and underwrite the shares. Where there are investment syndicates, they may purchase the whole issue of shares and sell them proportionately to their members.

Underwriting Conditions

(1) There should be a stipulation that the company will receive a minimum agreed amount of the whole issue of shares within a stated period.

(2) The payment of underwriting commission should be properly authorised by the Articles of Association.

(3) The amount of commission should not exceed the rate authorised by the Articles of Association or 5 per cent of the issue price of shares under the Companies Act, 1956, whichever is less. In the case of debentures the rates should not exceed 2-1/2 per cent of the issue price under tile Act.

(4) The amount of the rate of commission and the number of shares and debentures which the persons have agreed to subscribe for a commission should be "stated" in tile prospectus.

(5) The payment must be "strictly" by way of "commission and not merely a device to issue shares at a discount.

(6) The names of the underwriters and the opinion of the directors that the resources of the underwriters are sufficient to discharge their obligations must be "disclosed" in the prospectus.

A draft prospectus is given to the firm of underwriters to carefully examine and calculate the risk involved. If the underwriters are satisfied with it, they enter into an agreement with the company to that effect. It is presumed that the final prospectus will run on the same lines as those on the draft prospectus.

(4) Listing of Shares on Stock Exchanges. The inclusion of the shares in the list of securities dealt in on the stock exchange, is called *"listing of shares"*. The board of directors make an application to the authorities of the stock exchange which permits dealing of such shares to take place on the exchange. This will inspire confidence amongst the investors. The information that the permission has been obtained from the stock exchange authorities, or that an application for getting permission is made, must be mentioned in the prospectus of a company.

Procedure for Listing of Shares

1. Application. A company interested in listing its shares on the stock exchange, under the Securities Contracts (Regulation) Act, 1956, is required to apply to the stock exchange authorities along with prescribed fees.

2. Accompanying Documents. The company should also send the following documents along with its application :

(1) Copies of Memorandum of Association and Articles of Association.

(2) Underwriting agreements and directors' report.

(3) Specimen copies of letter of allotment, application forms, share certificates, etc.

(4) Details regarding capital Structure.

(5) Copy of the consent of the Controller of Capital Issues,

3. Examination on Stock Exchange. On receipt of such an application, the stock exchange authorities will examine the particulars including those of prospectus with a view to discouraging fraudulent companies in listing shares on the stock exchange. In case a public company wants an official quotation on recognised stock exchanges then it must issue 49 per cent of its issued capital to the public for subscription. If the stock exchange authorities are satisfied, they will ask the company to execute a Listing Agreement containing the terms and conditions of listing of shares which are to be complied with by the company concerned (listed company). Now shares and debentures of the company will be entered in the official list of the stock exchange. Thus, every application for listing shares will be considered on its own merit.

4. Appeal against Refusal. However, the company under Section 22 of the Securities Contracts (Regulation) Act, 1956, is empowered to appeal to the Central Government against the stock exchange authorities if its application to list securities is refused. Appeal should be made within 15 days of the refusal. Under same Act (S.C.R. Act) the Central Government is empowered to compel any public company for getting its shares listed on a recognised stock exchange.

5. Issue of Prospectus. According to the Section 2(36) of the Companies Act, "Prospectus means any document described or issued as a prospectus and includes any notice, circular, advertisement or other document (inviting deposits from the public or) inviting offers from the public for subscription or purchase of any shares in, or debentures of, a body corporate."

The words "inviting offers from the public" is an important clause or a condition in the definition of the prospectus as this clause determines whether a document is a prospectus or not. It is rather not easy to say what constitutes "the public. Any number of persons may constitute public." But Section 67 says that "the term of construed as including a reference to offering them to any section of the public, whether selected as members or debenture holders of the company concerned or as clients of the person issuing prospectus or in any other manner." The offers may be invited from a section of the public or from the existing shareholders or debenture holders of the company or from the clients of an investment company. If the offer is made to (i) only to a few friends and relatives of directors; or (ii) offer is to be accepted only a few persons to whom it is made then it is not an offer made to the public (Section 67). The construction of the meaning of "offers to the public" will depend upon the nature of the offer. If the offer is open to the persons other than those to whom it is made then it is made to the public. If the offer is made only to the friends and relatives of directors or if it is to be accepted only by the persons to whom it is made then it is not made to the public. A prospectus marked confidential was issued among selected circle of persons was not a prospectus. The offering of shares to relatives of directors is not an invitation to public. An offer to shareholders of an existing company "A" in a new company "B" in exchange of existing shares of "A" is not an offer to public. Act, 2000 lay down that an invitation by companies other than non-banking

Finance Companies or financial institutions, even though meant for subscription/purchase by only those who receive it, shall be construed as invitation to public, if it is made to 50 persons or more.

Section 64 of the Act states that if the whole share capital of the company is allotted to an "Issue House" whose principal business is to handle new issues and if this "Issue House" offers such shares to the public through an advertisement, the document by which such an offer is made shall be deemed to be a "Prospectus by Implication" provided it is shown that the offer was made within six months after the allotment or agreement to allot to the Issue House or that at the date of offer to the public, the whole consideration in respect of the shares has not been received by the company.

Provisions for the Issue of Prospectus

(i) *Filing a Copy with the Registrar :* Where a prospectus is issued as a newspaper advertisement, it shall not be necessary to specify therein the contents of the memorandum, the signatories thereto, or the number of shares subscribed by them, but it must contain all the particulars which are statutorily required in the case of an ordinary prospectus.

Every prospectus must state that a true copy of it has been filed for registration with the Registrar of Companies. Thus, a prospectus cannot be issued to the public before it is registered with the Registrar of Companies. Section 56 of the Act requires the prospectus to contain particulars given in that section. Any omission to this effect is heavily penalised. The issue of prospectus is essential when the company wishes the public to purchase its shares or debentures. But private companies are strictly prohibited from issuing the prospectus as they cannot invite the public to subscribe to their shares. Even a public company need not issue the prospectus. But in this case it will have to file with the Registrar a *Statement in Lieu of Prospectus* giving particulars as per Part I of Schedule III of the Companies Act, 1956 (Section 70).

(ii) *Dating of Prospectus :* Section 55 states that every prospectus issued by or on behalf of a company or in relation to a proposed company shall be dated and that date shall be taken as the date of the publication of prospectus unless the contrary is proved. The board has to pass a resolution for effecting the issue of the prospectus which authorises the secretary to deliver one copy of the prospectus to the Registrar of Companies. The date of publication of prospectus is also given in the resolution.

(iii) *The Contents of the Prospectus :* The contents of prospectus have not been provided under the statute. According to Section 56, every prospectus which is issued by or on behalf of the company, by or on behalf of any person who is or has been engaged or interested in the formation of a company, must contain particulars specified on Part I of Schedule II of the Companies Act, 1956, and set out reports contained in Part II of the schedule. The essential particulars to be specified in the prospectus and the reports attached to it are the following :

(1) Name and registered address of the Company.

(2) The main objects of the Company.

(3) Information with reference to listing of shares on a recognised Stock Exchange. Detailed information should be given.

(4) Particulars pertaining to voting right of different classes of shareholders and other details as regards rights of members to attend, speak or vote at meetings of the company.

(5) The names and addresses of the company promoters, if any, and a reference to their remuneration.

(6) Particulars about the borrowing powers.

(7) All details pertaining to various contracts entered in connection with :

    (a) appointment of officers;

    (b) remuneration of such officers;

    (c) any other matter not usually discussed in the normal course of business.

(8) Particulars of signatories of the memorandum and shares subscribed by them (A prospectus issued in the form of newspaper advertisement need not contain this clause).

(9) Particulars regarding the directors, managing director, manager etc., and of the contracts fixing the remuneration of managing director, manager etc.

(10) Nature and extent of interest of every director or promoter either in the promotion of the company or in any property purchased by company.

(11) Number and classes of shares issued and extent of interest of holders; particulars regarding debentures and redeemable preference shares should be shown separately.

(12) The rights in respect of capital and dividends attached to different classes of shares.

(13) Minimum subscription and amount payable on application and allotment.

(14) Preliminary expenses incurred.

(15) Particulars regarding purchase of property.

(16) Details of any premium or underwriting commissions paid and details of underwriting agreement.

(17) Time of opening and closing of a subscription list.

(18) Particulars of reserves including reserves capitalised.

(19) A report by the auditor should be attached showing the profit and loss; and assets and liabilities of the company; rates of dividend paid for five years preceding the issue of prospectus and particulars regarding subsidiaries being also shown.

(20) Whether the prospectus issued was at the time of formation of the company or subsequently.

(21) The names and addresses of auditors of the company.

Requirements from the Person Acquiring Shares

Section 68A provides that the following provision must be prominently printed in every prospectus and in every application form for shares issued by the company. "Any person who makes, in a fictitious name, an application to a company for acquiring any shares therein, or otherwise induces a company to allot or register any transfer of shares therein to him or any other person in a fictitious name, shall be punishable with imprisonment upto five years." As per the latest Government Guidelines, it must be printed in every prospectus and in every application form for shares issued that "An applicant should submit only one application for the total number of shares required. Applications may be made in single or joint names (not more than three). Two or more applications in single and/or joint names will be deemed to be multiple applications if the sale and/or the first applicant is one and the same. The Board of Directors reserves the right to reject in its absolute discretion all or any multiple applications. In case of applications under Power of Attorney or by limited companies or corporate bodies the relevant Power of Attorney or the relevant authority, as the case may be, or a duly certified copy thereof, must be attached to the Application Form or lodged separately at the office of the Registrar to the Issue."

Application for Shares

(1) The Section 56(3) now provides that no one shall issue any form of application for shares in or debentures of a company unless the form is accompanied "*by a memorandum containing such salient features of a prospectus as may be prescribed*" which complies with the requirements of this section. The Act now has substituted the words, "by a memorandum" in the place of old term, "by a prospectus". It is now further provided that a copy of the prospectus shall be furnished to a person who makes such a request before closing of the subscription list. A director or other person responsible for the prospectus shall not incur any liability by reasons of any non-compliance with any of the requirements of this section, if :

(a) As regards any matter not disclosed, he proves that he had no knowledge thereof; or

(b) He proves that the non compliance arose out of honest mistake of fact on his part.

An application form for shares or debentures of a company cannot be issued unless such form is accompanied by a copy of the prospectus, otherwise a heavy penalty extending to Rs. 5,000 is imposed under the Act. The above enumerated requirements do not apply to the following cases :

(a) Where the form of application is issued in connection with a *bonafide* invitation to a person to enter into an underwriting agreement with respect to the shares or debentures which were not offered to the public, or

(b) Where the prospectus is issued to existing members of debenture holders of the Company;

(c) Where application forms are issued pertaining to shares or debentures not offered to the public.

(2) Under Section 60(4), no prospectus is to be issued more than ninety days after the date on which a copy is delivered for registration; and if a prospectus is so issued, it shall be deemed to be a prospectus, a copy of which has not been delivered to the Registrar.

Expert's Opinion : Under Sections 57, 58 and 59, an expert may be an engineer, a valuer, an accountant or any other person whose profession gives authority to a statement made by him. A prospectus inviting the public to subscribe to the shares or debentures of a company must not include a statement purporting to be made by an expert unless :

(i) Such expert has never been engaged or interested in the formation or promotion, or in the management of the company;

(ii) He has given his written consent to the issue thereof;

(iii) He has not withdrawn such consent before the delivery of a copy of the prospectus for registration; and

(iv) A statement to that effect appears in the prospectus.

(iv) *Registration of prospectus :* Under Section 60, before issuing a prospectus to the public, a copy of it duly signed by every person who is named therein as a director or proposed director must be filed with the Registrar for registration. Such a copy of prospectus can even be signed by authorised agent of a director who gives his consent in writing to this effect. Similarly every prospectus on the face of it shall state that a copy has been delivered for registration and specify the documents required by Section 60 to be attached to the copy of the prospectus so delivered. The following documents shall be attached to the prospectus :

(1) Any report of an expert who has given his written consent.

(2) A copy of any material contract.

(3) A copy of the contract relating to the appointment, remuneration

of a managing director, managing agent, secretaries and treasurer or a manager.

(4) The consent in writing of any person named as the auditor, legal adviser, attorney, solicitor, banker or broker of the company.

The Registrar shall not register a prospectus unless :

(a) the prospectus is dated;

(b) matters stated in Part I of Schedule II are specified and

(c) the prospectus is certified by an expert who is unconnected with formation or management of the company.

(5) However, it should be noted that no prospectus shall be issued more than ninety days after the date on which a copy thereof is delivered for registration. If a prospectus is issued without a copy thereof being delivered under this Section to the Registrar, the company and every person who is knowingly a party to the issue of prospectus, shall be punishable with fine which may extend to five thousand rupees.

(v) *Newspaper Advertisements of Prospectus :* Section 66 provides that the contents of the memorandum or the signatories thereto or the number of shares subscribed for by them need not be mentioned in the prospectus published as a newspaper advertisement. It must have all other contents of a general prospectus. The Department of Company Affairs has laid down that such an advertisement must state at the top, "this is an announcement and not a prospectus." It should give information regarding the company and the proposed issue of shares under the following heads :

1. Name of the company.
2. Address of the company's registered office.
3. Existing and proposed activities.
4. Location of the industry.
5. Board of Directors.
6. Manager/Managing Director(s) if any.
7. Details about capital — authorised, subscribed. etc.
8. Proposed issue to the public.
9. Opening and closing dates of subscription list.
10. Address of brokers, and underwriters from whom prospectus and application forms can be had.

(vi) *Prospectus and application Forms :* Section 56(3) states that application forms are only to be issued for shares or debentures along with the prospectus. Unless accompanied by prospectus, no application forms can be issued. Those responsible for default are punishable with a fine which may extend to five thousand rupees (Rs. 5,000).

In the following cases, application forms without a prospectus can be sent out when the prospectus contains all the prescribed details :

(1) In the case of bonafide underwriting agreement [Section 56(3)(a)].

(2) Where the offer of shares or debentures is not made to the public [Sec. 56(3)(b)].

(3) Where the offer is made only to existing members or debenture holder, with or without the right of renunciation [Section 56(5)(a)].

(4) Where the issue of shares and debentures is similar with those previously issued and dealt in oil stock exchange [Section 56(5)(b)].

STATEMENT IN LIEU OF PROSPECTUS

Meaning

A public company is expected to raise its capital from the public. For this purpose, an invitation is usually extended to it through a prospectus. If a company raises its capital without approaching the public, it may not issue a prospectus. But, where no prospectus is issued, a company is not allowed to allot shares to any party. Section 70 of the Act provides that where no prospectus is issued, atleast three days before the first allotment of shares or debentures a statement called "Statement in Lieu of Prospectus" must be filed with the Registrar for registration, signed by every person who is named therein as a director or proposed director of the company, or by, an authorised agent. It will be drafted strictly in accordance with the particulars set out in Part I of Schedule III of the Act.

The above provisions are not applicable to a private company.

Where a statement in lieu of prospectus filed with the Registrar includes any untrue statement, any person who authorised the filing of the statement in lieu of prospectus for registration shall be punishable with imprisonment for a term which may extend to two years or with fine which may extend to five thousand rupees or with both. However, he will not be liable for imprisonment or fine if he proves either that statement was immaterial or what he had reasonable ground to believe that the statement was true [Section 70(5)].

If the shares are allotted by a company to an applicant in contravention of Sections 69 and 70 which provide for raising of minimum subscription amount and of filing a statement in lieu of prospects with the Registrar, shall be avoidable at the instance of the applicant. In this case, a director who is responsible for contravention of provisions of Section 69 or 70 of the Act is liable to compensate the company and the allottee for any loss or damages sustained. Under Section 71(3) proceeding to recover any such loss or damages must be commenced before the expiry of two years from the date of the allotment.

Prospectus by Implication

It is not a real prospectus but is deemed to be a prospectus under

Section 64 of the Act. Under this Section, when a company allots or agrees to allot shares or debentures of the company, either all or any of them being offered for sale to the public, then any document by which the offer for sale to the public is made shall, for all purposes; be deemed to be a prospectus issued by the company. But for this purpose it is necessary that an offer of the shares or debentures for sale to the public must be made within six months after the allotment or agreement to allot. Similarly the whole consideration to be received by the company in respect of the shares or debentures was not received by the company at the date when the officer was actually made.

Since this document is deemed to be a prospectus, all provisions pertaining to company prospectus shall be applicable to it. Under Section 64 (3) of the Act this document deemed to be a prospectus, must also state :

(a) the net amount of the consideration received or to be received by the company in respect of the shares or debentures offered for sale and

(b) the place and time at which the contract under which slid shares or debentures are allotted may be inspected.

Section 60 as applied by this Section shall have effect as if the persons making the offer were persons named in a prospectus as directors of a company.

Where the offer for sale of shares or debentures is made by a company, the relevant document containing the conditions of offer must be signed by two directors of the company and not less than one-half of other the partners when the offer is made by a firm. It can also be signed by the agent of a director or partner if such an agent is authorised in writing.

ABRIDGED FORM OF PROSPECTUS

A draft prospectus filed with SEBI would be made a public document. A company can issue an abridged prospectus under Section 56(3) and SEBI has laid down certain conditions to be met by the lead Merchant Banker. An abridged prospectus may not be issued (as well as prospectus) if it is a private company or if management feels that they can mobilise resources through personal relationship or in case of underwriting agreement or right issue of shares is made or when invitation is in the form of an advertisement (called prospectus announcement) (Section (66)) or the issue is uniform in all respects as perviously issued and dealt in and quoted in a recognised stock exchange.

SHELF PROSPECTUS AND INFORMATION MEMORANDUM (SECTION 60A AND 60B)

The Companies (Amendment) Act 2000 has introduced these sections. Shelf prospectus means a prospectus issued by any financial institution of bank for issue of securities specified in the prospectus. For subsequent offerings, information memorandum updating the information under various heads will be filed. A company filing shelf prospectus will not be required to file an information memorandum. Both will however, be issued to the public at the stage of first offer of securities.

'Information memorandum' means a process undertaken prior to the filing of a prospectus by which a demand for securities proposed to be issued by a company is elicited, the price and terms for such securities are assessed by means of a notice, circular, advertisement or document.

RED-HERRING PROSPECTUS

It is a prospectus which does not have complete particulars as the price and quantity of securities offered. It carries the same obligations as a prospectus. Any variation between 'Information Memorandum' and red-herring prospectus shall be highlighted by the company.

GOLDEN RULE IN FRAMING PROSPECTUS

The rule was laid down in re Brunswick and Canada Railways and land Co., Vs. Muggeridge. The rule states that everything in prospectus must be stated with strict and scrupulous accuracy. A half truth represented as a whole may tantamount to a false statement. It means a company not only should disclose particulars as required in Part I and Part II of Schedule II of the Act, but any information within the knowledge of the persons issuing it which may affect the decision of the prospective investor should be disclosed.

NOTICE OF SITUATION OF REGISTERED OFFICE

Another document to be filed with the registrar is a notice, regarding the situation of the registered office of the company. It is to be given within 30 days after the date of incorporation of the company or of the change, as the case may be, to the Registrar in the following form :

7.1 : Notice for Situation/Change of Situation of Registered Office

Pursuant to Section 146 of

THE COMPANIES ACT, 1956

(Name of Company).....................

Presented by.......................

The Registrar of Companies................

I hereby give you notice, in accordance with Section 146 of the Companies Act, 1956, that the registered office of the Company was situated at.......................has been removed from............... To....................on the day.............19.........

Dated the.......................day of................19............

(Sd.) ....

Designation

The inclusion in the annual return of a company of a statement as the address or its registered office shall not be taken to satisfy the obligation imposed by sub-section (2) of Section 146 of the Act.

If default is made in complying with the requirements of this section, the company and every officer of the company who is in default, shall be punishable with fine which may extend to fifty rupees for every day during which the default continues.

After the prospectus or statement in lieu of prospectus is filed with the Registrar for registration, the directors will now proceed to make arrangements for making the prospectus known to the public.

Reports to be set out in a Prospectus

1. A report by the auditors of the company with respect to profits, losses, assets and liabilities of the company. The report should refer to the rate of dividends paid during the Five financial years preceding the issue of prospectus. Such information should also be given in the report regarding company subsidiaries.
2. If the company proposes to acquire any business, a report by a Chartered Accountant regarding profits, losses, assets and liabilities of five financial years before the date of issue of prospectus. Name of the accountant making report should be mentioned in the prospectus.
3. A report of similar nature by a Chartered Accountant if the company proposes to acquire shares in another body corporate.

MIS-REPRESENTATION AND FRAUDULENT STATEMENT

Prospectus is a document which attracts or induces the general public to invest money in a company. For a person who is generally induced to purchase the shares and debentures of a company on the basis of contents of its prospectus, a prospectus becomes the basis of the contract between the company and the shareholder. It is likely to influence the judgement of a prospective investor in deciding whether to subscribe for the shares and debentures of a particular company or not. Therefore, no material fact should be concealed and it must not contain any statement which may be held fraudulent or misrepresentation.

Meaning of False Statement

A prospectus should be honestly framed and should not contain any incomplete or ambiguous statement. A false statement means any statement which may confuse the public or which may create a wrong impression in the minds of the public about the facts of the issue. A general recommendation, even if it is too highly coloured, cannot be a false statement. A statement that something is expected or it has been done, when it is not, will be a misstatement of the fact. If there is an omission of a material fact from a prospectus, it may also be deemed to be a misstatement. If a statement is ambiguous in the form in which it is included, it shall also be deemed to be untrue. Therefore, a prospectus containing false, misleading ambiguous or fraudulent statement, of a material facts, may be termed as a misleading prospectus. For examples in '*Rex* Vs. *Kylsant*' : A prospectus was issued in 1928 with a statement that the company has regularly been paying dividend ranging from 5 per cent to 8 per cent while the fact was that the company had been incurring substantial trading losses during the, 7 years preceding the date of prospectus. The court decided that the prospectus, was false, not because of what is stated, but because of what was not contained in it.

To be called a misleading prospectus there must be misrepresentation of facts and not of law. For example, if the prospectus of a company states that the shares of company will be issued at half of their normal value but it is not the real statement, the prospectus may not be held misleading because it is only a mis-representation of the law. Section 79 does not allow a company to issue its shares at a discount exceeding 10 per cent.

Remedies to the Misleading Statement

(I) Remedies Against Company

Following are the remedies available to a person against the company for the misrepresentation or misstatement in the prospectus : (i) Right of rescission of contract and (2) Right to claim the damages.

1. Right of Rescission of Contract. Under Indian Contract Act, 1872, a contract induced by a mis-statement of any material fact, either innocently or fraudulently, is voidable at the discretion of the aggrieved party. Hence a person induced by a mis-statement, is entitled to rescind his contract and to return his shares of the company and to receive back his money with the appropriate interest. He is empowered to go to the court for a declaration of rescission of the contract, if so required.

However, if a statement was true when it was made but subsequently becomes false before the final allotment of shares, the contract to take the shares may even be rescinded. The contract can also be rescinded for mis-representation made in a document by which an offer for sale is made to the public.

Conditions for Succeeding in a Suit of Rescission

1. Responsibility of the Company. The prospectus was issued by the company or on its behalf by the directors. If it was issued by the promoter, the board of directors has ratified and adopted the issue. Thus, the responsibility of the company to the issue of prospectus must be established by the subscriber.

2. Mis-representation of Facts. The prospectus contained a mis-representation of facts, and not of law or of opinion or of expectation.

3. Material Mis-representation. The mis-representation of the fact was material. The mis-represention must be such as likely to influence the judgement of a person in deciding whether to take the shares and debentures of a particular company or not. If the mis-statement is not material, the subscriber will not be allowed to rescind the contract.

4. Actual Reliance. It must be proved by the subscriber that while applying for shares he has actually relied upon the statement in question. Thus, if it is proved by the company that he did not read it or that he knew that the statement in question was untrue or that he made the investigation to verify the statement or that he purchased the shares in the open market or that he subscribed to the memorandum of the association before the company came into existence, the subscriber will not be allowed to rescind the contract in any of such cases.

Conditions of Loss of the Right of Rescission

1. No Proceedings in Time. If he does not start the proceedings within a reasonable time after knowing the mis-representation.

2. Confirmation of Contract. If he confirms his contract, either expressly or impliedly after becoming aware of the false statement. If a subscriber attends any of the meetings of the company, accepts any payment of dividend by the company, pays any call money on his shares or tries to sell his shares, it will be taken his affirmation of the contract by his acts and in all such cases, he will not be allowed to rescind the contract.

3. Company Liquidation. If a company goes into liquidation before he starts the proceedings to rescind the contract.

4. Calibre. If the company proves that he is a man of such calibre and such experience that he is not likely to be misled by the mis-statement in the prospectus.

Conditions of Right to Claim the Damages for Frauds

If a person has purchased any shares or debentures of a company induced by a mis-statement in the prospectus of the company, he does not enjoy only the right of rescission of contract but also to recover the damages for such statement. To avail this remedy, the subscriber must prove the following :

1. Fraud. That the mis-statement was made fraudulently and not innocently. If a fraudulent statement was made innocently, only the right of rescission of contract is available for the subscriber. The right to claim the damages for fraud is an elective right. The subscriber can sue the company or the Directors as he likes.

2. Actual Deception. That he has actually been deceived by the mis-statement. The right to claim any damages can be exercised only after the rescission of contract has been allowed by the court. Thus if the right to rescind a contract is lost, right to claim the damages will also be lost automatically.

(II) Remedies Against the Directors, Promoters and Experts

A subscriber enjoys some remedies against the directors, promoters and experts, liable for the mis-statement. These remedies are available to a subscriber whether he rescinds his contract or not. A subscriber may take action against all or any one of the following persons to pay the compensation or penalty for mis-statement in the prospectus under Section 62(l) :

1. The directors at the time of issue of prospectus.

2. Every person who has authorised himself to be named in the prospectus as the present or future director.

3. Every promoter.

4. Every other person who has authorised the issue of prospectus. Experts like an engineer, a valuer, auditor, accountant, legal experts etc., are not included under this clause unless the prospectus contains their name in untrue statement.

HEADS OF LIABILITY OF THE PERSONS LIABLE FOR THE MIS-STATEMENT

1. Damages for fraud,
2. Damages for mis-representation,
3. Criminal liability and
4. Liability for omission. The details are as follows :

1. Damages for Fraud. A subscriber may sue all or any one of the persons authorising the issue of prospectus to recover the damages for misstatement. This right can be exercised by the subscriber only if he does not sue the company for this right. For this, he will have to prove the following :

(i) That the person or persons were guilty of the mis-statement in question.

(ii) That he has actually been deceived by the mis-statement.

Such an action should be taken at the earliest but this action call be taken even if the company goes into liquidation because it is not an action against the company.

2. Damages for Mis-representation. Section 62 of the Indian Companies Act states that, if the subscriber suffers any loss because of any untrue statement in the prospectus he can claim the damages from the company whether the statement was made fraudulently or innocently. The true measurement of damages is the difference between the amount paid by him and the value of shares at the time of allotment. For this also, the subscriber will have to prove the following :

(i) That the prospectus contained untrue statement of material fact.

(ii) That he has actually sustained the loss by reason of the untrue statements.

3. Criminal Liability. Section 63 of the Companies Act states that if a prospectus contains any untrue statement, every person authorising the issue of such a prospectus, shall be punishable with an imprisonment for a term which may be upto 2 years or with fine which may be upto Rs. 5,000 or with both.

4. Liability for Omission. Section 56 of the Indian Companies Act states that if any material fact is not included in the prospectus (leaving out any of the items which the II Schedule of the Act requires to be disclosed in the prospectus), it creates the liability of the persons liable for such an omission. Omission need not make the prospectus false or misleading. All the persons responsible for the issue of such prospectus will be liable to be punished with a fine which may be upto Rs. 5,000 and to pay the damages to the subscriber. The subscriber must prove the following :

(i) That if the omission would not have been in the prospectus, he would not have purchased the shares.

(ii) That he has actually sustained the loss.

In case of omission in a prospectus, the subscriber does not have the right to rescind the contract.

DEFENCES AVAILABLE TO THE PERSONS LIABLE FOR MIS-STATEMENT

Section 62 of the Indian Companies Act, 1956 provides for defences available to the persons liable for mis-statement in prospectus.

1. Defences open to Directors etc.

2. Defences open to Experts. The details are as follows :

1. Defences Open to Directors etc. Section 62(2) of Companies Act states that a person liable for the mis-statement in the prospectus (other than experts) may escape from the liabilities if he proves :

(i) That he withdrew his consent to act as a director before the prospectus was issued and it was issued without his consent; or

(ii) That the prospectus was issued with his knowledge or consent and on becoming aware of this issue, he gave reasonable public notice that the said prospectus has been so issued; or

(iii) That he was ignorant of the mis-statement in question and on becoming aware of the same, after the issue of prospectus but before the allotment of shares, he withdrew his consent and gave a reasonable public notice to that effect; or

(iv) That he believed or he had reasonable grounds to believe that the statement in question was true and he believed it to be true; or

(v) That the statement has given his consent under Section 58 of the Companies Act and he had not withdrawn it; or

(vi) That the statement was a true and fair copy of an official document or that it was based on the authority of some official person.

2. Defences Available to Experts. Section 62(3) of the Companies Act states that an expert made liable regarding any false statement of a prospectus purporting to be made by him as an expert, may avoid or escape from liabilities if he proves :

(i) That having given his consent, he withdrew it in writing before delivery of a copy of the prospectus for registration; or

(ii) That after delivery of prospectus for registration but before allotment of the shares, he became aware of the untrue statement and withdrew his consent in writing and gave a reasonable public notice of the withdrawal of his consent and the reasons thereof; or

(iii) That he was competent to make the statement in question and believed it on a reasonable ground that it was true.

QUESTIONS

1. What is a 'Prospectus?' Is the issue of a prospectus compulsory for a company? Discuss the subject matter of a prospectus.
2. Define prospectus. Is the issue of prospectus compulsory? State in brief the meaning and contents of prospectus.
3. What is meant by a company prospectus? When is the issue of Prospectus deemed to be for public? Is the issue of prospectus compulsory on the part of a company?
4. What is a company prospectus? Explain fully the contents of prospectus issued by a company under Companies Act, 1956.
5. Discuss the Consequences of Omission, Misrepresentation and Fraud in connection with prospectus of a Company. Also narrate the circumstances under which a director may be realised from the liability?
6. Explain the legal formalities regarding the form and subject matter of prospectus. What are the consequences of fraud in the subject matter of prospectus?
7. What remedies are open to the allottees of Shares who had applied for them on the faith of a false and misleading prospectus and what are the defences available to the directors of company who have issued such a Prospectus?
8. Discuss the civil and criminal liabilities which arise as a result of an untrue and mis-representing statement in the prospectus. Explain the 'Golden Rule' of issuing prospectus.

9. Explain the following terms :
   (a) Information memorandum
   (b) Shelf prospectus
   (c) Abridged prospectus
   (d) Red herring prospectus
   (e) Deemed prospectus

8

Share Capital and Shares

A company needs finance to meet its various type of requirements. Of these some funds are required for a fairly long time, for the purpose of acquiring fixed assets, while some others are required for day to day working. The method of raising funds should be decided after taking into consideration the period for which funds are required. Long term funds should be raised in such a way that a company may have uninterrupted use of it for a sufficiently long time. It is unwise for a company to take loans from a bank to acquire a fixed asset as loan is a source of obtaining funds only for a short period.

TYPES OF SECURITIES

According to the mode of raising funds, sources for a company may be classified into two broad categories : (1) By issue of securities such as shares (equity and preference) and debentures and (2) By other methods such as ploughing back of profits, public deposits, bank loans, loans from special financial institutions etc. According to the Indian Companies Act 1956, a company can issue two types of securities (1) ownership securities and (2) creditorship securities. While the ownership securities include the equity and the preference shares, creditorship securities include debentures and bonds.

1. Ownership Securities. These may be classified into (i) equity shares and (ii) preference shares.

(i) *Equity Shares :* These are the shares the holders of which are the residual claimants and have no preference in capital as well as in the income of the company. They control the affairs of the company and carry with them the ownership responsibilities. They provide the "risk capital" or "venture capital" of the company.

(ii) *Preference Shares :* According to Section 85(l) of the Companies Act, preference shares are those which carry preferential rights as to the payment of dividend at a fixed rate either free of or subject to income-tax, and as to the repayment of capital. These shareholders enjoy two preferential rights over the other category of shares. Firstly, they are entitled to receive a fixed rate of dividend out of the net profits of the company prior to declaration of dividend on equity shares. Secondly, after the payment of debts of the company under liquidation, the remaining assets are first appropriated for returning the capital contributed by the preference shareholders.

2. Creditorship Securities. (i) *Debentures :* A debenture is an acknowledgement of debt by a company under its seal. Debentures are equal parts of a loan raised by a company. They are offered to the public through prospectus. They are always secured either by floating charge or by fixed charge.

(ii) *Bonds :* Bond is a agreement between the bondholders and the company, called bond indenture containing the terms and conditions. As appointed by the company a trustee acts as an agent of the bondholders and controls the affairs of the company on behalf of the bondholders. According to terms of issue bonds may be classified as secured and unsecured, redeemable and irredeemable bonds etc. A big majority of bonds carry a fixed rate of interest.

SIGNIFICANCE OF SECURITIES IN FINANCIAL STRUCTURE

1. Bonds or debentures are issued only when the future earnings of company are liberal and fairly constant. A public utility concern may collect a fairly large amount through debentures as its earnings are somewhat constant.

2. Equity shares should be issued and debt should be contracted in the beginning by basic and manufacturing industries.

3. Only equity shares should be issued when fresh capital is required by an existing concern whose previous earnings have been unstable.

4. Cheap borrowed funds may be used for expansion purposes, when a company has become well established and the earnings have stabilised. When debentures are issued to obtain these funds, it should be ensured that twice the interest charges are being earned by the public utility concerns and four times by other concerns.

5. If funds are obtained on the basis of mortgage issue, the total amount thus collected should not exceed half the depreciated value of the assets covered by the mortgage.

6. Industries having large fixed assets may issue irredeemable debentures or long term redeemable debentures.

7. When the earnings are irregular but average profits over a period of years give a fair margin over preference shares, dividend preference shares may be issued.

MEANING OF SHARE CAPITAL

No company can do without capital as Company is that form of business organisation which collects the required capital from a large number of persons. It needs a huge amount of capital to start and carry on its business. As no one can contribute the whole amount required, the company divides it into the parts of a very nominal amount, say Rs. 10 or Rs. 100. These are known as Shares. To raise the required amount of capital the company issues the shares to the general public. Therefore, a capital of a company is called Share Capital. Thus share capital denotes the amount raised or to be raised by the issue of shares by a company.

TYPES OF SHARE CAPITAL

1. Authorised Capital. Authorised Share Capital is the amount of share capital with which a company is registered. It is disclosed under the capital clause in the memorandum of the association of the company. It is the maximum amount of share capital which can ever be issued by the company. There is no limitation on the amount of authorised capital. A company can decide the amount of its share capital keeping in view both the present and future needs. It is also known as Registered Capital and Nominal Capital.

2. Issued Capital. The term 'Issued Capital', may be defined as follows : "the nominal value of that part of the authorised capital which has been offered for subscription to the public is called the issued capital. The remaining part of the authorised capital of the company which has not been issued so far, it called Unissued Capital."

Authorised capital of a company is issued in parts at different times according to the need of capital. It is not issued in full at the time of incorporation of the company. It is that part of the authorised capital of the company which is issued for cash or for consideration other than cash. It includes the shares subscribed by the signatories of the company to its memorandum.

3. Subscribed Capital. Subscribed capital is that part of the authorised shared capital which is allotted for cash or for consideration other than cash. It also includes the shares allotted to the signatories to the memorandum. The company issues a certain number of shares to the public called Issued Capital, Public subscribes for the shares of the company. The amount subscribed for by the public is called Subscribed Capital. There may be three conditions in this connection :

(i) The public may send the applications for the same number of shares as issued by the company.

(ii) The applications sent by the public are more than the issued share capital by company, it is called over subscription.

(iii) The number of applications received from public may be less than the issued by the company, it is called under subscription.

A company cannot allot more than shares issued. If the public subscribes for more shares, then either some applications will be totally rejected or a *pro rata* allotment will be made. In no case, the number of shares allotted can exceed the number of shares issued. If the public subscribes for less number of shares than issued, the company will have to issue the shares only in the number subscribed for by the public. If public subscribes for the equal number of shares as issued no such problem arises.

4. Called up Capital. The called up capital is that part of the allotted share capital which has been called up by the company. The remaining part of the value of share capital is called Uncalled Capital. The company allots the shares but the full amount of the share is not called on application. Practically the amount of share is called in instalment at different times as per the need of the company. The amount which has been called by the company on its share capital is called 'Called up Amount'.

5. Paid up Capital. The amount that has actually been paid up by the shareholders, is called Paid up Share Capital. The company makes the calls on its share capital as the need arises. In some cases the shareholders are not able to pay their due money. Such an amount is called calls in arrears. Sometimes, some shareholders pay the full money of the value of the shares held by them in order to avoid the difficulty of paying at different times. These are Calls-in-Advance, the amount, paid in advance by the shareholders that has not been called by the company so far.

RESERVE CAPITAL OR RESERVE LIABILITY

Reserve capital is that part of share capital which has been reserved by the company to be called in the event of its winding up. If a company does not require any more payments on its share capital, it may decide not to call the uncalled share capital. It is called Reserve Capital or Reserve Liability. It can only be created by a company under section 99 of the Indian Companies Act, 1956 which states that a company limited by shares or a limited company by guarantee having share capital, may, by a special resolution, determine that any portion of its uncalled share capital shall not be called up except in the event of winding up. This is given by a company with the object of providing additional security to the creditors. Once a company passes a special resolution to this effect, it cannot call the uncalled part of its share capital before its winding up under any circumstances whatsoever. A company cannot charge this part of capital as security for loans. Reserve capital cannot be turned into ordinary capital without permission of the court. Reserve capital can also not be cancelled by way of rejection of capital. A company can create the reserve capital only after its incorporation. The provision of reserve capital can not be introduced in the memorandum or articles of association of the company. This type of share capital is also known as the reserve liability because it is that part of the share capital which cannot be called up except in case of winding up of the company.

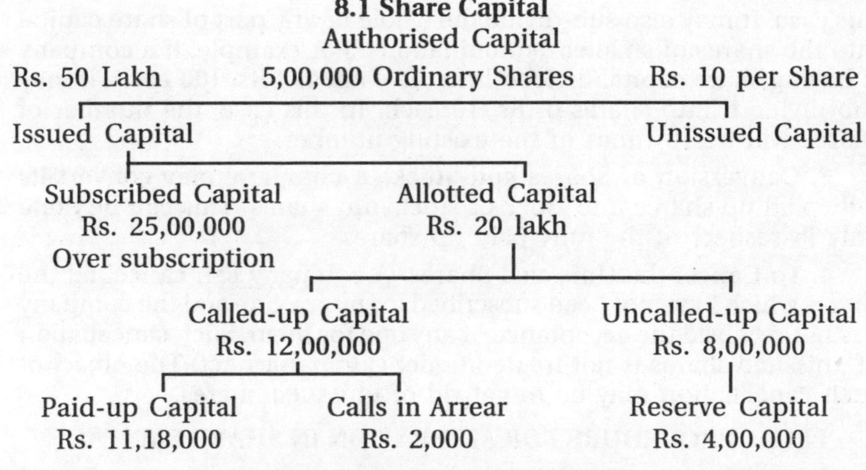

ALTERATION IN SHARE CAPITAL

A public company starts its business with a certain amount of share capital. After a certain period it may need to alter it, to reduce or increase or reorganise it. According to Section 94 of the Indian Companies Act, 1956, a company limited by shares and a company limited by guarantee with a share capital, are empowered to make alteration in their share capital if the articles of association of the concerned company permit to do so. According to Section 94(1) a company with a limited liability and having a share capital can alter its capital in any ways of the following :

1. Increase in Share Capital. A company may increase its share capital by issuing new shares. This increase may be of two types :

(i) *Further Issue of the Unissued Shares :* According to Section 81 of the Indian Companies Act, 1956, a company may issue the unissued shares within its authorised capital at any time it needs. For, this, a company will not have to make any alteration in its memorandum of association or articles of association. The Board of Directors may issue the unissued part of their authorised share capital only by passing a resolution at their meeting, if they are authorised to do so by their articles of association.

(ii) *Increase in Authorised Share Capital :* A company incorporated with certain amount of authorised share capital can, if it requires, increase its amount also by following a specific legal procedure.

2. Consolidation of Sub-division of Share Capital. A company may consolidate the whole amount or any part of its existing share capital into the shares of larger denominations. For example, if a company is having share capital, divided in the shares of Rs. 10 each, it may consolidate them into the shares of Rs. 100 each. The number of shares will be reduced to 1/10th of the existing number of shares in this case. It may also sub-divide the whole or any part of share capital into the shares of smaller denominations. For example, if a company is having share capital divided into the shares of Rs. 100 each, it may sub-divide it into shares of Rs. 10 each. In this case, the number of shares will be 10 times of the existing number.

3. Conversion of Shares and Stock. A company may convert its fully paid up shares into stock or stock into shares. This can be done only in respect of the fully paid up shares.

4. To Cancel the Unissued Shares. A company can cancel all the shares which have not been subscribed for by any one and the company has not received the acceptance of any one for them. Such cancellation of unissued shares is not treated under Companies Act. The object of such cancellation may be to get rid of unissued shares.

LEGAL PROCEDURE FOR ALTERATION IN SHARE CAPITAL

According to Section 94 a public company, limited by shares and a public company limited by guarantee, having share capital may alter their share capital. For making such alteration, the company is to follow the following legal procedures :

1. To be Authorised by Articles of Association. A company must be authorised to do so in its articles of association. Even if a company is not empowered to do so by its articles of association, it may very well do so making the alteration in its articles of association, first. This can be done by the company by passing a special resolution in its general meeting.

2. To Pass a Resolution. According to Section 94(2) a company should pass an ordinary resolution for making an alteration in its share capital. The permission of court or central government is not required for a company to make the alteration in its share capital.

3. To Inform the Registrar. According to section 95(1) and Section 95(2) the company is under obligation to inform the Registrar of Companies about the alteration in its share capital within 30 days of such change. The registrar will make the necessary changes in the memorandum of association or articles of association of the company on the basis of this information.

4. Provision of Penalty. According to Section 95(3), if the required information is not sent to the registrar alongwith a copy of resolution, the company and every officer of the company, in default may be penalised with a penalty upto Rs. 500 per day for the period of mistake.

5. Exemption from Passing a Resolution. According to Section 94 (1) and 94A(2) of the Companies (Amendment) Act, 1974 there is no need of passing a resolution for alteration of authorised share capital if it is increased by the reason of :

(a) An order made by the central government for conversion of any loan or debentures into the shares of company.

Or

(b) An order made by the central government on application of any public financial institution, which proposes to convert any loan or debentures into shares of the company.

According to Section 94A(3) of the Companies (Amendment) Act, 1974, a company must give the notice for the increase of capital to the Registrar of Companies, in the form of a return in the prescribed form within 30 days of getting the order of government. On such information, the registrar will make the necessary alterations in the memorandum and articles of association of the company.

REDUCTION IN SHARE CAPITAL

Meaning of Reduction

Reduction in share capital means to reduce the share capital. When a company reduces its existing share capital, it is called reduction in share capital. A company limited by shares or a company limited by guarantee having share capital, can alter its shares under the following legal procedure :

1. To reduce or to cancel the uncalled part of its partly paid up share capital. For example if a company has its shares capital divided in the shares of Rs. 10 each the company has called Rs. 7 each on its shares so far. The company may decide to cancel the remaining Rs. 3 on each share. This will reduce the share capital of the company to the extent of Rs. 3 per share.
2. In case of fully paid up shares, the company may reduce its share capital by writing off any of its assets.
3. If the paid up share capital of the company is more than its requirements, it may reduce its share capital by returning some money to its shareholders.
4. A company can reduce its share capital by cancelling its surrendered shares also.

Objects of Reduction

Indian Companies Act has not permitted the companies to reduce their share capital to the extent and in the manner they require. To ensure the best utilisation of the funds of a company and to protect the interests of the shareholders, debenture holders and creditors of the company, reduction of share capital is permitted only for the legitimate purposes. A company may be allowed to reduce its share capital only for the following purposes :

1. To Write off Lost Capital. In some cases, a part of the share capital of a company does not represent any tangible assets, because of the heavy trade losses or unsound investments. Such a part of the capital is called lost capital or watered capital. A company may reduce its share capital to write off such part of capital.

2. To Pay off Surplus Capital. Sometimes a company has more capital than its requirements. This is known as over capital or surplus capital. In this case, a company loses the earning of such part. It will be wise to decide to remove the surplus part of capital and the company may proceed to reduce its share capital for this purpose.

Procedure for Reduction

Assuming that the purpose of reduction in share capital is legitimate, a company limited by shares or a company limited by guarantee having share capital may reduce its share capital by adopting the procedure as specified under Sections 100 to 103 of the Indian Companies Act as follows :

1. To be Authorised by Articles of Association. A company may reduce its share capital only if it is authorised by its articles of association to do so. If a company is not authorised to do so by its articles of association, it will have to alter its Articles of Association by passing a special resolution.

2. To Pass a Special Resolution. According to Section 100 of the Companies Act the company must pass a special resolution for the reduction in share capital. A copy of the resolution should be filed with the Registrar of Companies within 15 days.

3. Petition of the Court. After passing a special resolution, the company must submit a petition to the court to get an order confirming reduction of share capital. Before confirming the share capital the court will satisfy itself that the interests of creditors and shareholders are not adversely affected by the proposed reduction in share capital. For this the court will ensure :

(i) That sufficient notice has been given to every person whose interests are likely to be affected by the proposed alteration.

(ii) That if any creditor or creditors object to the proposed change, he or they has or have been paid in full or his or their written consent has been obtained and

(iii) That the proposed reduction of share capital is quite fair and equitable to all kinds of shareholders.

Satisfied in all the above respects the court may issue an order confirming the reduction in share capital, subject to the terms and conditions, it thinks fit. It may order the company to furnish some more explanations about any point. It may also order the company to use the words "and reduced" after its name for a certain period.

4. To prepare the List of Creditors. According to Section 101 of the Companies Act if some of the creditors or debenture holders of the company do not agree on the proposed reduction of share capital, the court orders the company to prepare a list of such creditors and debentureholders. It fixes a date by which the creditors and debentureholders may check the list and file their objection in the court, if any. Such creditors and debentureholders are paid for by the company or the amount of their claim is deposited in the court.

5. Registration of Alteration. According to Section 102 of the Companies Act, after getting the copy of confirmation order of the court, the company may proceed accordingly and make alteration in its share capital and in its memorandum of associations, if so required, it must file a copy of the changed documents with the Registrar of Companies within 3 months of the court's order. The registrar shall register the same and shall issue a certificate of registration within one month. Reduction in share capital will be effective from the date of such registration.

6. Provision of Penalty. According to section 105 of the Companies Act, if any officer of the company conceals the name of any creditor deliberately to minimise the objections to the reduction of share capital or makes any mis-statement about the amount of loan of any creditor or gives any sort of co-operation for such concealment or such representation, he may be penalised with an imprisonment of one year or fine upto any amount or both. The forfeiture of shares and the redemption of redeemable preference shares are not treated as a reduction in share capital.

Effect of Reduction

1. Effect of Reduction in Share Capital on the Liability of Members. According to Section 104 of the Indian Companies Act, 1956, after the reduction of share capital, a member of the company is liable only to pay the difference between the new face value of a share after reduction and the amount paid by him so far. But, if the name of creditor is omitted from the list of creditors, and after reduction of share capital, the company is unable to pay his loan, the court, on the request of such a creditor, may order the member of the company to pay the original amount of shares held by them.

2. Effect of Reduction in Share Capital on Memorandum of Association. If surplus capita, is written off by cancelling a portion of the issued share capital, and the original face value of the shares is not reduced, no alteration will be required in the memorandum of association because the issued share capital is not stated in the capital clause of the memorandum. But if it is written off by reducing the face value of the shares, the alteration in the capital clause of the memorandum will be necessary. Similarly, if the issued share capital is reduced by converting the partly paid up shares into fully paid up, it will lead to reduction in the face value of the shares and consequently, the alteration in memorandum will be necessary.

SHARE

Meaning of Share

A share in a company is one of the units into which the total capital of the company is divided. For example, if capital of a company is Rs. 10 Lakhs is divided in 1,00,000 parts of Rs. 10 each, each part of Rs. 10 shall be called a share of the company.

Definition of Share

1. Section 2(46) of the Indian Companies Act. "Share means share in the share capital of the company, and includes stock except where a distinction between stock and share is expressed or implied."

2. Justice Lindley. "The Joint Stock (contributed by members) is expressed in money and is the capital of the company. The persons who contribute it or to whom it belongs, are members. The proportion of capital to which each member is entitled, is his share."

3. Justice Farewell. "A share is the interest of a shareholder in the company measured by a sum of money for the purpose of liability in the first place and of interest in the second, but also considering all mutual convents entered into by all the shareholders in terms of the Act and the Articles."

4. Section 82 of Indian Companies Act, 1956. "Share of any member in a company shall be a movable property which can be mortgaged, which can be pledged or which can be transferred."

Thus, a share is a fractional part of the capital of a company. It forms the basis of ownership and the interest of a subscriber in a company. The rights and duties of a shareholder are determined on the basis of shares held by him. Shares are the movable property which can be mortgaged as a security for any loan and can be pledged also. Shares are "goods" in India. A share is not a negotiable instrument. The company issues a certificate to every person who subscribes for its shares. Such a certificate is called share certificate. The shares are easily transferable.

Types of Shares

According to Section 66 of Indian Company Act, 1956 a company limited by shares which is established after the enactment of this Act can have only two types of shares : (1) Equity Shares and (2) Preference Shares.

The companies established before enactment of Companies Act, 1956, use the words "Ordinary Shares" in place of 'Equity Shares". Types of shares is clear by the following chart :

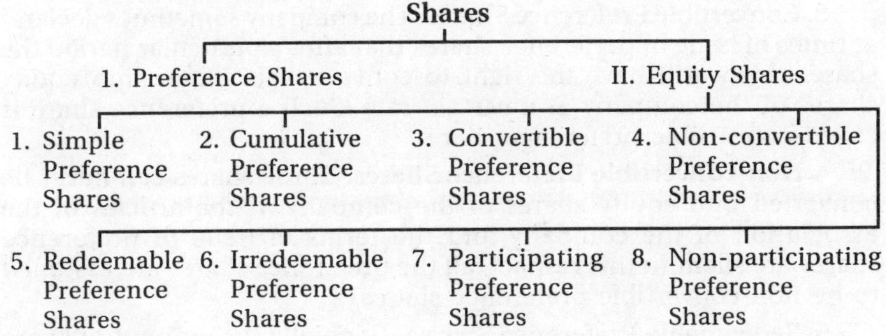

(I) Preference Shares

Preference shares are the shares that enjoy preferential rights : (a) as to the payment of dividend at a certain rate during the life of a company, and (b) as to the return of capital on the winding up of the company. If any class of shares enjoys only one of these two preferential rights, it will not be treated as preference shares, but as equity shares. The holder of these types of shares enjoys only preferential rights over the equity shareholders. He will receive the dividend at a certain rate, if a dividend is declared by the company. A preference shareholder will be entitled to get the dividend on his shares only if a divisible profit is available with the company and only if the company declares the dividend. The rate of dividend, declared with the issue of such shares, does not mean the guarantee of the payment of dividend at that rate. It only means that if dividend is declared by the company he will be preferred in the payment of dividend.

1. Simple Preference Shares or Non-cumulative Preference Shares. These shares get the preferential treatment as to the payment of dividend, if it is declared by the company. If the company fails to declare the dividend for a number of years, such shares do not carry the right to receive the arrears of their dividend in the year when the dividend is declared. If no dividend is paid in any particular year, it lapses.

2. Cumulative Preference Shares. If the company fails to pay the dividend in a particular year or years, the shareholders of such shares will be entitled to get the accumulated arrears of dividend on the declaration of dividend in subsequent years. The company can pay any dividend to its equity shareholders only when the arrears of dividend of such shareholders is fully paid off. However, no arrears of dividend are payable if the company goes into liquidation unless the Articles permits to do so or such dividend has already been declared. A preference share is assumed to be a cumulative preference share unless otherwise specified clearly either in the articles or in the terms of issue.

3. Convertible Preference Shares. The company sometimes declares at times of issue of preference shares that after a particular period the shareholders will have the right to convert their shares into equity shares of the company at a certain rate. Such a preference share is called convertible preference share.

4. Non-convertible Preference Shares. These shares can never be converted into equity shares of the company. If the articles of the association of the company and the terms of issue of preference shares are silent **in** this respect, all the preference shares are assumed to be non-convertible preference shares.

5. Redeemable Preference Shares. Generally the amount of share capital, raised by a company can be returned only on the winding up of the company. However, Section 80 of the Indian Companies Act, 1956, states that a company limited by shares can issue redeemable preference shares. The amount received on such preference shares can be returned to their shareholders after a certain period specified under terms of issue or after serving proper notice to the shareholders. Further, a company can issue such shares only when the following conditions are fulfilled :

(i) The articles of association of the company have a provision for the issue of such shares.

(ii) The shares are redeemable only if they are fully paid up.

(iii) For the redemption of such shares, the company creates either "Capital Redemption Reserve Account" out of the distributable profits of the company or redeems the shares out of the proceeds of a fresh issue of shares.

(iv) If any premium is payable on the redemption of such shares, the required amount is provided for either out of the profits of the company or out of the share premium account of the company and such a provision is made before the shares are redeemed.

This section further states that :

(i) Redemption of preference shares is not the reduction of capital.

(ii) Issue of new shares for the purpose of redemption of such shares, is not the increase in capital.

(iii) The company and its every officer found guilty if not fulfilling all the above provisions shall be punishable with a fine which may go upto Rs. 1,000.

The particulars of redeemable preference shares must be disclosed in the prospectus and in the every balance sheet of the company. When such shares are redeemed, the information must be duly furnished to the registrar within one month of redemption.

6. Irredeemable Preference Shares. These are the shares which can not be redeemed by the company in its life. These can be redeemed only on the winding up of the company. All preference shares issued by the company are assumed to be irredeemable preference shares unless specifically provided in the articles of association or in the terms of issue.

Note : The Companies (Amendment) Acts 1988 and 1996 have prohibited the issue of any preference shares which is irredeemable or is redeemed after expiry of period of twenty years from the date of issue [Sec. 80(5A)].

7. Participating Preference Shares. Participating preference shares are the shares that are entitled to get their fixed dividend in the normal way. If the company has any additional distributable profits, these shares can be further entitled to get additional dividend. Additional profits mean the profits available with the company after distributing the dividend to equity shareholders at a reasonable rate.

8. Non-participating Preference Shares. These shares are entitled to get their fixed dividend only, if it is declared. These cannot participate further even if the company has surplus distributable profits. If nothing is mentioned in the articles of association of the company or in the terms of issue, all the preference shares are assumed to be non-participating preference shares.

9. Cumulative Convertible Preference Shares (CCPS) have been allowed to be issued since 1985. They cannot exceed equity shares and can be issued for setting up new projects or expansion of old projects or working capital requirements.

(II) Equity Shares

According to section 85(3) of the Companies Act, Equity Shares are not the preference shares. All the shares issued by a company, other than the preference shares, are called equity shares. These have a right to get the whole of the distributable profits after paying out the dividend to preference shares, if any. If the company does not have any distributable profits or any profits left after the payment of dividend on preference shares, such shares do not get any dividend. They are paid at the last in regard to the payment of their amount. Equity shares are always irredeemable, they can be paid out only on the winding up of the company. According to Section 87 the equity shareholders have voting rights on every resolution placed before the company in its general meeting.

Equity share capital may be with voting rights or with differential rights as to dividend, voting or otherwise as per rules issued by Department of Company Affairs.

Distinction between Equity Shares and Preference Shares

Basis of Difference	*Equity Shares*	*Preference Shares*
1. Right to get the dividend	Entitled to get the dividend only after the company has distributable surplus profits after paying out the dividend to preference shares, if any.	Get a preference as to the payment of dividend.
2. Rate of dividend	Rate of dividend for equity share varies from year to year.	Get the dividend at a certain rate, fixed at the time of issue.
3. Accumulation of dividend	Never entitled to a cumulative dividend.	Entitled to get the accumulative dividend, if the shares are so issued.
4. Right to get the refund of Capital	Get the refund of their amount only at last.	Get a preference to get the accumulative dividend, if the shares are so issued.
5. Redemption in the life of company	A company can never redeem.	Get a preference to get the refund of capital over equity shares.
6. Convertibility	Can not be converted.	These can be redeemed during the life of the company also, they are redeemable.
7. Right of Voting	Equity Shareholders always have the right of voting.	Can be converted after a certain rate, if so provied at certain period.
8. Compulsion	A company with share capital must issue these.	Shareholders can vote only in the exceptional cases.
9. Risk	These are subject to the maximum risk as to the payment of dividend also as well as to the return of capital.	It is not necessary for any company to issue these. These bear the risk second to equity shares.

SHARE AND STOCK

Section 2(46) of the Indian Companies Act states that share means a share in the share capital of a company and includes stock except where a distinction between stock and share is expressed or implied.

Definition of Stock

Lord Cairns says, "The use of the word 'stock' makes it clear that the company has received the full payment on its shares and the appropriate time has come when the shares may be splitted into parts."

Stock means a bundle of duly paid up shares put together for convenience so that it may be divided into any amount and transferred into any fractions and sub-divisions with regard to the original face value of the shares. For example, a company having a share capital of 1,00,000 shares of Rs. 10 each can convert its share capital into the stock of Rs. 10,00,000, when the shares have been fully paid up. After such conversion, stock holders of the company can transfer their holdings to any other person in any fractions they like. Now if stockholder wants to transfer the holdings of Rs. 4355 and Rs. 8508 he may do so easily, while it was not possible in case of share capital.

A company can not issue stock originally. It can convert its share capital into stock only if shares are fully paid and the articles of association of the company empower the company to do so. Such conversion can be made only by passing an ordinary resolution by the members of the company and the stock may be converted into shares again by passing the ordinary resolution.

DISTINCTION BETWEEN SHARE AND STOCK

Basis of Difference	*Share*	*Stock*
1. Face Value	Has a definite face value.	Has no face value.
2. Time of Issue	A company can issues a share originally after its incorporation.	A company cannot issue stock originally. Only the fully paid up shares can be converted into stock.
3. Transfer in fractions	Can be transferered in its entirety or in its multiples only. No part of share can be transferred.	Stock is divisible into any amount and can be transferred in any fraction.
4. Serial No.	Has a serial number by which it is recognised.	Has no serial number.
5. Registration	It is necessary to get it registered.	It is not necessary to get it registered.
6. Fully paid up or partly paid up	It can be fully paid as well as partly paid.	It is not partly paid up.
7. Uniformity in the face value	Shares of one class have equal face value	The stocks may be of different values.

Conversion of Shares into Stock

1. Proviso 36 of Table 'A'. A company can convert its fully paid up shares into stock by passing an ordinary resolution in a meeting. Stock can again be converted into fully paid up shares by adopting same methods.

2. Proviso 37 of Table 'A'. The stock may be transferred in the same manner as the fully paid shares can be transferred. However, the board of directors may fix a minimum limit below which the transfer of stock may not be allowed but such limit can not exceed the face value of the shares which are converted into stock.

3. Proviso 39 of Table 'A'. All the rules, applicable for the shares in a company, will also be applicable for stock.

PROCEDURE OF CONVERSION OF SHARES INTO STOCK

1. Resolution. If the articles of association of the company do not have a provision for conversion of the shares into stock, the company will have to alter its articles, by calling a meeting of its shareholders and passing a special resolution to that effect.

2. Book Close. Books of share transfer are closed after getting the right to convert the shares into stock.

3. Notice. The company must give a proper notice to its shareholders for such conversion and must request them to surrender their certificates.

4. Receipt. The company must issue a receipt to its every shareholder, certifying the surrender of shares by him.

5. Certificate. After a certain time a company issues a stock certificate to its shareholder, whose amount must be equal to that of the share certificates of the shareholders.

6. Record. Stock certificates are recorded in the new register with full particulars and the shares are deemed to be converted into stock.

7. Information. The company must send an information to the Registrar of Companies within 15 days of such conversion.

SHARE CERTIFICATE

Meaning

According to Section 84(1) of Indian Companies Act, 1956 "A certificate, under the common seal of the company, specifying any shares held by any member, shall be prima facie endence of the title of the member to such shares." It is a registered proof of the ownership of shares issued by the company tinder its common seal. It is duly stamped and signed by one or more directors and countersigned by secretary of the company, as per the articles of association of the company.

Thus, a share certificate discloses the name of company, date of issue, name of the shareholder, serial number of the share certificate, number of shares held by the shareholder, serial number of shares, the amount paid on the shares etc. It must be signed by at least two directors of the company and countersigned by the secretary of the company, as per the provisions of its articles of association.

Contents of the Share Certificate

The share certificate bears the name and full address of the registered office of the company. It also specifies the name and address of the shareholders, number and class of shares, distinctive number of shares, amount paid on the share, day and date of the issue of certificate and certificate number etc. It is issued under the common seal of the company, be affixed in the presence of the two directors and the secretary and/or their property appointed attorneys. All these persons sign the share certificate which also bears a revenue stamp.

Legal Provisions

The Companies (issue of Share Certificate) Rules, 1960 have been by the central government in order to provide strict control of the issue of share certificates by the companies, followed by every company. Even the articles of association of the company can not go beyond these rules. The rules may be described as under :

1. **Issue of Share Certificates.** The board of directors must pass a resolution for the issue of share certificates. No fresh certificate should be issued unless the previous share certificates have been surrendered by the shareholder to the company. However, a fresh certificate may be issued in case of bonus shares or if it is proved to the satisfaction of the company that the original share certificate has been lost or destroyed.

2. **Issue of Duplicate Share Certificate.** If a shareholder requests the company to issue the duplicate share certificate, the company may impose some reasonable terms regarding the evidence of the loss of original certificate, indemnity bond and the payment of out of pocket expenses etc.

3. **Liability in Case of Fault in Issuing the Share Certificate.** If the company or any officer of the company commit any fault in issuing the share certificates, he may be punished upto Rs. 5000 per day for the period during which the fault continues.

4. **Form of Certificates.** Every certificate issued by a company must specify the name of shareholder, the shares for which it is issued and the amount paid up thereon. A duplicate share certificate must be stamped on the face of the certificate that it is a duplicate certificate.

5. **Stamping and Signing the Certificates.** Every certificate must be issued under the common seal of the company, affixed in the presence of at least 2 directors and the secretary of the company or their attorneys, These must sign every share certificate being issued by the company.

6. **Records of Share Certificate.** When a share certificate is issued all the relevant particulars must be entered in the register of members

and all the entries made in register of members must be authenticated by the person appointed by the board of directors for this purpose.

7. Printing of Forms. All the share certificates must be issued on printed forms numbered by a machine.

8. Custody of Books and Documents. A company must permanently preserve all the books and documents relating to the issue of share certificates. These books and documents must be preserved in the site custody of a responsible person, appointed by the directors for the purpose.

9. Penalty for Fraudulent Share Certificate. If a company issues or renews any share certificate, fraudulently, the company may be fined upto Rs. 10000, Every officer of the company, responsible for the mistake, may be penalised with a fine upto Rs. one lakh or may be imprisoned upto six months or with both.

Legal Effects

1. *Prima Facie* Evidence of the Title. According to Section 33(1) of the Indian Companies Act share certificate, once issued, is the *prima facie* evidence of the title of shares, mentioned therein. A company cannot deny the holding of shares by the person in whose favour it is issued, provided that he gets the shares in good faith, for the value or under a genuine transfer. But a share certificate is not a conclusive evidence of the title of shares. If a person has obtained transfer in his name, either innocently or fraudulently, the company can refuse to recognise him as the shareholder and the share certificate can be cancelled by the company.

2. Evidence of the Payment. A share certificate states the amount that has, been paid by the shareholder by the shares held by him. It is the conclusive evidence of the payment mentioned therein. The company may never deny the payment mentioned in the share certificate.

LIMITATION OF TIME FOR ISSUE OF SHARE CERTIFICATES

According to Section 113 of the Companies Act, it is obligatory for every company to issue the share certificates to all the allottees within a period of 3 months from the date of allotment or within a period of 2 months from the date of registration of transfer, in the absence of which the company and every officer of the company, liable for the mistake, may be fined upto Rs. 500 per day, so long as the default continues.

SHARE WARRANTS

Meaning

According to Section 114 of Indian Companies Act, "A share warrant is a bearer document of the title to the shares, issued by company under its common seal, duly stamped and signed by one or more director(s) of the company as per its Articles. Thus a share warrant is a document in which it is stated that the holder of the warrant is entitled to the shares, stated therein. It is just like a negotiable instrument. The shares, in such case, can be transferred only by delivery of warrant. Thus, it is said that the share warrant is a bearer share certificate. Because of the great risk involved, it is not very popular.

Legal Provision

1. Conditions for the Issue of Share Warrants. Section 114 of the Companies Act lays down the following conditions for issue of the share warrants :

(i) Only a public company limited by shares can issue such share warrants.

(ii) The company must be authorised to issue the share wan-ants by its articles of association.

(iii) The company must obtain the prior permission of the central government for issuing share warrants.

(iv) Share warrants cannot be issued originally. Only fully paid up shares can be converted into share warrants.

2. Preparation of the Share Warrants. If a shareholder wants to convert his share certificate into a share warrant, he must apply to the company on the printed application form depositing certain fees and surrendering his share certificate alongwith the application.

On receiving such application the secretary of the company issues a ticket to the shareholder as the acknowledgement of the application and share certificate. The secretary then scrutinises the application and orders for the preparation of share warrant if he is satisfied.

3. Form of Share Warrant. Share warrant forms are usually printed in the three parts (a) the counterfoil, (b) the main share warrant and (c) the dividend coupons. After these forms are duly completed a meeting of the board of directors is held to pass a resolution and share warrants are sealed and signed by the competent authorities. Now, the applicants are advised to take the delivery of share warrants from the registered office of the company. The tickets, earlier issued, are taken back while delivering the share warrants.

4. Dividend on Share Warrants. According to Section 114(1) the company may pay the dividend on share warrants. For this, the coupons should be attached with the share warrants. While declaring the dividend the company advertises the serial number of coupons, eligible for getting the dividend which is paid to the person who presents the appropriate coupons.

5. Procedure for Issuing the Duplicate Share Warrants. If a duplicate share warrant is required by any person he must surrender the original share warrant to the company. If the original share warrant is lost or stolen or destroyed, the duplicate share warrant is issued only upon satisfactory evidence and an appropriate indemnity bond. The procedure for issuing the duplicate share warrant is almost the same as for issue of the duplicate share certificate.

6. Surrender of Share Warrants. According to Section 115(2) of the Companies Act the bearer of the share warrant may surrender it to the company for cancellation and for entering his name in the register of members, provided the articles of association of the company have a provision to this effect.

7. Membership of the Holders of Share Warrants. Generally the holders of share warrants are not deemed to be the members of the company. But if the articles of association permit, they may be deemed to be the members for some specific objects.

8. Provision for Penalty. If a company or any officer of the company commits any mistake in the implementation of the above provisions they may be fined upto Rs. 500 per day for the period as long as the default continues.

Legal Effects

1. A company shall strike out the names of all the shareholders to whom the share warrants are issued and enter the facts of the issue of share warrants in the register in which the distinguished numbers of share warrants and the date of the issue will be mentioned.

2. According to Section 115(5) the bearer of a share warrant may or may not get the right of membership of the company depending upon the articles of the association of the company.

3. The share warrants do not constitute the qualification shares for the directors.

4. The company must prepare annual return giving full particular of the warrants.

SHARE CERTIFICATES AND SHARE WARRANTS

Basis of difference	*Share Certificate*	*Shares Warrants*
1. Right of issue	Can be issued by every company.	Only public limited companies can issues.
2. Paid up value	May he fully paid as well as partly paid also.	Only fully paid shares can be converted.
3. Original issue	A company can issue originally.	A company cannot issue originally. Only fully paid shares can be converted into the share warrants.

Basis of difference	*Share Certificate*	*Shares Warrants*
4. Transfer	Transfer must be registered with the company.	Can be transferred only by delivery.
5. Membership	Holders are definitely the members of the company.	Holders are not the members of the company usually.
6. Qualification shares of directors	Qualification shares of directors are constituted.	Qualification shares of the directors are not constituted.
7. Ownership	The owner is only a person whose name is given in share certificates and has been mentioned in the register of members.	Bearer is its owner.
8. Negotiable instrument	It is not a negotiable instrument.	It is a negotiable instrument.
9. Payment of dividend	It does not have coupon issued for the payment of dividend. Only the shareholders are paid the dividend.	It bears the coupon with it for the payment of dividend and dividend is paid to the person who presents these coupons to the company.
10. Approval for the	Authority of the articles of association and approval of the central government is not necessary for its issue.	Authority of the articles and the approval of the central government is necessary for its issue.
11. Evidence of title	It is *prima facie* evidence of title.	It is a conclusive evidence of title.
12. Stamp duty on transfer	Stamp duty is payable on its transfer.	No stamp duty is payable on its transfer.
13. Conditions for winding up of a company	The holders can file a petition in the court for the winding up of the company.	Holder cannot file any petition for the winding up of the company.

VOTING RIGHTS OF SHAREHOLDERS

Under the provisions of Indian Companies Act, 1956, a public company can issue two types of shares :

I. Preference Shares and

II. Equity Shares.

(I) Voting Right of Preference Shareholders

The provision of the Companies Act regarding voting rights of shareholders of both types may be describe as under :

1. On a Resolution Involving their Interests. If a resolution is to be passed by a company which may have a direct effect upon the rights of the preference shareholders; they are entitled to vote on a resolution for the winding up of a company or for the repayment of the capital or for the reduction of share capital. If it directly effects the rights of the preference shareholders, they may exercise the power of voting on such a resolution.

2. In Case of Non-Payments of Dividend. Preference shareholders can exercise the right of proportionate voting like equity shareholders. If the company, has issued cumulative preference shares and has not paid the dividend for a period of not less than 2 years preceding the date of meeting; in case of non-cumulative preference shareholders, if the company has not paid the dividend for a period of 2 consecutive years or for a total period of not less than 2 years during the last six years. The preference shareholders are entitled to vote on every resolution placed before the company at its general meeting.

If a company makes any distinction in the voting rights of the preference shareholders for the preference shares issued before Ist April, 1956 and after this date, the Companies (Amendment) Act, 1974, rejects such difference and all the preference shares, irrespective of the date of their issue, have been placed on the same voting right by this Fact.

(II) Voting Rights of Equity Shareholders

1. Sections 88 & 89. According to it, all the holders of equity shares of company have a voting right on any and every resolution placed before the company in proportion to the capital held by them. If the company had the equity shares of varying rights before the enactment of Companies Act, 1956, this Act has placed all the equity shares on the same looting. All the equity shares of the company are now treated in a single manner.

2. Section 90. According to it the above provisions regarding voting rights of shareholders of the company do not apply in case of private companies.

VARIATIONS IN THE RIGHTS OF SHAREHOLDERS

Different classes of shareholders of a company enjoy, different rights as to dividend and voting. These rights are conferred upon them either by the Indian Companies Act or by the memorandum of association of the company. Sections 106 and 107 of the Indian Companies Act, 1956 lay down the- following procedure for making any change in these.

1. Authorisation to make the Change. The company may make the change in the rights of its shareholders **only** if its memorandum or articles of association have a provision for such change. If these documents do not have such provision, there must be no provision prohibiting the company for such change.

2. Written Consent of the Concerned Shareholders. The company can make any change in the rights of its shareholders only if it gets the consent of the concerned shareholders in writing.

3. A Special Resolution. The company should call a meeting of all the shareholders whose rights are going to be changed and pass a special resolution for the purpose at this meeting.

4. Rights of the Dissatisfied Shareholder. Even though a company passes the change in the rights of its shareholders in all respects, there may be some shareholders feeling dissatisfied from such change. Section 107 of the Indian Companies Act, 1956 provides that if such shareholders are not less than 10 per cent of their class, they may apply to the court within 21 days of passing the resolution. The change will not be effective until the court confirms it. After hearing the arguments from both the sides the court may confirm the change or cancel it or confirm it with some modifications. The order of the court will be binding upon both the parties.

The company must file a copy of the order of the court with the Registrar of the Companies within 30 days of the order, following which the company and every officer of the company, liable for the mistake, may, be punished with a fine which may extend upto Rs. 500 per day.

NO-PAR STOCK

Meaning

The no-par shares are issued in the U.K., the U.S.A. and Canada and gaining popularity day by day. Such shares are not issued in India.

No-par stock means share having no face value. The total owned capital of the company is divided into a certain number of shares. Share certificate merely states the number of shares held by a particular holder without mentioning the face value of shares. The value of a share can be calculated by dividing the total owned capital (real net worth) with the number of shares. Hence the question of difference between nominal value and market price of shares does not arise. Thus it has no meaning to issue shares at premium or at discount. Dividend is paid by way of a given amount per share instead of as certain percentage of the fixed nominal value of shares.

Advantages of No-par Stock

1. True and Correct Position in the Balance Sheet. The balance sheet shows a true and correct position of the business as there is no need for inflating the assets to offset inflated or watered stock issues. The capital is always equal to the net worth and not an imaginary amount as with shares of nominal values.

2. Real Value of Holdings. As value of shares is related to the earnings, the shareholders know the real value of their holdings which is always determined on the basis of net assets of the company.

3. Marketing of Shares Easy. Issue of no-par shares avoids many legal formalities because the question of their issue at premium or at discount does not arise as there is no-par value of such shares. This makes marketing of such shares very easy.

4. No Need of Reduction of Capital. As the value of shares is automatically adjusted with the earning capacity, there is no question of reduction of capital at the time of reconstruction and reorganisation of companies.

5. No Liability of Future Calls. As the whole of the amount is collected in one sum at the time of issue of shares the shareholders have no liability beyond the initial payment.

6. Flexibility. No-par stock gives a complete freedom for fixing the price in the market that commensurates with the prevailing conditions in the market and provides relief from the rigid legal requirements. While at the initial stage a company can issue the shares at low prices its later achievements may make possible the subsequent issues at higher prices.

7. No Manipulation of Accounts. A company issuing no-par stock need not manipulate its accounts. It has no motive to conceal the stock discount, underwriting commission and other costs as these can be deducted from the sales proceeds of the shares.

8. Correction of Over Capitalisation. As there is no face value, directors have every right to adjust the value of capital to correct the over capitalisation.

9. Careful Financial Study. As the real value of share depends very much on the earning capacity of the company, it induces the investor to study the financial position of the company carefully.

Disadvantages of No-par Stock

1. No Standard. No-par shares have no standard on the basis of which valuation of assets may be compared with capitalisation. Because the price level is deceptive, the ignorant investors may be deceived. Investors cannot make valuation of their stock. In the absence of par value, they cannot judge the fairness of return.

2. Manipulation. It offers enough scope to management to manipulate the sale proceeds of shares and pay dividend out of capital. In the absence of any standard, the management split the sale proceeds of stock into two or more parts. A nominal amount may be credited to the stated paid up capital account and the balance to the capital surplus which may later on be utilised for dividend.

3. No Capital Planning. There cannot be any planning for the financial need of the concern which may lead the concern to over capitalisation or under capitalisation.

4. Under Payments for Promoters. The flexibility of capital account facilitates the promoters to pay themselves unduly high remuneration for their services and for goodwill and concealing the losses.

5. No Additional Security to Creditors. The uncalled share capital provides an additional security to creditors because it may be realised whenever necessary in case of par value shares. No-par value shares provides no such security to creditors because the whole of the amount is called in one sum.

6. Difficult to Understand. No-par value shares render the balance sheet of the company unduly complex and difficult to be understood by investors, creditors and tax authorities.

7. Tax Evasion. If no-par shares are issued, taxation becomes complicated and tax evasion is facilitated.

8. Difficult Calculation of Registration Fee. The fee for the registration of companies is charged on the amount of Authorised capital. On par value shares in almost all the countries of the world, however, it is very difficult to calculate registration fee on companies issuing no-par value shares.

As the above limitations of the no-par value shares have created certain doubts in the utility of the issue of no-par shares, no-par shares have now lost their popularity even in the U.S.A.

ISSUE OF SHARES

Timing of Issues

One of the most noteworthy problem of securities is concerned with the selection of security to be issued to the public according to prevailing capital market conditions. For example, suppose an existing company has already issued 20,000 equity shares of Rs. 10 each fully paid. The market value of its shares is Rs. 20. per share. Now the said company wants Rs. 4,00,000 as additional finance. The company should issue equity shares for this finance. The company can issue only 20,000 equity shares @ Rs. 20 each which share only a 5 per cent voting control, if the market value of existing shares is Rs. 8 per share.

Pricing of Issue

whenever shares are issued to the public they may be offered to them either at par, at a premium or at a discount. The price at which a new issue of shares is offered to the market is based mainly on the price and yields on comparable issues already quoted. It is decided by the Board of Directors after negotiations with share brokers, underwriters and stock exchange authorities etc. The offered price must also appear attractive to the investing public and underwriters.

It must be reasonable and commensurate with the risk involved and right of control attached therewith.

There is no problem if the Board of Directors decides to issue shares at par. But if it wants to charge a premium the investors must be attracted by a profit potential to purchase these shares at premium. The company's management must take into account the market rating of similar companies in determining the sale price of security. The strength of demand for new issues and the forecast of the level of maintainable profits is also relevant. Also important is the capitalisation factor *i.e.*, P/E ratio (Price : Earning ratio) and the denomination of the security. Lower denominations such as Rs. 10 per share are more appealing and convenient than higher denomination securities.

Effect of Trade Cycle on Issue

The total period of a trade cycle is divided into boom, recession, depression and recovery.

1. Boom. In boom period, the trend in the market is upward, the demand of capital increases and consequently the rate of interest goes up.

2. Recession. Under recession the demand of products is much less than the production. This period is just reverse of boom period. The trend is downward. The demand of capital and the rate of interest go down. As the investors prefer fixed income, the issue of preference shares or debentures should be preferred.

3. Depression. In depression period the market is pessimistic. Therefore, raising funds is quite difficult. Only fixed income securities are preferred.

4. Recovery. In recovery period the upward trend starts and the demand of risk capital begins.

To conclude in the words of Gerstenberg, "The best time to raise funds is when business is booming and people are optimistic."

RIGHT FINANCING

What is Right Financing?

When an existing company seeks to issue new series of equity shares to finance its additional activities, it should offer these shares to the existing shareholders at a specified price during a particular period. This is a 'right' or 'Pre-emptive right' which may be defined as an option to buy a security at the specified price, generally at par or at premium but much below the market price. The shares offered are called Right Shares. Financing the projects of a company by the issue of such right shares is 'right financing'.

According to Section 81 of the Companies Act, a company may increase its capital by issue of new shares at any time after the expiry of two years from the formation of the company limited by shares or of one year after the first allotment of shares in that company, whichever is earlier. These new shares must first be offered to the existing equity shareholders of the company in proportion, as nearly as circumstances admit, to the capital paid upon those shares at the time of offer.

Procedure of Right Issue

According to the Companies Act the procedure of right issue may be as follows :

Before making an offer to the existing shareholders the company will have to obtain the permission of Controller of Capital Issues. The Controller of Capital Issues takes decision on application for right issue in concurrence with the company. Certain conditions may be imposed on the company making an offer of rights. The company sends a 'Letter of offer' to the existing equity shareholders whose names are on the Register of Members mentioning therein the number of shares to which they are entitled in proportion to their old share holdings and the time within which the offer must be accepted. Such period shall not be less than 15 days from the date of offer. However, it may be more than 15 days keeping in mind that shareholders must have sufficient time to make up their mind judiciously. The offer must indicate that if it is not accepted within the specified period, it shall be deemed to have been declined. It must also state that they have the right to renounce all or any of the shares offered to them in favour of their nominee(s).

The shareholder shall inform the company within stipulated period about his acceptance of right or the name of the nominee to whom he wants to renounce his right.

An existing shareholder may also apply for the additional shares. But a shareholder who has renounced his right in favour of any person is not entitled to apply for additional shares.

If the right shares are not fully subscribed, the balance left over shall be distributed equally among the applicants for additional shares with reference to the shares held by them in the company. Subject to this requirement, preference shall be allowed to small holders in concurrence with the stock exchange on which the company's shares are listed. The company may deal in any manner it likes with any balance left after making allotment of additional shares.

Valuation of Right Shares

The right shares are issued by the company at par or at a premium but normally at less than the ruling market price, so that shareholders may offer the right with a hope of some capital gain. The gain on shares is the value of right. It may be calculated in the following manner.

First, calculate the market price of the existing shares. Add to it the issue price of right shares. The total of these two prices should be averaged. This average is the value of right share. The difference between the market price and the average price is the value of right. For example, suppose a company makes right issue of one share for every three shares held. The market value of existing shares is Rs. 50 (for Rs. 10 share). The issue price of right shares is Rs. 20 per share (Face value Rs. 10).

The value of right shall be calculated as under :

The total market price of three existing shares	= 50 × 3 = Rs. 150.
The issue price of right share	= 20
Total for 4 shares	= 170
Average Price Per share	= 170/4 = 42.50
Value of right (per share)	= Rs. 50 (–) Rs. 42.50
	= 7.50

Advantages of Right Issue

1. Maintain *Pro rata* Share. Right issue gives the existing shareholders an opportunity to maintain their *pro rata* share in the earning and surplus of the company and voting power as before.

2. Increase in Goodwill. The goodwill of the company increase in the eyes of existing shareholders.

3. Lower cost of Issue. The cost of issue of such shares will also be lower.

4. No Botheration of Selling. The financial management is relieved of the botheration of selling the shares.

5. Proof of Financial Status. If Right shares are accepted by the shareholders enthusiastically, it proves that financial position of the company is sufficiently good, and the company can obtain more loans at lower rate of interest.

Considerations for Pricing the Right Issue

1. What the Market can Bear. If the amount collected by issue of right shares is not invested in securities yielding a good return or normal return, the market price of shares in the long run will go down. In that case, rights will not be used and investors will invest their funds in alternative investments.

2. The State of Capital Market. The company should keep vigil on the market price and see how its shares have been moving in the market in the past and how these are likely to move, if the rights arc fixed at a particular price.

3. The General Price Trend in the Capital Market. This means the consideration whether the general prices are stable or fluctuating. If the trend is not stable, the investors will not like to invest funds in securities and rights cannot be favoured.

4. The Profit Earning Capacity of Shares. If the shares have no capacity or low capacity to earn profit, they will not be accepted by the shareholders howsoever low their price may be. On the other hand, if profit earning capacity of the shares is somewhat higher, regular and dependable, the rights will attract the existing shareholders as well as their nominees even if rights are priced a bit higher.

5. The Prospects of Proposed Plans of Expansion. If plans seem profitable, the right may be priced a bit high. On the other hand, if the plans are not attractive or slow, the price will be fixed differently.

6. Dividend Policy. If conservative policy of dividend is adopted by the company, the shareholders shall not be interested in purchasing the rights. Here the price may be fixed much lower. If the shareholders are getting good dividend, the price may be fixed somewhat higher.

7. The Resource Position of the Company. If financial resource position of the company is sound, the shareholders will be attracted to invest and the price may be fixed at somewhat higher level, otherwise the position will be reversed.

8. Proper Price. Whatsoever tire pricing policy of rights, the enterprise should fix the premium, not very low, nor very high. It should yield the shareholders a fair return, the enterprise should strike a judicious balance between the two.

Impact of Rights on Financial Policy

1. Fall in Market Price of Shares. Right shares are issued at a price much lower than the market price of existing shares. The market price is expected to fall by the issue of right shares to a considerable extent. This problem should be considered by the company well in advance taking in view the fall in market price of shares of the company.

2. Goodwill. If the existing shareholders decline the offer, the shares are offered to other persons at the same price. If the company has a good record of payment of dividend, the customers are tempted to purchase such shares at lower price even though, a decline in market price is obvious, because they expect an increase in the market price of shares after a short spell and if it is so, the goodwill of the company also goes up.

3. Dividend. Right issue has an adverse effect on the market due to lower payment of dividend. Due to increase in the number of shares the dividend per share will be lower. It is on the presumption that additional amount realised through the issue of rights will not be put to profit immediately and it will take time in increasing the profits. Accordingly, a situation might arise that even good shareholders might feel disinclined to continue with the enterprise and begin to sell their holdings. Such a trend will affect the market adversely and the price of shares will go down. The company should take proper care and ensure that a healthy balance is struck between the use of amount invited and the income from the investment, failing which market will be adversely affected.

4. Existing Shareholder's Capacity to purchase Shares. In case, shares are fully subscribed by the shareholders, the market will not be very adversely affected. But if the shareholders do not have capacity to purchase shares, they will either surrender their rights or renounce it in favour of their nominee. In that case even the nominee will also surrender such shares thereby making these shares available in the market and the market will be affected adversely. In such circumstances it is better to offer right in lower proportions.

5. Fluctuation in the Market Price of the Shares. If the shares are favourably traded in the market, without having any fluctuation in the price to a considerable degree, the rights will attract the shareholders and the price may be fixed somewhat higher. But if the shares invariably fluctuate, the issue will adversely affect the market and the company will have to fix the price of the right share much lower.

6. Pre-Offering Pressure. Usually in respect of that particular share market comes under heavy pressure in pre-offering period just after it is known to the public that the company is about to offer right shares. This pre-offering pressure is usually considerably great and the financial management should take every effort to check that pressure otherwise its financial policy will be adversely affected.

7. Downward Trends. There are usually downward trends during the period of right issue and even the existing shares will come under heavy strains. If the financial management does not move swiftly, its whole financial policy might come under unbearable heavy strains.

Modes of Issue of Shares

Issue of shares by a company means to invite the public to subscribe for the share of the company. A private company cannot invite public to subscribe for its shares. Only a public company can collect its required capital by shares from public. A company can issue its shares in the following three manners :

1. Issue of shares at par.
2. Issue of shares at premium
3. Issue of shares at discount.

1. Issue of Shares at Par. When a company issues its shares to the public at their face value, it is called issue of shares at par. For example, if the share capital of the company is divided into the shares of Rs. 10 each and the company makes the issue of these shares at Rs. 10 each, it will be called the issue of shares at par. Generally a new company issues its shares at par.

2. Issue of Shares at Premium. When a company issues its shares at a price above their face value, it is called the issue of shares at premium. For example if the share capital of a company is divided into share of Rs. 10 each and the company wants to issue the shares at Rs. 12 each, this will be called the issue of shares at premium. The difference between the face value of the share and its issue price, is called the premium, in this case it is Rs. 2 per share.

Legal Provisions

While issuing its shares at a premium, there are no legal norms to be observed by a company. Any company can issue its shares at premium. It is also free to charge any amount as premium on its shares. However, generally, only those companies take the advantage of issuing their shares at a premium which have acquired a high reputation in the share market and which have been paying dividend on their share capital regularly.

Section 78 of the Indian Companies Act, 1956, lays down some restrictions upon the use of the amount of premium collected by the company. It is compulsory for the companies that a Share Premium Account should be opened and the amount of premium must be deposited only in this account. Such amount must be disclosed in the balance sheet of the company, so long as it stands. This amount must not be used for any purpose other than the purposes mentioned above. The company can use the amount of share premium only for the following purposes :

(i) To issue the fully paid bonus shares to the members.

(ii) To write off the preliminary expenses of the company.

(iii) To write off the expenses of the issue of shares or debentures of the company or the commission paid or the discount allowed on such issue.

(iv) To provide for the premium payable on redemption of redeemable preference shares or debentures.

3. Issue of Shares at Discount. When a company issues its shares at a price less than their face value, it is called the issue of shares at discount. For example, if share capital of the company is divided into the shares of Rs. 10 each and the company issues the shares at Rs. 9 each, this will be called the issue of shares at discount and the difference between the face value and issue price of a share will be called the discount. In this case, it is Re. 1 per share.

Legal Provisions

Section 79 of the Indian Companies Act, 1956, states that a company can issue its shares at discount subject to the following conditions only :

(i) *Restrictions Regarding Time :* No company can issue its shares at discount immediately after the certificate of commencement of business. A new company cannot issue us shares at discount. The shares can be so issued only after a period, not less than one year of the certificate of commencement of business.

(ii) *First Issue of a Class of a Shares cannot be at Discount :* A company cannot issue a class of its shares at discount for the first time. It can issue the shares at discount of a class that have already been issued.

(iii) *To pass a Resolution :* For issue of shares at discount a company must pass in its general meeting an ordinary resolution specifying the rate of discount at which the shares will be issued.

(iv) *To get Sanction of Company Law Board (CLB) :* After passing a resolution in its meeting the company must obtain the sanction of Company Law Board for the issue of shares at discount. The Board does not allow the issue if the rate of discount specified in the resolution exceeds 10 per cent unless the board is convinced of the logic for a higher percentage of discount.

(v) *Period for the Issue of Shares :* A company must issue the shares within a period of 2 months after getting the permission of Company Law Board or within such period as may be extended by the board. The entire process will have to be repeated if the company fails to issue the shares within the stipulated time.

(vi) *Restrictions on Disclosure of Discount :* Every prospectus relating to the issue of shares of the company must contain the particulars of discount allowed on the issue of shares by the company till it is fully written off. Annual Return and the balance sheet of the company must also show the similar details every year after the issue till it is fully written off.

(vi) *Provision for Penalty :* If a company does not comply with the above provisions the company and every officer of the company who is in default will be liable for a fine which may extend upto Rs. 500 per day.

Thus a company must follow restrictions for issuing the shares at discount because it practically means the reduction of share capital. The above restrictions do not apply in case of issue of debentures at discount because they do not confirm a part of the share capital of the company.

GUIDELINES FOR ISSUE OF SECURITIES

The following guidelines have been issued by the Securities and Exchange Board of India on 11-6-1992 :

1. Guidelines for First Issue of New Companies

(i) *Definition of New Companies* : A new company is defined as one (a) which has not completed 12 months of commercial operations and its audited operatives results are not available, and (b) which is set up by entrepreneurs without a track record. Such a company will be permitted to issue capital to public only at par.

(ii) *Promoting Company :* Where a new company is being set up by existing companies with a 5-year track record of consistent profitability, it will be free to price its issue. The participation of the promoting companies in such a company should not be less than 50 per cent of the equity of such new company and the issue price should be made applicable to all new investors uniformly. Further the prospectus or offer documents of such company shall contain justification for issue price.

(iii) *Appraisal of Draft Prospectus :* A draft prospectus containing the disclosures will be voted (subjected to expert appraisal) by Securities and Exchanges Board of India (SEBI) before a public issue is made.

(iv) *Placement :* No private placement of the promoters share shall be made by solicitation of share contribution from unrelated investors through any kind of market intermediaries.

(v) *Listing :* The shares of the above companies can be listed on either Over the Counter Exchange of India or any other stock exchanges.

2. First Issue of Existing Private/Closely-held Companies

(i) With a 3-year track record of consistent profitability such companies shall be permitted to freely price the issue and list their securities on the stock exchanges.

(ii) Not less than 20 per cent of the equity should be offered.

(iii) The draft prospectus will be vetted by SEBI to ensure adequacy of disclosures.

(vi) The pricing would be determined by the issuer and the lead manager(s) to the issue and would be subject to specific disclosure requirements including :

(a) Disclosure of the net asset value of the company as per the last audited balance sheet.

(b) Justification for the price of the issue.

3. Guidelines for Public Issue by Existing Listed Companies

1. Fresh Capital. These companies will be allowed to raise fresh capital by freely pricing their further issues.

2. Pricing. The issue price will be determined by the issuer in consultation with the lead manager(s) to the issue.

3. Disclosures. (a) The draft prospectus will be vetted by SEBI to ensure adequacy of disclosures.

(b) The prospectus or offer documents shall contain the net asset value of the company and a justification for the price of the issue.

(c) High and low price of the shares for the last 2 years.

4. Guidelines for Underwriting

1. Mandatory. Underwriting is mandatory for the full issue and minimum requirement of 90 per cent subscription is also mandatory for each issue of capital to public. Number of underwriters would be decided by the issuer.

2. Refund. If the company does not receive 90 per cent of issued amount from public subscription plus accepted development (shares unsubscribed for by public to be taken up by the underwriters) from underwriters, within 120 days from the date of opening of the issue, the company shall refund the amount of subscription. In case of the disputed development, the company shall refund the subscription if the above conditions are not met.

3. Worth. The lead manager(s) must satisfy themselves about the net worth of the underwriters and the outstanding commitments and disclose the same to SEBI.

4. Filing. The underwriting agreements may be filed with the Stock Exchanges.

5. Guidelines about Composite Issues. Issue to the public by an existing company can be priced differently as compared to issues to the rights shareholders.

6. Guidelines about Reservation in Issues. (1) Unreserved offer of equity or instruments convertible into equity shall not be less than the minimum required for listing purposes in case of new issues made either by the new company or by the existing closely held/private companies going public.

(2) Reservations for employees of new companies, promoting companies, associate companies, working directors on a suitable, percentage is permissible in case of issues of capital by new companies.

(3) Shareholders of existing group companies can be offered capital on a preferential basis.

(4) Shareholders of promoters companies shall also be eligible for preferential allotment.

(5) Reservations for NRIs shall be according to the schemes prescribed by RBI from time to time.

7. Guidelines for Minimum Interval Time between Two Issues. (1) No bonus issue shall be made within 12 months of any public/rights issue.

(2) The promoters shall bring capital in full before public issue.

(3) The capital issued should be made fully paid up within 12 months from the date of issue.

To encourage employees to have a higher participation in the company, suitable percentage not more than 5 per cent of reservation can be made by the issuer for the employees of the company or the promoters company as the need may arise. Equitable distribution of shares among the employees contributes to the smooth working of the scheme. The issuer may like to have non transferability at his discretion in new issues. In other cases, employees participation upto 5 per cent (maximum 200 shares per employee) shall be non transferable for a period of 3 years.

8. Guidelines for Promoters' Contribution. (1) Equity capital to be subscribed in any issue to the public by the promoters, *i.e.*, those described in the prospectus as promoters, directors, friends, relatives and associates should not be less than 25 per cent of the total issue of equity capital upto Rs. 100 crores and 20 per cent for the issues above Rs. 100 crores.

In the case of FCDS, one-third of issue amount should be contributed by promoters, directors, friends, relatives and associates by way of equity before issue is made. In the case of PCDs one-third of the convertible portion should be brought in as contribution of promoters, directors, friends, relatives and associates before issue is made. Minimum subscription by each of the friends, relatives and associates under promoter quota should not be less than Rs. 1 lakh.

(2) The promoters' contribution shall not be diluted for a lock in period of 5 years from the date of commencement of the production or date of allotment whichever is later.

(3) Promoters must bring in their full subscription to issues in advance before public issue.

(4) All firm allotments, preferential allotment to collaborators, shareholders of promoters' companies whether corporate or individuals shall not be transferable for 3 years from the date of the commencement of production or date of allotment whichever is later.

(5) The share certificates issued to promoters, friends, relatives and associates etc. should carry the inscription, "not transferable" for a period of 3 or 5 years as may be applicable from the date of commencement of production or date of allotment whichever is later.

REDEEMABLE PREFERENCE SHARES

Ordinarily a company cannot refund the money in its life paid by its shareholders on their shares. However, under some legal provisions and some specific circumstances, a company can issue the preference shares redeemable by the company in its life. Section 80 of the Indian Companies Act, 1956, authorises a company to issue such redeemable preference shares. The amount received by the company on such shares can be returned as per the terms of issue, either after the certain period or whenever the company so decides after giving proper notice. Redemption of redeemable preference shares by a company is not deemed to be the reduction of share capital.

Issue

Section 80 of the Indian Companies Act, 1956, clearly states the following conditions for the issue of redeemable preference shares :

1. If the articles of association do not contain provision for the issue of such shares the company can provide for it by making an alteration thereto.

2. At its meeting for the issue of such shares the company must pass a special resolution specifying the terms and conditions for such issue and the period after which the shares can be redeemed.

Redemption

Section 80 of the Indian Companies Act, 1956 imposes the following restrictions upon the redemption of redeemable preference shares :

1. **Fully Paid up Shares.** A company can redeem the redeemable preference shares only after the shares are fully paid up. If the shares are not fully paid up, the company cannot redeem them.

2. **Redemption.** The company can redeem such shares only in two ways :

(i) If a company has sufficient balance of Profits for the redemption of preference shares in the previous years.

(ii) If the company makes any fresh issue of its share capital and the issue provides the sufficient funds for the redemption.

3. **Provision for the Premium Payable at Redemption.** If the company has to redeem these shares at premium, provided for sufficient amount of premium payable, out of the Share Premium Account of the company.

4. **Provision for the Redemption out of Profits.** If the company decides to redeem these shares out of the profits of previous years, it must transfer the amount required for the redemption out of the profits to the reserve fund, called "Capital Redemption Reserve Account." This account will be treated as the paid up share capital of the company. The redemption of these shares will not be treated as the reduction of share capital.

5. **Provision for Redemption out of the Proceeds from the Issue of Fresh Shares.** If a company decides to redeem the redeemable preference shares out of the proceeds available from the issue of fresh shares, it will not have to pay stamp duty on such issue.

6. **Use of Capital Redemption Reserve Account.** The company may use the amount of this account for the issue of bonus shares to its members.

7. **Information to the Registrar.** The company must inform the Registrar of Companies about the redemption of redeemable preference shares within 30 days of such redemption.

8. **Provision for Penalty.** According to Section 80 if a company or any officer of a company does not comply with the above provisions,

a penalty for such fault may be imposed and it may extend upto Rs. 1,000.

The Companies (Amendment) Act 1988, as further amended in 1996 has prohibited the issue of any preference share which is irredeemable or is redeemable after the expiry of 20 years from the date of its issue [Sec. 80(5A)].

EMPLOYEES STOCK OPTION SCHEME

The Employees Stock Option means as option is given to the whole time directors, officers or employees of a company which gives such directors, officers or employees the benefit or right to purchase or subscribe at a future date, the securities offered by the company at a predetermined price [Sec. 2 (15A)] added by the Companies (Amendment) Act 2000. Companies are allowed to offer this scheme to their employees subject to SEBI guidelines.

BOOK BUILDING

SEBI has allowed book building as an alternative to a firm allotment. Under the process of book building prospective buyers make offer to purchase specified number of shares at a particular price. SEBI guidelines 2000 define book building to mean a process undertaken by which demand for securities proposed to be issued by a body corporate is elicited and built up and price of such securities is assessed for determination of quantum of such securities to be issued by means of a notice, circular, advertisement, document or information memorandum as offer document. SEBI has also issued guidelines for (over the Counter Exchange of India) issues listed there and for preferential allotment. Issues of shares to a charitable institution by way of donation is not valid issue.

QUESTIONS

1. Describe different types of securities issued by a company. What is the significance of securities in the financial structure of a company?
2. What do you mean by share capital? Discuss the various types of share capital.
3. Explain the meaning and types of share capital. Also discuss the concept of reserve capital and its types or reserve liability.
4. What are the different methods of alteration of share capital of a company and what are the provisions regarding it?
5. How and in what manner can public company reduce, increase and reorganise its share capital? Discuss.
6. State briefly the circumstances in which and the manner by which a company can alter its share capital.
7. What is meant by reduction of share capital under Indian

Companies Act? State the consideration and the procedure laid down in the Act to reduce the share capital.

8. What is a share? Explain the different kinds of shares which a company can issue.
9. Explain the different kinds of share capital recognised by the Indian Companies Act, 1956.
10. What is stock? How does it differ from a share? Can the shares be converted into stock? If so, how?
11. Explain the meaning of stock and show how does it differ from a share? What are the provisions relating to the conversion of shares into stock.?
12. Distinguish between a share and stock. Can a company offer stock for subscription to public? Explain procedure of conversion of shares into stock and also explain its advantages.
13. What is share certificate? What are the provisions relevant to share certificate? What is a share warrant? What are the provisions relevant to share warrant? Distinguish between the two.
14. What voting rights are available to the preference shareholders of a company? What variations can be made by the company in this regard and to what extent?
15. What do you understand by no-par stock? Examine its advantages and disadvantages.
16. Write a Short Note on the timing and pricing of issues of securities. Discuss the effect of trade cycles on the issue of shares.
17. What is Right Financing? What is the procedure of Right Issue? How is the value of Right determined? Explain the advantages of Right Issue and the considerations in its pricing.
18. Explain the influence and impact of Rights on Financial policy of an enterprise?
19. Discuss the legal provisions relevant to the issue of shares at premium and at a discount.
20. What are the modes in which a company can issue its shares? What are the legal provisions in this regard.
21. Explain the statutory provisions relating to the issue and redemption of preference shares by the company.
22. What are the legal provisions regarding issue and redemption of preference shares by a company.

PRACTICAL PROBLEMS

1. The directors of Vijay Electronics Ltd. allotted to themselves certain right shares for which no application was made by certain shareholders to whom the offer was made as required by Section 81 of the Companies Act. Discuss the validity of their action

specially in view of the fact that the market price of shares of this company is 50 per cent above par.
[**Hint.** The Board of directors may dispose of the shares in such manner as they think moist beneficial to the company (Section 81)].

2. A public limited company has 2 classes of shares, namely, equity shares and 12 per cent non-cumulative preference shares. It wished to change the rights regarding the preference shares to 10 per cent cumulative preference shares. There is no provision in the Articles or Memorandum regarding such variation. Advise the company.
[**Hint.** Refer to Sections 106 and 107.].

3. A company has sufficient cash which it cannot profitably employ. Hence it proposes to repay 25 per cent of the capital and reduce the paid-up amount on each share from Rs. 100 to Rs. 75. State the procedure it must adopt for this purpose.
[**Hint.** Refer to Sections 100 to 103].

4. The secretary of a company issued in favour of R a certificate which apparently complied with the company's Articles as it purported to be signed by 2 directors and the secretary and it had the company's seal affixed to it. In fact the secretary had forged the signatures of the directors and affixed the seal without authority. Is the certificate binding on the company?
[**Hint.** No (Exceptions to the doctrine of indoor management : Ruben *Vs.* Great Fingal Consolidated)].

5. The nominal value of a share in a limited company is Rs. 100 out of which Rs. 40 is called and paid up. The company, as disclosed by its last balance sheet, is losing heavily. A shareholder surrenders his 10 shares to the company and the Board of directors of the company accept the surrender. Discuss the legality of surrender.
[**Hint.** The surrender is unlawful].

6. X Co. had no money to pay directors' fees. The directors thereupon paid into company's bank account the amount remaining due on their shares and retook the amount as fees. Does this give a discharge to directors' liability to pay on their shares?
[**Hint.** No (European Central Rly. Co., Re Skyes' Case)].

7. The directors of B Ltd. made a call on the shareholders but the resolution for making the call was defective as it did not mention the amount of the call or the time or place for its payment. On the failure of M, a shareholder, to pay the call, the directors purported to forfeit his shares. The directors subsequently discovered their mistake and rescinded their previous resolution as to forfeiture. They then made a proper fresh call on the shareholders and on M's failure to pay the call money, filed a suit against him to recover the amount due. M contended that

his shares had already been forfeited and as such he had ceased to be a shareholder and was, therefore, not liable for the call made. How would you decide the suit?
[**Hint.** M is liable to pay the call money. His shares could not be validly forfeited for non-payment of an invalid call. On his failure to pay the subsequent valid call, the company can proceed against him for the recovery of the call.].

8. To foster better industrial relations, directors of *A.B.* Ltd. agree with its trade union to offer 1,000 shares of Rs. 100 each, fully paid up to its employees and to receive amount thereon in 10 equal instalments of Rs. 10 per share. Can the company make such an issue?
[**Hint.** Yes. Section 77 permits such an issue of shares].

9. X buys 10 shares of a public company from Y through a stock broker. He also receives the share certificate and the blank transfer deed countersigned by Y but does not lodge the transfer deed for registration. Examine the legal effect of the unregistered transfer between the transferrer and the transferee.
[**Hint.** Y continues to be the legal owner of shares].

10. X transfers his shares in a public company to Y. The directors, however, refuse to register the transfer or to give reasons for their refusal.
   (*a*) Can the directors be compelled to state their reasons for so refusing?
   (*b*) Has Y any redress?
   [**Hint.** (*a*) Yes. (*b*) Y can apply to the Company Law Board against failure of the company to register transfer].

9

ALLOTMENT, TRANSFER AND BUY BACK OF SHARES

Allotment of Shares

The term 'allotment' means acceptance by the company of the offer made by a person on a prescribed application form to take shares. With regard to allotment there are general principles to the observed in addition to the legal provision under the Act. The general principles are :

(1) The allotment should be made by proper authority *e.g.*, the Board of Directors.

(2) Allotment must be made only when a person makes an application in writing.

(3) Allotment must be made within a reasonable time.

(4) The allotment must be communicated to the applicant.

(5) The allotment must be absolute and unconditional

LEGAL PROVISIONS

The following provision of the Act are applicable to 'application' for, and allotment of shares :

A. Minimum Subscription. No allotment shall be made of any share capital of a company offered to the public for subscription unless—

(a) the amount stated in the prospectus as the minimum amount has been subscribed, and

(b) the sum payable on application for such amount has been paid to and received by the company.

A company making any rights or public issues of shares, debentures, etc., must receive a minimum of 90 per cent subscription against *the entire issue* before making an allotment of shares or debentures to the public. If minimum amount of 90 per cent is not received, the entire amount collected with applications shall be refunded to the applicants at the end of 90 days from the closure of issue. If there is a delay in refund of such amount by more than 10 days, the company will pay interest at the rate of 15 percent per annum for the delayed period [Section 69(1)].

B. Application Money [Section 69(3) to (6)]. The amount payable on application on each share shall not be less than 5 per cent of the nominal amount of the share.

All money received from applicants for shares shall be deposited and kept deposited in a Scheduled Bank—

(a) until the certificate to commerce business is obtained; or

(b) where such certificate has already been obtained, until the entire amount payable on applications for shares in respect of the minimum of 90 per cent subscription has been received by the company. If these conditions are not complied with, all moneys received from applicants for shares shall be forthwith repaid to them without interest. If any such money is not repaid within 130 days after the issue of the prospectus, the directors of the company shall be jointly and severally liable to repay it with interest at the rate of 6 per cent per annum from the expiry of the 130th day [Section 69(3) to (6)].

Any condition requiring or binding any applicant for shares to waive compliance with any requirement of Section 69 shall be void.

C. Effect of Irregular Allotment (Section 71). Allotment of shares is irregular when it has been made by a company in violation of Section 69 or 70. Thus,

(a) where the company has issued a prospectus, the allotment is irregular if it—

  (i) has not been able to raise the amount of minimum subscription;

  (ii) has not collected application money (which shall not be less than 5 per cent of the nominal amount of the share); and

  (iii) has not kept the money so received in a Scheduled Bank.

(b) where the company has not issued a prospects, the allotment is irregular if it does not file with the Registrar for registration, a statement in lieu of prospectus at least 3 days before the first allotment of shares.

The effects of an irregular allotment are as follows :

(a) **Allotment is voidable.** An irregular allotment is voidable at the option of the applicant. The option must be exercised—

(i) within 2 months after the holding of the statutory meeting of the company, or

(ii) where the company is not required to hold a statutory meeting, or where the allotment is made after the holding of the statutory meeting, within 2 months after the date of the allotment.

The irregular allotment is voidable even if the company is being wound up.

(b) **Compensation.** Any director, who has knowledge of the fact of the irregular allotment of shares, shall be liable to compensate the company and the shareholder for any loss, damages or costs which the company or the allottee may have sustained or incurred thereby. Proceedings to recover any such loss, damages or costs can be only be commenced within 2 years from the date of the allotment.

D. Opening of the Subscription List. When shares or debentures of a company are offered in pursuance of a prospectus issued generally, these cannot be allotted at once. The allotment can be made only after the beginning of the 5th day from the date of the issue of the prospectus or on such later day as may be specified in the prospectus. The 5th day is to be counted from the date when the prospectus was published in a newspaper or was otherwise notified to the public. This beginning of the 5th day or the later day is known as 'the opening of the subscription list' (Section 72).

E. Shares and Debentures to be Listed on a Stock Exchange. Every company, intending to offer shares or debentures to the public for subscription by the issue of a prospectus, shall, before such issue, make an application to one or more recognized stock exchanges for permission for the listing of its shares or debentures. This provision has been made to lend liquidity and marketability to the shares or debentures issued to the public (Section 73).

The name of the stock exchange or, as the case may be, of each of the stock exchanges is to be stated in the prospectus.

Return of Money on Refusal of Permission. Where the permission has not been applied for under Section 73 or such permission having been applied has not been granted, the company shall forthwith repay without interest all moneys received from applicants in pursuance of the prospectus. If any such money is not repaid within 8 days after the company becomes liable to repay it, the company and every director of the company who is an officer in default shall, on and from the expiry of the 8th day, be jointly and severally liable to repay that money with interest at such rate (a) not less than 4 per cent and not more than 15 per cent as may be prescribed; (b) having regard to the length of the period of delay in making the repayment of such money.

Right of Appeal. Where a stock exchange refuses to grant an application or fails to dispose it of within 10 weeks (in which case it will be deemed to have been rejected), the company may, under Section 22 of the Securities Contracts (Regulation) Act, 1956, appeal to the Central Government against the refusal. The appeal shall be filed—

(i) within 15 days from the date of the refusal; or

(ii) within 15 days from the date of expiry of the 10 weeks.

The Central Government may after giving the stock exchange an opportunity of being heard—

(i) vary or set aside the decision of the stock exchange, or

(ii) where the stock exchange has omitted or failed to dispose of the application within the specified time, grant or refuse the permission.

Return of Excess Money where Permission Granted. Where permission has been granted by the recognised stock exchange or stock exchanges for dealing in any shares or debentures, all moneys received from applicants for shares or debentures in excess of the application money on shares or debentures allotted, shall be repaid *forthwith* without interest. If such money is not repaid within 8 days from the day the company becomes liable to pay it, the company and every director of the company who is an officer in default shall, on and from the expiry of the 8th day, be jointly and severally liable to repay the money with interest at such rate, not less than 4 per cent and not more than 15 per cent, as may be prescribed. The rate of interest shall be prescribed having regard to the length of the period of delay in making the repayment of such money.

All moneys to be kept in a separate Bank Account. All moneys received from applicants for shares shall be kept in a separate bank account maintained with a scheduled bank until the permission for listing of shares has been granted. Where an appeal has been preferred against the refusal to grant such permission, the money shall be so kept until the disposal of the appeal. Where the permission has not been applied for as aforesaid or has not been granted, the money standing in the separate account shall be repaid within the time and in the manner specified in Section 73.

F. Return as to Allotments (Section 75). Within 30 days of allotment of shares by a company, the company shall file with the Registrar a statement known as 'return as to allotments'. The return shall contain :

(a) Particulars about the shares allotted for cash, the names, addresses and occupations of the allottees, and the amount paid on each share. Shares should be shown as allotted for cash only when cash has actually been received in respect of them.

(b) Particulars about the shares (not being bonus shares) allotted as fully or partly paid up for any consideration other than cash.

(c) Particulars about the bonus shares and the names, addresses and occupations of the allottees and a resolution authorising the issue of such shares.

(d) A copy of the resolution passed by the company authorising issue of shares at a discount, and a copy of the Company Law Board's order sanctioning the issue.

CALLS ON SHARES

A call is a demand by a company on its shareholders to pay the whole or part of the balance remaining unpaid on each share. It is made in pursuance of a resolution of the Board of directors and terms of the Articles. It may be made any time during the lifetime of the company or during its winding up.

Legal Provisions Relating to Calls

1. *Resolution of the Board* : A call must be made under a resolution of the Board of directors passed at a meeting of the Board. In making a call, care must be taken—

(1) that the directors making it are duly appointed and duly qualified.

(2) the meeting of directors has been duly convened,

(3) that the proper quorum is present, and

(4) that the resolution making the call is duly passed [Section 292(1)]

2. *Bona fide and for the benefit of the company* : The power to make calls is in the nature of trust and must be exercised *bona fide* for the benefit of the company. A call should be made by the company only when it is *bona fide* need of capital.

3. *Uniform basis* : The calls must be made on a uniform basis on all shares falling under the same class. Shares of the nominal value on which different amounts have been paid up do not fall under the same class. If a call is made on some shareholders but not on others or a call of a greater amount is made on some shareholders than on others, the call is invalid (Section 91).

4. *Calls in Advance* : A company may, if so authorised by its Articles, accept from any member the whole or a part of the amount remaining unpaid on any shares held by him in advance. The payment of calls in advance does not give voting rights to the member in respect of that amount until that amount becomes presently payable (Section 92).

5. *In accordance with the Articles, amount, place and time of payment* : The call must be made strictly in accordance with the provisions of the Articles. It must specify the amount of the call and the time and the place of payment. If this is not done, the call will be invalid.

TRANSFER OF SHARES

The shares of a member in a company are movable property, transferable in the manner prescribed in the Act and the Articles of the company (Section 82).

Sections 82 and 111 permit the Board of Directors to assume powers under the Articles of Association to refuse registration of transfer of shares without assigning any reason. However, a provision has been provided for an appeal against such a refusal to the Company Law Board.

Provisions of the Act relating to transfer

Sections 108 to 112 deal with the transfer of shares. The provisions of these Sections are as follows :

1. *Transfer not to be registered except on production of transfer deed (Section 108)* : (1) *Transfer deed* : A company shall not register a transfer of shares unless a proper transfer deed duly stamped and executed and signed by both the transferor and the transferee is delivered to the company. The transfer deed shall specify the name, address and occupation, if any, of the transferee. It shall be delivered to the company along with the share certificate, or if no such certificate is in existence, along with the letter of allotment of the shares.

The instrument of transfer is not required in case of transmission of shares by operation of law.

(2) *Prescribed form* : (a) Every transfer deed shall be in the prescribed form.

(b) It shall be presented to the prescribed authority before it is signed by or on behalf of the transferor and before any entry is made therein. Normally the prescribed authority is the Registrar of Companies.

(c) The prescribed authority shall stamp or otherwise endorse thereon the date on which the instrument is so presented.

(3) *Period for delivery of transfer deed* : (a) The transfer deed shall then be delivered to the company in the case of shares quoted on a recognised stock exchange before the date on which the register of members is closed for the first time after the date of such presentation, or within 12 months from the date of presentation to the prescribed authority whichever is later. The period of currency of share transfer instruments has been raised from 2 months to 12 months in case of shares listed on the stock exchange.

(b) In any other case, the transfer deed shall be presented to the company within 2 months of the date of presentation to the prescribed authority.

Any instrument of transfer which is not in conformity with these provisions shall not be accepted by the company.

(c) *Extension of time* : In cases of hardship, the Central Government may extend the period for delivery of instrument of transfer to the company. For seeking this extension of time an application is to be made to the Central Government.

The transferee becomes member of a company only when the transfer is registered by the company.

2. *Transfer by legal representatives (Section 109)* : A transfer executed by the legal representative of a deceased member, although he is not himself a member, is as valid as the one executed by the member himself.

3. *Application for transfer (Section 110)* : An application for the registration of a transfer of shares of the company may be made either by the transferor or by the transferee. Where the application is made by the transferor and relates to partly paid shares, the transfer shall not be registered, unless the company gives notice of the application to the transferee and the transferee makes no objection to the transfer within 2 weeks from the receipt of the notice.

4. *Power to refuse registration and appeal against refusal (Section 111)* : With a view to providing adequate protection to investors against refusal of a company to register transfer of shares. Section 111 requires companies to give reasons before they refuse any transfer of shares. It also confers a right on the aggrieved investor to apply for relief to the Company Law Board on specified grounds.

The appeal shall be made by a petition in writing and shall be accompanied by the prescribed fee.

Forged Transfer

An instrument of transfer of shares on which the signature of the transferor is forged is called a forged instrument and any transfer of shares effected on such instrument is called a 'forged transfer.'

Consequences of a forged transfer. (1) A forged transfer is a nullity. It does not pass any legal title to the transferee. The true owner can have his name restored on the register of members. A forged document can never have any legal effect.

(2) If the company has issued a share certificate to the transferee on a forged transfer and he has sold these shares to an innocent buyer, the buyer gets no right to be registered as a shareholder. In such a case, he can claim damages from the company on the ground that he acted on the share certificate of the company [Balkis Consolidated Co. Ltd. *Vs.* Tomkinson, (1893) A.C. 396].

(3) If the company has been put to a loss by reason of the forged transfer, it may recover the loss from the person who procured registration, even though he might have acted in good faith.

Blank transfer

Blank transfer is a transfer of shares which is executed without the name of the transferee being filled in the transfer form or deed which a transferor hands over to a purchaser or pledgee. The transferor also hands over to the purchaser or pledge the share certificate alongwith the blank transfer form or deed. In the blank transfer deed he only fills in his name and signs it. The date of sale and the name of the transferee are left blank in the transfer deed. The idea of a blank transfer is that the buyer or pledge gets equitable interest in the shares and he may sell them on failure of the pledger to discharge the debt after giving him a reasonable time.

LIEN ON SHARES

'Lien' means a right to retain possession of some property of another until some claim attaching to it is settled. The right of lien on shares is not conferred on a company by the Statute. It must be clearly provided for in the Articles. A company has first and paramount lien on all shares (not being fully paid shares) for amounts payable on the shares or for any amount due from any shareholder or his estate to the company (Article 9 of Table A). The company's lien on shares operates even for debts due by a shareholder to the company in his capacity as a customer of the company. It also extends to all dividends payable thereon and the assets receivable by the shareholders upon winding up. It continues even after the death of a shareholder [Allen *Vs.* Gold Reefs of West Africa Ltd., (1900) 1 Ch. 656]. It is safer for a company to adopt such a regulation in the Articles of Association.

A lien is an equitable charge. It gives the company such rights as it would have had under the general law if the shares had been expressly charged. Note the following case :

Loss of lien. A company loses lien if—

(1) it registers a transfer of shares subject to the lien of the transferee;

(2) a member pledges his shares to a third party as security for a loan and the company has notice thereof, and then incurs a liability to the company. In such a case, the pledgee has priority over the lien of the company.

SURRENDER OF SHARES

When a shareholder of a company voluntarily gives up his shares in favour of the company, he is said to have surrendered them to the company. The Companies Act does not contain any provision relating to the surrender of shares and Table A gives no power to the company to accept a surrender. If it accepts the surrender of shares, it possibly amounts to a purchase by the company of its own shares. This is prohibited by Section 77. The Articles, however, sometimes give power to the directors to accept a surrender of shares.

The surrender of shares by a member to the company is valid in the following cases :

(1) *In case of partly paid shares where forfeiture is called for* : Where the Articles give power to the directors to accept surrender of shares and it is accepted in case of partly paid shares to save the company from going through the formalities of forfeiture, the surrender is valid. Any provision in the Articles for the acceptance of surrender in other circumstances is invalid.

Surrender of partly paid shares, not liable to forfeiture, is unlawful as it— (a) release the shareholder from further liability in respect of shares. It is not open to a shareholder to surrender at will his shares, especially when he has to meet further calls. It is also not open to a company to accept a surrender of shares unless the act of the company can be brought within the rule relating to forfeiture of shares, (b) amounts to a purchase by the company of its own shares, and (c) is a reduction of capital without the sanction of the Court.

(2) *In case of fully paid shares, where they are exchanged for new shares* : Where surrender of shares is in accordance with the Articles and accepted in case of fully paid shares in exchange for new shares of the same nominal value and the surrendered shares remain capable of re-issue, the surrender is valid [Rowell *Vs.* John Rowell & Sons Ltd., (1912) Ch. 609].

Surrendered shares can be validly re-issued in the same way as forfeited shares, if the Articles authorise their re-issue.

FORFEITURE OF SHARES

If a shareholder, having been called upon to pay any call on his shares, fails to pay the call, the company has two remedies against the shareholder, *viz.*,

1. It may sue him for the amount due.
2. It may *forfeit* his shares.

Forfeiture means depriving a person of his property as a penalty for some act or omission.

The company may forfeit the shares of a shareholder for non-payment of some call/calls if the following conditions are satisfied :

1. *In accordance with Articles* : A forfeiture must be authorised by the Articles of the company.

Forfeiture is in the nature of *penal proceedings*. It is valid only if the provisions of the Articles are strictly complied with.

2. *Notice prior to forfeiture* : Before shares can be forfeited, the company must serve a notice on the defaulting shareholder requiring payment of the unpaid call together with any interest which may have accrued (Article 29 of Table A). The notice must—

(a) give not less than 14 days' time from the date of service of notice for the payment of the amount due:

(b) state that in the event of non-payment of the amount due within the period mentioned in the notice, the shares in respect of which the call was made will be liable to be forfeited (Article 30 of Table A).

The notice of forfeiture must also specify the exact amount due from the shareholder. If the notice is defective in any respect, *e.g.*, where it does not specify the amount claimed by the company, or where it claims a wrong amount, the forfeiture will be invalid. The defect in the notice, even though slight, invalidates the notice and is fatal to the forfeiture.

3. *Resolution of the Board* : If the defaulting shareholder does not pay the amount within the specified time as required by the notice, the directors must pass a resolution forfeiting the shares (Article 31 of Table A). If this resolution is not passed, the forfeiture is invalid. If, however, the notice threatening the forfeiture incorporates the resolution of forfeiture as well, *e.g.*, when it states that in the event of default the shares shall be deemed to have been forfeited, no further resolution is necessary.

4. *Good faith* : The power to forfeit shares must be exercised by the directors in good faith and for the benefit of the company.

Effect of forfeiture

(1) *Cessation of membership* : A person whose shares have been forfeited ceases to be a member in respect of the forfeited shares. But notwithstanding the forfeiture he remains liable to pay to the company all moneys which, at the date of forfeiture, were payable by him to the company in respect of the shares [Article 33 (1) of Table A].

(2) *Cessation of liability* : The liability of the person whose shares have been forfeited ceases if and when the company receives payment in full of all such money in respect of the shares [Article 33 (2) of Table A].

If a company is wound up more than 1 year after the forfeiture, the member whose shares have been forfeited cannot be held liable as a contributory.

Forfeited shares become the property of the company. These may be re-issued or otherwise disposed of on such terms and in such manner as the Board thinks fit [Article 32 (1)].

NOMINATION AND TRANSMISSION OF SHARES

[New Sections. 109-A and 109-B as introduced by Companies (Amendment) Act, 1999]

Nomination of shares (Section 109-A)

Single holder : Every holder of shares in, or holder of debentures of, a company may, at any time, nominate a person to whom his shares in, or debentures of, the company shall vest in the event of his death. The nomination will be in the prescribed manner [Section 109-A (1)].

Joint holders : Where the shares in, or debentures of, a company are held by more than one person jointly, the joint holders may together nominate a person to whom all the rights in the shares or debentures of the company shall vest in the event of death of all the joint holders. The nomination will be in the prescribed manner [Section 109-A (2)], Where a nomination made in the prescribed manner purports to confer on any person the right to vest the shares in or debentures of the company, the nominee shall, on the death of the shareholder or holder of debentures of the company or, as the case may be, on the death of the joint holders become entitled to all the rights in the shares or debentures of the company [Section 109-A (3)].

Minor nominee : Where the nominee is a minor, it shall be lawful for the holder of the shares, or holder of debentures, to make the nomination to appoint in the prescribed manner any person to become entitled to shares in or debentures of the company, in the event of his death, during the minority [Section 109-A (4)].

Transmission of shares (109-B)

Any person who becomes a nominee by virtue of the provisions of Section 109-A, upon the production of such evidence as may be required by the Board of directors, may elect, either-

(a) to be registered himself as holder of the share or debenture, as the case may be; or

(b) to make such transfer of the share or debenture as the deceased shareholder or debenture holder could have made [Section 109-B (1)]

Right to decline : The Board shall, in the above cases, have the same right to decline or suspend registration as it would have had, if the deceased shareholder or debenture-holder, had transferred the share or debenture, before his death [Section 109-B (2)].

Right of the nominee : If the person being a nominee, so becoming entitled, elects to be registered as holder of the share or debenture himself, he shall deliver or send to the company a notice in writing signed by him stating that he so elects. Such notice shall be accompanied with the death certificate of the deceased shareholder or debenture-holder [Section 109-B (3)].

All limitations, restrictions and provisions of the Companies Act, 1956 relating to the right to transfer and the registration of transfers of shares or debentures shall be applicable to the notice or transfer referred to above as if the death of the member had not occurred and the notice of transfer were a notice signed by that shareholder or debenture-holder, as the case may be [Section 109-B (4)].

Dividend etc. : A person, being a nominee, becoming entitled to a share or debenture by reason of the death of the holder, shall be entitled to the same dividends and advantages to which he would be entitled if the were he registered holder of the share or debenture. But he shall not be entitled, before being *registered* as a member, to exercise any right conferred by membership in relation to meetings of the company [Section 109-B (5)].

Notice by the Board : The board of directors may, at any time, give notice requiring the person becoming entitled to a share or debenture by reason of the death of the holder to elect either to be registered himself or to transfer the share or debenture. If the notice is not complied with within 90 days, the Board may thereafter withhold payment of all dividends or bonuses or other moneys payable in respect of the share or debenture, until the requirements of the notice are complied with [Proviso to Section 109-B (5)].

PURCHASE BY COMPANY OF ITS OWN SHARES (SECTION 77)

Section 77 has become redundant in view of Section 77-A (which permits a company to buy-back its own shares) introduced by the Companies (Amendment) Act, 1999. The provisions of Section 77 are as follows :

A company limited by shares, and a company limited by guarantee and having a share capital, cannot buy its own shares unless the consequent reduction of capital is effected and sanctioned in accordance with the provisions of the Companies Act. Further a public company and a private company which is a subsidiary of a public company, cannot give, whether directly or indirectly, any financial assistance to any person for purchasing any shares in the company.

Purchase is ultra vires the company : The purchase of its own shares by a company is void and ultra vires the company. It cannot be permitted even if the power to do so is taken in the Articles.

Exceptions. In the case of a public company or a private company which is a subsidiary of a public company, the following kinds of transactions are not prohibited by Section 77 :

1. The lending of money by a banking company in the ordinary course of its business.

2. The provision of money by a company for the purchase of fully paid shares in the company by trustees for and on behalf of the employees of the company including any director holding a salaried office or employment in the company.

3. The lending of money by a company to its employees with a view to enabling them to purchase fully paid shares in the company and hold them by way of beneficial ownership. The word 'employee' does not include directors or managers. The loan made to an employee for this should not exceed the employee's salary for the period of 6 months.

BUY-BACK OF SECURITIES

[New Sections. 77-A, 77-AA and 77-B as introduced by the Companies (Amendment) Act, 1999]

Section 77-A, 77-AA permits a company to purchase its own shares or other specified securities (referred to as buy-back subject to certain conditions).

Section 77-B prohibits buy-back in certain circumstances.

Power of company to purchase its own shares (Section 77-A)

Buy-back : Notwithstanding anything contained in the Companies Act, 1956, a company may purchase its own shares or other specified securities (hereinafter referred to as buy-back). This is however subject to provisions as contained in Section 77-A (2) and Section 77-B.

Thus, a company may purchase its own shares or other specified securities from—

(i) out of its free reserves; or

(ii) out of the securities premium account; or

(iii) out of the proceeds of an earlier issue other than fresh issue of shares made specifically for buy-back purposes [Section 77-A (1)].

Conditions for buy back : No company shall purchase its own shares or other specified securities as referred to above unless :

(a) the buy-back is authorised by its Articles,

(b) a special resolution has been passed in general meeting of the company authorising the buy-back.

However, nothing contained in this clause no buy-back shall be made within a period of 365 days reckoned from the date of the trading offer of buy-back, if they added by the Companies (Third) Amendment Act, 2001. Where :

(a) the buy-back is or less than 10 per cent of the total paid-up equity capital and the reserves of the company;

(b) such buy-back has been authorised in the Board of Directors by means of a resolution passed at its's meeting;

(c) the buy-back does not exceed 25 per cent of the total paid-up capital and free reserves of the company purchasing its own shares or other specified securities;

(d) the ratio of the debt owed by the company is not more than twice the capital and its free reserves after such buy-back;

(e) all the shares or other specified securities are fully paid-up;

(f) the buy-back of shares or other specified securities listed on a stock exchange is in accordance with the regulations made by the Securities and Exchange Board of India (SEBI) in this behalf;

(g) the buy-back in respect of unlisted shares or other specified securities is in accordance with the guidelines as may be prescribed [Section 77-A (2)].

Notice of the meeting : The notice of the meeting at which special resolution is proposed to be passed shall be accompanied by an explanatory statement stating—

(a) a full and complete disclosure of all material facts;

(b) the necessity for the buy-back;

(c) the class of security intended to be purchased under the buy back;

(d) the amount to be invested under the buy-back; and

(e) the time limit for completion of buy-back [Section 77-A (3)].

Period for completion of buy-back : Every buy-back shall be completed or a resolution passed by the board of Directors at its next meeting within 12 months from the date of passing the special resolution [Section 77-A (4)].

Modes of buy-back : The buy-back referred to above may be :

(a) from the existing security holders on a proportionate basis; or

(b) from the open market; or

(c) from odd lots, that is to say, where the lot of securities in a listed public company is smaller than such market lot as may be specified by the stock exchange; or

(d) by purchasing the securities issued to employees of the company pursuant to a scheme of stock option or sweat equity [Section 77-A (5)].

Filing of declaration of solvency : Where a company has passed a special resolution or a resolution passed by the Board of Directors at its next meeting to buy-back its own shares or other securities, it shall, before making such purchases, file with the Registrar of Companies and the Securities and Exchange Board of India a declaration of solvency in the form prescribed. The declaration shall be verified by an affidavit to the effect that the Board of directors has made a full inquiry into the affairs of the company as a result of which it is capable of meeting its liabilities and will not be rendered insolvent within a period of one year of the date of declaration adopted by the Board. The declaration shall be signed by at least two directors of the company, one of whom shall be the managing director, if any.

The declaration of solvency is not required to be filled by an unlisted company [Section 77-A (6)].

Extinguishment and physical destruction of securities : Where a company buys-back its own securities, it shall extinguish and physically destroy the securities so bought-back within 7 days of the last date of completion of buy-back [Section 77-A (7)].

Restriction on further issue of securities within 24 months : Where a company complete a buy-back of its securities, it shall not make further issue of securities within a period of 24 months. It may however issue bonus shares. It may also discharge its subsisting obligations such as conversion of preference shares or debentures into equity shares [Section 77-A (8)].

Maintenance of register and filing of return : Where a company buys-back its securities, it shall maintain a register of the securities so bought, the consideration paid for the securities bought-back, the date of cancellation of securities, the date of extinguishing and physically destroying of securities and such other particulars as may be prescribed [Section 77-A (9)].

A company shall, after the completion of the buy-back, file with the Registrar of Companies and the Securities and Exchange Board of India, a return containing such particulars relating to the buy-back within 30 days of such completion, as may be prescribed [Section 77-A (10)].

Penalty : If a company makes default in complying with the provisions of Section 77-A or any rules made thereunder, the company or any officer of the company who is in default shall be punishable with imprisonment for a term which may extend to 2 years, or with fine which may extend to Rs. 50,000, or with both [Section 77-A (11)].

Transfer of certain sum (Section 77-A) : Where a company purchases its own shares out of free reserves, a sum equal to the nominal value of share so purchased shall be transferred to capital redemption reserve account and details of such transfer shall be disclosed in the balance sheet.

Issue of sweat equity shares [Section 79A)

'Sweat-equity shares' means equity shares issued by the company to employees or directors at a discount or for consideration other than cash. 'Sweat equity shares' may be issued for providing know-how or making available intellectual property rights (say, patents) or value additions, by whatever name called.

Section 79A allows companies to issue sweat equity shares subject to the following conditions :

(a) 'Sweat equity shares' must be of a class of shares already issued by the company;

(b) the issue of sweat equity shares is authorised by a special resolution passed by the company in the general meeting;

(c) the resolution specifies the number of shares, current market price, consideration, if any, and the class or classes of directors or employees to whom such equity shares are to be issued;

(d) not less than one year has, at the date of issue, elapsed since the date on which the company was entitled to commence business.

(e) The sweat equity shares of a company whose equity shares are listed on recognised stock exchange are issued in accordance with the regulation made by the Securities and Exchange Board of India in this behalf [Sec 79A(1)]. However, in the case of a company whose equity shares are not listed the same must be issued in accordance with the guidelines, as may be prescribed.

(f) All the limitations, restrictions and provisions relating to equity shares shall be applicable to such sweat equity shares issued under sub-section (1) [Section 79A(2)].

Explanation. For the purposes of section 79A, the expression "a company" means, company incorporated, formed and registered under this Act and includes its subsidiary company incorporated in a country outside India.

Bonus shares

A company may, if its Articles so provide, capitalise profits by issuing fully paid-up shares to the members thereby transferring the sums capitalised from the profit and loss account or Reserve Account to the Share Capital [Section 205(3)]. Such shares are known as bonus shares and are issued to the existing members of the company free of charge.

The issue of bonus shares is regulated by the guidelines issued by SEBI in this regard.

Guidelines for issue of bonus shares. These are :

(a) These guidelines are applicable to existing listed companies.

(b) The bonus issue shall only be made out of free reserves built out of genuine profits or share premium collected in cash only. However, SEBI guidelines relating to debentures provide that Debenture Redemption Reserve shall be considered as general reserve for consideration of bonus issue proposals.

(c) Reserves created by revaluation of fixed assets are not to be capitalised.

(d) The declaration of bonus issue, in lieu of dividend, is not made.

(e) The bonus issue is not made unless the partly-paid shares, if any, existing, are made fully paid-up.

(f) The company—

  (i) has not defaulted in payment of interest or principal in respect of fixed deposits and interest in existing debentures or principal on redemption thereof, and

  (ii) has sufficient reason to believe that it has not defaulted in respect of the payment of statutory dues of the employees such as contribution to provident fund, gratuity, bonus, etc.

(g) A company which announces its bonus issue after the approval of the Board of directors must implement the proposal within a period 6 months from the date of such approval and shall not have the option of changing the decision.

(h) There should be a provision in the Articles of association of the company for capitalisation of reserves, and, if not, the company shall pass a resolution at its general body meeting making provisions in the Articles of Association for capitalisation.

(i) Consequent to the issue of bonus shares, if the subscribed and paid-up capital exceed the authorised share capital, resolution shall be passed by the company at its general body meeting for increasing the authorised capital.

(j) No company shall, pending conversion of FCDs/PCDs, issue any shares by way of bonus, unless similar benefit is extended to the holders of such FCDs/PCDs through reservation of shares in proportion to such convertible part of FCDs/PCDs. The shares so reserved may be issued at the time of conversion of such debentures on the same terms on which the bonus issues were made.

Distinction between bonus shares and rights shares

Rights Shares	Bonus Shares
1. *To be paid for* : It only confers a privilege on the existing shareholders to have a claim on the shares offered after the first public issue. However, the shareholders must pay for the shares accepted.	1. Bonus shares are issued to the existing members free of charge.
2. *Partly paid* : The existing share-holding of the members as well as rights shares may be partly paid.	2. Bonus shares are always fully paid.
3. *Minimum subscription* : In the event of a company failing to receive a minimum of 90% subscription, the company shall have to return the entire money received.	3. There is no such requirement.
4. *Money to be kept in a separate bank account* : Till the concerned regional stock exchange approves the allotment, money received against rights must be kept in a separate bank account.	4. This is not relevant to bonus issues as no money is to be received by the company.

Underwriting

Meaning : underwriting is an expression used in company matters signifying a contract by which a person (known as the underwriter) agrees (usually for a commission) that if the shares, debentures, or debenture stock about to be offered for subscription or some specified proportion therefore, are not, within a specified time, taken up by the public, or by that section of the public to which they are to be offered, he will himself take them up and pay for what the public do not take up or some specified proportions thereof.

SEBI Guidelines, 2000 define 'underwriting' to mean an agreement with or without conditions to subscribe to the securities of a body corporate when the existing shareholders of such body corporate or the public do not subscribe to the securities offered to them.

Underwriting is thus in the nature of an insurance against the possibility of inadequate subscription.

(1) *Firm underwriting* : When an underwriter desires to take in a firm way, the whole or a portion of the number of shares he has underwritten, the effect will be that an allotment of that number would be made to him irrespective of whether the issue is over or undersubscribed. To the underwriter who takes on firm basis a given number of shares will be, so far as the rest of the shares are concerned, in the same position as other underwriters.

(2) *Revocation of underwriting agreement* : An underwriting letter is usually in the shape of an offer and, therefore, can be withdrawn at any time before acceptance. The revocation shall be valid even where made just by a word of mouth. However, if the underwriting is in the form of an application for shares, it cannot be withdrawn like other applications until the 5th day after the opening of the subscription list (Section 72).

An underwriting letter generally authorises the company or persons acting for it, to apply in the name of underwriter or sub-underwriter for the shares in case they fail to apply when called upon to do so. Such a letter amounts to an authority coupled with interest and therefore, after acceptance by the promoter, is irrevocable.

(3) *Liability of legal heirs* : The underwriting agreement can be enforced even against the executors, of the deceased underwriters. The duty imposed for finding capital is not such a personal contract as would come to an end with the life of the contractor.

SEBI guidelines. As per SEBI Guidelines, 2000 :

(i) Underwriting shall be optional.

(ii) The lead merchant banker shall satisfy themselves about the ability of the underwriters to discharge their underwriting obligations.

(iii) The lead merchant banker shall :

(a) incorporate a statement in the offer document to the effect that in the opinion of the lead merchant banker, the underwriters' assets are adequate to meet their underwriting obligations;

(b) obtain Underwriter's written consent before including their names as underwriters in the final offer document.

(iv) In respect of every underwritten issue, the lead merchant banker(s) shall undertake a minimum underwriting obligation of 5% of the total underwriting commitment or Rs. 25 lacs whichever is less.

(v) The outstanding underwriting commitments of a merchant banker shall not exceed 20 times its networth at any point of time.

(vi) In respect of an underwritten issue, the lead merchant banker shall ensure that the relevant details of underwriters are included in the offer document.

Underwriting commission. Section 76 permits the payment of underwriting commission subject to the compliance of the following conditions :

(i) It should be authorised by the Articles of the company. An authority in the memorandum is not sufficient.

(ii) The commission payable should not exceed 5 per cent in the case of shares and 2½ per cent in the case of debentures. Any lesser amount may be prescribed by the Articles and if it is so prescribed, it is the amount prescribed in the Articles that shall be payable as the underwriting commission by way of maximum.

(iii) Underwriting commission may be paid in cash or kind or as lump sum or by way of percentage but in no case can it go beyond the statutory limits of 5 per cent or 2½ per cent as the case may be. However, if the articles authorise payment by a certain percentage, a lump sum payment cannot be made.

(iv) Underwriting commission should be disclosed in the prospectus or statement in lieu of prospectus, as the case may be, or in a statement filed with the Registrar before the payment of the commission. However, the requirement of disclosure is relevant to the main underwriting agreements only; it does not cover sub-underwriting agreements.

(v) The number of shares or debentures which persons have agreed to subscribe absolutely or conditionally should also be disclosed as in (iv) above.

(vi) A copy of the contract relating to the payment of the commission should be delivered to the Registrar.

(vii) No underwriting commission shall be paid to any person on shares or debentures which are not offered to the public for subscription. But where a person has subscribed or agreed to subscribe under sub-section (1) (a) for any shares in or debentures of the company and before the issue of the prospectus or statement in lieu thereof any other person or persons has or have subscribed for any or all of those shares or debentures and that fact together with the aggregate amount of commission payable under this section in respect of such sub-section is disclosed in such prospectus or statement, then, the company may pay commission to the first-mentioned person in respect of such subscription [Section 76(4A)].

Underwriting commission may be paid in respect of debentures offered to the members on a rights basis.

Payment of underwriting commission by private companies : The provisions of section 76 are applicable to all companies, private and public. Where a private company pays commission, it must fulfil the conditions of section 76 as noted above. In particular, it will have to file a statement before the Registrar before paying commission.

Sub-underwriting : The underwriter usually chooses to spread his risk by using sub-underwriters who agree to take certain number of shares for which they receive a commission. The liability of sub-underwriter is contingent upon :

(a) the number of shares subscribed by the public;

(b) the intimation by the underwriter to the sub-underwriter that the latter shall subscribe or procure subscriptions.

A sub-underwriting letter authorising an underwriter to apply for shares for a valuable consideration, if the offer is accepted by the underwriter, amounts to an authority coupled with interest and is irrevocable. In case of discrepancy between an underwriting agreement and sub-underwriting, say where the sub-underwriting mentions the shares at par whereas it was a premium issue, it was held that the sub-underwriter was bound by the allotment at premium.

SEBI Guidelines for Preferential Allotments

A listed company making issue of capital by way of shares/FCDs/PCDs/warrants and any other financial instrument on a preferential basis to any select group of persons, must fulfil the following requirements as prescribed in the Guidelines :

1. *Pricing of the Issue* : The issue of shares on a preferential basis can be made at a price not less than the higher of the following :

(A) The average of the weekly high and low of the closing prices of the related shares quoted on the stock exchange during the six months preceding the relevant date.

Or

(B) The average of the weekly high and low of the closing prices of the related shares quoted on a stock exchange during the two weeks preceding the relevant date.

"Relevant date" for this purpose means the date thirty days prior to the date on which the meeting of general body of shareholders is convened, in terms of section 81 (1A) of the Companies Act to consider the proposed issue.

The explanatory statement to the notice for the general meeting in terms of section 173 of the Companies Act, 1956 shall contain :

(i) The object/s of the issue through preferential offer,

(ii) intention of promoters/directors/key management persons to subscribe to the offer,

(iii) proposed time within which the allotment shall be completed,

(iv) proposed time within the allotment shall be completed,

(v) the identity of the purposed allotees and the percentage of post preferential issue capital that may be held by them.

2. *Pricing of shares arising out of warrants, etc.* : Where warrants are issued on a preferential basis with an option to apply for and get shares allotted, the issuer company shall determine the price of the resultant shares in accordance with the above.

However, the relevant date for this purpose may, at the option of the issuer, be either the one referred to above or the date of their allotment.

3. *Upfront payment on warrants* : An amount equivalent to at least ten per cent of the price as above shall become payable for the warrants on the date of their allotment. This amount would be adjusted against the price payable subsequently for acquiring the shares by exercising an option for the purpose. This amount would stand forfeited if the option to acquire shares is not exercised.

4. *Pricing of shares on conversion* : Where PCDs/FCDs/other instruments are issued on a preferential basis providing for the issuer to allot shares at a future date, the issuer shall determine the price at which the shares are to be allotted in lieu of the aforesaid instruments.

5. *Currency of financial instruments* : In case of Warrants/PCDs/ FCDs/or any other financial instruments with a provision for the allotment of equity shares at a future date, either through conversion or otherwise, the currency of the instruments should not exceed beyond 18 months from the date of issue of the relevant instrument.

6. *Non-transferability of financial instruments* : Warrants/FCDs/ PCDs/ or any other financial instruments issued on a preferential basis will be subject to 3 years lock-in-period from the date of allotment.

In any case, not more than 20% of the total capital of the company, including capital brought in by way of preferential issue, shall be subject to lock-in of three years form the date of allotment.

In addition to the requirements for lock-in of instruments allotted on preferential basis to promoters/promoter group, as above, the instruments allotted on preferential basis to any person including promoters/promoters group shall be locked-in for a period of one year from the date of their allotment except for such allotment on preferential basis which involve swap of equity shares/securities convertible into equity shares at a later date, for acquisition.

The lock-in on shares acquired by conversion of the convertible instrument/exercise of warrants, shall be reduced to the extent the convertible instrument/warrants have already been locked in (w.e.f. 4-8-2000).

7. *Currency of shareholders resolutions* : Action on any resolution passed at a meeting of shareholders of a company granting consent for preferential issues of any financial instrument shall be completed within a period of three months from the date of passing of the resolution. If such a resolution is not acted upon within the said period, a fresh consent of the shareholders will have to be obtained (w.e.f. 4-8-2000).

The equity shares and securities convertible into equity shares at a later date, allotted in terms of the aforesaid resolution shall be made fully paid up at the time of their allotment. However, in case of warrants, allotment may be made subject to the guidelines relating to upfront payment [discussed under (3) above] (w.e.f. 4-8-2000).

8. *Certificate from Auditors* : In the case of every issue of shares/warrants/FCDs/PCDs/or other financial instruments, the statutory auditors of the issuer company must certify that the issue of said instruments is being made in accordance with the requirements contained in these guidelines. Copies of the certificate shall also be laid before the meeting of the shareholders convened to consider the proposed issue.

9. *Disclosures with respect to utilisation of preferential issue proceeds* : The details of all monies utilised out of the preferential issue proceeds shall be disclosed under an appropriate head in the balance sheet of the company indicating the purpose for which such monies have been utilised. The details of unutilised monies shall also be disclosed under a separate head in the balance sheet of the company indicating the form in which such unutilised monies have been invested (w.e.f. 4-8-2000).

Preferential Allotments to FIIs-Additional Guidelines : Foreign Institutional Investors (FIIs) are free to invest in all securities traded on the primary and secondary markets including equity and other securities/instruments of companies listed/to be listed on stock exchanges in India including the OTC Exchange of India. In view of the requests received from industry to allow listed companies to make preferential allotment in favour of registered FIIs for meeting the immediate response requirements especially of medium and small sized companies, SEBI has allowed making of preferential allotment in favour of FIIs. However, this is subject to the following conditions which are in addition to the above mentioned guidelines :

(i) Consent of shareholders is to be obtained by the company at a general meeting under section 81(1A) of the Companies Act.

(ii) FII investments by way of preferential allotments should not exceed 15% of the equity of the company and the aggregate of FII investments should not exceed 49% subject to approval of the Board/General Body of the equity of the company. Besides, investments by NRIs/PIOs/OCBs through stock exchanges under portfolio investment scheme shall not be more than 10% (24%, if special resolution is passed by the general body) of the paid-up equity capital. Thus, the total investments by FIIs/NRI/OCB may be upto 73% of the equity capital of the company. In case of debt instruments FIIs have been allowed to invest upto 100 per cent.

(iii) The holding of a single FII (or a sub-account wherever applicable) in a company should not exceed the ceiling of 10% of the equity of the company. In case of foreign corporates or individuals, each of such sub-account shall not invest more than 5% of the total issued capital of the company [Notification No. SO 946(E), dt. 20-10-2000]

(iv) FIIs investing through the 100% debt route would be permitted to invest in unlisted securities also.

(v) To facilitate the participation of FIIs in open offers, SEBI has permitted FIIs to tender their securities directly in response to an open offer made in terms of the SEBI (Substantial Acquisition of Shares and Takeovers) Regulations, 1997.

(vi) FIIs shall be entitled to buy and sell derivative contracts which are traded on a stock exchange. They will also be permitted to trade in derivatives without requiring them to take delivery and give delivery.

(vii) The preferential allotment shall be made at a price not less than the highest price during the last 26 weeks on all the stock exchanges where the securities of the company are listed. There relevant date for the purpose of 26 weeks would be the date thirty days prior to the date on which the general body meeting of the shareholders is convened in terms of section 81(1A) of the Companies Act to consider the proposed issue.

(viii) In case of an offer by a company to buy-back its securities, the FII may sell the securities held by it to such company, in accordance with SEBI (Buy-back of Securities) Regulations, 1998.

(ix) Prior approval of the RBI under FERA, 1973 is necessary in all cases. For this purpose, an application is to be made to the

Controller, Exchange Control Department, Foreign Investment, Division-II, Reserve Bank of India, Central Office, Bombay-400 023.

In addition, any other guideline or circular issued by RBI will also be complied with by the company making preferential allotments to FIIs.

DEPOSITORY SYSTEM

The Depositories Bill, 1995 has introduced an alternate mode of effecting transfer of shares in place of share certificate. Under the Act one or more depositories can be established. Every depository will be required to be registered with SEBI and receive a certificate of commencement of business. The investors who want to join the system will be required to be registered with one or more participants who will be agent for the depository. These participants can be only custodial agents like banks, financial institutions and large corporate brokerage firms. Upon entry into the system, share certificates belonging to the investor will be dematerialised and their names will be entered in the books of the participants as beneficial owners. In the books of the company the name of the depository instead of the investor shall be registered as the owner of shares etc.

In case of initial issue, the investor will indicate in the application form if he wants to avail this system. The shares in depositary mode shall cease to have distinct numbers. This system operates through electronic account transfer system.

QUESTIONS

1. Can a Company purchase its own shares? Explain the law in this regard.
2. What is meant by allotment of shares? How a valid allotment is made? What is irregular allotment and what are its effects?
3. How shares can be forfeited? What is minimum subscription?
4. Point out the differences between "transfer and transmission of shares".
5. Write Notes on :
   (a) Bonus Shares
   (b) Depositary system
   (c) Right of pre-emption in case of further issue of capital
   (d) Types of convertible debentures

PRACTICAL PROBLEMS

1. A applies for shares on 1.1.2003 to Delhi Metro Corporation. The Corporation allots him shares on 31.4.2003. A refuses to take shares. Advise.

2. A, the secretary of a company, forges the signature of directors and affixes seal on a share certificate issued to Mr. Y. Can Y hold the company liable?
3. Can a company issue shares against a promissory note?

10

Membership and Register of Members

Who is Member?

From legal point of view a member is one whose name appears on the register of members. Section 41 of the Act lays down following rules relating to the term 'member' :

(1) The subscribers of the memorandum of a company shall be deemed to have agreed to become members of the company, and on its registration, shall be entered as members in its register of members.

(2) Every other person who [1][agrees in writing] to become a member of a company and whose name is entered in the register of members shall be a member of the company.

Ways of Membership

Thus, a person can become a 'member' or 'shareholder' of a company in any one of the following ways :

(1) By being a subscriber to the memorandum.

(2) By agreeing in writing to become a member and whose name is entered in the register of members.

(3) [Every person holding equity share capital of a company and whose name is entered as beneficial owner in the records of the depository shall be deemed to be a member of the concerned company.][2]

The second is comprised of two classes :

(i) Persons who are members because they have applied for shares which have been allotted to them and

(ii) Persons who have taken a transfer from a member.

1. Subscription to Memorandum. Mere subscription to the memorandum is enough to make them members, and neither allotment nor entry in the register of members is essential (Channler & 48 All 580).

1. Substituted by Act 65 of 1960, Section 13 for "agrees."
2. Inserted by the Depositaries Act, 1996 w.r.e. 20-9-1995.

2. Membership by Allotment. As to the membership by allotment an agreement to take shares coupled with registration of the name in the company's register must be shown, otherwise the person cannot be called a shareholder or member. There must be an agreement to take shares. Now by the amendment to Section 41, such an agreement must be in writing. If there is no valid agreement neither allotment nor entry in the register will make a person a member. The principles of law of contract to proposal and acceptance apply to shares. The contract to take shares is not completed till the fact of allotment is communicated to the applicant (Pellet's Case, 2 ch. 527). Where the shares applied for, are subject to a condition, the applicant is not a member till the condition is satisfied even though his name might be on the register of members (Roger's Case, 1868 3 Ch. App. 936), A person whose name has been entered in the register by mistake is not a member since there is no agreement.

The transferee does not become a member by merely obtaining a transfer of shares. The transferee's title is not complete till his name is actually entered in the register of members (Fazal *Vs.* Mangaldas, 23 B. LR. 1944).

A legal representative of a deceased member is not a member unless and until he establishes his legal title to the shares held by the deceased member.

In the case of shares held jointly by two or three persons, all of them are deemed to be the members of the company as the joint possession of shares indicates their agreement to become members of the company.

3. Membership in Depository. It is necessary that the name must be entered as beneficial owner in the depository.

Minor as a Member

As a minor is not competent to enter into a legal contract, he cannot be a member. Though the guardian of a minor can purchase shares on his (minor) behalf, but the name of the guardian will be entered in the Register of Members instead of the minor without mentioning that the guardian holds shares on behalf of the minor. Thus, the guardian acts as a trustee for the minor and a trustee cannot become a member. A company cannot be compelled to admit a minor as a member. It may refuse to register a transfer of shares in his favour unless the shares are fully paid.

CONDITIONS OF ELIGIBILITY

(1) Those who can enter into a Contract. Any person who fulfils the conditions laid down in the Indian Contract Act, 1872, about competency of a person's entering into a contract and about agreement, can become a member of a company. Thus a minor, who is not eligible to enter into a contract, cannot become a member of a public limited company. Where lie is entitled to hold shares as a heir, the name of his guardian or executor will be entered in the Register of Members and not the name of such a minor. If by mistake the shares are allotted to a minor, the allotment is subject to repudiation by both the company and the minor during his minority.

(2) A Company. Apart from an individual a company also can become a member of another company, if the company's memorandum so allows. It can attend meetings of that other company through its duly appointed representative.

A company cannot be a member of itself because that will be tantamount to purchasing its own shares (Section 42).

(3) Trustee. Section 153 of the Act lays that no notice of any trust express, implied or constructive, should be entered in the register. The Central Government may appoint a person as public trustee to discharge the functions and to exercise the rights and powers, conferred on him by this Act (Section 153A).

(4) Joint-holder. Every joint-holder of a share is a member of a company (Narandas *Vs.* Indian Manufacturing Co. 55, Bom. L.R. 567). But they are treated as a single member in a private company.

(5) A Partnership Firm. As a partnership firm is not recognised by law as a person it cannot become a member of a public company in its own name. However, a partner of a firm is entitled to be a member of any company provided he is not a person disqualified under any law.

(6) A Subsidiary Company. A subsidiary company is not allowed to become a member of its holding company. But there are following exceptions to this general provision :

(i) Legal representative of a deceased member of the company of which it is a subsidiary company.

(ii) Trustee of the shares of the holding company where such a subsidiary company has no insurable interest in the trust.

(iii) Subsidiary company which is already a member of a holding company before the commencement of the Act.

METHODS OF ACQUIRING MEMBERSHIP

(1) Subscription. If a person subscribes his name to the memorandum of a company and signs it, he is deemed to be a member of that company.

(2) Application and Allotment. A person can apply for shares issued by a company, when the shares, applied for, are allotted to him by the board of directors and this fact is communicated to him through a letter of allotment, he is entitled to the membership. However, mere allotment is not sufficient; he must see that his name appears in the register of members.

(3) **Allotment of Shares for Consideration other than Cash.** One can be a member by accepting fully paid or partly paid shares as a consideration for some services rendered or property sold to the company. In this case also his name must be entered in the register.

(4) **Transfer.** When a person purchases shares from a member of a company he is termed as the transferee and a member of the company. The transfer must be made strictly according to the procedure laid down by the articles. Transferee's name must be entered in the register.

(5) **Succession.** A person becomes a member by succeeding to the shares of a deceased. The official assignee or a liquidator, or a lunatic or bankrupt shareholder, may have his name put on the register by producing documentary evidence to that effect.

(6) **Conversion of Share Warrants into Share Certificates.** If one is a holder of share warrants of a public company and if the articles allow conversion of such warrants into share certificates he can get his warrants converted into share certificates. After that his name must be entered in the Register of Members and he acquires membership by this method.

(7) **Agreeing to become a Director.** By agreeing to become a director of a company a person *ipso facto* becomes a member. For this purpose, he must purchase qualification shares necessary for directorship as laid down by the articles.

(8) **Estoppel or Acquiescence.** If he allows his name to be entered in the register or allows himself to be held out as a member after selling all his shares or holds himself a member, he will be deemed to be a member of the company. He will be liable to the liquidator, if the company is wound up and he will be estopped from denying the fact that he was a member without his knowledge or consent.

(9) **Corporation Sole/Society.** A corporate sole like the President of India/Governor of State (not a Collector of a district) Administrator General (Under A.G. Act 1963) or a society registered under Act of 1860 can become member of a company. Similarly, Trade Union registered can became a member.

MEMBER AND SHAREHOLDER

There is no difference between a shareholder and a member except in case of a bearer of share warrant or member of an unlimited company or company limited by guarantee, a person is not a shareholder but a member. In case of a company limited by share, a person will be a member, not a shareholder in case when one acquires shares through a sale, on death of shareholder as legal representative or official receiver/assignee recurring shares on insolvency of a shareholder. A person who subscribes to memorandum, till shares are not allotted to him, is a member.

TERMINATION OF MEMBERSHIP

Membership of a person may he terminated under the following conditions :

1. If he transfers all his shares according to the procedure laid down by the articles.
2. By a valid forfeiture or surrender his shares.
3. If he becomes a lunatic, a bankrupt or dies.
4. When he repudiates the contract of membership on grounds of misrepresentation in the prospectus, irregular allotment or minority of the shareholders.
5. On sale of shares by the company when it exercises its rights by lien on shares.
6. If the company goes into liquidation.
7. When share certificates are converted into share warrants.
8. When redeemable preference shares have been redeemed.

RIGHTS OF MEMBERS

(1) Claiming Share Certificate. Where a company has been registered with a share capital, every person whose name is entered in the register of members has a right to claim one or several share certificates within three months after allotment or registration of transfer of shares.

(2) Duplicate Certificate. The member has a right to get a duplicate share certificate on payment of prescribed fees and giving an indemnity bond, if the original share certificate is lost, defaced or destroyed.

(3) Transfer of Shares. The member have a right to make an appeal to the Central Government in case the company refuses to register the transfer of shares.

(4) Legal Heir. A person becoming entitled to shares by reason of death or insolvency of a holder shall be entitled to the dividends and other advantages to which he could have been entitled if he were the registered holder of share.

(5) Voting regarding Dividend. Every holder of equity shares has a right to vote in favour or against the declaration of dividend when this matter is placed before the general meeting for its approval.

(6) Payments of Dividend, Where members have been granted special rights as to dividends, they can claim that the dividends must be declared and paid according to the amounts paid or credited as paid on the shares possessed by them.

(7) If a company has declared dividend and the same has been approved by the general meeting, then a member has two rights :

(i) He can claim the amount of dividend due to him on his shares.

(ii) He can vote for reducing the rate of dividend fixed by the Board.

(8) Bonus Shares. A member has a night to decline the offer made by the company issuing bonus shares. Instead he can demand the amount in cash as a matter of right.

(9) Free Access. Under Section 163 of the Act, every member has a right to have free access to the books of accounts. He can make extracts from any register or index of members of the company.

(10) Issue of further Capital. Under Section 81 of the Act if a company issues further capital, the equity shareholders whose names appear on the Register of Members on the date of the offer, have the first right to receive such offer before the same is offered to the general public.

(11) Copies of PIL A/c. A member has a right to receive copies of the profit and loss account and balance sheet before the commencement of the annual general meeting.

(12) Attending Meeting. The members have a right to :

(i) Receive notice of the meeting;

(ii) Attend and vote at the meetings;

(iii) Call extraordinary general meeting on requisition.

(13) Appointing Proxy. Any member of a company entitled to attend and vote at a meeting of the company shall be entitled to appoint another person (whether a member or not) as his proxy to attend and vote on his behalf.

(14) Appointing and Removing Directors. Members at annual general meeting are not only entitled to elect directors of the company but also to remove them before the expiry of their period of office.

(15) Appointing Auditors. In respect of the auditors of the company, members have the rights to :

(i) make appointments,

(ii) fix their remuneration and

(iii) remove them from office.

(16) Approaching Court. Any member of a company has a right to approach the court if he complains :

(i) that the affairs of the company are being conducted in a manner oppressive to any one of them, or

(ii) they are of the opinion that the affairs of the company are being conducted in a manner prejudicial to the interest of the company; or

(iii) a material change in the management has taken place, then under all these circumstances members have a right to make an application to the Court for relief.

LIABILITIES OF MEMBERSHIP

(1) Every member, who has been allotted shares, is liable to pay to the company the total nominal value of shares held by him.

(2) If a member fails to pay any call or instalment of a call, and he is served with a notice to pay call money as is unpaid thereon, he is liable to pay interest which may have accrued.

(3) A person whose shares have been forfeited shall, notwithstanding the forfeiture, remain liable to pay to the company all moneys which, at the date of forfeiture, were presently payable by him to the company in respect of his shares.

(4) Where a member transfers his shares, he is held liable to pay the unpaid amount on his shares to the company till such time the name of the transferee is entered in the register of members.

(5) In a company limited by guarantee, a member who undertakes that in the event of winding up of the company he will contribute such amount as already fixed for setting the debts and meeting the cost of winding up of the company if it goes into liquidation will be liable to pay his share when he is a member. This liability also continues provided the company is wound up within one year from the cessation of his membership.

(6) The liability of every member is unlimited so far as the unlimited companies are concerned.

(7) A member who ceases to be a member as a result of transfer of all his shares, will be held liable to pay such amount as falls due on the shares transferred by him in case the company goes into liquidation within one year of the cessation of his membership.

REGISTER OF MEMBERS

Keeping of Register

Section 150 of the Act provides that :

(1) Every company shall keep in one or more books a register of its members, and enter therein the following particular :

(a) the name and address, and the occupation if any of each member,

(b) in the case of a company having a share capital, the shares held by each member, [distinguishing each share[1] by its number, expect where such shares are held with the depository][2] and the amount paid or agreed to be considered as paid on those shares,

(c) the date at which each person was entered in the register as a member and

1. "The words distinguishing each share by its number" omitted by the Depositories Act, 1996, w.r.e.f. 20-9-1995
2. Inserted by the Depositories Related Laws (Amendment) Act 1997, (8 of 1997) w.e.f. 15-1-1997

(d) the date at which any person ceased to be a member.

Provided that where the company has converted any of its shares into stock and given notice of the conversion to the Registrar, the register shall show amount of stock held by each of the members concerned instead of the shares so converted which were previously held by him.

(2) If default is made in complying with sub-section (1), the company, and every officer of the company who is in default, shall be punishable with fine which may extend to [five hundred rupees][1] for every day during which the default continues.

Contents of Register

When the period, if any allowed for renunciation, has lapsed and the list of allotment is finally settled, the work of writing up the share register or register of members should proceed with as rapidly as possible, because according to Section 150 of the Act, reproduced above, every company is required to keep in one or more books, a register of its members. The register must be maintained from the date of registration of the company. When the period of renunciation of allotment has lapsed, the names and other information appearing on the allotment sheets will be written down in the register of members. Thus, the allotment sheets form a provisional register. The register of members is a document giving the information about the shareholders. What information must be there in the register has been given in Section 150 of the Act. This Section states that a company shall enter in its register the following particulars :

(i) The name, address and the occupation, if any, of each member;

(ii) In the case of a company having a share capital, the shares held by each member distinguishing each share by its number, and the amount paid or agreed to be considered as paid on those shares;

(iii) The date at which the name of each person was entered in the register as a member and

(iv) The date at which any person ceased to be a member.

If a company has convened any of its shares into stock and has given notice of the conversion to the Registrar, the register must show the amount of stock held by each of the members instead of the shares so converted which were previously held by him.

Information in Register

Thus, the register of a company must give the following information: name, address, occupation of every member, the number of shares with their distinguishing members, or the amount of stock held by

1. Substituted for "fifty rupees" by the Companies (Amendment) Act 2000, w.e.f. 15-1-1997

him, the dates of his becoming and ceasing to be a member. If a company makes any default in this respect, the Section lays down that the company and every officer of the company who is in default shall be punished with fine extending to fifty rupees a day till the default continues.

Benami Holding of Shares

These shares are held by the ostensible owner whose name is entered in the Register of Members. As he has no beneficial interest in such shares he is called Benamidar and the person who has got real interest in such shares is called Beneficial Owner. Thus, real owner of shares can manage to get dividends without disclosing his identity. A new Section 187C has been introduced to control such benami holding of shares. It makes the following provisions :

(1) Every benami holder of shares is required to file a declaration with the company stating the particulars of beneficial owner.

(2) The beneficial owner 'Is also required to file a declaration specifying his own interest in such shares and the details of benami holder within 30 days of his becoming beneficial owner'.

(3) The beneficial owner should communicate to the company any change in his beneficial interest in such shares within 30 days of the change taking place.

(4) If required declarations are not filed by persons concerned they are punishable with a fine upto Rs. 1000 for every day till the default continues.

Share Ledger

In practice, the register of members is often styled as the register of members and share ledger, because generally, shares are partly paid. Therefore most companies find it necessary in their own interest to maintain a *"Share Ledger"*. It contains an account of each shareholder, showing the number of shares held by him and the amount due and paid-up in respect thereof, thus showing in detail the total issued and paid-up capital as appearing in the financial books.

The register of members and share ledger are conveniently combined in such a way as to comply with the statute and serve also as a subsidiary ledger. If the shares become fully paid, the cash account portion of the ruling can be dispensed with.

A register and share ledger may take the form of a bound book or a loose-leaf book with a separate card index. Small companies find it advantageous to have a bound book, and an alphabetical index in the front of the book because the number of shares is small, but for large companies, this form is not convenient.

Some companies issue both preference and equity shares and different methods are used to record this information. Sometimes, separate loose-leaf sheets of different colours are used for each class of shares, as there is less likelihood of error and confusion when recording payment of calls, transfers, etc. If shares are fully paid, a register with analysis columns to record different holdings is used. If a member holds two types of shares, the two sheets are kept together so that the repetition of a certain information in the case of such a member may be avoided.

If a company uses the bound book system and issue different types of shares, then each is divided into two parts, the upper portion being allotted to preference shares, while the remaining part is reserved for equity shares. As the information when written in one part need not be repeated in the other part, considerable amount of labour is saved. As per Section 151, the company requires to maintain an index of its members. It is convenient to keep the register in loose-leaf form, so as to constitute the index in itself.

Index of Members

(1) Every company having more than fifty members shall, unless the register of members is in such a form as in itself to constitute an index, keep an index (which may be in the form of a card index) of the names of the members of the company and shall, within fourteen days after the date on which any alteration is made in the register of members, make the necessary alteration in the index.

(2) The index shall, in respect of each member, contain a sufficient indication to enable the entries relating to that member in the register to be readily found.

(3) The index shall, at all times, be kept at the same place as the register of members.

(4) If default is made in complying with sub-section (1), (2) or (3), the company, and every officer of the company who is in default, shall be punishable with fine which may extend to [*five hundred rupees*].[1]

Advantages of a Loose-leaf Book

If a company follows the method of keeping its register to loose-leaf books of small dimensions so as to constitute in itself the index, it is not necessary to keep a separate card index. This method has the following advantages :

(i) A loose-leaf book can be easily written upon, while a card has to be extracted for the purpose.

(ii) The back of the page can be written upon without disturbing its position, a fact not possible with a card-index.

(iii) There is less possibility of up-setting the pages.

(iv) The use of a loose-leaf book is simple, effective and economical.

1. Substituted for "fifty rupees" by the companies (Amendment Act 2000, w.e.f. 13-12-2000

Importance of Register of Members

Register of Members is compulsory for every company. Information contained therein must be up-to-date, clear and sufficient, because entries made in it are treated as *prima facie* proof. As the entry on the register is considered the crucial test of determining the membership of a person, hence, every change effected in the case of a member must be incorporated as early as possible. The register is open for public inspection and extracts are to be given if demanded by any person.

Closure of Register of Members

Section 154 of the act authorises a company to close its register for any period or periods not exceeding 30 days at anytime. Thus, the company has the power to close its register for 45 days in a year. As this fact of closure must be made known to the members and the public, a company must give a previous notice of not less than seven days in the form of an advertisement in some newspaper circulating in the district in which the registered office of the company is situated. Provisions regarding the closure of register must be strictly followed by the company, otherwise the company and every officer of the company who is in default shall be punishable with fine extending to five hundred rupees a day as long as the default continues. In practice the companies generally close the register half yearly or prior to the holding of the annual general meeting of the shareholders. This provision helps companies to determine their membership and then to send dividend warrants and notices of annual general meeting to their members. The register is also closed when the half-yearly dividend is declared or a call is made. No transfers can take place during the period when the register is so closed.

Provisions for Inspection of Register

Section 163 of the Act has laid down following provisions regarding the place of keeping and inspection of register of members :

Section 163 of the Companies Act, 1956, provides that the register of members commencing from the date of the registration of the company as well as index of members be kept at the registered office of the company. The same section further empowers the company to keep the register, index and returns at any place within the city, town or village in which the registered office is situated provided :

(i) Such other place is approved by the general meeting by passing a special resolution to this effect.

(ii) That the Registrar has been supplied in advance with a copy of the proposed special resolution.

However, the Central Government may make rules either for preservation or destruction of such documents — register of members, indexes, returns, etc.

Such register index must be kept open for inspection of the general public every day not less than two hours during business hours. The register is not open for inspection when it is statutorily closed. Every member or a debenture-holder has a right to inspect and to take extracts from such register without paying any fee. But if he requires a copy of such register or index, he must pay 37 paise for every hundred words or a fraction thereof. The company is bound to send such a copy to that member within a period of ten days commencing from the day next after the day on which the request to that effect has been received by the company. Non-working days are to be excluded while counting these ten days. An outsider can inspect the register and make extracts from it by paying a fee of one rupee for each inspection. If he desires to have a copy of it, he can get it by paying 37 paise per hundred words. If a company refuses to give facilities for inspection or to make extracts from the register and to give a copy of it, then the company and every officer in default is liable in respect to each offence to a fine extending to fifty rupees a day till the default continues. On an application by a member the Court can compel an immediate inspection and direct the company to allow to make extracts and to send a copy forthwith.

Rectification of Register of Members

1. The Companies (Amendment) Act, 1988 omitted Sections 155 and 156 relating to the rectification of register of members Section 21 with effect form 13-5-1991. The provisions regarding rectification are incorporated under Section 111 from sub-sections 4 to 7. The powers granted to the Court have now been entrusted in the Company Law Board which is empowered to decide applications for rectification of register of members. It is empowered to exercise judicial and quasi judicial powers. It may reject an application for rectification of pass interim orders. It can decide the title of the rightful holders. It may pass orders as regards payment of dividend, bonus shares and issue of rights shares. Thus it has been invested with wide powers and can pass any orders it deems fit after hearing all the parties to the case.

2. Section III of the Act. It gives power to the company or any of its member or the outside party to get the order of rectification from the Company Law Board. This Section provides that if the name of any person (a) is without sufficient cause is entered in the register of the company or (b) after having been entered in the register is without sufficient cause omitted therefrom or (c) if default is made or (d) unnecessary delay takes place in entering on the register the fact of having become or ceased to be a member, such a person can apply to the Company Law Board for rectification of register of members accordingly. On an application by the aggrieved party the Board can either reject the application or order rectification. If the Board orders rectification, it can direct the company to pay any damages and costs to the aggrieved party. The Board has power to take into consideration any question which is necessary or expedient to decide in connection with the application for rectification. Section 156 of the old Act regarding notice to the Registrar of rectification of register has been deleted under the Amendment Act of 1988.

3. The Sub-section 11. It provides that "In the case of a private company which is not a subsidiary of a public company where the right to any shares or interest of a member in or debentures of a company is transmitted by a sale thereof held by a Court or other public authority, the provisions of Sub-sections 4 to 7 shall apply as if the company were a public company." According to this Sub-section, the Board can entertain an application and pass orders for transmission of shares or debentures of a private company which is not a subsidiary of a public company if such transmission is by way of a sale held by a Court or other public authority. However, it appears that in the aforesaid situation no petition will lie against a private company which is a subsidiary of a public company which is not perhaps the intention of the Parliament.

4. The Sub-section 9. It provides, "If any default is made in giving effect to the orders of the Company Law Board under this Sub-section, the company, and every officer of the company who is in default shall be punishable with fine which may extend to one thousand rupees and with a further fine which may extend to one hundred rupees for every day after the first day after which the default continues." According to this Sub-section the company and every officer of the company who is in default may be fined upto rupees one thousand and a further fine of rupees one hundred per day till the default continues.

Foreign Register

A. (1) A company which has a share capital or which has issued debentures, may, if so authorised by its articles, keep in any state or country outside India a branch register of members or debenture holders resident in that state or country (in this Act called a foreign register).

(2) The Company shall, within [1][thirty days] from the date of the opening of any foreign register, file with the Registrar notice of the situation of the office where such register is kept; and in the event of any change in the situation of such office or of its discontinuance, shall, within [2][thirty days] from the date of such change or discontinuance, as the case may be, file notice with the Registrar of such change or discontinuance.

1. Substituted by Act 31 of 1965, section 62 and Schedule for "one month" w.e.f. 15-10-1965.
2. *Ibid.*

(3) If default is made in complying with the requirements of sub-section (2), the company, and every officer of the company who is in default, shall be punishable with fine which may extend of [1][five hundred rupees] for every day during which the default continues (Section 157).

B. Provisions as to foreign registers.—(1) A foreign register shall be deemed to be part of the company's register (in this section called the "principal register" of members or of debenture holders, as the case may be.

(2) A foreign register shall be kept, shall be open to inspection and may be closed, and extracts may be taken therefrom and copies thereof may be required, in the same manner, *mutatis mutandis*, as is applicable to the principal register under this Act, except that the advertisement before closing the register shall be inserted in some newspaper circulating in the district wherein the foreign register in kept.

(3) (*a*) The Central Government may, by notification in the Official Gazette, direct that the provisions of clause (*b*) shall applies for the time being, the decision of any competent Court in that State or country outside India.

(*b*) If a foreign register is kept by a company in any State or country to which a direction under clause (*a*) applies for the time being, the decision of any competent Court in that State or country in regard to the rectification of the register shall have the same force and effect as if it were the decision of a competent Court in India.

(4) The company shall—

(a) transmit to its registered office in India a copy of every entry in any foreign register as soon as may be after the entry is made; and

(b) keep at such office a duplicate of every foreign register duly entered up from time to time.

(5) Every such duplicate shall, for all the purposes of this Act, be deemed to be part of the principal register.

(6) Subject to the provisions of this section with respect to duplicate registers, the shares of debentures registered in any foreign register shall be distinguished from the shares or debentures registered in the principal register and in every other foreign register; and no transaction with respect to any shares or debentures registered in a foreign register shall, during the continuance of that registration, be registered in any other register.

(7) The company may discontinue the keeping of any foreign register; and thereupon all entries in that register shall be transferred

1. Substituted for "fifty rupees" by the companies (Amendment) Act, 2000, w.e.f. 13-12-2000.

to some other foreign register kept by the company in the same part of world or to the principal register.

(8) Subject to the provisions of this Act, a company may, by its articles, make such regulations as it thinks fit in regard to its foreign registers.

(9) It default is made in complying with sub-section (4), the company, and every officer of the company who is in default, shall be punishable with fine which may extend to [*five hundred rupees*].

Principal Register *Vs.* Foreign Register

(1) Compulsory. While principal register is compulsory for every company, a company having share capital and having authority given by its articles in that behalf may keep a foreign register.

(2) Maintenance. While the principal register is to be maintained at the companys' registered office only a duplicate copy of a foreign register is kept at the company's registered office.

(3) Continuation. While principal register cannot be discontinued so long as the company carries on its business it is not so in the case of a foreign register.

(4) Rectification. While the principal register can be rectified by an Indian Court, the foreign register can be rectified by a Court of the foreign country where company's branch office is situated if the Indian Government approved the same by notification in its Official Gazette.

QUESTIONS

1. What is the meaning of membership of a company? How will you test the membership of a company? Distinguish between a member and a shareholder.
2. Explain the meaning of membership. Is it essential that a member of a company should also be the shareholder of company?
3. "Every shareholder of a company is also known as the member of company while every member may not be its shareholder." Comment.
4. Who can become the member of a company? What is the position of a minor in this regard?
5. Who may become the member of a company? Explain the methods of acquiring and termination of membership of a company.
6. How can a person become and cease to become a member of a company?
7. Explain Rights and Duties of the Members of a company.
8. "The members of a company collectively have Statutory Rights, some of which are enforceable by only a majority and others by a particular majority and still others by a particular minority." Discuss.

9. Describe the individual and collective rights of the members of a company.

PRACTICAL PROBLEMS

1. X allows his name, apart from any agreement to become a member, to appear on the register of members. He also holds himself out as a member of the company. The company goes into liquidation and his name is put on the list of contributories. He now seeks to avoid liability. Advise him.
   [**Hint.** X will be deemed to be a member of the company on the ground of acquiescence or estoppel].
2. An application was made by a father as a guardian of his minor daughter for certain shares. The company registered the shares in the name of the daughter described as minor. The company went into liquidation and the name of the father was placed on the list of contributories. Is he liable as such?
   [**Hint.** No (Palaniappa Mudaliar *Vs.* Official Liquidator. Pasupathi Bank Ltd.)].
3. S carried on business under an assumed name. He took shares in that name and became insolvent. His trustee in insolvency tries to avoid liability as a shareholder. Is S liable?
   [**Hint.** Yes (Central Klondyke Gold Mining Co., Re, Savigny's Case, (1899) W.N. 1)].
4. G agreed that he would 'place' 1,000 shares for a company in consideration of being appointed its agent. The company registered G as a holder of 1,000 shares but did not inform him of the fact? Is G a shareholder?
   [**Hint.** No (Monarch Insurance Co., Gorrisen's Case, Re (1973) 8 Ch. App. 507)].
5. A member requested the company in which he held shares to provide a copy of the register of members and paid the necessary fees. The company did reply but after 15 days. What remedy does he have?
   [**Hint.** Refer to Section 1631].
6. X, a builder, wrote to a company offering to take 300 shares on the condition that a contract for certain repairs to the company's property would be given to him. The application was accepted, X received his shares and the directors resolved that he should be given the contract. Before any contract was given to him, the company went into liquidation. Is X liable as a contributory for the unpaid balance on his shares?
   [**Hint.** No (Aldborough Hotel Co. Re, Simpson's Case)].

11

Borrowing Power : Debentures, Public Deposits and Investments

Indian Companies Act does not express explicitly any powers for the companies to borrow money. A company has, however, an implied power to borrow money on the security of its assets. It can borrow money even though its memorandum and articles of association are silent in this regard. But Non-trading Companies, which are formed to promote Art, Science, Commerce, Religion etc., are not empowered to borrow money. They can borrow money only if they are empowered by their memorandum of association which decides the maximum limit of the loan to be taken by the company and its articles of association explain the procedure to borrow. Generally, the memorandum fixes a limit on the borrowing capacity of the company. The directors of the company are entitled to borrow upto the specified amount. If the company requires more loans than this limit, it can do so only after getting the resolution passed in its general meeting.

RESTRICTIONS ON THE BORROWING POWERS OF A COMPANY

1. To Obey the Provisions of the Act. A company must obey the provisions of Indian Companies Act, given under various sections from 149 to 293, while borrowing the money. No company can borrow the money outside of the powers conferred under the provisions of the Act.

2. Time to Borrow. According to Section 149(l) of the Companies Act, a private company is entitled to exercise its borrowing powers immediately after its incorporation. But a public company can exercise its borrowing powers only after getting the certificate of commencement of business. According to Section 149(10) of the Act, however, a simultaneous issue of shares and debentures can be made by a public company just after its incorporation.

3. Borrowing Limits of Memorandum of Association. Though the trading companies have an implied power to borrow money but a company can borrow money subject to the restrictions placed by the memorandum of association or articles of association or any statute.

The directors are free to exercise the powers specified in the memorandum and articles of association of the company in any manner, they consider fit.

4. Loan not Exceeding the Total of Capital and Reserves. Section 293 states that the directors of a public company shall not borrow money, without the consent of their company taken in general meeting, which, together with the money already borrowed by them, exceeds the total of paid up share capital and its free reserves.

5. Restriction on the Charge of Assets. A trading company is empowered to borrow money for its requirements. If the articles of association of the company do not contain anything to the contrary, the loans raised by a company also create a charge on the uncalled money of the company. But the loans do not create any charge on the reserve capital of company. A company can take loan on the charge on its reserve capital.

6. Temporary Loans. They are loans repayable on demand or repayable within six months from the date of such loan. It does not include loans raised for purpose of financing expenditure of capital nature *e.g.* debts on account of purchase of machinery on deferred payment basis and acceptance by a bank of deposits from the public repayable on demand or otherwise.

CONDITIONS OF LAWFUL BORROWING

1. Trading Company. A trading company can borrow money even if its memorandum of association and articles of association do not speak anything in this regard. However, this power may be restricted by its memorandum or articles of association. The trading company has the power to borrow money, as well as to charge its assets by way of security for the amount borrowed by it.

2. Non Trading Company. A company which is not established to earn profit but for the purpose of promotion of art, science, culture and commerce etc., has no implied power to borrow. It can borrow money only if there is an express power in its memorandum of association in this regard.

While borrowing, a company must observe the restrictions placed upon it in this regard by Indian Companies Act, its memorandum of association and its articles of association. If a company violates any of the restrictions placed upon it in this regard, the borrowing will be treated *ultra vires.*

ULTRA VIRES BORROWINGS

Meaning

A company can borrow money for its various requirements and create a charge on its assets as security for the borrowed money within the limits of the provisions of Indian Companies Act, its memorandum of association and its articles of association. Borrowings beyond these provisions will be *ultra vires.* Such borrowing and the security given for the borrowing is *null* and *void*, and it cannot be ratified.

Types

1. Borrowings *ultra vires* the company or the borrowings beyond the authority given to the company by its memorandum and articles of association.

2. Borrowings are *ultra vires* if these are beyond the authority of the directors.

Legal Effects

1. Borrowings *Ultra Vires* the Memorandum of a Company. Any act *ultra vires* the memorandum of association of a company is completely *null and void.* It can never be ratified by the company, even if all the shareholders agree to do so. This also applies in the case of the borrowing powers of a company. If something is given in the memorandum of association regarding the borrowing powers, the company is bound to follow that. If the company borrows money beyond that power, it will be called borrowing *ultra vires* the memorandum of the company. Such a loan is completely void and not recognised as a loan against the company. Lender of such loan cannot sue the company, nor can he confiscate any security given on such loan. But the following remedies are available in such a case :

(i) *Injunction Order :* If the company has not used the money borrowed so far, the lender may get an injunction order against the company and restrain the company from using the amount for any purpose and may recover the money.

(ii) *A Tracing Order :* If the money so borrowed has been spent in purchasing some asset and the asset can be traced out, the lender may get tracing order against the company and he may claim that particular asset. If no specific asset could be recognised, the lender is still entitled to have restored to him any increase to the assets, which is shown to be due to the *ultra vires* borrowings, in the event of winding up of the company.

(iii) *Subrogate the Creditors :* If the company has used the borrowed money in paying off the loans of the company, the lender is empowered to step into the shoes of the creditors who have been paid off and he can subrogate their right. Thus he can be creditor of the company to the extent to which the money has been so used but he has no right to any security held by such creditors.

(iv) *Claim the Damages from Directors :* The lender may claim damages from the directors. But this can be possible only if he acted in good faith while granting the loan. He cannot claim the damages from directors upon the ground that he was misled because the

Memorandum of Association of a company is a public document which can be inspected by anyone.

2. Borrowings *Ultra Vires* the Articles of Association but *Intra Vires* the Memorandum. If the loan taken by the company is, *ultra vires* its Articles of Association only but is *intra vires* its memorandum, it can be made valid. For this, the company will have to alter its Articles of Association to that effect by passing a special resolution.

3. Borrowings *Ultra Vires* the Directors. Sometimes the directors of a company borrow the money which is *ultra vires* their powers but *intra vires* the memorandum and articles of association of their company. In this case, the legal position is very simple. The company may in its general meeting, ratify such acts of the directors and the loan shall become valid and binding upon the company. Even if the company does not ratify the acts of its directors, the doctrine of indoor management will apply and protect a lender who has lent the money to the company. For getting protection under this doctrine in the circumstances, he will have to prove that he granted the money in good faith and no knowledge of the fact that it was *ultra vires* the directors. Thus, in case of borrowings *ultra vires* the directors, the lender has almost no risk. However, the company can claim an indemnity from the directors.

DEBENTURE

A debenture means a document which certifies that the company has taken loan from the person, of the amount and on the terms mentioned in it. When company wants to raise some loan for a long period, it issues debentures.

Definition

1. Section 2 (12) of the Indian Companies Act, 1956. "Debenture includes debentures stock, bonds and any other security of a company, whether constituting a charge on the assets of the company or not." This definition presents only the legal form and meaning of debenture. It does not specify the real meaning and nature of a debenture.

2. Palmer. "The term debenture signifies any instrument issued under common seal of the company, evidencing a debt, the essence of it being the admission of indebtedness."

3. Tophan. "Debenture is a document issued by a company as evidence of debt to the holder, usually arising out of a loan and most commonly secured charge.

On the basis of above definitions, it may be said that a debenture is a certificate issued by a company under its common seal which certifies the loan taken by the company.

KINDS OF DEBENTURES

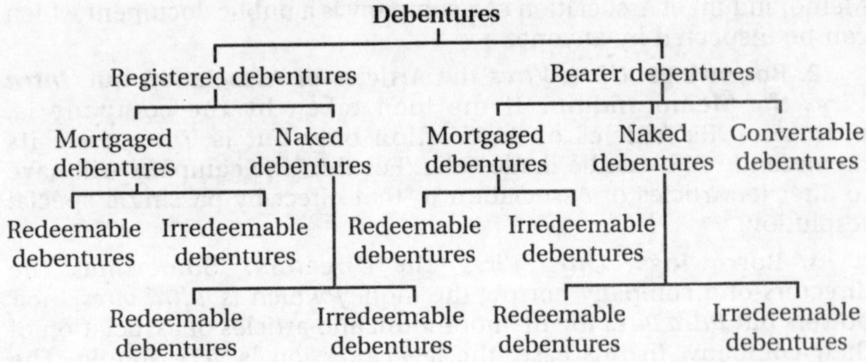

1. Registered Debentures. These are the debentures registered in the register of debentures of the company. The company maintains a register for the debentures issued by it. The date of the issue, the amount of the debentures, the rate of interest, maturity date and the relevant terms and conditions are mentioned in this register. The holders of such debentures can transfer their debenture according to the procedure laid down by the Act.

2. Bearer Debentures. It means the debenture which can be transferred only by delivery. The interest and the principal amount of such debentures are paid to the holders of such debentures who have not to adopt any procedure or to pay any stamp duty for the transfer.

3. Mortgaged Debentures. These are also called secured debentures. These create a charge on the fixed assets of the company. If the company is unable to make the payment the debenture holders can realise their money from the assets of the company that have been mortgaged.

4. Naked Debentures. These are also called Unsecured Debentures. The company does not offer any guarantee for the payment of principal amount or interest of such debentures. If the company is liquidated, the holders of such debentures will be 'treated as unsecured creditors only.

5. Redeemable Debentures. These are the debentures issued by the company for a certain period and after the expiry of this period company makes the payment of these debentures. Such debentures can be reissued, if articles allow it.

6. Irredeemable Debentures. These are the debentures not redeemed by the company during its life. Such debentures can be redeemed by the company only on the winding up of the company. But the interest on such debentures is paid regularly.

7. Convertible Debentures. In this case option is given to the debenture holder to convert them into equity or preference shares after a certain period, but vice versa is not allowed. They can be fully or partly convertible debentures.

SHAREHOLDER AND DEBENTURE-HOLDER

A person who holds the shares of a company, is called shareholder of the company. A person who has given loan to the company and hold its debentures, is called debenture-holder.

DISTINCTION BETWEEN A SHAREHOLDER AND A DEBENTURE-HOLDER

Basis of difference	*Shareholder*	*Debenture-holder*
1. Membership	He is a member of the company.	He is not a member of the company.
2. Right to Vote	He is empowered to present and vote at the meetings of the company. company.	He is not empowered to be present and vote at the meetings of the company.
3. Rate of Return	He gets dividend from the company at the rate which is not certain.	He gets the interest at certain rate.
4. Certainty of Return	He is not assured of getting the dividend on his share. The company may or may not declare the dividend on its share capital.	A company will have to pay the interest on debentures compulsorily.
5. Refund of money	He gets the refund on his money only in case of winding up of the company.	He gets refund of his money after a certain period.
6. Preference	He is paid at the last if a company goes into liquidation.	He gets a preference in the payment of their money if the company goes into liquidation.
7. Capital or Loan	These constitute the capital of a company.	These constitute the loan for a company.

ISSUE OF DEBENTURES

Legal Provisions

Section 292 of the Indian Companies Act states that :

1. Power to issue debentures rests with the board of directors of a company.

2. Debentures can be issued at any time by all the companies, *i.e.*, a public company or a private company.

3. Debentures may be issued at par, at premium or at discount.

4. Debentures can be issued by a company through prospectus or privately, as it may think fit.

5. The legal requirements for the issue and allotment of debentures are the same as in case of the issue and allotment of shares except the following provisions :

(i) The provision of minimum subscription does apply for the issue of debentures.

(ii) A company can freely issue its debentures at discount.

(iii) The company is not bound to file return of debenture allotment with the registrar of companies.

6. The debenture's certificate must be delivered within three months of the allotment, unless otherwise specified in the terms of issue.

Procedure

1. Permission of Controller of Capital Issue. If the company wants to issue the debentures of more than Rs. 25,000,000, it must get the permission of controller of capital issues. If the proposed issue, together with the debentures already issued by the company, exceeds the aggregate of paid up share capital and free reserves of the company, the company must get the permission of its general body by passing an ordinary resolution.

2. Resolution by Board of Directors. After getting the permission of controller of capital issues, if required, the board of directors must pass a resolution stating the terms of issue.

3. Permission of Reserve Bank. To issue the bearer debentures, company must obtain the permission of Reserve Bank of India.

4. Consent of Trustees. If the debentures are issued under a trust deed, a company must obtain the written consent of all the trustees and must prepare the trust deed.

5. Filing the Particulars of Charge with the Registrar. If the debentures to be issued create any charge on the assets of the company, the company must file a statement regarding such a charge with the Registrar of Companies within 21 days of creating the charge and must obtain a certificate from the registrar to this effect.

6. Prospectus or Statement in lieu of Prospectus with the Registrar. If the company wants to make the issue of debentures to the public, it must issue a prospectus or a statement in lieu of prospectus and copy of the same must be filed with the registrar.

7. Register of Debentures. After the allotment has been made, all the particulars about each debenture-holder must be entered in the register of debenture-holders.

8. Restriction Regarding Stock Exchange. If the company has specifically mentioned in its prospectus that proposed debentures are being transacted in a particular stock exchange or that the company is applying to get the permission for such transactions, the allotment of debentures will be void if the company does not get permission of the stock exchange.

SEBI guidelines, 2000 for disclosure and investor protection pertaining to debentures - Fully Convertible Debentures/Partially Convertible Debentures/Non-Convertible Debentures (FCDs/PCDs/NCDs)

(1) *Purpose of Issue* : Companies can issue debentures for any purpose except for acquiring shareholding or providing loan to any company in the same group. The restriction is, however, not applicable to the issue of fully convertible debentures providing conversion within a period of 18 months.

(2) *Issue of fully convertible debentures with a conversion period of more than 36 months* : If the FCDs are proposed to be issued having a conversion period of more than 36 months, the conversion is to be made optional with 'put' and 'call' option.

(3) *Compulsory credit rating :*

(i) No public or rights issue of debt instruments shall be made unless credit rating from a credit rating agency has been obtained and disclosed in the prospectus/offer document.

(ii) In case of Issue of Rs. 100 crores or more, two ratings from two different credit rating agencies must be obtained.

(iii) All credit rating including the unaccepted credit ratings must be disclosed.

(iv) Besides, all credit ratings obtained during the three years preceding the issue for any listed security of the issuer company must be disclosed in the prospectus/offer document.

(4) *Pre-determination of premium on conversion and time of conversion :* The premium on conversion of FCDs and PCDs and time of conversion, in stages, if any, is to be predetermined and stated in the prospectus.

(5) *Interest rate :* The interest rate on debentures is freely determinable.

(6) *Appointment of debenture trustees :* The names of debentures trustees should be stated in the prospectus and the trust deed should be executed within six months of the closure of the issue. In the case of debentures with maturity period of 18 months or less, the appointment of debenture trustees is not required. The trustees must be vested with the requisite power for protecting the interest of debenture holders including a right to appoint a nominee director in consultation with institutional debentures holders.

(7) *Debenture redemption reserve :* Creation of Debentures Redemption Reserve (DRR), on the prescribed basis, is compulsory

except for debentures with maturity period of 18 months or less. Again, the requirement of creation of DRR shall not be applicable in case of infrastructure companies. Creation of DRR is required to be done on the following basis :

(i) A moratorium upto the date of commercial production can be provided for creation of DRR in respect of debentures raised for project finance.

(ii) The DRR may be created in equal instalments or higher amounts, if profits so permit.

(iii) In the case of PCDs, DRR should be created in respect of non-convertible portion of debenture issue on the same lines as applicable to fully non-convertible debenture issue. In respect of convertible issues by new companies, the creation of DRR should commence from the year the company earns profits for the remaining life of debentures.

(iv) Companies may distribute dividends out of general reserves in certain year if residual profits after transfer to DRR are inadequate to distribute reasonable dividends.

(v) DRR will be considered as part of general reserve for consideration of bonus issue proposals and for price fixation related to post tax return.

(vi) Company must create DRR equivalent to 50 per cent of debenture before debenture redemption commences.

(vii) Drawal from DRR is permissible only after 10 per cent of the debenture liability has been actually redeemed by the company.

(8) *Distribution of dividends* :

(i) In case of new companies, distribution of dividend shall require approval of the debenture trustee and the lead institutions, if any.

(ii) In the case of existing companies, prior permission of the lead institutions for declaring dividend exceeding 20 per cent or as per loan covenants is necessary if the company does not comply with institutional condition regarding interest and debt service coverage ratio.

(iii) (a) Dividends may be distributed out of profits of particular years only after transfer of requisite amount to DRR.

(b) If residual profits after transfer to DRR are inadequate to distribute reasonable dividends, the company may distribute dividends out of general reserve.

(9) *Redemption of Debentures :* Company shall redeem debentures as per the offer document.

(10) *Conversion to be optional :* Where the conversion of debentures (in part or whole) is to take place at or after 18 months from the date

of allotment but before 36 months, such conversion should be made optional at the hands of the debenture holder.

(11) *Disclosure of redemption amount, Period of Maturity, Yield:* Redemption amount, period of maturity, yield on redemption for the PCDs/NCDs are to be indicated in the prospectus.

(12) *Discount on non-convertible portion of PCD :* Discount on the non-convertible portions of PCD in case they are traded and procedure for their purchase on spot trading basis should be disclosed in the prospectus.

(13) *Rollover of PCD/NCD :* If the non-convertible portion of PCD/NCD issued by a listed company, value of which exceeds Rs. 50 lacs, are to be rolled over without change in the interest rate, a compulsory option is to be given to those debenture holders who want to withdraw and encash from the debenture programme. Roll over must be done only in cases where the debenture holders have sent their positive consent and not on the basis of the non-receipt or their negative reply.

Before roll over of any NCDs or non-convertible portion of the PCDs, fresh credit rating must be obtained with a period of six months before roll over and fresh trust deed should be made. There is, however, no need to create fresh security in the event of roll over of debentures, if the existing trust deed or the securities documents provide for continuation of the security till redemption of debentures.

The letter of option for roll over or conversion of debentures, value of which exceeds Rs. 50 lakhs issued by a listed company, must be forwarded to SEBI for vetting through an eligible merchant banker.

(14) *Other disclosures :* The offer document/prospectus shall contain :

(a) Premium amount on conversion, time of conversion.

(b) In case of PCDs/NCDs, redemption amount, period of maturity, yield on redemption of the PCDs/NCDs.

(c) Full information relating to the terms of offer or purchase including the name(s) of the party offering to purchase the khokhas (non-convertible portion of PCDs).

(d) The discount at which such offer is made and the effective price for the investor as a result of such discount.

(e) The existing and future equity and long-term debt ratio.

(f) Servicing behaviour on existing debentures, payment of due interest on due dates on term loans and debentures.

(g) That the certificate from a financial institution or bankers about their no objection for a second or *pari passu* charge being created in favour of the trustees to the proposed debenture issue has been obtained.

(15) *Disclosure and Creation of charge :* The offer document shall specifically state the assets on which security shall be created and

shall also state the ranking of the charge(s). In case of second or residual charge or subordinated obligation, the offer document shall clearly state the risks associated with such subsequent charge. The relevant consent for creation of security such as *pari passu* letter, consent of the lessor of the land in case of leasehold land, etc. shall be obtained and submitted to the debenture trustee before opening of issue of debentures.

Further, the offer document shall also state the security/asset cover to be maintained, the basis for computation of the security/asset cover, the valuation methods and periodicity of such valuation. The security/asset cover shall be arrived at after reduction of the liabilities having a first/prior charge, in case debentures are secured by second or subsequent charge. Where the debentures have been issued having a maturity period not exceeding eighteen months, it is not necessary to appoint a trustee. If the company proposes to create a charge for such debentures, it must be filed with ROC. Where no charge is to be created, *i.e.*, in respect of unsecured debentures, the compliance of the provisions of Deposit Rules must be ensured. Since unsecured debentures have been treated as deposits under the Companies (Acceptance of Deposits) Rules, 1975.

The proposal to create a charge or otherwise must be disclosed in the prospectus along with its implications.

(16) *Monitoring* : The lead financial institution/investment institution is required to monitor the progress in respect of debentures for project finance modernisation/expansion/diversification/normal capital expenditure. If debentures are raised for working capital funds, the lead bank should monitor.

(17) *Certificate from auditor* : Trustee shall obtain from the auditors a certificate in respect of utilization of funds during the implementation period of projects. In the case of debentures for working capital, certificate should be obtained at the end of each accounting year.

(18) The Merchant Banker shall file with SEBI along with the draft offer document, a certificate from the bankers that the assets on which security is to be created are free from any encumbrances and the necessary permission to mortgage the assets, has been obtained or a no objection certificate has been obtained from the financial institution or banks for a second or *pari passu* charge, if the assets are encumbered.

(19) *Creation of security* : The security must be created within six months from the date of issue of debentures. If for any reasons, the company is not in a position to create security within 12 months from the date of issue of debentures, the company shall be liable to pay 2 per cent penal interest to debenture holders. If security is not created even after 18 months, a meeting of the debenture holders should be called within 21 days to explain the reason and the date by which the security would be created. The issue proceeds shall be kept in an

escrow account until the documents for creation of security as stated in the offer document are executed. The trustees are required to supervise the information of the conditions regarding creation of security and the debenture redemption reserve.

Additional Guidelines

(1) *Prohibition of debt instruments :* A listed company shall not make an issue of debentures unless a Category I Merchant Banker, holding a valid certificate of registration issued by SEBI has been appointed to manage the issue.

(2) *Duty of Merchant Banker :* The Merchant Banker, acting as the Lead Manager, shall ensure that the offer document provides a true, correct and fair view of the state of affairs of the company which is adequate for the investors to arrive at a well informed investment decision and is in compliance with SEBI Rules, Regulations and Guidelines and requirements of other laws.

The draft of the offer document shall be submitted by the Merchant banker to SEBI at least 6 weeks before the issue is scheduled to open. SEBI shall make suggestions, if any, within 3 weeks. The Merchant Banker shall submit to SEBI the offer document containing the modifications suggested by SEBI.

(3) *Listing of debt instruments :* SEBI has removed the restriction regarding prior listing of equity before listing of debt on the stock exchanges. Thus, debentures of even unlisted companies may be listed.

Some New Financial Instruments

Many new financial instruments have come up in the money and capital markets. Some of them are given below :

(1) *Zero coupon debentures/bonds :* Zero coupon bonds are those bonds that are sold at a large discount on the nominal value. The maturity period of these bonds vary from 5 to 12 years. On maturity, the debenture is redeemed at par value.

In India, zero interest convertible bonds have also been issued by companies. Since the investor is not entitled to any interest on the bonds, the conversion price is suitably adjusted to take care of the interest loss of the investor. These bonds were first issued in India by Mahindra and Mahindra Ltd.

Advantages to the company : The main advantage to the company is that there is no burden of servicing the debentures during the gestation period of the project. By linking the redemption/conversion period with the commissioning of the project, the company can ensure that there are considerable savings in project cost and there is no cash outflow for servicing of the debentures during the implementation stage of the project.

Advantages to the investors : The interest being only notional is not subject to tax. However, on sale or disposal it would attract capital gains tax.

Zero coupon bonds are attractive to investors particularly during periods when interest rates are declining.

(2) *Warrants :* A warrant confers an option to the investor to buy a specified number of equity shares at a specified price over a specified period of time. The warrant holder has to surrender the warrant and pay some cash known as the exercise price of the warrant to purchase the shares. On exercise of the option, the warrant holder becomes the shareholder. A number of companies in India have issued such warrants. Presently, SEBI guidelines, in this regard, require 10 per cent of the price to be payable at the time of allotment of warrants and compulsory conversion of warrants into shares within a period of 18 months. For detailed SEBI guidelines in this regard, refer to discussion entitled 'SEBI Guidelines for Preferential Allotments'—Chapter 9.

(3) *Detachable warrants :* These warrants are issued with debentures-convertible or non-convertible-or with equity and are immediately detachable. The detached warrants can be traded in the secondary market as separate instruments.

Puttable warrants : These warrants confer a right on the investor to sell the warrant back to the company at a fixed price before the expiry of a fixed period.

Wedding warrants : These warrants are attached to the host debentures and can be exercised only if the host debenture is surrendered.

Deep discount bonds : These bonds are sold at a large discount on their nominal value and mature at par value. There are no interest payments on these bonds and the investors obtain their return as accretion to the par value of the instrument over its life. The maturity period of this bond can extend as far as 25 years with an option to the investors to withdraw at the end of certain period, say 3 years or 5 years from the date of allotment. IDBI in January 1992 and again in Feb.-March 1996 (Rs. 5,300 to become Rs. 2,00,000 at the end of 25 years) issued such bonds as an unsecured instrument.

4. *PCD/NCD with buy-back arrangements :* PCD/NCD may be offered to the investors along with a facility to buy-back the non-convertible portion of the debentures (khokha) by financial institution/bank/ financial services company at a discount on the face value.

As per SEBI guidelines, buy-back of 'khokha' has to be made on spot delivery basis and procedure for their buy-back and their tradability should be disclosed in the offer document.

5. *Secured Premium Notes (SPN) :* SPN is a new kind of instrument which was issued by the TISCO Ltd. to its shareholders in June 1992. The salient features of the instrument are :

(i) The SPN is issued at a nominal value and does not carry any interest.

(ii) The SPN is redeemed by repayment in several instalments at a premium over its face value. The premium amount is distributed equally over the period of maturity of the instalment.

(iii) The SPN may carry a detachable warrant which will give the holder a right to claim allotment of certain share or shares for cash at a certain price. This right can be exercised by the holder after a certain period from the date of allotment of SPN.

(iv) The instrument is secured by a mortgage of all the immovable properties of the company.

6. *Zero coupon convertible notes :* These are debts convertible into equity shares of the issuer. If investors choose to convert, they forego all the accrued and unpaid interest. These convertibles are generally issued with put option (*i.e.*, buy-back arrangement) to the investor. The investor gains in the event of appreciation in the value of the equity shares. Even if the appreciation does not materialise, the investor has the benefit of a steady stream of implied interest income.

Promoters' Contribution and Lock in Period

The term "promoters contribution" will mean contribution by promoters, directors, friends, relatives and associates. In the case of FCDS, the intention is that over and above the proposed issue amount of FCDS, the promoters, directors, friends, relatives and associates should bring in by way of contribution to equity amount equivalent to one-third of the amount proposed to be issued as FCDS. Likewise in case of PCDS, one-third amount of equity should be with reference to convertible portion of PCDS. Alternatively out of total issue of FCD or total issue of PCD, they can take promoters' quota of 25 per cent or 20 per cent, as the case may be, at the time of issue, with the same conversion price as stipulated for public.

The trustees to the debenture-holders will supervise the implementation of the conditions regarding creation of security for the debentures and regarding the DRR.

Debentures with voting rights not to be issued hereafter.—No company shall after the commencement of this Act, issue any debentures carrying voting rights at any meeting of the company, whether generally or in respect of particular classes of business.

Debenture trust deed.—(1) A trust deed for securing any issue of debentures shall be in such form and shall be executed within such period as may be prescribed.

(2) A copy of the trust deed shall be open to inspection to any member or debenture holder of the company and he shall also be entitled to obtain copies of such trust deed on payment of such sum as may be prescribed.

(3) If a copy of the trust deed is not made available for inspection or is not given to any member or debenture holder, the company and every officer of the company who is in a default, shall be punishable, for each offence, with fine which may extend to five hundred rupees for every day during which the offence continues.

CHARGE

Meaning

The loan raised by a company may be of two types : unsecured and secured. When the company does not furnish any security to the loan lender for the loan taken by it, it is called unsecured loan. On the other hand, when the company furnishes some security for the loan, it is called secured loan. There are several methods of giving the security for the loan. Generally, the title over the security is transferred in favour of the lender with an assurance that if the company is unable to pay off its loan, the lender can realise his claim by the sale of that security. Such a transfer of title or such an assurance is called a charge created on the security. A charge is created by the borrowing company on its assets in favour of the lender.

Kinds of Charge

1. Fixed Charge. It is one which is created on particular assets of a permanent nature. It is created only through a mortgage and is created on the fixed assets such as building, machinery, land etc. It prevents the company from selling the property so charged so long as the loan is completely paid off. The mortgage may be either legal or equitable.

In case of legal mortgage, the legal ownership of the property is transferred to the creditor but the real possession of the property is not delivered. In case of equitable mortgage, the title deeds of the property are deposited with the creditor and the legal ownership and the possession of the property are not transferred. In both the cases, the borrowing company undertakes to deliver the possession of property, if it fails to pay the money of loan.

2. Floating Charge. It means a charge which is created by a company or, its assets for the time being. It is a charge on the assets of the company in general and covers all the assets and keeps on floating with the property which it is intended to cover. It does not attach to any specific property till the event, on which it is fixed, happens. In it the legal ownership or possession of properties is not transferred to the lender.

Section 125 of the Indian Companies Act states that a floating charge can be created only by a company and requires the registration with the registrar.

DISTINCTION BETWEEN FIXED CHARGE AND FLOATING CHARGE

Basis of difference	*Fixed Charge*	*Floating Charge*
1. Right to sell the property	The company cannot sell the property under it.	The company can sell the property under it.
2. Particular Assets	It is created only on particular assets.	It is created in generation of all the assets of the company.
3. Present and Future assets	It can be created only on the existing assets.	It can be created on the existing as well as the future assets.

Crystallisation of a Floating Charge

Crystallisation of a floating charge means that a floating charge becomes a fixed charge on the happening of a event specified in the document creating the charge. If a floating charge becomes a fixed charge by this method, the assets charged come under the same restrictions as are applicable in the case of fixed charge. A floating charge becomes fixed charge under the following circumstances :

1. When the company goes into liquidation.
2. When the company ceases to carry on its business.
3. When the debenture-holders have become entitled to realise their security for that purpose such as appointing a official receiver.

DISTINCTION BETWEEN MORTGAGE AND CHARGE

Basis of distinction	*Mortgage*	*Charge*
1. Creation	It is created by a contract between the parties.	It has a limited scope. It is created by the acts of the parties or by the operation of law.
2. Transfer of interest in the property	The interest for the property is transferred to the creditor.	Interest in the property is not transferred.
3. Period	Generally, it is for a certain period.	Generally it is forever.
4. Scope		Its scope is wider.

REGISTRATION OF CHARGES

Sections 124 to Sections 145 of the Companies Act deal with registration of charges. The expression "charge" includes a mortgage (Section 124).

Certain charges to be void against liquidator or creditors unless registered.—(1) Subject to the provisions of this part, every charge created on or after the 1st day of April, 1914, by a company and being a charge to which this section applies shall, so far as any security on the company's property or undertaking is conferred thereby, be void against the liquidator and any creditor of the company, unless the prescribed particulars of the charge, together with the instrument, if any, by which the charge is created or evidenced, or a copy thereof verified in the prescribed manner, are filed with the Registrar for registration in the manner required by this Act within [thirty] days after the date of its creation :

[Provided that the Registrar may allow the particulars and instrument or copy as aforesaid to be filed within thirty days next following the expiry of the said period of thirty days on payment of such additional fee not exceeding ten times the amount of fee specifies in Schedule X as the Registrar may determine, if the company satisfies the Registrar that it had sufficient cause for not filing the particulars and instrument or copy within that period.]

(2) Nothing in sub-section (1) shall prejudice any contract or obligation for the repayment of the money secured by the charge.

(3) When a charge becomes void under this section, the money secured thereby shall immediately become payable.

(4) This section applies to the following charges :

(a) a charge for the purpose of securing any issue of debentures;

(b) a charge on uncalled share capital of the company;

(c) a charge on any immovable property, whereever situate, or any interest therein;

(d) a charge on any book debts of the company;

(e) a charge, not being a pledge, on any movable property of the company;

(f) a floating charge on the undertaking or any property of the company including stock-in-trade;

(g) a charge on calls made but not paid;

(h) a change on a ship or any share in a ship;

(i) a charge on goodwill, on a patent or a license under a patent, on a trade mark, or on a copyright or a license under a copyright.

(5) In the case of a charge created out of India and comprising solely property situate outside India, [thirty] days after the date on which the instrument creating or evidencing the charge or a copy thereof could, in due course of post and if dispatched with due diligence, have been received in India, shall be substituted for [thirty] days after the date of the creation of the charge as the time within which the particulars and instrument or copy are to be filed with the Registrar.

(6) Where a charge is created in India but comprises property outside India, the instrument creating or purporting to create the charge under this section or a copy thereof verified in the prescribed manner, may be filed for registration, notwithstanding that further proceedings may be necessary to make the charge valid or effectual according to the law of the country in which the property is situated.

(7) Where a negotiable instrument has been given to secure the payment of any book debts of a company, the deposit of the instrument for the purpose of securing an advance to the company shall not, for the purposes of this section, be treated as a charge on those book debts.

(8) The holding of debentures entitling the holder to a charge on immovable property shall not, for the purposes of this section, be deemed to be an interest in immovable property (Section 125).

Date of notice of charge. Where any charge on any property of a company required to be registered under section 125 has been so registered, any person acquiring such property or any part thereof, or any share or interest therein, shall be deemed to have notice of the charge as from the date of such registration (Section 126).

Registration of charges on properties acquired subject to charge. (1) Where a company acquires any property which is subject to a charge of any such kind as would, if it had been created by the company after the acquisition of the property, have been required to be registered under this Part, the company shall cause the prescribed particulars of the charge, together with a copy (certified in the prescribed manner to be a correct copy) of the instrument, if any, by which the charge was created or is evidenced, to be delivered to the Registrar for registration in the manner required by this Act within [thirty] days after the date on which the acquisition is completed :

Provided that, if the property is situated and the charge was created, outside India, [thirty] days after the date on which a copy of the instrument could, in due course of post and if dispatched with due diligence, have been received in India shall be substituted for [thirty] days after the completion of the acquisition as the time within which the particulars and the copy of the instrument are to be delivered to the Registrar.

(2) If default is made in complying with sub-section (1), the company, and every officer of the company who is in default, shall be punishable with fine which may extend to [*five thousand rupees*] (Section 127).

Particulars in case of series of debentures entitling holders *pari passu.* Where a series of debentures containing, or giving by reference to any other instrument, any charge to the benefit of which debentures holders of that series are entitled *pari passu* is created by a company, it shall, for the purpose of section 125, be sufficient, if there are filed with the Registrar, within [thirty] days after the execution of the deed containing the charge or, if there is no such deed, after the execution of any debentures of the series, the following particulars:

(a) the total amount secured by the whole series;

(b) the dates of the resolutions authorizing the issue of the series and the date of the covering deed, if any, by which the security is created or defined;

(c) a general description of the property charged; and

(d) the names of the trustees, if any, for the debenture holders;

together with the deed containing the charge, or a copy of the deed verified in the prescribed manner, or if there is no such deed, one of the debentures of the series :

Provided that, where more than one issue is made of debentures in the series, there shall be filed with the Registrar, for entry in the register, particulars of the date and amount of each issue; but an omission to do this shall not affect the validity of the debentures issued (Section 128).

Particulars in case of commission, etc., on debentures. Where any commission, allowance or discount has been paid or made either directly or indirectly by a company to any person in consideration of his subscribing or agreeing to subscribe, whether absolutely or conditionally, for any debentures of the company, or procuring or agreeing to procure subscriptions, whether absolute or conditional, for any such debentures, the particulars required to be filed for registration under sections 125 and 128 shall include particulars as to the amount or rate per cent of the commission, discount or allowance so paid or made but an omission to do this shall not affect the validity of the debentures issued :

Provided that the deposit of any debentures as security for any debt of the company shall not, for the purpose of this section, be treated as the tissue of the debentures at a discount (Section 129).

Register of charges to be kept by Registrar. [(1) The Registrar shall, in respect of each company, cause to be kept a register containing the particulars of all the charges requiring registration under this Part.

(1A) Every company shall forward to the Registrar for being entered in the registrar kept under sub-section (1) the particulars of all the charges requiring registration under this Part in such form and manner, and after payment of, such fees as may be prescribed.

(1B) The particulars of the charges referred to in sub-section (1) shall relate to :

(a) in the case of a charge to the benefit of which the holders of a series of debentures are entitled, such particulars as are specified in sections 128 and 129;

(b) in the case of any other charge :

(i) if the charge is a charge created by the company, the date of its creation, and if the charge was a charge existing on property acquired by the company, the date of the acquisition of the property;

(ii) the amount secured by the charge;

(iii) short particulars of the property charged; and

(iv) the persons entitled to the charge.

(1C) The pages of the register shall be consecutively numbered and the Registrar shall :

(a) cause to be kept in such register in the prescribed form the documents of charges filed in such form and manner as may be prescribed; and

(b) sign or initial every page of such register.

(2) After entering the particulars of all the charges required under sub-section (1), the Registrar shall return the instrument, if any, or the verified copy thereof, as the case may be, filed in accordance with the provisions of this Part to the person filing it.]

(3) The register kept in pursuance of this section shall be open to inspection by any person on payment of [such fee as may be prescribed] for each inspection (Section 130).

Index to register of charges. The Registrar shall keep a chronological index, in the prescribed form and with the prescribed particulars, of the charges registered with (Section 130).

Certificate of registration. The Registrar shall give a certificate under his hand of the registration of any charge registered in pursuance of this Part, stating the amounts thereby secured; and the certificate shall be conclusive evidence that the requirements of this Part as to registration have been complied with (Section 132).

Endorsement of certificate of registration on debenture or certificate of debenture stork. (1) The company shall cause a copy of every certificate of registration given under section 132, to be endorsed on every debenture or certificate of debenture stock which is issued by the company and the payment of which is secured by the charge so registered :

Provided that nothing in this sub-section shall be construed as requiring a company to cause a certificate of registration of any charge so given to be endorsed on any debenture or certificate of debenture stock issued by the company before the charge was created.

(2) If any person knowingly delivers, or wilfully authorizes or permits the delivery of, any debenture or certificate of debenture stock which, under the provisions of sub-section (1), is required to have endorsed on it a copy of a certificate of registration without the copy being so endorsed upon it, he shall, without prejudice to any other

liability, be punishable with fine which may extend to [*ten thousand rupees*] (Section 133).

Duty of company as regards registration and right of interested party. (1) It shall be the duty of a company to file with the Registrar for registration the particulars of every charge created by the company, and of every issue debentures of a series, requiring registration under this Part; but registration of any such charge may also be effected on the application of any person interested therein.

(2) Where registration is effected on the application of some person other than the company, that person shall be entitled to recover from the company the amount of any fees properly paid by him to the Registrar on the registration (Section 134).

Provisions of Part to apply to modification of charges. Whenever the terms or conditions, or the extent or operation, of any charge registered under this Part are or is modified, it shall be the duty of the company to send to the Registrar the particulars of such modification, and the provisions of this Part as to registration of a charge shall apply to such modifications of the charge (Section 135).

Copy of instrument creating charge to be kept by company at registered office. Every company shall cause a copy of every instrument creating any charge requiring registration under this Part to be kept at the registered office of the company (Section 136) :

Provided that, in the case of a series of uniform debentures, a copy of one debenture of the series shall be sufficient.

Entry in register of charges of appointment of receiver or manager. (1) If any person obtains an order for the appointment of a receiver of, or of a person to manage, the property of a company, or if any person appoints such receiver or person under any powers contained in any instrument, he shall, within [thirty] days from the date of the passing of the order or of the making of the appointment under the said powers, give notice of the fact to the Registrar; and the Registrar shall, on payment of the prescribed fee, enter the fact in the register of charges.

(2) Where any person so appointed under the powers contained in any instrument ceases to act as such, he shall, on so ceasing, give to the Registrar notice to that effect; and the Registrar shall enter the notice in the register of charger.

(3) If any person makes default in complying with the requirements of sub-section (1) or (2), he shall be punishable with fine which may extend to [*five hundred rupees*] for every day during which the default continues (Section 137).

Company to report satisfaction and procedure thereafter. (1) The company shall give intimation to the Registrar of the payment or satisfaction, [in full], of any charge relating to the company and requiring registration under this Part, within [thirty] days from the date of such payment or satisfaction.

(2) The Registrar shall, on receipt of such intimation, cause a notice to be sent to the holder of the charge calling upon him to show cause within a time (not exceeding fourteen days) specified in such notice, why payment or satisfaction should not be recorded as intimated to the Registrar.

(3) If no cause is shown, the Registrar shall order that a memorandum of satisfaction [***] shall be entered in the register of charges.

(4) If cause is shown, the Registrar shall record a note to that effect in the register, and shall inform the company that he has done so.

(5) Nothing in this section shall be deemed to affect the power of the Registrar to make an entry in the register of charges under section 139 otherwise than on receipt of an intimation from the company (Section 139).

Power of Registrar to make entries of satisfaction and release in absence of intimation from company. The Registrar may, on evidence being given to his satisfaction with respect to any registered charge;

(a) that the debt for which the charge was given has been paid or satisfied in whole or in part; or

(b) that part of the property or undertaking charged has been released from the charge or has ceased to form part of the company's property or undertaking;

enter in the register of charges a memorandum of satisfaction in whole or in part, or of the fact that part of the property or undertaking has been released from the charge or has ceased to form part of the company's property or undertaking, as the case may be, notwithstanding the fact that an intimation has been received by him from the company (Section 139).

Copy of memorandum of satisfaction to be furnished to company. Where the Registrar enters a memorandum of satisfaction in whole or in part, in pursuance of section 138 or 139, he shall furnish the company with a copy of memorandum (Section 140).

Rectification by Company Law Board of register or charges. [(1) the [Company Law Board], on being satisfied :

(a) that the omission to file with the Registrar the particulars of any charge created by a company or of any charge subject to which any property has been acquired by the company or of any modification of any such charge or of any issue of debentures or a series, or that the omission to register any charge within the time required by this Part, or that the omission to give intimation to the Registrar of the payment or satisfaction of a charge, within the time required by this Part, or that the omission or mis-statement of any particular with respect to any such charge, modification or issue of debentures of a series or with respect to any memorandum of satisfaction or other entry made in pursuance of section 138 or 139, was accidental or due to inadvertence or to some other sufficient cause or is not of a nature to prejudice the position of creditors or shareholders of the company; or

(b) that on other grounds it is just and equitable to grant relief; may on the application of the company or any person interested and on such terms and conditions as seem to the [Company Law Board] just and expedient, direct that the time for the filing of the particulars or for the registration of the charge or for the giving of intimation of payment or satisfaction shall be extended or, as the case may require, that the omission or misstatement shall be rectified.]

(2) The [Company Law Board] may make such order as to the costs of an application under sub-section (1) as it thinks fit.

(3) Where the [Company Law Board] extends the time for the registration of a charge, the order shall not prejudice any rights acquired in respect of the property concerned before the charge is actually registered (Section 141)

Penalties. — (1) If default is made in filing with the Registrar for registration the particulars :

(a) of any charge created by the company :

(b) of the payment or satisfaction [***] of a debt in respect of which a charge has been registered under this Part; or

(c) of the issues of debentures of a series;

requiring registration with the Registrar under the provisions of this Part, then unless the registration has been effected on the application of some other person, the company, and every officer of the company or other person who is a default, shall be punishable with fine which may extent to [*five thousand rupees*] for every day during which the default continues.

(2) Subject as aforesaid, if any company makes default in complying with any of the other requirements of this Act as to the registration with the Registrar of any charge created by the company or of any fact connected therewith, the company, and every officer, of the company who is in a default, shall without prejudice to any other liability, be punishable with fine which may extent to [*ten thousand rupees*] (Section 142).

Company's register of charges. (1) Every company shall keep at its registered office a register of charges and enter therein all charges specifically affecting property of the company, and all floating charges on the undertaking or on any property of the company, giving in each case :

(i) a short description of the property charged;

(ii) the amount of the charge; and

(iii) except in the case of securities of bearer, the names of the persons entitled to the charge.

(2) If any officer of the company knowingly omits, or wilfully authorizes or permits the omission of, any entry required to be made in pursuance of sub-section (1), he shall be punishable with fine which may extend to [*five thousand rupees*] (Section 143).

Right to inspect copies of instruments creating charges and company's register of charges. (1) The copies of instruments creating charges kept in pursuance of section 136, and the register of charges kept in pursuance of section 143, shall be open during business hours (but subject to such reasonable restrictions as the company in general meeting may impose, so that not less than two hours in each day are allowed for inspection) to the inspection of any creditor or member of the company without fee, at the registered office of the company.

(2) The register of charges kept in pursuance of section 143 shall also be open, during business hours but subject to the reasonable restrictions aforesaid, to the inspection of any other person on payment of a fee of [such sum as may be prescribed] for each inspection, at the registered office of the company.

(3) If inspection of the said copies or register is refused, the company and every officer of the company who is in default, shall be punishable with fine which may extend to [*five hundred rupees*] and with a further fine which may extend to [*two hundred rupees*] for every day during which the refusal continues.

(4) The [Company Law Board] may also by order compel an immediate inspection of the said copies or register (Section 144).

Application of Part to charges requiring registration under it but not under previous law. In respect of [any charge created before and remaining unsatisfied at, the commencement of this Act,] which, if this Act had been in force at the relevant time, would have had to be registered by the company in pursuance of this Part but which did not require registration under the Indian Companies Act, 1913 (7 of 1913), and in respect of all matters relating to such charge, the provisions of this Part shall apply and have effect in all respects, as if the date of commencement of this Act had been substituted therein for the date of creation of the charge, or the date of completion of the acquisition of the property subject to the charge as the case may be.

Nothing contained in this section shall be deemed to affect the relative priorities as they existed immediately before the commencement of this Act, as between charges on the same property (Section 145).

REDEEMABLE DEBENTURES

Meaning

Redeemable debentures are those that will be repaid by the company under the terms of issue at the end of a specified period or at any time within a specified period by giving them a notice of its intention to redeem them at the end of the notice period or by instalments during the existence of the company. Redeemable debenture may be reissued even after they have been redeemed until they been cancelled.

Merits of Redeemable Debentures

1. Flexibility in Capital Structure. By issuing redeemable debentures the company can make its capital structure more flexible. It can issue the debentures as and when it needs the money of loan.

2. Check on Over Capitalisation. An over capitalised company may redeem the redeemable debentures and may control the state of over capitalisation.

3. Best Solution for Fixed Term Loan. If a company requires funds for a fixed period it may issue redeemable debentures because such debentures can be redeemed after a certain specified period.

4. Preferred by Fixed Term Investors. Redeemable debentures are preferred by those investors who wish to invest their funds for a fixed term at a fixed rate of interest and at minimum risk.

Demerits of Redeemable Debentures

1. Liquidation of Company. Redeemable debentures are repaid at the end of a certain specified period or at any time within the specified period by giving them notice of redemption. If the company fails to arrange the necessary amount to redeem them the debenture-holders can take action for its winding up. The company's existence is always at stake if its financial position is not sound enough.

2. Redemption at any Time. If debentures are repayable at any time within a specified period under the terms of issue, it may create a problem before the debenture-holders to invest the amount as soon as it is repaid by the company. There remains uncertainty in the minds of debenture-holders regarding its redemption.

3. Adverse Effect on Liquidity. If a company has to repay a large sum at the time of redemption of debentures it may adversely affect the liquidity of assets unless it is planned wisely by creating sinking fund so that the company may get the required amount at the time of redemption of debentures at the end of the specified period.

CONVERTIBLE DEBENTURES

Meaning

Convertible debentures are debentures which are convertible into shares at the option of the holders after a specified period. These are considered as a means of deferred equity financing. A company intending to raise additional equity capital at a particular time may find that the prevailing conditions in the capital market are not congenial for the issue of equity shares. It may be that the investment project which is not likely to yield profit may not succeed initially. Under such circumstances, the company may issue debentures with the provision that holder will have the option of converting them into equity shares after a few say 3 to 5 years.

Advantages of Issue

1. Raise in Equity Capital. By such issue a company can raise equity capital indirectly without diluting the earnings of the existing shareholders. By the time debentures are converted into shares the additional investment starts earning an added return to support the additional shares.

2. Sale of Shares. In a period of low market prices of shares the company can sell equity shares in disguise. Investors who may be unwilling to purchase equity shares initially, may like to convert their debentures into equity shares if they find, later on, it to be a profitable proposition.

3. Funds from Institutions. By issuing convertible debentures, a company can attract funds from the institutions which may not otherwise purchase equity shares due to restrictions imposed by their bye-laws.

4. Tax Benefit. As the interest on debentures is a charge on profits, the company gets tax advantage until the bond are converted into shares.

5. More Appeal. Convertible debentures may have greater appeal among the investors particularly in a period of tight money. The addition of conversion right allows the company to offer comparatively a lower rate of interest in a period when prices of other bonds are falling due to rise in the interest rates.

6. Saving in Security. As convertible debentures are unsecure and therefore the borrowing capacity of the company remains intact by the issue of such bonds, the company can provide security against its other debts.

7. Flexibility of Capital Structure. The issue of convertible debentures results in an element of flexibility to the company's capital structure.

8. Double Benefits. Convertible debentures offer benefits of both debt financing and equity financing.

RIGHT DEBENTURES

Provision

Under Section 81 of the Indian Companies Act, 1956, there are specific provisions regarding the issue of "right shares" by the public companies while no such specified provision has been made regarding the issue of rights debentures. However public companies are authorised to issue such debentures for raising long term resources. The Central Government has formulated certain guidelines to regulate the issue of rights debentures by public companies for working capital requirements. While seeking consent of the Controller of Capital Issue, companies are required to follow these guidelines.

Points of Guideline

The main points of the guideline are as follows :

1. The rights debentures may be issued by only public limited companies.

2. The rights debentures may be issued to augment working capital on a long term basis. Issue of debenture for any other purpose such as financing of expansion project or addition to fixed assets will not fall under this category.

3. The amount of the debenture issue will not exceed 20 per cent of the gross current assets, loans and advances minus the long term funds currently available for working capital; or 20 per cent of the paid up share capital, including preference capital and free reserve, whichever is lower of the two.

4. The debt equity ratio including the proposed debenture issue, should not exceed 1 : 1.

5. The debentures will carry a rate of interest 10.5 per cent payable half yearly where the period of maturity is up to and including 7 years and 11 per cent where the period of maturity is from 8 to 12 years.

6. Such debentures can be issued at a discount or additional interest of 1/2 per cent can be offered for any year, if in that year the rate of dividend on equity shares is highest in the preceding three years.

7. The debentures will be redeemable as follows :

(i) Where the maturity period is upto 7 years, 33-1/3 per cent of the debentures will be repaid uniformly to all debenture-holders in the 5th. 6th and 7th year.

(ii) Where the maturity period is from 8 to 12 years, 20 per cent of the debentures will be repaid uniformly to all the debenture-holders in the 8th, 9th, 10th, 11 th and 12th year.

8. The face value of each debenture will be Rs. 100.

9. The debentures will be listed with the stock exchange.

10. The company should be a listed company. Its equity shares must be quoted on the stock exchanges at or above par value in six months prior to the date of application for the issue.

11. The debentures shall first be offered to the existing Indian shareholders of the company on a *pro rata* basis and thereafter must be kept open for at least two months. The unsubscribed debentures, if any, will be offered on a rational basis to (a) shareholders interested

in taking up additional allotment; (b) the directors of the company and (c) the employees and business associates of the company.

12. Allotment of debentures will be made only after a minimum subscription of 75 per cent of the amount of debentures has been secured.

13. The company should ascertain beforehand the prospects of at least 75 per cent of the issue being taken up by the shareholders of the company and other categories of investors mentioned above.

INVESTMENTS

Inter-corporate Loans and Investments

The Companies (Amendment) Act, 1999, the provisions of S. 370 relating to inter-corporate loans and those of S. 372 relating to inter-corporate investments have been revised by substituting them by a single section, Section 372-A. The amendment has the effect of saying that the provisions of Section 370 and 372 shall not apply and those of Section 372-A will take over the matter of such loans and investments. The main and the most primary change is that the requirement of the Central Government approval has been dispensed with. Companies are now thus free from the shackles of control on inter-corporate loans and investments. The only control mechanism now is wholly internal. The Board of directors can invest or advance up to 60% of their own decision and beyond that with the special resolution of the shareholders.

The new provisions under Section 372-A are as follows :

(1) A company can advance loans to other companies or invest in the securities of other companies up to 60% of the paid-up share capital and free reserves or up to 100% of free reserves, which is more. The transactions covered under the provision are :

(a) loans to any body corporate;
(b) guarantee or security for any loan given or taken by a body corporate;
(c) acquiring, by way of subscription, purchase or otherwise the securities of any body corporate.

(2) The notice of the meeting of shareholders called for the purpose of giving previous approval of loans and investment beyond 60% must disclose clearly the specific limits, the particulars of the body corporate in which the investment is proposed to be made or loan or security or guarantee to be give, the purpose of the investment, etc. specific sources of funding and other allied details.

(3) The Board of directors can give a guarantee without the authority of a special resolution :

(a) if the Board is so authorised by its own resolution to give the guarantee in accordance with the provisions of the section;

(b) if some exceptional circumstances are preventing the process of obtaining a special resolution;

(c) if the resolution of the Board is confirmed at a general meting within 12 months or at the annual general meeting held after the guarantee whichever is earlier.

The requirements of sub-section (1) and (2) are not to apply to any loan made by a holding company to its wholly-owned subsidiary, any guarantee given on any security provided by a holding company in respect of loans made to its wholly-owned subsidiary, or acquisition by a holding company, by way of subscription, purchases or otherwise, the securities of its wholly owned subsidiary.

(4) A company which has defaulted in making payment of fixed deposits or interest due on them cannot, during the period of such default, make any loans, investments or provide any guarantee.

(5) The rate of interest to be charged on loans must not be less than the prevailing bank rate of interest, which shall mean the standard rate made public under Section 49 of the RBI Act, 1934.

(6) The decision of the Board of directors must be at a meeting sanctioning the transaction by a resolution passed with the consent of all the directors present at the meeting and also prior approval of any such public financial institution must be taken whose term loan with the company is subsisting. Prior approval of a financial institution is not required where the 60% limit is not to be exceeded and there are no defaults in payments towards the institution.

Register of investments-loans. The company has to keep a register showing the particulars about investments, loans, guarantees and securities :

1. the name of the body corporate;
2. the amount, terms and purpose of the investment or loan or security or guarantee;
3. the date on which the investment or loan has been made;
4. the date on which a guarantee or security has been provided in connection with a loan.

The particulars should be entered in the register chronologically within seven days of the making of loans or investment, etc.

This register has to be kept at the registered office of the company. It should be available for inspection to members who may also take extracts and may demand copies on a similar fee as is applicable in respect of the register of members.

Exceptions. The provisions of the section do not apply in respect of the following transactions:

1. a banking company, insurance company or a housing finance company for transactions made in the ordinary course of

business, a company established with the sole object of financing industrial enterprises or for providing infrastructural facilities;

2. a company whose principal business is the acquisition of shares, stock, debentures or other securities.
3. a private company, unless it is the subsidiary of a public company.

Sub-section (8) exempts subscription of shares pursuant to Section 81(1)(a) (further issue of capital) from compliance with the provisions.

Penalty. Two kinds of default have been identified and given different treatment, one is the violation of the main provision and the second is default in maintaining the register. A very light penalty is provided in the matter of the register. The company and every officer of the company who is in a default is punishable with fine extending to Rs. 5000 and also with a further fine up to Rs. 500 for every day during which the default continues.

For failure to comply with the main provisions of the section, the company and every officer of the company who is in the default is liable to be punished with fine extending to fifty thousand rupees or imprisonment which may extend to two years. Where any loan or investment made in violation of the section has been recovered, the punishment by way of imprisonment is not to be inflicted and where recovery is only partial, the term of imprisonment is to be appropriately reduced.

Where the company suffers any loss because of the contravention, as for example, loans have become irrecoverable, the investment has been lost, or the security has been attached by the security holder or payment under guarantee has been enforced, all the persons who were knowingly a party to the contravention would be jointly as well as severally liable to make good the company's loss.

Loans. The *Explanation* to the section says that for the purposes of the section "loan" includes debentures or any deposit of money made by one company with another company, except where the depositee company is a banking company.

Free reserves. "Free reserves" means those reserves which, as per the latest audited balance sheet of the company, are free for distribution as dividend. It also includes the amount of premium received on issue of securities but does not include share application money.

Investment in own name

Section 49 requires that "all investments made by a company on its own behalf shall be made and held by it in its own name". If the company's nominee or director becomes on its behalf a director in another company and is required to hold qualification shares, they may be held jointly in the name of the company and such person. Where a company advances money to another company by way of a loan to enable the borrowing company to make investment in its shares, that does not amount to investment in shares by the lending company in another company's name.

The section recognises a few exceptions also. Firstly, the section does not apply to investments made by a company whose principal business consists of buying and selling of shares or securities. Secondly, a company may hold shares in its subsidiary company in the name of one or more nominees if it is necessary to ensure the number of members from going below the statutory minimum. Thirdly, a company may deposit with its bankers, shares or securities for collection of dividends or to facilitate their transfer. If the transfer is not effected with six months, they shall be held back by the company in its own name. Fourthly, a company may transfer its shares or securities to another person as a security for a loan or the performance of an obligation.

A further exception has been added under the consequential amendment of the section by the Depositories Act, 1996. A company can hold investments in the name of a depository when such investments are in the form of securities held by the company as a beneficial owner. All such exceptional transactions have to be entered in a register so as to enable their identification and the name in which they are held.

Form of contracts [Section 46]

The brief purpose of the section is to declare that contracts of a company can be made in the same manner in which they can be made by an individual whether they be written or oral. Accordingly, the section says that a written contract can be made on behalf of a company by any person acting under its authority, whether express or implied. An oral contract can also be made in the same manner. Where a debenture was signed not by the director of a company but by the person to whom the director had given his power of attorney, the company was not permitted to question the validity. Section 9(1) of the European Communities Act, 1972 presumes good faith in favour of a person dealing with a company and he is not bound to inquire either into the limitations on the powers of directors or the capacity of the company. (New provisions in the 1989 Act [English] are in Sections 35-A and 35-B).

No personal liability arises under contracts signed for the company. A clause in the contract providing for personal liability of the signatory would be ineffective unless both sides understand that the contract is being on the basis of personal liability.

Execution of deeds and seal [Section 48]

Formal deeds can be executed only through a power of attorney. Section 48 accordingly provides that a company may, by writing under its common seal, appoint any person as its attorney and he may, in the exercise of his power, execute deeds on behalf of the company. Such a deed binds the company to the same effect as if it were under the company's common seal. The seal is a method of making a physical impression upon the documents of the company of its name etc. The seal can be used by the authority of the directors or of a committee of directors authorised by directors. The directors may determine who shall sign any instrument to which the seal is affixed, otherwise such a document has to be signed by a director and by the secretary. A company transacting business in foreign countries may have in accordance with its articles its official seal in a foreign country, which is a facsimile of the company's common seal and should include the name of the place where it is to be used.

Deposit of employees' securities

Money received from employees by way of security deposit must be deposited in the manner prescribed by the section within 15 days from the date of receipt. The openings for depositing the money which are allowed are a Post Office account or a special account with the State Bank or a Scheduled Bank or, where the company itself is a Scheduled Bank, in a special account to be opened by the company in itself, or in the State Bank or any Scheduled Bank.

The money or securities so received are not to be used for any purposes except those agreed to in the contract of service. A receipt granted for money deposited with the company is not a security for the purposes of this section and, therefore, ought to be treated as money received. Any other way of handling such money may amount to breach of trust (Section 417).

Provident funds of employees

A company constituting a provident fund for its employees or any section of them must deposit contributions from both sides and accruals within 15 days in a Post Office account or in a special account in the State Bank or any Scheduled Bank. But where the company itself is a Scheduled bank, it may keep the amount with itself in a special account or in the State Bank or any Scheduled Bank. Alternatively, the amount may be invested in trust securities as enumerated in clauses (a) to (e) of Section 20 of the Indian Trusts Act, 1882. The interest yielded by the investment is the maximum that an employee can claim even if the rules governing the fund or the contract with the employees contain different provisions.

Where the fund becomes a recognised fund, an employee shall have the right to withdraw the sum standing to the credit of his account or take advances from it.

Where a trust has been created of such a fund, the money must be given to the trustees within 15 days. Other things will remain the same except that instead of the company, it shall be the responsibility of trustees to administer the fund.

Employees or their trustees have the right to look at the bank receipts (Section 418).

PUBLIC DEPOSITS

Meaning

The term "public deposit" implies any money received by a non banking company by way of deposit or loan from the public including the employees, customers and shareholders of the company other than in the form of shares and debentures. Public deposits have been a peculiar feature of industrial finance in India. In order to meet their medium term and long term requirements, finance companies have been receiving public deposits for a long time. Prior to independence, banking facilities in the country were not well developed and people preferred to deposit their savings with reputed companies. Public deposits has again become popular in the recent years. Rates of interest offered by companies are higher than those offered by banks while the cost of deposits to the company is less than the cost of borrowings from banks. Companies generally accept public deposits for a minimum period of one year and for a maximum period of 3 years. However, the deposits may be renewed from time to time. The rate of interest on deposits varies from 12 per cent depending on the period of deposit and reputation of the company.

Procedure of Public Deposit

According to the Companies (Acceptance of Deposits) Rules, 1975 as amended in 1984, no company can receive secured and unsecured deposits in excess of 10 per cent and 25 per cent respectively of the paid up share capital plus free reserves. Since April 1, 1980, public sector companies have been also permitted to invite public deposits. The company which intends to raise public deposits approaches the public through an advertisement in the press. It advertises the progress and prospects of the company to induce the public to deposit their surplus money with the company. The depositors can withdraw their balances after the specified period or after giving notice. The receipt of public deposits is governed by the rules made by the Central Government under section 58 A and B of the Companies Act and directions issued by the Reserve Bank of India.

Advantages

1. Simplicity. Raising capital through public deposits is a relatively simple affair. There are few legal formalities. The company receiving deposits is only required to issue a receipt to each depositor.

2. Economy. Public deposits are cheaper to raise. By only advertising in the newspapers for public deposits, the company can collect the necessary funds in a short period. It can save on underwriting commission, brokerage etc. Thus interest on public deposits works out to be much less than liability in the form of dividend on shares or interest on debentures.

3. Trading on Equity. Funds raised through public deposits enable the company to trade on the equity. As interest on public deposits is paid at a fixed rate, the entire remaining profits is available for distribution among equity shareholders of the company.

4. Valuable Source of Short Term Finance. Public deposits serve as a valuable source of short term finance. They prove very useful in case of companies depending on raw materials which is available only in a particular season of the year and for meeting other short term liabilities. Through such deposits these companies can buy enough quantities of raw material. As the sale of their finished product picks up, they are enabled not only to pay interest on the deposits but also to save for the eventual repayment.

5. No Mortgage of Assets. Public deposits do not create any charge or mortgage on the company's assets like debentures. Thus the company may raise loans against the security of its assets to meet other requirements.

Disadvantages

(i) *Uncertainty :* A person who has made a deposit with a company can withdraw his money at any time he pleases with the only condition that he has to give a prior notice to the company. Though this facility helps the depositors, it may affect the company adversely. Premature withdrawals of depositors, may affect the company's financial position, particularly if its earnings have become unstable. The company may find it difficult to honour its commitment as to repayment, if a large number of depositors decide to withdraw their deposits at a time when the business in general is faced with depression and slump.

(ii) *Fair Weather Friend :* The company may be flooded with deposits when its earnings show a higher trend. But in times of financial crisis the depositors might desert it as a sinking ship is deserted by its crew.

(iii) *Reckless Trading and Speculation :* Raising of deposits from the public is relatively simple and inexpensive affair. Therefore sometimes this tempts the companies to raise more funds than they can profitably use. This gives rise to overtrading or speculation activities on their part, with harmful consequences for the business of the undertaking.

(iv) *Lack of Attraction for Professional Investors :* As a mode of investment public deposits do not hold much attraction for professional investors. While the investors do not opt for deposits because of low return and absence of capital appreciation the conservative investors keep away from making deposits due to absence of proper security in the form of a mortgage or charge on the assets of the company.

(v) *Hindrance to Growth of Capital Market :* Public deposits hamper the growth of a sound capital market in the country. As the companies find it easy and economical to raise money through public deposits they are not very keen to raise money by issue of shares and debentures. Thus, investors are deprived of the benefits accruing from good securities.

(vi) *Uneconomical :* If better investment opportunities are freely available, the public will not be keen to make deposits unless very high rates of interest are offered. Payment of high rates of interest may be quite uneconomical but for a regular kind of business. The company raising money through public deposits has to spend a lot by way of commission and brokerage. Thus, in the ultimate analysis, this source of capital is costly.

METHODS OF EXTINCTION OF LONG TERM DEBTS

A company has to redeem every debt except the irredeemable debentures. Even the irredeemable debentures are to be repaid at the option of the company at any time after giving a due notice to the debenture-holders. Following are the three principal methods of retiring long term indebtedness :

1. Redemption involving cash payment.
2. Refunding or substitution of new debt for the old one.
3. Conversion of loan shares of the company.

1. Redemption. Redemption involves cash payment to the debenture-holders or bondholders either at or before the date of maturity according to the terms of contract. Payment is made (a) at maturity, (b) before maturity under terms of issue and (c) maturity and not under the terms of contract but under a subsequent agreement.

(a) *At Maturity :* Payment is made on due date out of cash which may be made available either out of current earnings or out of sinking fund created out of profits established to ensure payment of debentures at maturity. Investments against sinking fund are sold out and loan is redeemed in order to make each available.

Sinking Fund

As a company cannot redeem its entire bond issue from the earnings of any one year, sinking fund is built up out of profits over a number of years without injuring the financial operations of the company. The fund so set aside is invested in various securities, especially in gilt-edged securities, in such a way that total amount of indebtedness is collected including interest on investment after a fixed period. The main reasons for creating sinking fund are :

(i) It adds the element of security.

(ii) It tends to inspire the confidence in the capacity of the issuing company.

(iii) It acts as a check on the financial policies of the management due to sizable appropriations of profits for the fund.

(iv) The credit of the company is rated high because the company invests the amount equal to the fund in the open market securities, which tend to stabilize the market value of bonds at a relatively high level.

(v) It makes up the depreciation in the value of assets purchased out of the sale proceeds of bonds.

(b) *Before Maturity :* A company may redeem debentures even before maturity which may be mandatory or solicited.

(i) If it is mandatory, the bonds are chosen by lot for redemption and the issuing company reserves the right to redeem the debentures as given under the terms of debenture agreement at the time of issue. Payment may be made in fixed instalments year after year. The number of debentures to be redeemed in a year is drawn by lot. For this purpose slips containing distinct number of debentures or bonds are put in a drum and then as many slips are taken out as the debentures to be redeemed. The debentures thus drawn by lot are repaid in cash and in full under terms of contract.

(ii) If redemption is solicited before maturity, an agreement is entered into between the company and the debentures as per agreement.

(iii) A company may redeem debentures before maturity by purchasing them in the open market. If the terms of issue do not restrict the company from doing so the company may cancel these debentures after their purchase in the open market.

Reasons for Redemption on Maturity

Due to the following reasons a company is prompted to redeem before maturity :

1. To eliminate fixed charge on the earnings of the company provided the liquidity position of the company is not adversely affected.
2. To get rid of onerous terms and conditions of the bond.
3. If a company has idle funds to invest, it is better to redeem debentures either by taking them back direct from the debenture-holders or by purchasing them from the open market.
4. To provide flexibility to the financial plan of the company.

2. Refunding. Refunding of indebtedness means replacement of old debt into new debt instead of extinguishment of debt altogether as is done in redemption. This may take place either on maturity or before maturity.

(a) *On Maturity this may take Two Forms :*

1. By issuing new bonds and paying of the old bonds with the proceeds of new bonds.

2. By direct exchange of bonds for new bonds. Following are the main reasons for refunding the debt before maturity :

(i) To extend the obligation of the old debt on account of shortage of liquid funds.

(ii) To continue the indebtedness *i.e.*, trading on equity.

(b) *Before Maturity :* This is done by exercising call option given under the terms of issue or if no such option is given in the agreement, the company may enter into a first agreement with the bondholders inducing them to accept new series of debenture or to accept cash before maturity.

Inducements

Varied types of inducements are offered to the bondholders for persuading there to accept new bonds which may take one of the following forms :

(i) New bonds may be issued at a discount to the existing debentures.

(ii) It is likely to find favour with the old bondholders.

(iii) The bondholders of small issues may have the advantages of better security by consolidating the issue with after acquired property clause.

(iv) New issue may be guaranteed by the parent company, affiliated company or government or financial company.

(v) Old debentures may be redeemed at premium.

(vi) Debenture may be paid partially in cash and bonds for the balance.

If the bondholders insist on cash payment, it may be arranged to make the new issue underwritten with the bankers.

Reasons for Refunding before Maturity

(i) To reduce fixed charge.

(ii) To eliminate bonds containing prohibitive terms and conditions by offering new bonds in favourable market.

(iii) To consolidate several bonds containing different terms and conditions.

3. Conversion. Conversion means issue of shares to the existing debenture-holders in exchange of their bondholdings under the terms and conditions specified in the contract of issue. The debenture-holder is given a right to convert the debentures within a specified period according to the terms given in the bond indenture. This the company retires as debt by converting debentures into equity or preference shares. The main purpose of issuing convertible debentures is to make the financial plan of the company highly elastic because such debentures may be redeemed at any time before maturity.

Thus, the redemption of debenture is preferred when the company has sufficient cash to pay off the debentures. On the other hand, if the company lacks funds to pay off debentures in cash, a new series of debentures are issued and the old debt is replaced by the new series of debentures. If the company likes to continue the indebtedness for the purpose of trading on equity or due to favourable market conditions, it may adopt the method of refunding.

DEBT FINANCING

Reasons for Recommendation

(i) The rate of interest payable on long term debt is lower than the normal rate of return.

(ii) The cost of debt financing is always fixed.

(iii) The interest payable on debt is an admissible deduction for income tax purposes which reduces tax liability of the corporation.

(iv) Debt carries flexibility in the capital structure of the company because it can be redeemed at any time at the sweet will of the company.

Circumstances of Debt Capital

1. The sales and earnings are relatively small.

2. The marginal cost of debt is less than the cost equity or so long as it lowers the average cost of capital or trading on equity is advantageous.

3. The general price level is expected to be high, which will result in higher profits in future.

4. The existing debt ratio is relatively low.

5. Price earnings ratio on equity shares is low in relation to the levels of interest rates.

6. Retention of existing control pattern is the most important consideration in raising finances because debentures carry no voting rights.

7. Debt capital does not affect the cash flow situation of the company adversely or terms of debt agreement are not burdensome on the cash position of the company.

8. Terms and conditions of debt agreements are not onerous and prejudicial to the interest of the fin-n and its shareholders.

The management should bear the above factors in mind while deciding upon the use of debt vs. equity financing. However, there may be several other factors to be considered, depending upon the nature of the business and the situation.

Suitable Debt Management Policy

An optimum debt policy depends on expected ratio of returns and the rates at which these expected revenue streams will be capitalised. No matter how much it shifts towards debts (a cheaper form of finance) a company can never lower its average cost of capital unless it chalks out or maintains a suitable debt management policy, which means a balanced and cautious debt policy to remove the fluctuations in the earnings per share.

(i) *In the Years of Prosperity :* Earning per share will increase if the company relies more on debts rather than equity financing. However, it creates its own problems that all managers cannot appreciate because it restrains the freedom on the working of financial policies.

(ii) *In the Period of Depression :* It is not in the interest of the organisation and the shareholders to raise capital (fixed bearing debt) because the average rate of earning is much lower than the rate of interest payable on such debts. Equity shares should be issued otherwise earning per share will be lowered down. The company must follow the policy of balanced debt financing policy in order to avoid sharp fluctuations in the earning per equity share.

TRADE CREDIT FINANCING

Definition

Trade credit is the credit extended by one business firm to another as incidental to sale or purchase of goods and services. It is also known as mercantile credit. It may be defined as credit extended by sellers to buyers at all levels of the production and distribution process down to the retailer. It arises out of transfer of goods. If it is unsecured it is usually granted for periods ranging from 15 days to three months. It reflects the buyer's power to purchase now and pay later. It is available in the ordinary course of business and no security is required forgetting it. It does not make available the funds in cash.

It is an important source of short term finance and an important constituent of current liabilities. Its amount and terms depend upon the financial strength and goodwill of the buyers, the custom of trade, financial resources of the supplier, the amount and frequency of purchases, degree of competition in the market, location of the customer, the nature of products etc.

Advantages of Trade Credit

1. It is a simple and convenient method of raising short term finance.
2. It involves no formalities.
3. Credit is readily available to reputed business firms.
4. It does not require any security.
5. No interest is payable.
6. It is a flexible source of finance as no charge is created against the assets of the company.
7. It is more economical than bank loans.

Cost of Short Term Credit

It is not correct to say that trade credit is cost free. Although no explicit cost is levied on the recipient of trade credit the firm extending the credit does incur a cost. The supplier has to bear the loss of bad debts in addition to the costs of administering credit accounts. It requires a larger working capital to supply goods on credit. Initially the cost of trade credit may be absorbed by the supplier. But in the long run he tries to pass it on to the buyer in the shape of increased prices depending upon the type of goods and elasticity of demand. The buyer loses cash discounts. Thus trade credit is not cost free. It always carries implicit cost of capital.

QUESTIONS

1. Write a note on the borrowing powers of a company.
2. What is the position of a person who has lent money to a company where the borrowing is *ultra vires* the company?
3. A company borrows money beyond its powers. What remedies are available to the lender where the money has been used to pay the debts of the company? Will it make any difference if the money is still in the hands the company?
4. What is the statutory limitation to the borrowing power of the directors of a company?
5. What charges must be registered with the Registrar? What particulars must be entered in the Registrar's register of charges?
6. "Certain charges are void against liquidators." Explain. Also enumerate the charges which require registration, and state the effect of their non-registration.
7. By whom are the charges created on the property of a company to be registered?
8. What particulars must be entered in a company's register of charges?
9. When can the Company Law Board order for the rectification of the register of charges?

10. What is a debenture? What is meant by a debenture payable *pari passu*?
11. What are the different kinds of debentures? What remedies are available to debenture-holders for realisation of their security?
12. Under what circumstances may a company issue, re-issue, debentures?
13. Why are trustees for debenture-holders appointed and what are their duties?
14. What is a floating charge? What is the consequence if a floating charge created by a company on its undertaking is not registered with the Registrar of Companies?
15. Distinguish between (a) a floating charge and a fixed charge, (b) debentures and debenture stock.

PRACTICAL PROBLEMS

1. A joint stock company borrows money from Y beyond its powers. Has Y, a shareholder, any remedy against (a) the company and (b) the directors of the company?
[**Hint.** (a) No. (b) He can recover damages from the directors (Refer to lender's rights when borrowing is *ultra vires* the company)].
2. The Articles of a company provide that the Managing Director may, with the previous sanction of the Board of directors, take a loan of Rs. 1 lakh. The Managing Director, without such sanction takes a loan of Rs. 2 lakhs and misappropriates the amount. Can the creditor sue the company for the recovery of the loan?
[**Hint.** No. The borrowing is ultra vires the company].
3. A company by a special resolution declared that Rs. 50 out of each Rs. 100 share should be the reserve capital. The company then issued debentures charging its undertaking and property including its uncalled capital. Two years later the company went into liquidation. The debenture-holders claimed a first charge on the reserve capital. Is their claim justified? Give reasons.
[**Hint.** No (Mayfair Property Co., Re)].
4. The debentures issued by a company created a floating charge on the company's property and stock-in-trade, with the condition that the company was not to create any prior charge. The manager of the company having forgotten this commitment deposited the title deeds of the company's property with a bank by way of security for a loan obtained. The bank also happened to hold some of the company's debentures on deposit for one of its customers. How would you decide the issue of priority of charges between the debenture-holders and the bank?

[**Hint.** The bank has priority over the floating charge (Valletort Sanitary Steam Co. Ltd. Re (I 903) 2 Ch. 6441)].

5. On January 10, 1998 a company, In consideration of a past debt of Rs. 2 lakhs and a future advance of Rs. 1 lakh, issued debentures to a creditor accompanied by a floating charge over its assets. On June 25, 1998 an order for the winding up was passed. State the rights of the creditor in winding up.

   [**Hint.** The charge is void as to the past debt of Rs. 2,00,000, and is valid as to the fresh advance of Rs. 1.00,000 (Section 534)].

6. A company had power in its Memorandum to sell the whole of its undertaking. The company sold the undertaking. The debenture-holders whose loan was secured by a floating charge which was to become fixed (crystallised) on an order or resolution to wind up claimed that by the act of sale the charge became fixed (crystallised) and the property was still subject to the charge. Will their claim succeed?
   [**Hint.** No (Borax Co., Re)].

12

COMPANY MANAGEMENT

A Joint Stock Company is an artificial person created by law. It is not a natural person though it acts as a natural person. As an impersonal creation of law it can act only through some human persons. In the public interest, the persons authorised for the management of a company should be competent, honest and intelligent. Director is the person who performs all the functions of a company.

DIRECTOR

Definition

1. Section 2(12). "Director includes any person verifying the position of director, by whatever name called." This is not satisfactory definition. It does not clear the meaning or the nature of the word director.

2. Websters Dictionary. "Director means the person who is appointed for the management of a company. As a company has a large number of shareholders and all these shareholders cannot participate in the management of the company, the management of the company is delivered to some selected persons who are called directors. These persons are dominating and proficient in the business activity."

Thus, a director is a person who directs, conducts, manages, supervises and controls the functioning of a company. All the directors of a company are collectively known as the Board of Directors or the Management Committee or the Governing Board.

Provision Regarding Number of Directors

1. Minimum Number of Directors (Section 252). Every public company must have a minimum of 3 directors and every private company must have a minimum of 2 directors.

2. Maximum Number of Directors (Section 258). The Companies Act does not specify any maximum number for the directors of a company. The articles of association may prescribe the maximum number of directors for its management and the number of directors constituting the board of directors may also be fixed by the articles of the company. The number so fixed may be increased or decreased within the limits prescribed by the articles of association by passing an ordinary resolution only.

3. Increase in the Number of Directors (Section 259). The number of directors of a public company or a private company subsidiary of a public company, cannot be increased without the approval of central government. However, the company is not required to get the approval of central government if the increase in the number of directors does not make the total number of directors more than 12.

QUALIFICATIONS OF DIRECTORS

Indian Companies Act does not lay down any particular qualification for a director. He may or may not be the shareholder of the company but, the articles of association of a company may make it obligatory for its directors to be its shareholders also. Section 270 of the Indian Companies Act, states that if the articles of association of a company so provide, the directors must obtain their qualification shares within two months after their appointment and if the company is a newly floated one, the directors must pay for their qualification shares before the certificate of commencement of business is obtained by the company. It further states that if the directors are required to purchase the qualification shares by the articles of the company, the nominal value of such shares must not exceed Rs. 5,000. The bearer shares are not to count for this purpose. Proviso 66 of Table 'A' provides that the directors of the company must hold at least one share each in the company.

According to Section 282(1) if the directors do not acquire the required qualification shares within the prescribed time, they cease to be the directors. They will also be liable to a penalty which may extend upto Rs. 500 per day for the period in which they continue to act as directors after the expiry of such period. The provisions of the qualification shares do not apply in the following cases :

1. Technical Directors.
2. Directors representing some special interest.
3. Directors appointed by the Central Government.
4. Directors of a Private Company.

APPOINTMENT OF DIRECTORS

1. Appointment of First Directors (Section 254). The first directors of a company are appointed by its promoters. Their names and addresses are disclosed in the articles of association, otherwise the subscribers to memorandum of association of the company shall be deemed to be the first directors of the company. Such directors shall retire at the first annual general meeting of the company because the company appoints its directors at this meeting.

2. Appointment of Subsequent Directors. (i) Section 255. The shareholders must appoint the directors for the company at the first annual general meeting and then at every subsequent annual general meeting of the company.

(ii) Section 256. The minimum of two-thirds of the total number of directors must retire by rotation every year in case of a public company and a private company which is a subsidiary of any public company. Such a company cannot have more than one-third of the total number of directors as permanent directors. A company may provide by its articles of association that all the directors will retire every year and the fresh directors will be appointed and the retiring directors shall be eligible for re-election.

(iii) Section 257. A new person must inform the company, at least 14 days before, when he wants to be elected as a director. The company is required to inform the members about this fact at least 7 days before the annual general meeting.

(iv) Section 263. Every director has to be appointed through a separate resolution and the resolution must be passed by a simple majority.

(v) Section 264. It is compulsory that for the appointment of a director, who is not a retiring director, the company must file his written consent to act as a director within 30 days of appointment.

(vi) Section 265. It empowers the company to provide a system of proportional representation of the minority shareholders by its articles of association.

3. Appointment of Additional Directors (Section 260). If the articles of association of a company have a provision, that the board of directors can also appoint additional directors subject to the maximum number of directors fixed by the articles. These will hold the office only upto the date of next annual general meeting.

4. Alternate Directors (Section 313). The board of directors may appoint an alternate director only if a director remains absent from the state in which the meetings of the board are ordinarily held for a period of more than three months. The articles of association of the company must provide for the appointment of such alternate director, who shall hold office till the expiry of the term of original director or till he returns to the state.

5. Appointment of Directors in Case of Casual Vacancies (Section 262). If the office of a director falls vacant due to the death or resignation of a director before the expiry of his term, the board of directors may fill up such vacancies. The casual director, so appointed, will hold the office till the term of the original director.

6. Appointment of Directors by the Central Government (Section 408). On the application of minimum one hundred members of the company or on the application of members holding 10% voting rights or on its own motion the central government can appoint such number of directors in company as it may deem necessary, in case of mismanagement of the company. Such directors can be appointed for a period of not more than 3 years.

7. Appointment of Directors by other Parties. If the articles of association of a company have a provision, other parties may also appoint the directors for the company. These include the bank, financial institution or debenture-holders etc.

Restrictions in Respect of Appointment

1. Only an Individual may be a Director (Section 253). Only an individual can be appointed as a director of a company. It means that a partnership firm or a company or an institute cannot be appointed as a director.

2. Restriction on Qualification Shares. A person cannot be appointed as director unless he has complied with the following provisions :

(i) He must have submitted his written consent with the registrar of companies to act as the director.

(ii) Section 270. He must purchase the qualification share or he must have promised to purchase such shares within 2 months of his appointment. The nominal value of qualification shares must not exceed Rs. 5000.

3. Number of Companies Directors (Section 275). A person cannot be a director of more than 15 companies at one time.

4. Legal Restriction (Section 263). A separate resolution must be passed for the appointment of every director. He must be appointed by passing an ordinary resolution. This provision can be waived if the meeting of the company unanimously passes an otherwise resolution.

5. Restriction on Remaining Absent. If any director remains absent in three consecutive meetings of the board of directors or in the meetings of the board held in three months, whichever is a longer period, without the permission of board of directors, he cannot continue to work as a director.

6. Other Disqualifications of Directors (Section 274). The following persons can not be appointed as a director or an additional director or an alternate director :

(i) Declared to be of unsound mind.

(ii) An undischarged insolvent.

(iii) Adjudicated insolvent.

(iv) Convicted by a Court of Law and sentenced to at least 6 months of imprisonment for an offence and a period of not less than 5 years has not lapsed from the date of expiry of such sentence.

(v) Failed to pay call on his shares for the last six months.

(vi) Has been disqualified by the Court of Law for fraudulent activities in the promotion or management of the company.

However, by notification in the official gazette the central government is empowered to waive the disqualifications mentioned at number (iv) and (v) above.

(vii) A private company may add any other disqualifications in its article of association for appointment of a director.

Remuneration of Director

The directors are the agents and not servants of the company. They have no right to get any remuneration unless there is a specific provision to that effect in the articles of association or unless the shareholders resolve for the remuneration in the general meeting because they are appointed by the shareholders and not by the company. However, generally the articles of association of every company provide for the remuneration of directors.

Minimum and Maximum Limit of Remuneration

1. Section 198. The total managerial remuneration payable to directors, managing director, manager and whole-time director should not exceed 11 per cent of the net profits of the company in a financial year. In the years of inadequate profits, the amount not exceeding Rs. 50 thousand per annum may be paid to all the managerial personnel without the prior approval of the central government. The central government has been empowered to allow a greater sum by way of managerial remuneration provided it is satisfied about the genuineness of the case and a monthly payment is being made or is proposed to be made.

2. Section 309(3). Under the above limits, a full time director cannot be paid any remuneration exceeding 5 per cent of the net profits of the company for a particular financial year. If the number of full time directors is two or more than two, they all cannot be paid the total remuneration exceeding 10 per cent of the net profits of the company.

3. Section 309(4). If the company has no full time director or manager, the remuneration of such part time director can be increased upto 3 per cent of the net profits of the company.

4. A company will not pay remuneration free of tax to any officer or employee.

POWERS OF DIRECTORS

As representatives of the shareholders of a company the directors manage, administer and control the functions of the company in the interests of the shareholders. Their powers are mentioned in the articles of association of the company. These can be divided into two parts : (I) General Powers and (II) Special Powers. The details are as follows :

(I) General Powers. According to section 291 of the Indian Companies Act, the directors of a company have the power to do all such acts which a company is authorised to do, subject to the articles of association of the company and of the provision of the Indian Companies Act. The shareholders of a company cannot interfere and control the acts of directors provided if they act within their limits and in the best interests of the company. However, they can alter the articles of association to restrict the powers of the board of directors or they can refuse to reappoint the director or the directors whom they disapprove.

Individual directors have no power to manage the company unless the articles of association of the company provide otherwise. Directors must exercise their powers as a board. The articles of association may authorise board of directors to delegate their powers to a committee of directors or to the managing director or to the manager.

(II) Special Powers. According to Section 292 of the Act, subject to the restrictions placed by the articles of association of tire company the following powers can be exercised by the board of directors only by passing a resolution at their meeting :

1. To fill up the casual vacancies.
2. To make unpaid calls.
3. To issue debentures.
4. To borrow money in any, other form.
5. To invest the funds of the company.
6. To lend the money.
7. To enter into contract for the company.
8. To appoint the managing director.
9. A public company with share capital of not less than 5 crores of rupees is required to constitute an "audit committee of the Board of Directors." Its membership is not less than three directors and other directors which Board may decide. The committee can investigate in any matter relating to audit.

Restrictions on the Powers of Board of Directors

1. Restriction on the Powers of Board of Directors (Section 293). In public company and its subsidiary, the board of directors cannot exercise any of the following powers without the consent of the shareholders in their annual general meeting :

(i) To sell, lease or otherwise dispose off the whole or a part of the undertaking of the company. However, the title of the purchaser and lessee who have acted in the good faith, with due care and precaution, and without having the knowledge of non compliance of the above restriction, will not be affected. These restrictions will not apply in case of a company whose ordinary business is to sell or lease the property.

(ii) To write off or allow more time for the payment of any debt due by a director.

(iii) To borrow the money more than the aggregate of the paid up share capital of the company and its free reserves. Temporary loans are not included in this limit. Section 293(v) protects interest of a lender who has advanced the loan in the good faith and without having the knowledge that the above limit has been exceeded.

(iv) To invest the money received in respect of compulsory acquisition of any fixed assets of the company, in the securities other than the trust securities.

(v) To contribute an amount exceeding Rs. 50,000 or 5 per cent of the average net profit for the last three financial years, whichever is greater, to any charitable fund which is not directly related with the business of company or with the welfare of the employee of the company.

2. Restrictions upon the Appointment of Sole Selling Agent. (i) **Section 294(2).** The board of directors of a company cannot appoint any sole selling agent. However, such an agent can be appointed on the conditions that if the annual general meeting of the company does not approve the appointment it will be treated as terminated since the date of the meeting.

(ii) Section 294AA. The central government can restrict the appointment of such sole selling agent in any company in which, the government is of the opinion, that there is no need of the appointment of such agent because the demand of the products of the company is already higher than its supply. A company having a paid up share capital of Rs. 50 lakhs or more, can appoint the sole selling agent only if it passes a special resolution to the effect and gets the permission of the central government.

3. Restrictions upon Granting the Loans to Directors (Section 295). A company can neither sanction any loan to the following parties, either directly or indirectly, without the prior permission of the central government, nor take the guarantee of any loan taken by these persons :

(i) Any of its directors.

(ii) Any of the directors of its subsidiary company.

(iii) Any partner or relative of such directors.

(iv) Any firm in which any of such directors or his relative is a partner.

(v) Any private company in which any of such directors is a director or a member.

(vi) Any incorporated body of which a minimum of 25 per cent of voting rights is controlled by any of such directors or two or more such directors.

(vii) Any incorporated body whose board of directors or managing director or manager is in a position to be controlled by the orders of directors or board of directors of the company granting such loan.

POLITICAL CONTRIBUTIONS

Before the substitution of a new section 293-A by the Companies (Amendment) Act, 1985, there was a blanket ban on political contributions by companies. New Section 293-A allows some companies to make contributions to political parties or for political purposes to any person, directly or indirectly, out of their profits.

Section 293-A(1) however continues the existing blanket ban against political contributions in the case of :

1. Government Companies.

2. Companies which have been in existence for less than 3 financial years.

Section 293-A(2) permits any other company to contribute any amount or amounts, directly or indirectly, to any political party or for any political purpose to any person subject to the following conditions :

1. Proviso I to the Section 293-A(2). The amount or aggregate of the amounts so contributed by a company in any financial year shall not exceed 5 per cent of its average net profits during the 3 immediately preceding financial years.

2. Proviso 2 to the Section 293-A(2). Before any such contribution is made by the company, a resolution authorising the making of the contributions shall be passed at a meeting of the board of directors. Such resolution shall be deemed to be justification in law for the making and accepting of the contributions authorised by it.

3. Section 293-A(4). The company shall disclose in its Profits and Loss Account the amount or amounts of such contributions during the financial year to which that account relates, giving :

(i) Particulars of the total amount contributed.

(ii) The name of the party or person to which or to whom such amount has been contributed.

What is included in Political Contribution. Section 293-A(3) of the Indian Companies Act, states that the contribution of any amount, directly or indirectly, to any political party or for any political purpose to any person includes :

(i) A donation or subscription or payment to be given by a company on its behalf or on its account to a person who, to its knowledge, is carrying on any activity which can reasonably be regarded as likely to affect public support for a political party at the time of donation, subscription or payment.

(ii) The amount of expenditure incurred, directly or indirectly, by a company on advertisement in any publication (being a publication in the nature of a souvenir, brochure, tract, pamphlet or the like) by or on behalf of a political party or for its advantage.

Penalty. If a company makes any contribution in contravention of the provisions of Section 293-A, the company shall be punishable with fine which may extend to 3 times the amount so contributed; and every officer of the company who is in default shall be punishable with imprisonment for a term which may extend to 3 years and shall also be liable to fine.

CONTRIBUTION TO NATIONAL DEFENCE FUND

Section 293-B of the Indian Companies Act, states that a company may contribute such amount as it thinks fit to National Defence Fund or any other fund approved by the central government for the purpose of national defence. The power of contributing amount to National Defence Fund or any other fund approved by the central government for the purpose of national defence may be exercised by the board of directors of the company or any person or authority exercising the powers of the board of directors of the company. The company shall, however, disclose in its Profit and loss Account the total amount or amounts contributed by it to National Defence Fund drum the financial year to which the amount relates.

DUTIES OF DIRECTORS

Directors play a key role in the management and administration of a company. They have to perform a large number of duties. There are statutory duties of the directors under the Companies Act. Besides, there are many duties of a general nature under the general law. The directors have to obey their duties right from the incorporation of the company till its liquidation. The duties of directors can be studied under three heads : (I) Duties under Companies Act, (II) Duties under Articles of Association and (III) Duties described by the Justices.

(I) Duties Under Indian Companies Act

1. To disclose Personal Interest. If the directors of a company have done any work of the company in which their personal interest is involved or may be involved, they are under the obligation to disclose their personal interest at the meeting of the board of directors.

2. To disclose the Post Held and Resigned. Every director of a company is under the obligation to disclose his name, address, occupation, date of birth, and the particulars of all other posts held by him within 20 days of his appointment. If while working as a director of a company, he joins some other post or resigns from any post held by him, he must inform the same to the company within a proper time.

3. To disclose the Shares Held by Him. Every director is under the obligation to disclose the full details of the shares held by him so that the appropriate entries may be entered in the register of directors.

4. Other duties. Under the Indian Companies Act the directors of a company have to perform the following duties :

(i) **Section 56.** To verify the truth of a prospectus to be issued by the company.

(ii) **Section 149.** Not to start the business of the company until the amount of minimum subscription is collected and the amount on the shares taken by directors has been collected in the same proportion as others have paid.

(iii) **Section 165.** To call a statutory meeting within a period of minimum one month and maximum 6 months from the date of certificate of commencement of business.

(iv) **Section 166.** To call an annual general meeting of the company within 18 months of the incorporation of the company and then every year.

(v) **Section 169.** To call the extraordinary meeting of the company if it is demanded by the members having a minimum of 10 per cent voting right.

(vi) **Section 209.** To maintain the accounts and the books of accounts of the company in proper way.

(vii) **Section 210.** To present the Profit and Loss Account and the Balance street of the company in its annual general meetings.

(II) Duties Under Articles of Association

A company may have some provisions in its Articles of Association regarding the duties of its directors. If it is so, the directors must follow them also.

(III) Duties Described by Justices

Justices have described following duties of the directors of a company while deciding the cases on the issue :

1. To work in the good faith and for the benefit of the company.
2. To have fiduciary relations with the company. Therefore, they must disclose all the relevant facts to the company and they must not make any secret profit.
3. To perform their duties with such amount of care as a reasonable person would have done under the same circumstances.
4. Not to be negligent in performing their duties.
5. To perform the duties delegated to them by the shareholders. "A delegate cannot delegate further." Therefore, the directors must perform their duties personally and they must not delegate any of their powers to some other person, unless specifically permitted by the articles of association.
6. To attend every meeting of the board of directors unless otherwise impossible.

LIABILITIES OF DIRECTORS

The directors, if they incur no personal liability, act *intra vires* the Companies Act, the memorandum of association and the articles of association and in the good faith, for the benefit of the company and take reasonable amount of care in discharging their duties. But under certain circumstances the directors may be held personally responsible for the acts done by them. The liabilities of directors may be divided into three parts : (I) Liability of Outsiders, (II) Liability to the company and (III) Liability for the criminal acts.

(I) Liabilities to the Outsiders

(1) As an Agent. The directors may be held liable to the outsiders in the capacity of an agent of the company in the following two cases :

(i) If they enter into any contract with any outsider in their personal name, they will be held personally responsible to complete the contract.

(ii) If they have knowingly entered into any *ultra vires* contract, they will be held responsible to make good the loss caused to other parties.

2. In Case of Mis-Statement in the Prospectus. If the prospectus of the company contains any misstatement and the investors suffer any loss because of that misstatement, the directors who have signed the prospectus will be held personally responsible for such loss.

3. In Case of Irregular Allotment. Allotment made not in accordance with Section 69 and 70 of the Companies Act, is called an irregular allotment. If the directors have made irregular allotment of the shares they will be held responsible to refund the money paid by the applicants along with the interest.

(II) Liabilities to the Company

1. Liability for *Ultra Vires* Acts. If the directors have entered into any contract *ultra vires* the memorandum or *ultra vires* the articles or *ultra vires* their powers, and the company suffers any loss because of such contract, they will be held responsible to make good the loss of the company.

2. Liability for Breach of Trust. If the directors make any secret profits or use the funds of the company for their personal use and the company suffers any loss, they will be held liable to compensate the company.

3. Liability for Breach of Duties. If the directors do not discharge their duties, they will be held liable to compensate the loss caused to the company because of the fault at their part.

4. Liability for Negligence. If the directors are held responsible for the negligence in the performance of then duties, they will have to make good the loss to the company caused because of such negligence.

5. Liability for Fraudulent Acts. If any director has done any act in a fraudulent manner and the company suffers any loss because of such acts, the concerned director will be held personally liable to compensate the loss of the company.

6. Liability for the Acts of Co-Directors. If a director habitually absent himself from the meetings of the board of directors and the company suffers any loss by the acts of his co-directors, he will be held liable to compensate such loss.

(III) Liability for the Criminal Acts

1. If the Prospectus Contains an Untrue Statement (Section 63). If the prospectus issued by the company contains any untrue statement, every director responsible for the statement may be punished with an imprisonment of 2 years or with a fine of Rs. 50,000 or with both.

2. If the Application Money on Shares is not deposited in a Scheduled Bank (Section 69). If the application money received on shares is not deposited in a scheduled bank, every responsible director for this may be punished with a fine which may extend upto Rs. 50,000.

3. If the Statement in lieu of Prospectus in not Submitted with the Registrar (Section 70). If a company has not issued the prospectus for the issue of shares, a statement in lieu of prospectus must be filed with the registrar at least 3 days before the allotment of shares. If it is not filed, every responsible director may be punished with a fine which may extend upto Rs. 10,000.

4. If the return of Allotment is not filed with the Registrar (Section 75). A Public Company, having share capital, must file a return of the allotment of shares with the registrar within 30 days of the allotment. On non compliance of this provision, every responsible director may be punished with a fine which may extend upto Rs. 50,000.

5. If the Re-Organisation of Share Capital or the Conversion of Share Capital into Stock is not informed to the Registrar (Section 95). If reorganisation of the share capital or the conversion of share capital into stock or the conversion of stock into share capital is not informed to the registrar, the responsible directors may be punished with a fine of Rs. 500 per day for the period in which the fault continues.

6. If the List of Members is not maintained (Section 151). If a company having more than 50 members, does not maintain the list of members, all the liable directors may be punished with a fine of Rs. 500.

7. If the Statutory Meeting is not called within Specified Time (Section 165). If the statutory meeting is not called within the time specified for the purpose, the liable directors may be punished with a fine which may extend upto Rs. 5000.

8. If the General Meeting is not called within Specified Time (Section 166 and 167). If the general meeting of the company is not called within the specified time, the responsible directors may be punished with a fine which may extend upto Rs. 50,000 and if the fault continues they may be punished with an additional fine of Rs. 2500 per day till the fault continues.

9. If the Profit and Loss Account and the Balance sheet are not presented in the Annual General Meeting (Section 210). If the profit and loss account and the balance sheet of the company are not presented in its annual general meeting, all the responsible directors may be punished with an imprisonment of 6 months or with a fine of Rs. 10,000 or with both.

In addition to the above, the directors of a company also incur criminal liability for the non compliance of the various provisions of the Indian Companies Act under Sections 113, 192, 217, 272, 299, 300, 305, 407 and 513 etc.

LEGAL POSITION OF DIRECTORS OF A COMPANY

As the Companies Act is silent about the legal position of directors in a company it is very difficult to define it. Though the directors are treated as the agents, trustees and managing partners of their company but they are not in any such position. In fact the directors have fiduciary relationship with the company and discharge their duties in accordance with the Companies Act, memorandum of association and articles of association of the company. While deciding the case of 'Imperial Hydropathic Co. *Vs.* Hampson' Lord Justice Bowen observed, "Directors are described sometimes as agents, sometimes as trustees and sometime as managing partners. But each of these expressions is used not as exhaustive of their powers and responsibilities but as indicating useful points of view from which they may for the particular moment and for the particular purpose be considered."

1. Directors are the Agents of the Company. As company is an artificial person created by law, it cannot do its works itself. As the directors work on behalf of the company, the relationship between a company and its directors is of the principal and the agents. The company is responsible for the work done by its directors in the same manner as a principal is held liable by the act done by its agents.

While deciding the case of 'Fergoson *Vs.* Wilson' Lord Cairns observed, "They are merely the agents of the company. The company itself cannot act in person, it can act only through directors. Wherever an agent is liable, those directors would be liable : where the liability touches to the principal, the liability is of the company." Following are the results of this type of relationship between a company and its directors :

(i) If the directors have done their works within the scope of their authority, these will be deemed to be done by the company itself and the company is liable for them.

(ii) The directors can enter into contracts and put their signature on behalf of the company like an agent.

(iii) Directors must conduct the business of the company with reasonable care and must abide by the memorandum and articles of association of the company.

(iv) If the directors have done something out of their authority, they may be held personally liable for those acts.

But while the agents are appointed and not elected, the directors owe their office to election. Hence the directors cannot be the agents in the true sense.

2. Directors are Trustees of the Company. In certain respects, directors are in the position of trustees for the company. They are elected to manage the affairs of the company in the interests of shareholders. They have to perform their duties with honesty and in good faith in the best interests of the company.

In Sykes Case Justice Bacon observed, "It is the plain duty of the directors, who are trustees for the company, to deal in all matters of business with which the company is concerned for the benefit of the company and not with regard to their own particular interests." Practically, all the powers of directors to accept or reject the share transfer etc. are the powers in trust. They stand in fiduciary capacity to protect the interests of the company. The directors are trustees for the company and not for the shareholders individually or for the third parties who have entered into contracts with the company.

Though the directors are the trustees of their company but their position is not like trustees in the legal sense. A trustee, in the legal sense, is one who is the owner of the property and deals with it as principal owner subject only to an obligation to account for to those to whom he stands in the relation of trustee. On the other hand, directors are the trustees only for the wealth, properties and powers of the company and not for the loans and liabilities. They cannot sue and cannot be sued for the contracts while acting *intra vires.* Therefore, they cannot be called the trustee in the real sense.

3. Directors are the Managing Partners of the Company. As the directors are elected by the shareholders to carry on the business of company on their behalf, they may be called the managing partners of the company. As shareholders of the company they are partners with other shareholders. They do almost all the functions of the company in the capacity of its proprietor. But they are not the managing partners of the company in full sense, because if they are the managing partners, they are not authorised to bind other directors and shareholders by their acts and they compulsorily retire.

4. Directors are the Officers of the Company. According to the provisions of Indian Companies Act, the directors of a company are its employees. They get the remuneration for their work and are held personally liable by their acts if they violate the provisions of Indian Companies Act or of memorandum of association of the company.

However, directors cannot be regarded as the full-fledged officers of the company because they are the elected representatives of the shareholders. They are not appointed and the company is not bound to pay the remuneration to them in some cases.

Thus, the directors of a company are neither its agents, nor managing partners, nor trustees, and nor the officers in the full sense of the term. They combine all these positions in themselves. They have the fiduciary relationship with the company. Section 2(30) of Indian Companies Act, 1956 terms the directors of a company as its officers.

REMOVAL OF DIRECTORS

Following are the provisions for the removal of directors from their post :

1. Removal by the Shareholders (Section 284). The directors of a company may be removed by its shareholders if it is proved that they are performing their duties in unsatisfactory manner or in any other manner undesirable. The company must give a special notice for the meeting of shareholders, at least 14 days before the date of meeting, specifying the intention to move resolution for the removal of directors. A company notice must be sent to the director concerned also. He should be given the opportunity of being heard at the general meeting. If the shareholders are not satisfied with the qualification furnished by him they may remove him by passing an ordinary resolution to that effect and with this the director is taken to be removed from his post with immediate effect.

The vacancies so created may be filled at the same meeting or may also be filled as casual vacancies. The director so appointed will hold his post till expiry of the term of the removed director. A removed director can not be reappointed but he can claim compensation if he has been removed in a wrong manner. The amount of compensation will be calculated with reference to the income he has lost.

Exceptions to this Rule. The shareholders cannot remove the following types of directors :

(i) If the director was appointed by the Central Government under Section 408.

(ii) Director of a private company holding office for life as on Ist April 1952.

(iii) If the director represents the interests of a particular class.

(iv) If the director was elected by the proportionate representation under Section 265.

2. Removal by Central Government (Section 388 E). If any High

Court has given any judgement, on a reference made by the government for the detection of fraud, misfeasance, negligence, or breach of trust, existing in carrying out his duties, the Central Government may order for the removal of such director. The person so removed, cannot hold the office of a director of any company for a period of 5 years from the date of judgement, unless the period is reduced. No compensation will be payable to such a director. For the vacancies so created, the company may appoint any other person to that office with the prior permission of Central Government.

3. Removal by the Court. If an application is moved to the court for the prevention of mismanagement of a company, the court has the power to remove the director of the company under Section 397 and 398 of the Companies Act. The director so removed cannot hold any managerial post in any company for a period of 5 years from the date of his removal, without the order of the court. Section 407 further states in this regard that such a director cannot claim any compensation for his removal.

VACATION (DISQUALIFICATION) OF OFFICE BY DIRECTORS

Vacation of office by a director is the disqualification because of which the director himself resigns from his post. Section 283 of the Indian Companies Act, 1956 states that an office of director shall be deemed to have been vacated on the happening of any of the six disqualifications, already discussed under Section 274. In addition to those six disqualifications, his office shall be treated as vacant in the following circumstance as well :

1. If he does not purchase the qualification shares, if any, within a period of two months of his appointment.
2. If he is declared insolvent.
3. If he is declared a person of unsound mind by any court.
4. If he is removed by the shareholders by passing an ordinary resolution in the annual general meeting of the company. Before passing such resolution, a special notice must be given to the director to be removed.
5. If he moves an application in any court for being declared insolvent.
6. If he is declared disqualified to work as a director by any court.
7. If he does not disclose his interest in any contract entered into with the company.
8. If he was appointed the director because of being the employee of the company or because of any post held by him in the company and he is removed from his service or from his post.
9. If he absents himself from three consecutive meetings of the board of directors or from all the meetings of the board of

directors for a period of three months, whichever is longer, without obtaining the leave of absence from the board.

10. If he has been convicted of any offence by any court under Section 209A. Under this section, every director must produce the books of accounts and must furnish all the information and explanations required by the inspecting officer.
11. If he has been removed from office by any court under Section 402. This section relates to the prevention of oppression or mismanagement of the companies.
12. If he has been removed from his office for fraud or misfeasance or breach of trust by the Central Government under Section 388E.
13. If he holds any office of profit without obtaining the prior permission of shareholders by a special resolution, in the company or its subsidiary company.
14. If he or the partnership firm in which he is a partner or a private company in which he is a director, borrows from the company without prior approval of the Central Government.
15. If he does not pay the amount of call made on his shares within six months from the last date of payment.

Any person, functioning as a director in a company, must vacate his office immediately after coming to know that the office of director held by him has become vacant on account of any of the above disqualifications. If he does not comply with this provision, he may be punished with a fine which may extend upto Rs. 5000 per day for the period in which he continues to be the director.

APPOINTMENT OF DIRECTORS TO AN OFFICE OF PROFIT

Section 314 of the Indian Companies Act, 1956, imposes a restriction upon the directors and their associates to hold an office of profit in the company or in any subsidiary company thereof This section provides the following unless the company approves by a special resolution :

1. No director of the company shall hold any office of profit, however small the remuneration attached to it may be.
2. No director; or any relative of such director; or the partnership firm in which the director or his relative is a partner; or the private company in which a director or his relative is the director, can hold the post of profit in the company or in subsidiary company thereof, carrying total monthly remuneration of Rs. 5000 or more.
3. According to the Companies (Amendment) Act, 1974, if the remuneration of such posts is Rs. 20,000 or more, such post may be held with the prior permission of the Central Government. If a person holds such appointment before the

enactment of this amendment act, it must be approved by the central government within a period of six months from Ist Feb. 1975.

4. A company may offer an office of profit to its directors by passing a special resolution.
5. If any such appointment has been made without the permission of shareholders, the permission of shareholders by a special resolution must be obtained in the first annual general meeting of the company held after such appointment.
6. If the appointment of a relative of a director, or the firm in which such a relative is a partner is made without the knowledge of the concerned director, the consent of the company may be obtained either in the general meeting or within three months from the date of appointment whichever is later.
7. If the remuneration of any such office is increased at a larger time, it must also be approved by the special resolution, except where time scale was approved by the first resolution itself.

Meaning of Office of Profit

1. If it is held by a director, and the director holding it obtains anything by way of remuneration over the remuneration to which he is entitled as a director.

2. If it is held by a relative of the director or by a firm in which the relative, is the partner, and he or the firm obtains from the company anything by way of remuneration as salaries, fees, commission or otherwise.

Exceptions. Section 314 does not apply in the following cases :

1. For holding of office of a managing director, a manager, a banker, or a trustee.

2. Where the relative of a director or the firm in which such relative is a partner was already holding any office of profit before such director becomes a director of the company.

Provisions for Penalty

If any office or place of profit is not held in accordance of the above provisions, it will result in the following :

1. The director, partner, relative, partnership firm, private company or the manager concerned will have to vacate such office of profit from the date next following the date of the general meeting of the company at which the appointment was not approved.
2. The concerned director, partner, relative, partnership firm, private company or manager will have to refund the amount of remuneration or the perks enjoyed by him while remaining on such post. The company cannot exempt such refund without

the prior permission of Central Government. Section 312 applies to all companies, whether a public company or a private company.

LOANS TO DIRECTORS

According to Section 295 of the Indian Companies Act, 1956, a public company cannot sanction any loan to the following persons without prior permission of the Central Government :

1. To its directors or their relatives.
2. To any institution in which the director or any relative of the director has any interest.
3. To any partnership firm in which the director or his relative is a partner.
4. To any private company in which any such director or his relative is a director or a member.
5. To any company in which such directors may control 25 per cent of the total voting power.
6. To any company in which the persons in charge of its management, act in accordance with the direction of the board of directors of the lending company.

This section prohibits the company from giving any guarantee or security for a loan made by any other person or institution to any of the above parties.

Provision for Penalty

Every person who is liable for the non compliance of the above provisions shall be punishable with a fine which may extend upto Rs. 50,000 or with simple imprisonment for a period which may extend upto 6 months or with both. Every liable person shall be jointly and severally liable to refund the amount of loan or guarantee to the lending company. The liable director shall also have to vacate his office.

Exceptions. The provisions of Section 295 do not apply to the following :

1. A private company which is not a subsidiary of a public company.
2. A banking company.
3. A holding company while making loans to its subsidiaries or providing any guarantee for the loans of its subsidiary.

NUMBER OF DIRECTORSHIPS

Section 275 of the Indian Companies Act, 1956 (as amended by Act 2000) states that a person cannot be a director in more than 15 companies at one time. If a person who is already holding the office of director in twenty companies, is also appointed as a director by any other company, such new appointment shall become void. It cannot be effective unless the person vacates some or the other office of director in any company, within 15 days from the date of such new appointment. It is tip to him to decide which company to resign and which to join and which companies to continue.

While calculating the number of fifteen offices of directorship the following are not included :

1. Private Company. Directorship of a private company is not counted while calculating this number of twenty. But the private company to be exempted must neither be a subsidiary company of any public company nor a holding company of a public company.

2. Unlimited Company. If a person holds the office of director in any unlimited company, such office is also not counted while calculating the number of twenty under this restriction.

3. Association. If a person holds any post of directorship in an association which is not established for making the profits or an association which prohibits the payment of dividend, such office is also not included in this number of twenty.

4. Alternate Directorship. If a person is holding the office of director in a company only as alternate director, such office shall also be excluded from the number of twenty.

Except the above four conditions, a person can hold the office of director in the maximum number of twenty companies at one time. If he gets any new appointment as director, he will have to vacate any of the present appointments so that the total number of directorship held by him at one time, does not exceed twenty.

Provision for Penalty. A person who holds the office as director in more than fifteen companies at a time, shall be punishable with a fine which may extend upto Rs. 50,000 for every company after the first fifteen companies.

COMPENSATION FOR LOSS OF OFFICE

Section 318 of the Indian Companies Act states that the directors other than the managing director or the whole time directors who are in the employment of a company, are not entitled to any compensation for loss of office or for the retirement from office. This section further states that a managing director or a whole time director or a director holding the office of manager may be entitled for getting the compensation for loss of office.

Meaning of Compensation for Loss of Office

It means the compensation for the abolition of office because of the following changes :

1. A change in the constitution of a company. For example, a company is amalgamated with any other company and the person concerned does not get the office in the new undertaking.

2. A change in the nature of a company.
3. A change in the mode of management. As a consequence of it, the person concerned does not get his office.

Conditions of no Compensation (Section 318)

1. When the person concerned has resigned from his office in view of the reconstruction or amalgamation of the company and he has obtained similar appointment in the new undertaking.
2. When the person concerned has resigned otherwise, other than due to re-construction or amalgamation.
3. When he has vacated his office by virtue of the power of the court to restrain fraudulent person or by virtue of vacation of office by directors under Section 283.
4. When the company is being wound up and the situation of winding up has arisen due to the negligence or default of the director.
5. When the person concerned has been guilty of fraud or breach of trust or negligence of duty or mismanagement in the affairs of the company.
6. When he himself has taken part in bringing about the termination of his office.

Amount of Compensation

Under Section 318, the amount of compensation should not exceed the remuneration which one would have earned for the unexpired term of his office or for the next three years, whichever is shorter. Further in case the winding up of the company commences within 12 months from the date of termination of the director, no compensation shall be paid to the person if the assets of the company are not sufficient to pay to the shareholders the share capital contributed by them.

REGISTER CONCERNING DIRECTORS

According to Indian Companies Act, 1956 every company, whether a public company or a private company, must maintain the following registers concerning directors :

1. Register of Directors. (i) Section 303. Every company shall keep a register of directors at its registered office. This register must disclose full details *viz.* the names of directors with their surname, name of their father or husband, their residential address, nationality, occupation and the particulars of other directorships held by them. The company must submit a return in the duplicate in the prescribed form to the Registrar of Companies within a period of 30 days from the date of first appointment of directors. If any change takes place in such register, it must also be notified to the registrar within a period of 30 days of such change.

(ii) Section 304. The register of directors shall be free for inspection by any of the member of the company without any charge. It can be inspected by an outsider also on the payment of nominal fee of one rupee for each inspection. Such inspection can be made in the business hours as fixed by the company but it should not be less than 2 hours per day.

2. Register of Shareholdings of Directors. (i) Section 307. Every company must keep a register in which the shares held by the directors in the company and in the subsidiary companies of the company and in the holding company of the company and in all other subsidiaries companies of the same holding company must be disclosed. In this register, the number of shares held by each director, and amount paid on such shares must be disclosed. This register must remain open for the inspection of shareholders or debenture-holders of that company for a period of 14 days before the annual general meeting and 3 days after the meeting.

(ii) Section 308. Every director must give in writing a notice of the transfer or sale of shares by him to the company so that the company may get its register up to date.

3. Register of Contracts, Companies and Firms in Which Directors are interested. Section 301. Every company must keep a register in which all the contracts in which the directors of the company are interested, the companies and the partnership firms in which the directors of the company are holding the position of a director or a partner respectively, must be disclosed. Regarding contracts in which the directors are interested, the register must disclose the following information :

(i) The date of contract.
(ii) The names of all the parties of the contract.
(iii) The terms and conditions of contract.
(iv) The date on which the contract was placed before the board of directors.
(v) The names of directors voting for and against the approval of the contract.

This register must be open for inspection for not less than two hours per day. The register must be kept at the registered office of the company. Only members of the company can inspect this register.

DIRECTORS WITH UNLIMITED LIABILITY

According to Section 322 of the Indian Companies Act a company may have the directors with unlimited liability, only if the following conditions are fulfilled :

1. The memorandum of association of the company contains the provision for the unlimited liability of the directors,

2. The concerned director or directors have been informed in writing by the promoters or directors or manager of the company that his or their liability in the company will be unlimited and he or they must have consented to it in writing.

3. If the memorandum of association of a company does not contain any such provision, the company may alter its memorandum of association by passing a special resolution to make the liability of any of its directors unlimited. But such an alteration can be made by the company only if it is allowed by its articles of association to do so and the directors concerned must have consented in writing to their unlimited liability.

(I) Disclosure of Interests in Contracts by Directors

According to Section 299 of the Indian Companies Act, 1956 every director of a company who is in any way, whether directly or indirectly concerned or interested in a contract or arrangement or proposed contract or arrangement, entered into or to be entered into, by or on behalf of the company shall disclose the nature of his concern or interest at a meeting of the Board of Directors. If the director was not interested in the contract at that time and becomes interested after the contract has been finalised, he must disclose his interest at the first meeting of board of directors after he became so interested in the contract. If the contract has been made by the company with a partnership firm in which he is a partner or with any other company in which he is a member, he must disclose his interest in the contract by giving a general notice to the board of directors disclosing this fact. If the director is interested in any contract entered into by the company and he does not disclose his interest in the contract, he may be punished with a fine which may extend upto Rs. 50,000 and the contract in which the director was so interested, becomes voidable at the discretion of the board of directors.

Section 300 of the Companies Act provides that the directors so interested can neither participate in the discussion nor vote on any such matter in the meeting of board of directors. His presence shall not be counted for the purpose of quorum of the meeting in which the said proposal is to be discussed. If any director violates this provision, he may be punished with a fine which may extend upto to Rs. 5,000.

NECESSITY OF THE SANCTION OF BOARD OF DIRECTORS

According to Section 297 of the Indian Companies Act, when a company wants to enter into any contract for the sale or purchase or supply of any material or service or any underwriting contract with any of its directors or his relatives, or his partners, the consent of board of directors must be obtained. Such consent must be accorded by a resolution passed at the meeting of board of directors. Consent by means of a resolution passed by circulation will not be enough for this purpose.

Except with the consent of the Board of directors of a company, a director of the company or his relative, a firm in which such a director or relative is a partner, any other partner in such a firm, or a private company of which the director is a member or director, shall not enter into any contract with the company—

(a) for the sale, purchase or supply of any goods, material of services; or

(b) after the commencement of this Act, for underwriting the subscription of any shares in, or debentures of, the company:

[1][Provided that in the case of a company having a paid-up share capital of not less than rupees one crore, no such contract shall be entered into except with the previous approval[2] of the Central Government.[3]]

[4](2) Nothing contained in clause (a) sub-section (1) shall affect—

(a) the purchase of goods and materials from the company, or the sale of goods and materials to the company, by the director, relative, firm, partner or private company as aforesaid for cash at prevailing market prices; or

(b) any contract or contracts between the company on one side and any such director, relative, firm, partner or private company on the other for sale, purchase or supply of any goods, materials and services in which either the company or the director, relative, firm, partner or private company, as the case may be, regularly trades or does business:

Provided that such contract or contracts do not relate to goods and materials the value of which, or services the cost of which, exceeds five thousand rupees in the aggregate in any year comprised in the period of the contract or contracts or;

(c) in the case of a banking or insurance company any transaction in the ordinary course of business of such company with the director, relative, firm partner or private company as aforesaid.

(3) Notwithstanding anything contained in sub-sections (1) and (2) a director, relative, firm, partner or private company as aforesaid may, in circumstances of urgent necessity, enter, without obtaining the consent of the Board, into any contract with the company for the sale, purchase or supply of any goods, materials or services even if the value of such goods or cost of such services exceeds five thousand rupees in the aggregate in any year comprised in the period of the

1. Inserted by Act 41 of 1974, Section 28, w.e.f. 1-2-1975.
2. See Form 24A, Companies (Central Government's) General Rules and Forms, 1956.
3. Powers delegated to Regional Director vide Notification No. GSR 563(E), dated 19-8-1993.
4. Substituted by Act 65 of 1960, section 104, for sub-sections (2) to (5).

contract; but in such a case, the consent of the Board shall be obtained at a meeting within three months of the date on which the contract was entered into.

(4) Every consent of the Board required under this section shall be accorded by a resolution passed at a meeting of the Board and not otherwise; and the consent of the Board required under sub-section (1) shall not be deemed to have been given within the meaning of that sub-section unless the consent is accorded before the contract is entered into or within three months of the date on which it was entered into.

(5) If consent is not accorded to any contract under this section, anything done in pursuance of the contract shall be voidable at the option of the Board.

(6) Nothing in this section shall apply to any case where the consent has been accorded to the contract before the commencement of the Companies (Amendment) Act, 1960 (65 of 1960).

MANAGING DIRECTOR

Definition

According to Section 267 of the Indian Companies Act, 1956 "A director who, by the virtue of an agreement with the company or by a resolution passed by the company in general meeting or by its board of directors, or by virtue of its memorandum or articles of association, is entrusted with substantial powers of management which would not otherwise be exercisable by him, and includes a director occupying the position of a managing director, by whatever name he may be called, provided that a managing director of a company shall exercise his powers subject to the superintendence, control and direction of the board of directors."

Thus, Managing Director must be a director enjoying the substantial powers of the management. He may be appointed by an agreement or by memorandum or by articles of association or by resolution passed by the board of directors or by resolution passed at the general meeting. Generally the articles of association of a company refer to the office of managing director. The board of directors may appoint any director to the office of managing director by passing a resolution at its meeting. A separate service contract is set out for specifying the terms and conditions, powers and duties and liabilities of the appointment managing director. A director acts under the supervision and control of the board of directors.

Characteristics

1. A Director. A managing director must necessarily be a director. So, first of all a person should hold the office of director and only then he can be appointed as managing director of the company. If he ceases to act as a director his appointment as a managing director is automatically terminated.

2. Substantial Powers of Management. Managing director is practically head of the company. He controls all the activities of the company. Hence he must have substantial powers of management other than the administrative acts of routine nature to discharge his duties properly because the routine nature acts are done by other directors.

3. Appointment Under a Separate Service Contract. A managing director may be appointed by virtue of an agreement with the company, or by virtue of a resolution passed by the company in its general meeting, or by virtue of a resolution passed at the meeting of board of directors of the company, or by virtue of its memorandum of association, or by virtue of its articles of association. Generally, the managing director is appointed by a resolution passed at the meeting of board of directors of the company. The terms and conditions of this appointment, his duties, liabilities, rights and powers are generally decided by a separate service contract.

4. Under the Supervision of the Board of Directors. Managing director has to discharge his duties under the control and supervision of the board of directors of the company. As he is the chief executive officer of the company, he cannot go beyond the provisions of the Indian Companies Act, and the memorandum of association and articles of association of the company.

Statutory Provisions Regarding Appointment

Indian Companies Act, 1956 imposes following conditions regarding the appointment of a person to the office of managing director in case of a public company or a private company which is a subsidiary of any public company.

1. Method of Appointment [Section 2(28)]. The managing director of a company can be appointed by any of the following methods :

(i) By an agreement between company and the person concerned.

(ii) By passing a resolution at the general meeting of the shareholders.

(iii) By passing a resolution at the board of directors.

(iv) By the provisions of memorandum and articles of association of the company.

2. Only an Individual. Only an individual can be appointed to the office of managing director. A partnership firm, or an association of persons, or a company cannot be appointed to hold the office of managing director.

3. Person cannot be a Managing Director of Two or More Companies (Section 316). The person to be appointed as a managing director in a company can hold the office of managing director in one company only. He cannot hold such office in two or more companies at the same time, unless specifically permitted by the Central Government.

4. Term of the Office [Section 317(3)]. Normally a managing director is appointed for a ten-n of five years, but the central government may increase or decrease the period of his term, if it thinks it in the interest of the company to do so.

5. Sanction of the Central Government. On and from the commencement of the Companies (Amendment) Act, 1988, no appointment of a person as a managing or whole-time director or a manager in a public company or a private company which is a subsidiary of a public company shall be made except with the approval of the Central Government unless such appointment is made in accordance with the conditions specified in Part I and II of Schedule XIII (the said Parts being subject to the provisions of Part III of that Schedule) and a return in the prescribed from is filed within ninety days from the date of such appointment.

Every application seeking approval to the appointment of a managing or whole-time director or a manager shall be made to the Central Government within a period of ninety days from the date of such appointment.

The Central Government shall not accord its approval to an application made under sub-section (3), if it is satisfied that—

(a) the managing or whole-time director or the manager appointed is, in its opinion, not a fit and proper person to be appointed as such or such appointment is not in the public interest; or

(b) the terms and conditions of the appointment of managing or whole-time director or the manager are not fair and reasonable.

It shall be competent for the Central Government while according approval to an appointment under sub-section (3) to accord approval for a period lesser than the period for which the appointment is proposed to be made.

6. No Change without Approval of Central Government. According to Section 268 no such change can be made by the company without prior approval of the Central Government.

Duration of the Office

According to the provisions of Companies (Amendment) Act, 1974 a public company cannot appoint any person to the office of managing director for a term exceeding five years. After the expiry of this term he may be reappointed for another five years. For this, either the prior approval of Central Government must be obtained or such approval must be obtained within a period of 3 months from the date of such re-appointment. Under Section 317 the reappointment must be made within the last two months of his present term. There is, however, no restriction regarding the term of appointment of a whole time director. No restriction applies to the appointment of managing director or whole lime director in the private companies.

Remuneration

1. Monthly or Percentage of Profit. The managing director of a company may be paid the remuneration either on monthly basis or in the form of percentage on the net profits of the company or in both ways.

2. No other Remuneration. A person getting the remuneration from a company as a managing director can get no remuneration from any of its subsidiary company, in any capacity.

3. Limits to Remuneration. If the company is having only one full time managing director, remuneration payable to such managing director cannot be more than 5 per cent of the net profits of the company. If the company is having more than one full time managing directors, their total remuneration cannot be more than 10 per cent of the profits of the company. For any remuneration exceeding this limit, prior approval of the Central Government must be obtained.

4. According to Section 637A. The Central Government is empowered to fix a limit for the remuneration of managing director, at the time of giving approval of such appointment.

Disqualifications

According to Section 274 of the Companies Act, 1956 a person suffering from any of the following disqualifications cannot be appointed as a managing director or whole time director of a company.

1. One who has been declared insolvent at any time.
2. Suspends or has, at any time, suspended payment to his creditors or makes or has made a composition with them.
3. Is or has been convicted by a court of an offence involving moral turpitude.

A person to be appointed as a managing director or a whole time director of a company, should be a man of character and integrity. He should never have been declared insolvent, or sustained payment or made any compromise with his creditors of convicted or an offence involving moral turpitude. This restriction applies to the private companies as well.

Restriction on the Number

According to Section 316 a person cannot act as a managing director of more than two companies at one time including both public and private companies. At least one of the two companies should be a public company. Thus, a person can work as a managing director of more than two independent private companies at one time. If a person who already working as a managing director of a company, is to be appointed as managing director in some other company, an unanimous resolution of the board of directors must be passed for such appointment. If the Central Government is satisfied that the companies must have a common managing director for their proper work it may permit a person to be appointed as a managing director of more than two companies. But in practice, the Company Law Board does not approve appointment of any person as managing director in two companies of large size.

Compensation on Termination of Office

According to Section 318(4) of the Companies Act, a managing director may claim the compensation from the company if he is terminated from his office. Section 318(1) provides that a managing director cannot be entitled to any compensation in the following cases :

1. If his office is vacated because of the re-construction or amalgamation of the company.
2. If he has resigned from his office because of the operations of Section 263 or Section 283 of the Companies Act.
3. If the company has gone into liquidation because of the faults of managing director himself.
4. If he has been terminated, by the company, on the allegation of negligence of duty or breach of trust.
5. If he has directly or indirectly made an effort for the vacation of his office.
6. He will not be paid any compensation for the loss caused to him because of transfer of business.

In the above six conditions a managing director, terminated from his office, cannot claim any compensation from the company. But in other conditions the managing director may claim the compensation from the company for termination of his office and the company shall be held liable to pay such compensation.

Amount of Compensation

The compensation to managing director cannot exceed the total remuneration payable to him for his unexpired term or the total remuneration for a period of three years. But if the company goes into winding up within a period of 12 months from the date of termination of his office and the assets of the company are insufficient to make the payment of shareholders, the terminated managing director cannot be paid any compensation in any circumstances.

QUESTIONS

1 . What are the provisions of the Indian Companies Act, 2000, as to the number, appointment and remuneration of directors of a company?

2. What are the legal restrictions on the appointment of directors in a public Company?
3. How are the directors appointed? What provisions have been made regarding restrictions on the appointment of directors in the Company Law?
4. Who are the directors? How can they be appointed? How is their remuneration fixed in a company?
5. What are the powers of the directors of the company? What statutory restrictions have been imposed upon these directors?
6. Explain the Duties and Liabilities of the directors of a company.
7. "Directors of a company are not only tile agents but they are also in some sense and to some extent trustees or in the position of trustees." Discuss.
8. "The act does not define the status of directors and it is difficult to define their precise position." Discuss.
9. "The exact position of directors with regard to the company is hard to define. They are not servants of tile company but are rather in the position of managing partners." Discuss.
10. Write short notes on the following :

    (A) Removal of directors. (B) Vacation of office by director. (C) Appointment of directors to an office of profit. (D) Loan to directors. (E) Number of directorship (F) Compensation for loss of office. (G) Register of director. (H) Directors with unlimited liability. (I) Disclosure of interests in contracts by directors. (J) Necessity of the consent of Board of directors.
11. State the provisions of the Indian Companies Act in regard to the appointment, qualifications, the duration of office and compensation on termination of appointment of a managing director.
12. Who is managing director? How is he appointed'? What are the qualifications and disqualifications for the appointment of a managing director? How can he be terminated and what is the legal position regarding compensation on termination of appointment of a managing director?

PRACTICAL PROBLEMS

1. A contract between N.W. Ltd. and B, one, of its directors, is referred to a general meeting for its approval. At the meeting, B voted for the resolution and all others against it. But as B held majority of shares and was entitled to majority of votes, the resolution was passed. Is the contract binding on the company?
   [**Hint.** No (Section 300)].

2. A public limited company has 15 directors, 4 of whom are not subject to retire by rotation. Is it a validly constituted Board? [**Hint.** Yes (Section 255)].
3. A private company having 2 directors has just become a public company by virtue of Section 43-A. Is it obligatory for the company to appoint a third director?
[**Hint.** No (Section 252)].
4. Three persons were appointed as directors of a company by a single resolution. A member who did not object to this in the meeting later filed a complaint to Magistrate under Section 629-A of the Companies Act, who sentenced them to a fine of Rs. 250 each and in default 15 days' simple imprisonment. The directors appealed against the conviction. Decide.
[**Hint.** Section 629-A provides for penalty in case of certain offences where no specific remedy is provided elsewhere in the Act. The appointment of 2 or more persons as directors by a single resolution is void (Section 263). The decision of the Magistrate is correct and the appeal of the directors against conviction will be set aside].
5. The Board of directors of X Ltd. met only 3 times in the previous year. A fourth meeting was adjourned twice for lack of quorum. Does this constitute a violation of Section 285 of the Companies Act, 1956?
[**Hint.** No (Section 288)].
6. The directors of a company bought some of its shares from a shareholder while they were negotiating for a transaction financially advantageous to the company and which, if successful, would have substantially raised the market value of its shares. They did not disclose this information to the shareholder when buying his shares. This erstwhile shareholder sued the directors for rescission of sale on the ground of fraud. State, giving reasons, whether he will succeed.
[**Hint.** No (Percival *Vs.* Wright)]
7. The Articles of a company incorporated in 1988 provided that a director should hold 200 shares of the value of Rs. 10 each as a qualification. At the annual general meeting of the company held in September 1998 an ordinary resolution was passed increasing the share qualification to be held by directors to 600 shares. The company then issued notice to the directors who did not hold 600 shares to acquire additional shares within one month. M, a director, who was asked to acquire the additional qualification shares, received the notice. He seeks your advice. What advice would you give him?
[**Hint.** The alteration is invalid because (a) special resolution required to alter the Articles is not passed, (b) it violates the provisions of Section 270].

8. The Board of directors of A & Co. Ltd. appointed Rajan the managing director and gave him full powers of management of the company's affairs and authorised him to sign all papers. Rajan borrowed money on a promissory note.
   Is the company bound by this transaction
   [**Hint.** Yes (P. Rangaswamy Reddiar *Vs.* R.K. Reddiar, (1973) 43 Comp. Cas. 232)].

9. The Secretary of a company purchased some stationery for the company but he took it home and put it to his private use. The company refused to pay to the supplier of the stationery on the plea that it never received the stationery.
   Is the company liable?
   [**Hint.** Yes [Panorama Development (Guildford) Ltd. *Vs.* Fidelis Furnishing Fabrics Ltd.].

13

THE COMPANY MANAGER

MEANING AND DEFINITION

Manager is the chief executive officer of a company. The term Manager does not refer to such executive personnel as Sales Manager, Advertisement Manager, Factory Manager, Production Manager etc. It means the manager to supervise and to control all the activities of the company. He is :

1. Only an individual.

2. Liable for the management of the whole, or substantially the whole of the affairs of the company.

3. A manager may be or may not be appointed under the contract of service.

4. A director can also work as a manager.

5. Discharges his duties under the supervision, control and direction of board of directors.

Section 2(24) of Company Act 1956, defines a Manager, "A manager means an individual who, subject to the superintendence, control and direction of the board of directors, has been appointed for the management of the whole, or substantially the whole of the affairs of a company and includes a director or any other person occupying the position of a manager, by whatever name called, and whether under contract of service or not."

LEGAL PROVISIONS REGARDING APPOINTMENT

Under Sections 381 to 388 of Indian Companies Act, legal provisions of appointment of a manager may be summarised as under :

1. To Observe the Provision of Articles of Association. If the articles of association of a company contain some provisions regarding the appointment of manager, the company must observe all these provisions while appointing a person as a manager.

2. Appointment in accordance with Table 'A'. The company must observe the proviso 28 of Table 'A'. If the company has not drafted its own articles of association or if the articles of a company do not contain any provision regarding the appointment of a manager according to this proviso, a manager may be appointed with the consent of board of directors. A director may also be appointed as the manager. The board of directors is empowered to remove a manager from his post.

3. Only an Individual can be a Manager. Only an individual can be appointed as manager in a company. A partnership firm or a company cannot be appointed to hold the post of manager.

4. A Manager cannot hold the Office of Manager in more than Two Companies. A person can be appointed as manager at the most only in two companies at one time. No person can hold the office of manager in more than two companies at one time.

5. Prior Approval of Central Government. A public company must obtain the prior approval of the Central Government for appointing the manager. However, such approval may be obtained within a period of three months of such appointment in case of a newly incorporated company. If the Central Government does not approve, the appointed person will have to vacate his office.

6. Term of the Manager. A manager may be appointed by a company for a term of five years. However, a retiring manager may be re-appointed. A manager cannot assign his post.

DISQUALIFICATIONS FOR THE POST

According to Section 385 of the Indian Companies Act a person with any of the following disqualifications cannot be appointed as a manager by any company :

(i) *Insolvent :* A person who is an undischarged insolvent or has at any time been declared as insolvent within the preceding five years.

(ii) *Suspended :* A person who has at any time suspended any payment to his creditors within the preceding five years; or has made a confrontation with them at any time within the preceding five years.

(iii) *Convicted :* A person who is or has been convicted by a court in India at any time within the preceding five years for an offence involving moral turpitude.

Thus, while appointing a person to the office of manager, a period of five years preceding the date of his appointment is to be taken into account. However, the Central Government may waive any or all of the disqualifications for a person to be appointed to the office of manager.

REMOVAL OF MANAGER

1. The Central Government may remove any person holding the office of manager on the basis of judgement given by any High Court (Adjudged as fraudulent, liable for negligence of duty or liable for breach of trust or liable for negligence by the Court) under Section 388 of the Indian Companies Act, 1956.

2. The person so removed from his office cannot be appointed to the office of manager for a period of five years from the date of such removal.

3. If the Central Government is of the opinion that the person may be appointed to the post of manager before the expiry of the term of five years from the date of removal, it may do so with the consultation of High Court.

4. The managers so removed will not be eligible for any compensation for his removal.

5. However, if the person so removed succeeds in giving evidence before the High Court that he had discharged his duties with proper care and honesty, he may be freed of the charge against him by the High Court and in this case he may be re-appointed to the office of manager under Section 633.

REMUNERATION OF THE MANAGER

A manager may be remunerated by way of monthly salary or by way of a certain percentage on the net profits of the company or in both the ways. If he is entitled to get a percentage of net profit of the company, it should not exceed 5 per cent. However, this percentage may be increased with the approval of the Central Government. All the provisions of the Companies Act relating to the remuneration of managing director apply to the remuneration of manager also.

MANAGER AND MANAGING DIRECTOR

1. Both are the officers of the company.

2. Only an individual can be appointed for both the posts.

3. Both perform their duties in accordance with the instructions of board of directors.

4. Both have substantial powers for the management of the company.

5. Provisions of the Indian Companies Act apply almost similarly for both the posts.

Difference

1. Compulsion of being Director. For the post of managing director, the person must be a director of the company. If he is not a director, he cannot be appointed to the office of managing directors. On the other hand, the person to be appointed to the office of manager may or may not be a director of the company.

2. Need of Separate Service Contract. For the office of a managing director, a separate service contract must be signed between the company and the person holding the office of managing director. But for the post of a manager, there is no need of any such contract.

3. Rights. When compared with the rights of a managing director the rights of a manager are comparatively limited.

4. Possibility of waiving the Disqualifications. The Central Government may, if it thinks fit, waive the disqualifications for the appointment of a person to the office of the manager. But it cannot be possible for the appointment to the office of a managing director.

5. Number of Officers. There cannot be more than one manager in a company but there may be as many managing directors in a company as required, each of which will be in charge of a division or an activity of the business.

6. Maximum Remuneration. Under Section 387 the maximum remuneration payable to a person holding the office of a manager cannot exceed 5 per cent of the annual net profits of the company. But, if the company has more than one managing directors, the total remuneration payable to all of them should not exceed 10 per cent of the total net profits of the company.

MANAGERIAL PERSONNEL

As an artificial person created by law, a company cannot work like a natural person. Therefore, it is to be managed by its agents or representatives, who are called its managerial personnel, appointed in accordance with the provisions of Indian Companies Act, memorandum of association and articles of association of the company. The terms and conditions of their appointment and their remuneration are also decided under the same provisions. Following three offices are included in the term managerial personnel of a company :

1. Director,
2. Managing Director,
3. Manager.

RESTRICTIONS BY THE INDIAN COMPANIES ACT

Managerial Personnel are the persons authorised and liable for the management, administration and control of a company. The success of a company depends to a large extent, upon the discharge of duties by these personnel. They are also the agents and trustees of the shareholders of the company. Therefore, the persons appointed to all these offices must be honest, of high character and moral and capable enough to discharge the duties of their respective office. Keeping in view the importance of these offices, the Indian Companies Act has declared following persons as undesirable for the appointment to these offices and cannot hold any of the above offices in any company.

1. Undischarged Insolvent. Under Section 202 of the Indian Companies Act, 1956 an undischarged insolvent cannot be appointed to any office of the managerial personnel in any company. If any such person holds any such office in any company, either fraudulently or innocently, he may be punished with imprisonment for a term which may extend upto two years or with a fine which may extend upto

Rs. five thousand or with both. It is to remember that this provision does not apply on foreign companies.

2. A Defaulter in the Formation or Management of the Company. Under Section 203 of the Indian Companies Act, any person who has been proved defaulter for the formation, incorporation or management of the company or is liable for any fraudulent dealing with the company, may be declared by the court as undesirable person for the appointment to the office of managerial personnel of a company. If any such person holds any such office in any company, either fraudulently or innocently, he may be punished with an imprisonment for a term which may extend upto two years or with a fine which may extend upto Rs. five thousand or with both. In addition to this, he may also be debarred from holding any such post for the next five years.

3. Representative of a Firm or An Incorporated Body. A representative of any firm or any incorporated body cannot be appointed to any office of managerial personnel in any company for a term of five years. However, this provision does not apply for the appointment of the representative of debenture-holders or contributories.

4. Appointment of a Managing Agent or Secretary or Treasure. Section 324, 324A, 325, 326 and 348, regarding prohibition of appointment of managing agents have been omitted by the Companies (Amendment) Act 2000, as provisions relating to managing agents etc., had become redundant after abolition of system by Act 17 of 1969.

POWERS OF THE CENTRAL GOVERNMENT

The Indian Companies Act, 1956 empowers the Central Government to remove any of the managerial personnel of any company on the recommendation of the Company Law Board. The Central Government has the following powers also in this regard :

1. Order of Enquiry. The Central Government may order an enquiry by any court regarding any of the managerial personnel in any company in the following circumstances :

(i) If the company suffers any loss or expects to suffer any loss because of the conduct of such person.

(ii) If such person violates the principles of business of the company.

(iii) If the business activities of the company are being carried out by such person in a manner as to deceive the shareholders or debenture-holders of the company or the acts of such person are held against the interests of general public.

(iv) If any such person is held liable for fraud or negligence of duty or breach of trust in the discharge of his duties.

Under Section 388(B) of the Indian Companies Act, in any of the above circumstances, the Central Government may order for an enquiry by any court regarding the managerial competence of such person or persons.

2. Record of the Facts by the Court. If any such enquiry is ordered, the court going into the enquiry will collect and study all the facts regarding the case and will try to ascertain whether the person concerned is competent for the managerial post or not.

3. Interim Order. Under Section 388(C) of the Indian Companies Act, on the recommendations of the court enquiring the facts, the Central Government may order for the removal of any managerial personnel of any company and may appoint any person in place of Such removed person.

4. Action by the Government. Under Section 388(D), the Central Government, on the recommendations of the court, may declare any of the managerial personnel of a company as undesirable person to hold the office of managerial personnel in the company. The Central Government may also debar such person from holding any such post for a term of five years from the date of order.

MANAGERIAL REMUNERATION

Meaning

Managerial remuneration means the remuneration which is paid by a company to its managerial personnel *i.e.*, Director, Managing Director and Manager, or their services under Section 198 of the Indian Companies Act. The term remuneration includes the following perquisites also :

1. Any expenditure incurred by the company in providing any rent free accommodation or any other benefit in respect of accommodation free of charge or at concessional rate.

2. Any expenditure incurred by the company in providing any other benefit free of charge or at concessional rate.

3. Any expenditure incurred by the company in respect of any obligation or service, which, but for such expenditure, would have been incurred by the person himself.

4. Any expenditure by the company to effect any insurance on the life of, or to provide any pension, annuity or gratuity for, the person or spouse or his children.

The above provision has been made to prevent directors from drawing more money than allowed by the Indian Companies Act in the guise of collateral benefits.

Limit of Managerial Remuneration

The term remuneration shall not include the following :

1. Any expenses payable to the managerial personnel for attending the meeting of the board of directors or a committee, thereof, of the company, or

2. Any remuneration payable to managerial personnel for acting as technical consultant or management consultant or financial advisor having professional qualification under Section 309(1).

Under Section 637AA of the Indian Companies Act, the central government should consider the following factors while deciding the limit for the maximum managerial remuneration for a particular company :

1. Financial position of the company.

2. The commission or remuneration withdrawn by the person concerned in any other form.

3. The commission or remuneration withdrawn by the person concerned from any other company.

4. The qualification and experience of the business activities of the person concerned.

5. Public policy to eliminate the gap in the income.

MAXIMUM MANAGERIAL REMUNERATION

Section 198 of the Indian Companies Act lays down overall maximum managerial remuneration which can be paid by a public company or a private company which is a subsidiary of a public company. The total managerial remuneration to the directors and the manager in respect of any financial year must not exceed 11 per cent of the net profits of the company for that financial year computed in the manner laid down in section 349 and 350. This percentage shall be exclusive of the fees payable to the directors for attending the meetings of the board of directors or a committee thereof.

Within 11 per cent limit of the overall maximum remuneration, a company may pay monthly remuneration to its :

(a) Managing or whole time director in accordance with the provisions of Section 3 which deals with remuneration of directors, or

(b) Manager in accordance with the provisions of Section 387 (which deals with remuneration of Manager).

The persons having additional qualifications will not be subject to the limit of maximum remuneration.

REMUNERATION IN CASE OF NIL OR INADEQUATE PROFITS

If in any financial year a company has no net profits or its net profits are inadequate, the company shall not pay to its director, including any managing or whole time directors or manager by way of remuneration any sum excluding any fees payable to directors under Section 309(2) except with the previous approval of the Central Government. This is subject to the provisions of Section 269 which deals with appointment of managing or whole-time director, and with

Schedule XIII [Section 198(4) as amended by the Companies (Amendment) Act, 1988]. Prior to the amendment of Section 198(4) by the Companies Amendment Act, of 1988, a company could pay, by way of minimum remuneration, upto Rs. 50,000.

In the event of loss or inadequacy of profits, approval of the central government is not required for payment or remuneration if :

(a) the appointment had been made in accordance with the terms and conditions as specified in Schedule XIII and

(b) the resolution passed in the general meeting provides for a cut of 10 per cent of the salary proposed to be paid, in terms of para 2 of Part III of Schedule XIII of the Companies Act.

Rules Regarding Managerial Remuneration

The managerial remuneration payable to directors is a part of the overall managerial remuneration which cannot exceed 11 per cent of the net profits. The managerial remuneration payable to the directors, including any managing or whole time or part time directors, must be determined in accordance with the provisions of section 198 and 309 either by the articles of association or if articles of association so require, by a special resolution passed by the company in general meeting. In case of a public company and a private company which is a subsidiary company of a public company, the provisions relating to managerial remuneration of its directors are as follows :

1. Section 309(3). A managing or whole time director may be paid remuneration either by way of a monthly payment or at a specified percentage of net profits of the company for that financial year computed in manner laid down in section 349 and 350 or partly by one way or partly by the other. Except with the approval of the central government such remuneration must not exceed 5 per cent of the net profits for one such director or 10 per cent of the net profits or all of them in case there is more than one such director.

2. Section 309(4). A. director who is neither in the whole time employment of the company nor managing director (*i.e.* part time director) may be paid remuneration either by way of a monthly, quarterly or annual payment with the approval of the central government, or by way of commission if the company by special resolution authorise such payment. The remuneration paid to such category of directors must not exceed :

(i) 1 per cent of the net profits of the company if the company has a managing or whole time director or manager and

(ii) 3 per cent of the net profit of the company in any other case.

However, the company in general meeting may, with the approval of the central government, increase these rates of remuneration.

3. Section 309(9). The above rules do not apply to a private company unless it is a subsidiary company of a public company.

4. Section 387. The manager of a company may, subject to the overall limit of managerial remuneration, receive remuneration either by way of a monthly payment or by way of specified percentage of the net profits of the company. Except with the approval of the Central Government, such remuneration must not exceed in the aggregate 5 per cent of the net profit of the company.

5. Section 200. A company cannot pay to any officer or employee remuneration free of tax.

COMPUTATION OF NET PROFITS OF THE COMPANY

Under Section 349 of the Indian Companies Act, 1956 the following method is adopted for computing the net profits of the company for specified percentage of managerial remuneration :

1. Items to be included in Profits. The following items are included in gross profits in computing net profits of a company :

(i) Bounties (money offered as a premium to encourage industry).
(ii) Subsidies received from any Government or any Public Authority constituted or authorised in this behalf by any Government.

2. Items not to be included in Profits. The following items of incomes are not to be included, in computing the net profits of a company :

(i) Premium on the issue of shares or debentures.
(ii) Profits on re-issue of forfeited shares.
(iii) Capital profits including those arising from the sale of the undertaking or any of the undertakings of the company or any part thereof.
(iv) Capital profits from the sale of any immovable property of fixed assets.

Under Section 349(3) where the amount for which any fixed asset is sold exceeds its written down value (*i.e.*, Original Cost less depreciation), credit shall be given for so much of the excess as is not higher than the difference between the original cost of the fixed asset and its written down value.

3. Items to be deducted from Profits. In computing net profits of a company the following items of expenses and losses are to be deducted :

(i) All the usual working charges.
(ii) Directors remuneration (fee for attending meeting of board of directors or a committee thereof or any remuneration payable to managerial personnel for acting as technical consultant, or management consultant or financial advisor having professional qualifications).

(iii) Bonus or commission paid or payable to any employee of the company.

(iv) Any tax notified by the Central Government on abnormal profits.

(v) Any tax on business profits.

(vi) Interest on debentures issued by the company.

(vii) Interest on unsecured loans and advances.

(viii) Expenses on repairs, whether to immovable or to movable property, provided the repairs are not of capital nature.

(x) Contributions to charitable and other funds to the extent specified in Section 293(l)(e).

(xi) Depreciation to the extent specified in Section 350.

(xii) Past losses arising after lst April, 1956, to the extent not already deducted in any subsequent year.

(xiii) Any compensation or damages to be paid in virtue of any legal liability, including in a liability arising from a breach of contract.

(xiv) Any sum paid by way of insurance against the risk of meeting any liability such as is referred to in the relevant section.

(xv) Bad debts written off during the year.

4. Items not to be deducted from Profits. The following items of expenses and losses are not to be deducted in computing net profits of a company.

(i) Income tax, Super tax and any other tax paid on the income of the company not falling under clauses (iv) and (v) above.

(ii) Any compensation, damages or payments made voluntarily and not in virtue of any legal liability.

(iii) Capital losses [Section 349(5)].

Ascertainment of Depreciation. Under Section 350 of the Indian Companies Act, 1956 the amount of depreciation to be deducted is the amount calculated with reference to the written down value of the assets as shown by the books at the end of each financial year at the rate specified in Schedule XIV. Schedule XIV [added by the Companies (Amendment) Act, 1988] gives the Rates of Depreciation for various assets.

If any asset is sold, discarded, demolished or destroyed for any reason before depreciation of such assets has been provided in full, the excess, if any, of the written down value of such asset over its sale proceeds or its scrap value, shall be written off in the financial year in which the asset is sold, discarded, demolished or destroyed.

Guidelines Regarding Remuneration

The Companies (Amendment) Act, 1988 has introduced Schedule XIII regarding Managerial Remuneration. The Schedule was amended by Companies (Amendment) Act 2000. The Schedule deals with appointment of managerial personnel (Part I) and their remuneration (Part II) and provisions applicable to Part I and II of this Schedule (Part III). The Schedule XIII is reproduced below :

SCHEDULE XIII

(See Sections 198, 269, 310 and 311)

Conditions to be fulfilled for the appointment of a managing or whole time director or a manager without the prior approval of the central government.

PART I
APPOINTMENTS

No person shall be eligible for appointment as a managing or whole-time director or a manager (hereinafter referred to as managerial person) of a company unless he satisfies the following conditions, namely :

(a) he had not been sentenced to imprisonment for any period, or to a fine exceeding one thousand rupees, for the conviction of an offence under any of the following Acts, namely :

(i) the Indian Stamp Act, 1899 (2 of 1899),

(ii) the Central Excise Act, 1994 (1 of 1944),

(iii) the Industries (Development and Regulation) Act, 1951 (65 of 1951),

(iv) the Prevention of Food Adulteration Act, 1954 (37 of 1954),

(v) the Essential Commodities Act, 1955 (10 of 1955),

(vi) the Companies Act, 1956 (1 of 1956),

(vii) the Securities Contracts (Regulation) Act, 1956 (42 of 1956),

(viii) the Wealth-tax Act, 1957 (27 of 1957),

(ix) the Income-tax Act, 1961 (43 of 1961),

(x) the Customs Act, 1962 (52 of 1962),

(xi) the Monopolies and Restrictive Trade Practices Act, 1969 (54 of 1969),

(xii) the Foreign Exchange Regulation Act, 1973 (46 of 1973),

(xiii) the Sick Industrial Companies (Special Provisions) Act, 1985 (1 of 1986),

(xiv) the Securities and Exchange Board of India Act, 1992 (15 of 1992),

(xv) the Foreign Trade (Development and Regulation) Act, 1992 (22 of 1992);

(b) he had not been detained for any period under the Conservation of Foreign Exchange and Prevention of Smuggling Activities Act, 1974 (52 of 1974);

Provided that where the Central Government has given its approval to the appointment of a person convicted or detained under sub-paragraph (a) or sub-paragraph (b), as the case may be, no further approval of the Central Government shall be necessary for the subsequent appointment of that person if he had not been so convicted or detained subsequent to such approval;

(c) he has completed the age of 25 years and has not attained the age of 70 years :

Provided that where—

(i) he has not completed the age of 25 years, but has attained the age of majority; or

(ii) he has attained the age of 70 years; and

where his appointment is approved by a special resolution passed by the company in general meeting, no further approval of the Central Government shall be necessary for such appointment;

(d) where he is a managerial person in more than one company he draws remuneration from one or more companies subject to the ceiling provided in Section III of Part II;

(e) he is resident in India.

Explanation : For the purpose of this Schedule, resident in India includes a person who has been staying in India for a continuous period of not less than twelve months immediately preceding the date of his appointment as a managerial person and who has come to stay in India,—

(i) for taking up employment in India, or

(ii) for carrying on a business or vocation in India.

PART II
REMUNERATION

Section I.—*Remuneration payable by companies having profits*

Subject to the provisions of sections 198 and 309*, a company having profits in a financial year may pay any remuneration, by way of salary, dearness allowance, perquisites, commission and other allowances, which shall not exceed five per cent of its net profits for one such managerial person, and if there is more than one such managerial person, ten per cent for all of them together.

* These sections do not apply to government companies.

Section II.—*Remuneration payable by companies having no profits or inadequate profits*

1. Notwithstanding anything contained in this Part, where in any financial year during the currency of tenure of the managerial person, a company has no profits or its profits are inadequate, it may pay remuneration to a managerial person by way of salary, dearness allowance, perquisites and any other allowances,—

(A) not exceeding the ceiling limit of Rs. 24,00,000 per annum or Rs. 2,00,000 per month calculated on the following scale :

Where the effective capital of Company is	Monthly remuneration payable shall not exceed (Rupees)
(i) less than rupees 1 crore	75,000
(ii) rupees 1 crore or more but less than rupees 5 crores	1,00,000
(iii) rupees 5 crores or more but less than rupees 25 crores	1,25,000
(iv) rupees 25 crores or more but less than rupees 50 crores	1,50,000
(v) rupees 50 crores or more but less than rupees 100 crores	1,75,000
(vi) rupees 100 crores or more	2,00,000

Provided that the ceiling limits specified under this sub-paragraph shall apply, if—

(i) payment of remuneration is approved by a resolution passed by the Remuneration Committee;

(ii) the company has not made any default in repayment of any of its debts (including public deposits) or debentures or interest payable thereon for a continuous period of thirty days in the preceding financial year before the date of appointment of such managerial person.

(B) not exceeding the ceiling limit of Rs. 48,00,000 per annum or Rs. 4,00,000 per month calculated on the following scale:—

Where the effective capital of Company is	Monthly remuneration payable shall not exceed (Rupees)
(i) less than rupees 1 crore	1,50,000
(ii) rupees 1 crore or more but less than rupees 5 crores	2,00,000
(iii) rupees 5 crores or more but less than rupees 25 crores	2,50,000

(Contd.)

Where the effective capital of Company is	Monthly remuneration payable shall not exceed (Rupees)
(iv) rupees 25 crores or more but less than rupees 50 crores	3,00,000
(v) rupees 50 crores or more but less than rupees 100 crores	3,50,000
(vi) rupees 100 crores or more	4,00,000

Provided that the ceiling limits specified under this sub-paragraph shall apply, if—

(i) payment of remuneration is approved by a resolution passed by the Remuneration Committee;

(ii) the company has not made any default in repayment of any of its debts (including public deposits) or debentures or interest payable thereon for a continuous period of thirty days in the preceding financial year before the date of appointment of such managerial person;

(iii) a special resolution has been passed at the general meeting of the company for payment of remuneration for a period not exceeding three years;

(iv) a statement along with a notice calling the general meeting referred to in clause (iii) is given to the shareholders containing the following information, namely:—

I. General Information

(1) Nature of industry

(2) Date or expected date of commencement of commercial production

(3) In case of new companies, expected date of commencement of activities as per project approved by financial institutions appearing in the prospectus

(4) Financial performance based on given indicators

(5) Export performance and net foreign exchange collaborations

(6) Foreign investments or collaborators, if any.

II. Information about the appointee

(1) Background details

(2) Past remuneration

(3) Recognition or awards

(4) Job profile and his suitability

(5) Remuneration proposed

(6) Comparative remuneration profile with respect to industry, size of the company, profile of the position and person (in case

of expatriates the relevant details would be w.r.t. the country of his origin)

(7) Pecuniary relationship directly or indirectly with the company, or relationship with the managerial personnel, if any.

III. Other information

(1) Reasons of loss or inadequate profits

(2) Steps taken or proposed to be taken for improvement

(3) Expected increase in productivity and profits in measurable terms

IV. Disclosures

(1) The shareholders of the company shall be informed of the remuneration package of the managerial person

(2) The following disclosures shall be mentioned in the Board of Director's report under the heading "Corporate Governance", if any, attached to the annual report:—

(i) All elements of remuneration package such as salary, benefits, bonuses, stock options, pension etc. of all the directors;

(ii) Details of fixed component and performance linked incentives along with the performance criteria;

(iii) Service contracts, notice period, severance fees;

(iv) Stock option details, if any, and whether the same has been issued at a discount as well as the period over which accrued and over which exercisable;

(C) exceeding the ceiling limit of Rs. 48,00,000 per annum or Rs. 4,00,000 per month calculated on the following scale :

Where the effective capital of Company is	Monthly remuneration payable shall not exceed (Rupees)
(i) less than rupees 1 crore	1,50,000
(ii) rupees 1 crore or more but less than rupees 5 crores	2,00,000
(iii) rupees 5 crores or more but less than rupees 25 crores	2,50,000
(iv) rupees 25 crores or more but less than rupees 50 crores	3,00,000
(v) rupees 50 crores or more but less than rupees 100 crores	3,50,000
(vi) rupees 100 crores or more	4,00,000

Provided that the ceiling limits specified under this sub-paragraph shall apply, if—

(i) payment of remuneration is approved by a resolution passed by the Remuneration Committee;

(ii) the company has not made any default in payment of any of its debts (including public deposits) or debentures or interest payable thereon for a continuous period of thirty days in the preceding financial year before the date of appointment of such managerial person;

(iii) a special resolution has been passed at the general meeting of the company for payment of remuneration for a period not exceeding three years;

(iv) a statement along with a notice calling the general meeting referred to in clause (iii) is given to the shareholders containing the following information, namely :—

I. General Information

(1) Nature of industry

(2) Date or expected date of commencement of commercial production

(3) In case of new companies, expected date of commencement of activities as per project approved by financial institutions appearing in the prospectus.

(4) Financial performance based on given indicators

(5) Export performance and net foreign exchange collaborations

(6) Foreign investments or collaborators, if any

II. Information about the appointee

(1) Background details

(2) Past remuneration

(3) Recognition or awards

(4) Job profile and his suitability

(5) Remuneration proposed

(6) Comparative remuneration profile with respect to industry, size of the company, profile of the position and person (in case of expatriates the relevant details would be w.r.t. the country of his origin)

(7) Pecuniary relationship directly or indirectly with the company, or relationship with the managerial personnel, if any

III. Other information

(1) Reasons of loss or inadequate profits

(2) Steps taken or proposed to be taken for improvement

(3) Expected increase in productivity and profits in measurable terms

IV. Disclosures

(1) The shareholders of the company shall be informed of the remuneration package of the managerial person.

(2) The following disclosures shall be mentioned in the Board of Director's report under the heading "Corporate Governance", if any attached to the annual report :—

(i) All elements of remuneration package such as salary, benefits, bonuses, stock options, pension etc. of all the directors;

(ii) Details of fixed components and performance linked incentives along with the performance criteria;

(iii) Service contracts, notice period, severance fees;

(iv) Stock option details, if any, and whether the same has been issued at a discount as well as the period over which accrued and over which exercisable:

Provided further that the conditions specified in sub-paragraph (C) shall apply in the case the effective capital of the company is negative :

Provided also that the prior approval of the Central Government is obtained for payment of remuneration on the above scale.

2. A managerial person shall also be eligible to the following perquisites which shall not be included in the computation of the ceiling on remuneration specified in paragraph 1 of this section :

(a) contribution to provident fund, superannuation fund or annuity fund to the extend these either singly or put together are not taxable under the Income Tax Act, 1961.

(b) gratuity payable at a rate not exceeding half a month's salary for each completed year of service, and

(c) encashment of leave at the end of the tenure.

3. In addition to the perquisites specified in paragraph 2 of this section, an expatriate managerial person (including a non-resident Indian) shall be eligible to the following perquisites which shall not be included in the computation of the ceiling on remuneration specified in paragraph 1 of this section :

(a) *Children's education allowance* : In case of children studying in or outside India, an allowance limited to a maximum of Rs. 5,000 per month per child or actual expenses incurred, whichever is less. Such allowance is admissible upto a maximum of two children.

(b) *Holiday passage for children studying outside India/family staying abroad* : Return holiday passage once in a year by economy class or once in two years by first class to children and to the members of the family from the place of their study or stay abroad to India if they are not residing in India with the managerial person.

(c) *Leave travel concession* : Return passage for self and family in accordance with the rules specified by the company where it is proposed that the leave be spent in home country instead of anywhere in India.

Explanation I : For the purpose of Section II of this Part, "effective capital" means the aggregate of the paid-up share capital (excluding share application money or advances against shares); amount, if any, for the time being standing to the credit of share premium account, reserves and surplus, (excluding revaluation reserve), long-term loans and deposits repayable after one year (excluding working capital loans, overdrafts, interest due on loans unless funded, bank guarantee, etc., and other short-term arrangements) as reduced by the aggregate of any investments (except in the case of investment by an investment company whose principal business is acquisition of shares, stock debentures or other securities), accumulated losses and preliminary expenses not written off.

Explanation II : (a) Where the appointment of the managerial person is made in the year in which company has been incorporated, the effective capital shall be calculated as on the date of such appointment;

(b) In any other case, the effective capital shall be calculated as on the last date of the financial year preceding the financial year in which the appointment of the managerial person is made.

Explanation III : For the purpose of Section II of this Part, family means the spouse, dependent children and dependent parents of the managerial person.

[1][*Explanation IV* : For the purposes of this section, 'Remuneration Committee' means that a committee which consists of at least three non-executive independent directors including nominee director or nominee directors, if any.

Explanation V : For the purposes of this clause, the Remuneration Committee while approving the remuneration under this section shall,—

(a) take into account, financial position of the company, trend in the industry, appointee's qualification, experience, past performance, past remuneration etc.

(b) be in a position to bring about objectivity in determining the remuneration package while striking a balance between the interest of the company and the shareholders.

Explanation VI : For the purpose of Paragraph I, "negative effective capital" means the effective capital which is calculated :—

1. Inserted by Notification No. GSR 36(E), dated 16-1-2002.

(a) in accordance with the provision contained in the Explanation I of this Part;

(b) less than zero.]

[1][Section III - Remuneration payable to a managerial person in two companies

Subject to the provisions of Sections I and II, a managerial person shall draw remuneration from one or both companies, provided that the total remuneration drawn from the companies does not exceed the higher maximum limit admissible from any one of the companies of which he is managerial person.]

PART III

PROVISIONS APPLICABLE TO PARTS I AND II OF THIS SCHEDULE

1. The appointment and remuneration referred to in Parts I and II of this Schedule shall be subject to approval by a resolution of the shareholders in general meeting.

2. The auditor or the secretary of the company or where the company has not appointed a secretary, a secretary in whole-time practice shall certify that the requirements of this Schedule have been complied with and such certificate shall be incorporated in the return filed with the Registrar under sub-section (2) of section 269.]

Example. The amount of 'effective capital' and 'monthly salary' payable to the Managing Director of Confident Ltd. from the details given below shall be calculated as follows :

Liabilities (as on 31st March 2001). Equity Share Capital Rs. 3,00,000; 12% Preference Share Capital Rs. 1,00,000; Share Premium Account Rs. 50,000; General Reserve Rs. 5,80,000; Profit and Loss Account Rs. 1,70,000; 14% Debentures Rs. 5,00,000; Public Deposits Rs. 1,00,000; Creditors Rs. 1,20,000; Bills payable Rs. 80,000 = Total Rs. 20,00,000.

Assets (as on 31st March 2001). Fixed Assets (Net) Rs. 9,50,000; Investments Rs. 2,00,000; Current Assets, Loans and Advances Rs. 8,00,000; Preliminary Expenses Rs. 50,000 = Total Rs. 20,00,000.

Effective Capital = Equity Capital + 12% Preference Share Capital + Share Premium Account + General Reserve + Profit and Loss Account + 14% Debentures + 14% Public Deposits – Investments – Preliminary Expenses

= Rs. 3,00,000 + Rs. 1,00,000 + Rs. 50,000 + Rs. 5,80,000 + Rs. 1,70,000 + Rs. 5,00,000 + Rs. 1,00,000 – Rs. 2,00,000 – Rs. 50,000

= Rs. 18,00,000 – Rs. 2,50,000 = Rs. 15,50,000

1. Inserted by Notification No. GSR 418(E), dated 12-9-1996.

As effective Capital is less than Rs. 20,00,000, the managing director can be paid maximum monthly salary of Rs. 75,000.

Reimbursement of Medical Expenses – The Department of Company Affairs vide its Circular No. 2/10/99/6L-VII dated 28-10-1999 has clarified that in case of reimbursement of medical expenses incurred beyond the celing mentioned in the total managerial package, the approval shall be granted only in exceptional and deserving cases. Therefore, all proposals for reimbursement on specialised medical treatment abroad must be accompanied by certificate issued and signed by Director General of Health Services of the concerned State Government/Union Territory. The requirement may, however, be waived on the satisfaction of the Central Government in genuine and deserving cases of medical emergency as a special case.

Such proposals may be considered on merits on the basis of the circumstances of the case, financial position of the company, period of association of the concerned managerial personnel with the company, amount of total managerial remuneration and medical reimbursement paid to him in the past and other relevant factors.

Sitting fee (Section 310) – The fee payable to a director for each meeting of the Board of Directors or a Committee thereof is called sitting fee. According to section 310, sitting fee shall not exceed such amount as may be prescribed by the Central Government (presently, five thousand rupees - *vide notification dated 17-1-2000*). Companies will have discretion to pay such amount by way of sitting fee as may be considered appropriate within this revised ceiling of Rs. 5,000.

Increase in remuneration – Section 310 provides that any provision or an amendment thereof, either in the company's memorandum or Articles or in an agreement entered into by the company or in any resolution of the shareholders or of the Board, which purports to increase or has the effect of increasing, whether directly or indirectly, the remuneration of any director, shall not have any effect (a) unless the increase is in accordance with the conditions specified in Schedule XIII, or (b) unless it is otherwise approved by the Central Government.

Thus, approval of the Central Government shall not be required if the fixation or the increase in remuneration is in accordance with the conditions specified in Schedule XIII. It may be noted that Schedule XIII does not specify any conditions for increase in remuneration. It simply specifies the limits within which salary, commission and other perquisites can be paid without Government approval.

Schedule XIII does, however, specify the conditions which must be fulfilled for making an appointment without Government approval. Clause (a) of sub-section (1) of section 310, therefore, in effect, means that in case an appointment or re-appointment is made by fulfilling the conditions specified in Schedule XIII, read with Part III of that

Schedule, approval of the Central Government will not be required, insofar as increase in remuneration is concerned.*

MANAGING DIRECTOR AND WHOLE TIME DIRECTOR

A Managing Director is a director enjoying the specified powers of management. He must have power other than the administrative works of routine nature.

Companies Act does not define the term whole time director. A whole time director may be used in the sense that he is a director in the whole time employment of the company and is not entrusted with the substantial powers of management. For example, if one director is appointed as Personnel Director, one director is appointed as Financial Director, one director, is appointed as Production Director and one director is appointed as Marketing Director, these directors may be termed as Whole time Directors.

The main provisions of the Indian Companies Act equally apply to both managing director and whole time director. They are different from each other in following respects :

MANAGING DIRECTOR AND WHOLE TIME DIRECTOR

Basis of Difference	*Managing Director*	*Whole time Director*
1. Substantial powers of Management	Entrusted with the substantial powers of Management. Enjoys the powers other than of routine nature.	Does not enjoy the Substantial powers of the management. Is just an ordinary officer of the company. Does not enjoy any discretionary powers to take the decision on policy matter.
2. Appointment	The appointment is done by passing a resolution at the meeting of board of directors. It does not require the consent of the shareholders.	The appointment must be approved by the share-holders by means of a special resolution passed at their meeting, except when he is appointed as a trustee for debenture-holders.
3. Simultaneous existence	A managing director and a manager cannot exist simultaneously in any company.	There is no such restriction regarding a whole time director. A whole time director may be appointed along with managing director as well as a manager.
4. Holding Appointment in Number of Companies	Can be appointed as a managing director in more than one companies at the same time.	Cannot work as a whole time director in more than one company because he is a whole time employee of the company.

* The provisions of Section 310 also apply to a manager.

QUESTIONS

1. State the provisions of the Companies Act relating to the appointment of manager of a company.
2. Bring out clearly the difference between manager and managing director.
3. How are the manager and managing director of a company remunerated for their services?
4. Who is a manager of a company? How can he be appointed? What is the difference between a manager and a managing director?
5. What is meant by managerial personnel of a company? What are the provisions in the Indian Companies Act to prevent undesirable persons from the management of a company? Discuss the powers of the Central Government to remove managerial personnel.
6. What is the Law regarding Managerial Remuneration? Explain the restrictions imposed by the Indian Companies Act upon the managerial remuneration?
7. Distinguish between a managing director and a whole time director.
8. Are the terms managing director and whole time director different from each other? If so, how?

14

ACCOUNTS AND AUDITORS

Provisions Relating to Accounts

The Companies Act, 1956 contains a number of provisions relating to accounts and audit. These are designed :

(1) Primarily, to ensure that the members of a company are furnished with all the necessary information relating to its affairs, and

(2) Secondarily, to put such information which is, at any rate, in large companies a matter of public importance at the disposal of the creditors of the companies, employees and public at large.

ACCOUNTS

Books of Account to be kept by Company (Section 209)

The Act requires every company to maintain at its registered office proper books of account with respect to—

(1) all receipts and disbursements of money and the matters in respect of which the receipts and disbursements take place;

(2) all sales and purchases of goods of the company;

(3) the assets and liabilities of the company and

(4) in the case of a company engaged in production, processing, manufacturing or mining activities, such particulars relating to utilisation of material or labour or to other items of cost as may be prescribed by the Central Government in the case of such class of companies. The object of this clause is to make efficiency audit possible.

Where a company has a branch office, books of account relating to the transactions effected at the branch office shall be kept at the branch and at intervals of not more than 3 months summarised accounts shall be sent to the company at its registered office.

Books to give a True and Fair View. The books of account shall give a true and fair view of the company or the branch office, as the case may be. Proper books of account shall be deemed to be kept with respect to the matters specified in Section 209 :

(1) if such books give a *true and fair* view of the state of affairs of the company or branch office, as the case may be, and explain its transactions and

(2) if such books are kept on *accrual basis* and according to the double entry system of accounting.

Location of Books of Account. The books of account should ordinarily be kept at the registered office of the company. These may, however, be kept at any other place in India if the Board of directors so decides. The company shall, within 7 days of the decision of the Board, notify the full address of the place to the Registrar.

Where a company has a branch office, whether in or outside India, the company shall be deemed to have complied with the above provisions if proper books of account relating to the transactions effected at the branch office were kept at that office.

Preservation of Books of Account. The books of account of every company together with the vouchers relevant to any entry in such books shall be preserved for a period of *not less than 8 years* immediately preceding the current year. In the case of a company incorporated less than 8 years before the current year, the books of account for the entire period together with vouchers relevant to any entry in the books of account shall be so preserved.

Inspection of Books of Account (Section 209-A). The books of account and other books and papers shall be open to inspection during business hours—(l) by the Registrar; (2) by such other officer of the Government as may be authorised by the Central Government in this behalf. The Registrar or such officer may do the inspection without giving any previous notice to the company or any officer of the company.

The person making the inspection under Section 209-A may during the course of inspection :

(1) make or cause to be made copies of the books of account and other books and papers;

(2) place or cause to be placed any marks of identification thereon in token of the inspection having been made.

It shall be the duty of every director, officer or employee of the company :

(1) to produce to the Registrar or officer of the Government or SEBI the required books of account and other books and papers of the company in his custody or control and to furnish him with the required statement or explanation relating to the affairs of the company. The inspection by SEBI shall be made in respect of matters covered under Section 55-A. This section has been added by Companies (Amendment) Act 2000. The matters covered mostly relate to issue and transfer of securities and non payment of dividend.

(2) otherwise to give to the Registrar or such officer of the Government all assistance in connection with the inspection which the company is reasonably able to give.

STATUTORY BOOKS

In addition to the books of account required to be maintained by a company under Section 209 the company is also required to maintain some other books called statutory books to safeguarding the interest of shareholders. Such books are as follows :

1. Register of investments not held in company's name (open to Inspection of members and debenture-holders) [Section 49 (7)].

2. Register of charges (open to inspection of all) [Section 143 (1)].

3. Register of members (open to inspection of all) [Section 150 (1)]

4. Index of members where their number is more than 50 (open to inspection of all) [Section 151 (1)].

5. Register of debenture-holders (open to inspection of ail) [Section 152 (1)].

6. Index of debenture-holders where their number is more than 50 (open to inspection of all) [Section 152 (2)].

7. Foreign register (and a duplicate) of members and debenture-holders, if any (open to inspection of all) (Section 158).

8. Minute books containing minutes of proceedings of general meetings (open to inspection of members) [Section 193 (1)].

9. Books of account and annual accounts [Sections 209(1) and 210].

10. Register of contracts, and companies and firms in which directors are interested (open to inspection of members) [Section 301 (1)].

11. Register of directors, managing director, manager and secretary (open to inspection of all) [Section 303 (1)].

12. Register of directors' shareholdings (open to inspection of members and debenture-holders during 14 days before and 3 days after the annual general meeting and to the Registrar and the Central Government) [Section 307 (1)].

13. Register of loans made, guarantees given or securities provided to companies under the same management (open to inspection of all) [Section 370 (1-C)].

ANNUAL ACCOUNTS AND BALANCE SHEET

True and Fair View. The annual accounts of a company consist of a balance sheet as at the end of a financial year and a profit and loss account (or an income and expenditure account in the case of a non-trading company) for the financial year. The accounts shall give a true and fair view of the state of affairs of the company.

Annual Accounts and Balance Sheet (Section 210). At every annual general meeting of a company, the Board of directors shall lay before the meeting :

(1) a balance sheet for the year and

(2) a profit and loss account for the period and also directors' report (Section 217).

In the case of a company not carrying on business for profit, an income and expenditure account shall be laid before the company at its annual general meeting instead of a profit and loss account.

Period of Accounts. The profit and loss account or income and expenditure account shall relate, in the case of the first annual general meeting of a company, to the period from the date of incorporation to a day which shall not precede the day of the meeting by more than 9 months. In the case of any subsequent annual general meeting of the company, it shall relate to the period beginning on the day immediately after the period for which the account was last submitted and ending with a day which shall not precede the day of the meeting by more than 6 months. The power to approve annual accounts is that of directors and cannot be delegated.

Constitution of National Advisory Committee on Accounting Standards [New Section 210-A as introduced by the Companies (Amendment) Act, 1999].

The Central Government may, by notification in the Official Gazette, constitute an Advisory Committee to be called the National Advisory Committee on Accounting Standards (referred to as the 'Advisory Committee') to advise the Central Government on the formulation and laying down of accounting policies and accounting standards for adoption by companies or class of companies under the Companies Act, 1956 [Section 210-A-11)].

Constitution of the Advisory Committee

(1) a chairperson who shall be a person of eminence well versed in accountancy, finance, business administration, business law, economics or similar discipline;

(2) one member, each nominated by the Institute of Chartered Accountants of India constituted under the Chartered Accountants Act, under Section 38 to 1949, the Institute of Cost and Works Accountants of India constituted under the Cost and Works Accountants Act, under Section 23 of 1959 and the Institute of Company Secretaries of India constituted under the Company Secretaries Act, 1980, 56 of 1980;

(3) one representative of the Central Government to be nominated by it;

(4) one representative of the Reserve Bank of India to be nominated by it;

(5) one representative of the Comptroller and Auditor General of India to be nominated by him;

(6) a person who holds or has held the office of professor in accountancy, finance or business management in any university or deemed university;

(7) the chairman of the Central Board of Direct Taxes constituted under the Central Boards of Revenue Act, 1963, 54 of 1963 or his nominee;

(8) two members to represent the chambers of commerce and industry to be nominated by the Central Government and

(9) one representative of the Securities and Exchange Board of India to be nominated by it [Section 2 1 O-A (2)].

Function. The Advisory Committee shall give its recommendations to the Central Government on such matters of accounting policies and standards and auditing as may be referred to it for advice from time to time [Section 210-A (3)].

Term of Office. The members of the Advisory Committee shall hold office for such terms as may be determined by the Central Government at the time of their appointment. Any vacancy in the membership in the Committee shall be filled by the Central Government in the same manner as the member whose vacancy occurred was filled [Section 210-A (4)].

Board's Report (Section 217)

These shall be attached to every balance sheet laid before a company in general meeting (a report by its board of Directors).

Contents of Board's Report

(1) the state of the company's affairs.

(2) the amount which it proposes to carry to reserves.

(3) the amount recommended by way of dividend.

(4) material changes affecting the financial position of the company which have occurred between the date of the balance sheet and the date of report.

(5) the conservation of energy, technology absorption, foreign exchange earnings and outgo, in such manner as may be prescribed.

(6) changes which have occurred during the financial year :

(a) in the nature of the company's business,

(b) in the company's subsidiaries or in the nature of business carried on by them and

(c) generally in the classes of business in which the company has an interest.

(7) Statement of Employees. The Board's report shall also include a statement showing the name every employees of the company getting remuneration at a rate which is not less than such sum per month as may be prescribed. The statement shall also indicate (i) whether any such employee is a relative of any director or manager of the company and if so, the name of such director and (ii) such other particulars as may be prescribed.

Fullest information to be given in Report. The Board shall be bound to give the fullest information and explanations in its report on every reservation, qualification or adverse remark contained in the auditor's report. The Board's report shall be signed by its chairman if he is authorised in that behalf by the Board. Where the chairman is not so authorised, the report shall be signed by such number of directors as are required to sign the balance sheet and the profit and loss account of the company.

Form and Contents of Balance Sheet and Profit and Loss Account (Section 211). Balance sheet to give true and fair view. Every balance sheet of a company shall give a true and fair view of the state of affairs of the company as at the end of the financial year. It shall also be in the form set out in Part I of Schedule VI or in such other form as may be approved by the Central Government.

Profit and loss account to give true and fair view. Every profit and loss account of a company shall give a true and fair view of the profit or loss of the company for the financial year. It shall also comply with the requirements of Part II of Schedule VI, so far as they are applicable thereto.

The above provisions shall not apply to any insurance, banking, or electricity company or to any other class of company for which a form of balance sheet and profit and loss account has been specified in or under the Act governing such class of company.

Compliance with Accounting Standards. The following three Sub-Sections have been added to Section 211 [by the Companies (Amendment) Act, 1999] which deals with the form and contents of balance sheet and profit and loss account.

(3-A) Every profit and loss account and balance sheet of the company shall comply with the accounting standards.

(3-B) Where the profit and loss account and the balance sheet of the company do not comply with the accounting standards, the company shall disclose in its profit and loss account and balance sheet, the following, namely :

(a) the deviation from the accounting standards;

(b) the reasons for such deviation and

(c) the financial effect, if any, arising due to such deviation.

(3-C) For the purposes of Section 210, the expression "accounting standards" means the standards of accounting recommended by the Institute of Chartered Accountants of India, as may be prescribed by the Central Government in consultation with the National Advisory

Committee on Accounting Standards established under Section 210-A (1).

However, the standards of accounting specified by the Institute of Chartered Accountants of India shall be deemed to be the Accounting Standards until the National Advisory Committee on Accounting Standards is established under Section 210-A (1).

FILING OF ACCOUNTS WITH THE REGISTRAR (SECTION 220)

Three copies of the balance sheet and profit and loss account along with reports and documents of a company shall be filed with the Registrar within 30 days from the date on which the balance sheet and the profit and loss account were laid before the company at an annual general meeting.

If the annual general meeting of the company before which the balance sheet is laid does not adopt the balance sheet, or is adjourned without adopting the balance sheet or if the annual general meeting of the company for any year has not been held, a statement of that fact and of the reasons therefore shall be annexed to the balance sheet and to the copies thereof required to be filed with the Registrar.

AUDITORS

A joint stock company carries on business with capital furnished by persons who buy its shares. The subscribers of the capital are, however, not in direct control of its application which is left to the control of the directors and the superior officers of the company. To safeguard the interest of shareholders the companies Act provides for the employment of an auditor who is the servant of the shareholders. His duty is to examine the affairs of the company on their behalf at the end of a year and report to them what he found. That examination by the auditors is practically the only safeguard which the shareholders have against the enterprise being carried on in an unbusiness like manner or their money being misapplied or misappropriated without their knowing anything about it.

QUALIFICATIONS OF AUDITOR [SECTION 226(1)]

A person shall not be qualified for appointment as auditor of a company unless he is a chartered accountant within the meaning of the Chartered Accountants Act, 1949 (38 of 1949). A chartered accountant means a person who is a member of the Institute of Chartered Accountants. A firm whereof all the partners practising in India are qualified for appointment may be appointed by its firm name to be the auditor of a company. In such a case any partner may act as auditor in the name of the firm.

Appointment of Auditors (Sections 224 and 225)

1. Appointment in Annual General Meeting. Every company shall, at each annual general meeting, appoint an auditor or auditors to hold office from the conclusion of that meeting to the conclusion of the next annual general meeting. The company shall, within 7 days of the appointment, give information thereof to every auditor so appointed. Before any such appointment in the annual general meeting, a written certificate shall be obtained by the company from the auditor proposed to be appointed that the appointment will be within the number of companies that he can audit [Section 224 (1)].

2. Restriction on the Appointment of Auditors. A company shall not appoint or re-appoint any person who is in full-time employment elsewhere or firm as its auditor if such person or firm is, at the date of such appointment or re-appointment, holding appointment as auditor of more than the *specified number* of companies. The specified number shall mean :

(a) in the case of a person or firm holding appointment as auditor of a number of companies each of which has a paid-up share capital of less than Rs. 25 lakhs, 20 such companies;

(b) in any other case, 20 companies, out of which not more than 10 shall be companies each of which has a paid-up share capital of Rs. 25 lakhs or more [Section 224 (1-B) and (1-C)].

In the case of a firm of auditors, 'specified number of companies' shall be construed as the number of companies specified for every partner of the firm who is not in full-time employment elsewhere.

3. Compulsory Re-appointment. At any general meeting a retiring auditor, by whatsoever authority appointed (Board of directors, general meeting, annual general meeting or Central Government), shall be reappointed except In the following cases :

(a) if he is not qualified for re-appointment;

(b) if he has given to the company notice in writing of his unwillingness to be re-appointed;

(c) if a resolution has been passed to the effect appointing somebody instead of him or providing expressly that he shall not be re-appointed; or

(d) where notice has been given of an intended resolution to appoint some person or persons in the place of a retiring auditor, and by reason of death, incapacity or disqualification of that person or of all those persons, the resolution cannot be proceeded with [Section 224 (2)].

4. Appointment by the Central Government. Where at an annual general meeting no auditors are appointed or re-appointed, the Central Government may appoint a person to fill the vacancy. The company shall, within 7 days of the Central Government's power becoming exercisable, give notice of that fact to the Government. If the company fails to give such notice, the company, and every officer of the company who is in default, shall be punishable with line which may extend to Rs. 500 [Section 224 (3) and (4)].

5. Appointment of Auditors by a Special Resolution. Section 224-A puts another restriction on the appointment of auditors. It lays down that in the case of a company in which not less than 25 per cent of the subscribed share capital is held, whether singly or in any combination, by :

(a) a public financial institution (For definition of "public financial institution", refer to Chapter on "Kinds of Companies") or a Government company or Central Government or any State Government, or

(b) any financial or other institution established by any State Act in which a State Government holds not less than 51 per cent of the subscribed share capital, or

(c) a nationalised bank or a general insurance company, the appointment or re-appointment at each annual general meeting of an auditor or auditors shall be made by a special resolution.

In this case, the appointment or re-appointment of an auditor or auditors shall be made by a special resolution.

6. First Auditors. The first auditors of a company shall be appointed by its Board of directors within 1 month of Its incorporation. The auditors so appointed shall hold office until the conclusion of the first annual general meeting. The company may, at a general meeting, remove any or all such auditors and appoint any other person or persons who have been nominated for appointment by any member of the company and of whose nomination notice has been given to the members of the company at least 14 days before the date of the meeting. If the Board fails to exercise its power to appoint first auditors, the company in general meeting may appoint the first auditors [Section 224 (5)].

7. Subsequent Appointment (Section 225). At the expiry of the term of an auditor, the members may, in the annual general meeting, appoint another person in his place. But a special notice for a resolution to nominate a person other than a retiring auditor at the annual general meeting shall be given to the company. On receipt of notice of such a resolution, the company shall forthwith send a copy thereof to the retiring auditor. The auditor shall have a right of making a representation in writing to the company (not exceeding a reasonable length). The company shall send a copy of the representation, if so desired by the auditor, to every member of the company to whom notice of the meeting is sent. If a copy of the representation is not sent as aforesaid, the representation shall be read out at the meeting. If the company or any other person claims to be aggrieved, it or he may apply to the Company Law Board that the copies of the representation need not be sent out or the representation need not be read out at the meeting. The Company Law Board may pass the necessary orders if it is satisfied that this right is being abused to secure needless publicity for some defamatory matter.

8. Casual Vacancy. The Board of directors may fill any casual vacancy in the office of an auditor. While any such vacancy continues, the remaining auditor or auditors, if any, may act. Where such vacancy is caused by the resignation of an auditor, the vacancy shall only be filled by the company In general meeting. Any auditor appointed in a casual vacancy shall hold office until the conclusion of the next annual general meeting [Section 224 (6)].

Removal of Auditors

The first auditors of a company appointed by the directors prior to the first annual general meeting of the company may be removed by the members in a general meeting even if their tenure of office has not expired. The general meeting may, in their place, appoint any other person, notice for whose nomination has been given by any member not less than 14 days before the date of the meeting [Section 224 (5)].

In any other case, an auditor may be removed from office before the expiry of his term by the company In general meeting after obtaining the previous approval of the Central Government in that behalf [Section 224 (7)].

Remuneration of Auditors

The remuneration of the auditors of a company shall be fixed by the company in general meeting or in such manner as the company in general meeting may determine. But in the case of an auditor appointed by the Board of directors or the Central Government, his remuneration may be fixed by the Board or the Central Government, as the case may be. Any sums paid by the company in respect of the auditor's expenses shall be deemed to be included in the expression 'remuneration' [Section 224 (8)].

Auditor's Report

Contents of Report

(a) the accounts examined by him,

(b) balance sheet and profit and loss account and

(c) every document annexed to the balance sheet and profit and loss account laid before the company in general meeting during his tenure of office.

The report shall state whether in his opinion and to the best of his information and according to the explanations given to him, the accounts give the information required by the Act *(i.e.,* as per Schedule VI of the Act) and give a true and fair view of the state of the company's affairs and of the profit or loss.

Obligation to make an Inquiry [Section 227 (1-A)]

(1) whether loans and advances made by the company, on the basis of security, have been properly secured and whether the terms on which they have been made are not prejudicial to the interests of the company or its members;

(2) whether transactions of the company which are represented merely by book entries are not prejudicial to the interests of the company;

(3) where the company is not an investment company or a banking company, whether so much of the assets of the company as consist of shares, debentures and other securities have been sold at a price less than that at which they were purchased by the company;

(4) whether loans and advances made by the company have been short as deposits;

(5) whether personal expenses have been charged to revenue account;

(6) where any shares have been allotted for cash, whether cash has actually been received in respect of such allotment and if no cash has been received, whether the position shown in the books and balance sheet is correct, regular and not misleading.

This duty of inquiry has been cast on the auditors to safeguard the public money from being indirectly drained off for the personal benefit of the persons, directly or indirectly, in control of the affairs of a company.

Matters to be stated in Auditor's Report

(1) whether he has obtained all the information and explanations which to the best of his knowledge and belief were necessary for the purposes of his audit;

(2) whether proper books of account as required by law have been kept by the company, and proper returns adequate for the purposes of his audit have been received from branches not visited by him;

(3) whether the report on the accounts of any branch office audited by some person other than the company's auditor has been forwarded to him and how he has dealt with it in preparing his report;

(4) whether the company's balance sheet and profit and loss account dealt with by the report are in agreement with the company's books of account and returns;

(5) whether, in his opinion, the profit and loss account and balance sheet complied with the accounting standards referred to in Section 211 (3C). This clause has been introduced by the Companies (Amendment) Act, 1999 and

(6) whether the accounts examined by him, in his opinion, give the information required by the Act and whether the balance sheet

and profit and loss account laid before the company in general meeting render a true and fair view of the state of affairs of the company and of its profits or losses for the financial year for which they have been prepared.

Where any of these matters is answered in the negative or with a qualification, the report shall state the reason for it.

Signatures of Audit Report (Section 229). Only the person appointed as auditor of the company, or where a firm is appointed as the auditor, only a partner in the firm practising in India, may sign the auditor's report, or sign or authenticate any other document of the company required by law to be signed or authenticated by the auditor.

RIGHTS, POWERS AND DUTIES OF AUDITORS

Section 227 deals with rights, powers and duties of auditors. The rights and duties are interrelated. Where a duty is cast upon a person, to be a corresponding right to enable him to discharge such duty and *vice versa* Section 227 is based on this principle.

The several rights conferred upon an auditor of a company relate to the matters in respect of which he has to make a report to the holders of the company on its annual accounts.

Rights and powers of auditors

1. Right of Access to Books, Accounts and Vouchers (Section 227). The auditor of a company shall have right of access, at all times, to the books and accounts and vouchers of the company, whether kept at the head office of the company or elsewhere.

2. Right to obtain Information and Explanations (Section 227). The auditor shall be entitled to require from the officers of the company such information and explanations as he thinks necessary for the performance of his duties as auditor. As to what information and explanations are necessary is left entirely to the discretion of the auditor. If the directors refuse any information or explanation on the ground that it is not necessary for the performance of the duties of the auditor, the auditor shall report to the members that he has not obtained all the information and explanations required by him.

3. Right to visit Branch Offices and Right of Access to Books, etc. (Section 228). Where the accounts of any branch office are audited by a person other than the company's auditor, the company's auditor shall :

(a) be entitled to visit the branch office, if he deems it necessary to do so, for the performance of his duties as auditor; and

(b) have a right of access at all times to the books and accounts and vouchers of the company maintained at the branch office.

5. Right to receive Notice of General Meetings and to Attend Them (Section 231). The auditor has a right to receive notice of, and other communications relating to, any general meeting of the company.

6. Right to receive Remuneration. The auditor shall have the right to receive remuneration for auditing the accounts of the company.

Duties of Auditors

1. Acquaintance with the Articles and the Companies Act. The auditor of a company shall acquaint himself with his duties under the Articles of the company and the Companies Act, 1956 [Republic of Bolivia Exploration Syndicate Ltd., Re (1914) 1 Ch. 139].

2. Report to Members (Section 227). The main duty of the auditor is to make a report to the members of the company on the accounts examined by him and the balance sheet and the profit and loss account of the company and on every document which is annexed to the balance sheet or profit and loss account laid before the company in general meeting. The auditor owes a duty to the members to state whether the accounts give a true and fair view of the affairs of the company at the end of the financial year and of the profit and loss account of the year.

3. Duty of Care and Caution. The auditor shall be honest and shall exercise reasonable care and skill in the performance of his duties otherwise he may be sued for damages, As to what is reasonable care and skill depends upon the circumstances of the case.

It is not the duty of the auditor to give advice either to directors or to shareholders as to what they ought to do. He has nothing to do with the way in which the business is carried on. He is also not concerned with the policy of the company whether the company is well or ill-managed.

London & General Bank, Re (1895) 2 Ch. 673. The greater part of the capital of a company was advanced as loans upon securities which were insufficient and difficult to realise. For several years the auditors pointed out to the directors the unsatisfactory nature of these securities; and the auditor's report to the members on the balance sheet only stated that "the value of the assets as shown in the balance sheet is dependent on realisation." On the faith of this balance sheet dividends were declared, which were really paid out of capital. *Held*, it was the duty of the auditors to ascertain the true financial position of the company and to report to the members. The auditors had failed in this duty and were, therefore, liable.

Further Duties. In addition to the duties of the auditor discussed above, he has also to perform the following duties :

1. Statutory Report (Section 165). After the statutory report has been certified as correct by not less than two directors of the company, the auditor of the company shall certify the report as correct, so far as it relates to :

(a) the shares allotted by the company,

(b) the cash received in respect of such shares and

(c) the receipts and payments of the company.

The above provision does not apply to private companies as they are not required to hold a statutory meeting.

2. Prospectus (Section 56). Section 56 requires a report by the auditor of the company with respect to profits and losses, assets and liabilities and the rates of dividends, if any, paid by the company, to be included in a prospectus (Clause B- I of Part II of Schedule II). The auditor has to certify these as correct.

3. Assistance in Investigation (Section 240). It is the duty of all the officers and other employees and agents (and for Section 240, the expression 'agent' includes 'auditors') of a company —

(a) to preserve and to produce to an inspector (appointed under Section 235 to investigate the affairs of the company) or any person authorised by him in this behalf with the previous approval of the Central Government all books and papers of, or relating to, the company which are in their custody and power and

(b) otherwise to give to the inspector all assistance in connection with the investigation which they are reasonably able to give.

SPECIAL AUDIT (SECTION 233-A)

The Central Government may in certain cases direct that the special audit of the accounts of a company shall be conducted. It shall do so where it is of the opinion :

(a) that the affairs of the company are not being managed in accordance with sound business principles or prudent commercial practices; or

(b) that the company is being managed in a manner likely to cause serious injury or damage to the interest of the trade, industry or business to which it pertains; or

(c) that the financial position of the company is such as to endanger its solvency.

The Central Government may appoint a chartered accountant or the company's auditor himself to conduct the special audit of the company's accounts for such period or periods as may be specified. The auditor so appointed to conduct special audit shall be known as the special auditor.

Powers and Duties of Special Auditor. The special auditor shall have the same powers and duties as an auditor of the company. But he shall, instead of making his report to the members of the company, make the report to the Central Government. The report of the special auditor shall include all the matters required to be included in an auditor's report under Section 227. The Central Government may also direct that the report shall include a statement on any other matter. It may also direct any person to furnish to the special auditor such information as may be required by the special auditor in connection with the special audit.

Action by the Central Government. On receipt of the report of the special auditor, the Central Government may take such action as it considers necessary. If it does not take any action on the report within 4 months from the date of the receipt of the report, it may send the report to the company requiring the company to circulate the same to the members or read the report to them at the next annual general meeting.

AUDIT OF COST ACCOUNTS (SECTION 233-B)

Proper books of account in the case of companies engaged in production, processing, manufacturing or mining activities shall include particulars relating to utilisation of material, labour or other items of cost. This is in addition to information relating to all sums of money received and expended, all sales and purchases of goods and assets and liabilities of the company to be included in books of account.

Auditor to be Cost Accountant. The Central Government may, by order, direct that the audit of cost accounts of a company shall be conducted by an auditor who shall be a cost accountant within the meaning of the Cost and Works Accountants Act, 1959.

If, however, the Central Government is of opinion that a sufficient number of qualified cost accountants is not available for conducting the audit of the cost accounts of companies generally, it may, by notification in the Official Gazette, direct that for a specified period chartered accountants may also conduct the audit of the cost accounts of companies.

Appointment. The cost auditor shall be appointed by the Board of directors of the company in accordance with the provisions of Section 224 (1-B) and with the previous approval of the Central Government. But before the appointment of any cost auditor is made by the Board, a written certificate shall be obtained by the Board from the auditor proposed to be so appointed to the effect that the appointment, will be in accordance with the provisions of Section 224 (1-B).

SEIZURE OF DOCUMENTS BY REGISTRAR (SECTION 234-A)

Where, upon information in his possession or otherwise, the Registrar has reasonable ground to believe that the books of account and papers of, or relating to, a company or its managerial personnel, may be destroyed, mutilated, altered, falsified or secreted, he may make an application to the Magistrate of the First Class or, as the case may be, the Presidency Magistrate, for an order for the seizure of such books and papers.

After considering the application and hearing the Registrar, the Magistrate may authorise the Registrar :

(a) to enter the place or places where such books and papers are kept;

(b) to search that place or those places in the manner specified in the order and

(c) to seize such books and papers as he considers necessary.

The Registrar shall return the books and papers seized within 30 days of the seizure to the company or the managing director or the manager or any other person from whose custody or power they were seized and inform the Magistrate of such return. But he may, before returning such books and papers, take copies of or extracts from them or place identification marks on them or any part thereof.

QUESTIONS

1. What books of account is a company registered under the Companies Act, 1956 bound to maintain? Do you know of any other statistical books that a company maintains?
2. Give the provisions of the Companies Act, 1956 relating to the preparation, authentication, circulation, adoption and filing of the annual accounts of a company?
3. What are the statutory restrictions on the appointment of the auditors of a company?
4. What are the provisions of the Companies Act, 1956 relating to
   (a) the special audit of a company;
   (b) the audit of cost accounts of a company;
   (c) the seizure of documents by the Registrar;
   (d) the number of companies an auditor can audit?
5. How is an auditor of a company appointed? How is his remuneration fixed and by whom?
6. Who appoints :
   (a) the first auditors of a company;
   (b) auditors to fill casual vacancies;
   (c) auditors at each annual general meeting?
7. Can a 'chartered accountant' member of a company who holds 90 per cent of its issued share capital be its auditor?
8. Under what circumstances are auditors automatically re-appointed? Give the statutory provisions regarding (a) qualifications and (b) disqualifications of an auditor.

PRACTICAL PROBLEMS

1. The directors of a company are prosecuted for default in filing the balance sheet and the profit and loss account with the Registrar of Companies. Their defence is that the annual meeting for the

relevant year was not held for some reason and, therefore, since the occasion for placing the same before the general meeting did not arise, they are not guilty of contravention of Section 220. The Registrar contends that the directors cannot take advantage of their own default in holding the annual general meeting and should therefore be held guilty. What are your views?

[**Hint.** The directors are guilty of violating the provisions of Section 2201.

2. The auditors of a company made a confidential report to the directors calling their attention to the fact that the security for some loans was insufficient and that there was a difficulty in their realisation. They also reported that in their opinion no dividend should be paid for the year. In their report to the shareholders, however, they merely stated that the value of the assets was dependent upon realisation. A dividend of 7 per cent was declared by the company out of capital. Are the auditors liable for their omission?

   [**Hint.** Yes, they are guilty of misfeasance (Section 227 (2) : London & General Bank, Re)].

3. In 1999 when a company went into liquidation, A claimed a time-barred debt from it. Balance sheet of the company for the year 1998 referred to the debt and was signed by 2 directors of the company (one of whom was (A) and certified by the auditors. A argued that these signatures constituted a written acknowledgement of the debt by the company. Is A right in making this claim?

   [**Hint.** No (Transplanters (Holding Co.) Ltd., Re)].

15

MEETINGS AND PROCEEDINGS

A meeting in a company may be of either shareholders or Board of Directors or creditors or contributories or debenture holders. A property convened meeting must be by proper authority (*e.g.*, Board of Directors or C.L.B. or shareholders), and a proper and adequate notice must be given. The notice must contain place, day, time and agenda of meeting. There shall be a chairman of a meeting and proper quorum should be present.

MEETINGS OF THE BOARD

Under Section 285 of the Act, the meeting of the Board of Directors must be held at least once in every three months and at least four such meetings shall be held in every year. This provision is applicable to every company limited by guarantee and having a share capital. As per amendment, in every year, there must be four meetings of the Board and at least one in every three calendar months. In other words, no three months should pass without a directors' meeting being held and at least four directors meetings are held during the calendar year. This has been specifically provided to ensure that Board meetings are held at reasonably frequent intervals so that the directors may be in touch with the affairs of the company.

Duty. Director is supposed to attend important meetings though he is not bound to attend each and every Board meeting. In case, deliberately or willingly, without sufficient cause, he remains absent, he will be held liable for negligence.

Place. The above Section 285 does not provide that the Board meeting must be held at Registered Office. Thus, it can be held at any place convenient to directors. Generally such meetings are held at "*Administrative Office*" by the companies having such offices.

LEGAL PROVISIONS ABOUT BOARD MEETINGS

In the case of every company, a meeting of its Board of directors shall be held at least once in every three months; and at least four such meetings shall be held in every year.

Provided that the Central Government may, by notification in the Official Gazette, direct that the provisions of this section shall not apply in relation to any class of companies or shall apply in relation thereto subject to such exceptions, modifications or conditions as may be specified in the notification.

Section 286

(1) Notice of every meeting of the Board of directors of a company shall be given in writing to every director for the time being in India, and at his usual address in India to every other director.

(2) Every officer of the company whose duty is to give notice aforesaid and who fails to do so shall be punishable with fine which may extend to one hundred rupees.

Section 287

(1) In this section —

(a) "total strength" means the total strength of the Board of directors of a company as determined in pursuance of this Act, if any, whose places may be vacant at the time and

(b) "interested director" means any director whose presence cannot, by reason of Section 300, count for the purpose of forming a quorum at a meeting of the Board, at the time of the discussion or vote on any matter.

(2) The quorum for a meeting of the Board of directors of a company shall be one-third of its total strength (any fraction contained in that one-third being rounded off as one), two directors, whichever is higher.

Provided that where at any time the number of interested directors exceeds or is equal to two-thirds of the total strength, the number of the remaining directors, that is to say, the number of the directors who are not interested, (present at the meeting being not less than two), shall be the quorum during such time.

Section 288

(1) If a meeting of the Board can not be held for want of quorum, then unless the articles otherwise provide, the meeting shall, automatically stand adjourned till the same day in the next week, at the same time and place, or if that day is a public holiday, till the next succeeding day which is not a public holiday, and the same time and place.

(2) The provisions of Section 285 shall not be deemed to have been contravened merely by reason of the fact that a meeting of the Board which had been called in compliance with the terms of that section could not be held for want of a quorum.

Section 289

No resolution shall be deemed to have been duly passed by the Board or by a committee thereof by circulation, unless the resolution has been circulated in draft, together with the necessary papers, if any, to all directors, or to all the members of the committee then in

India (not being less in number than the quorum fixed for a meeting of the Board or committee, as the case may be), and to all other directors or members at their usual addresses in India and has been approved by such of the directors as are then in India, or by a majority of such of them, as are entitled to vote on the resolution.

Section 290

Acts done by a person as a director shall be valid notwithstanding that it may afterwards be discovered that his appointment was invalid by reason of and defect or disqualification or had terminated by virtue of any provision contained in this Act or in the articles.

Provided that nothing in this section shall be deemed to give validity to acts done by a director after his appointment has been shown to the company to be invalid or to have terminated.

Board's Powers and Restrictions Thereon

Section 291

(1) Subject to the provisions of this Act, the Board of directors of a company shall be entitled to exercise all such powers, and to do all such acts and things as the company is authorised to exercise and do.

Provided that the Board shall not exercise any power or do any act or thing which is directed or required, whether by this or any other Act or by the memorandum or articles of the company or otherwise, to be exercised or done by the company in general meeting.

Provided further that in exercising any such power or doing any such act or thing, the Board shall be subject to the provisions contained in that behalf in this or any other Act, or in the memorandum or articles of the company, or in any regulations not inconsistent therewith and duly made thereunder, including regulations made by the company in general meeting.

(2) No regulation made by the company in general meeting shall invalidate any prior act of the Board which would have been valid if that regulation had not been made.

Section 292

(1) The Board of directors of a company shall exercise the following powers on behalf of the company; and it shall do so only by means of resolutions passed at the meeting of the Board :

(a) the power to make calls on shareholders in respect of money unpaid on their shares;

(b) the power to issue debentures;

(c) the power to borrow moneys otherwise than on debentures;

(d) the power to invest the funds of the company and

(e) the power to make loans.

Provided that the Board may, by a resolution passed at a meeting, delegate to any committee of directors, the managing director, the managing agent, secretaries and treasurers, the manager or any other principal officer of the company, a principal officer, of the branch office, the powers specified in clauses (c), (d) and (e) to the extent specified in sub-sections (2), (3) and (4) respectively, on such conditions as the Board may prescribe.

Provided further that the acceptance by a banking company in the ordinary course of its business of deposits of money from the public repayable on demand or otherwise and withdrawable by cheque, draft, order or otherwise or the placing of moneys on deposit by a banking company with another banking company on such conditions as the Board may prescribe, shall not be deemed to be a borrowing of moneys or as the case may be, a making of loans by a banking company within the meaning of this section.

Explanation I. Nothing in clause (c) of sub-section (1) shall apply to borrowings by a banking company from other banking companies or from the Reserve Bank of India, the State Bank of India or any other banks established by or under any Act.

Explanation II. In respect of dealings between a company and its banks, exercise by the company of the power specified in clause (c) of sub-section (1) shall mean the arrangement made by the company with its banks for the borrowing of money by way of overdraft or cash credit or otherwise and not the actual day-to-day operation on overdraft, cash credit or other accounts by means of which the arrangement so made is actually availed of.

(2) Every resolution delegating the power referred to in clause (c) or sub-section (1) shall specify the total amount (outstanding at any one time) up to which moneys may be borrowed by the delegate.

(3) Every resolution delegating the power referred to in clause (b) of sub-section (1) shall specify the total amount upto which the funds may be invested, and the nature of the investments which may be made by the delegate.

(4) Every resolution delegating the power referred to in clause (e) of sub-section (1) shall specify the total amount up to which loans may be made by the delegate, the purposes for which the loans may be made, and the maximum amount of loans which may be made for each such purpose in individual case.

(5) Nothing in this section shall be deemed to affect the right of the company in general meeting to impose restrictions and conditions on the exercise by the Board of any of the powers specified in sub-section (1).

PROCEDURE OF BOARD'S MEETING

Notice of the Meeting

The articles of the company may provide that meeting should be held at regular intervals or on fixed days of the month. Notice of every meeting of the Board of Directors of a company is given in writing to every director at his usual address in India. The notice should contain the date, time and place of the meeting. If any director is out of India and it is not possible to trace out his new address notice of meeting need not be sent to him. The proceeding of the meeting will be deemed to be invalid when some of the directors remain absent from attending the meeting on account of notice being not received by them.

Therefore, under Section 286(2) of the Act, it is further provided, that if any officer of the company who is assigned this work fails to do so as said above, he shall be punishable with fine which may extend to one hundred rupees.

Form 20.1 : Notice of the Board Meeting

Notice

ABC India Ltd.
Partapur, Meerut
25th May 1996

Dear Sir/Madam,

I shall feel highly obliged if you kindly note that a meeting of directors of the above-named company will be held at its registered office on Monday, the 19th June 1996 at 3-00 p.m. when you are required to be present.

R.N. Sharma Esq.

Yours faithfully,
B.A. Gupta
Secretary.

Encl : Agenda

Notices to all directors must be posted to their registered addresses before the Board meeting is held. If the company fails to do so, all the resolutions passed at such meeting held without notice will be invalid. Where the meeting is adjourned, notice for adjourned meeting need not be sent unless there is a special provision in the Articles of Association that the company must give notice of such a meeting. If all directors attend the meeting without notice being given to them or absentee directors do not complain of want of notice, the proceedings at the meeting will not be invalid provided they are ratified at the next meeting attended by absentee directors.

Form 20.2 : Agenda of Board Meeting

For the Board Meeting to be held on Monday, the 19th June 1996, at the registered office of the Company.

1. To approve the minutes of the last meeting.
2. To consider matter arising out of the minutes.
3. To consider and pass the statement of accounts for payment.
4. To seal and sign the equity share certificates Nos. 1 to 10 and redeemable preference share certificates Nos. 15 to 25.
5. To declare dividend 4% (free of tax) on preference shares of Rs. 200 each on which Rs. 100 per share are paid-up and 2% (free of tax) on equity shares of Rs. 100 each on which Rs. 50 per share are paid up.
6. To consider any other business with due permission of the chair.
7. To fix the date and time of next meeting.

Quorum for Board Meeting

The requisite quorum for a meeting of the Board of Directors of a company is one-third of the total strength of its directors or two directors whichever is higher. Any fraction contained in that one-third should be rounded off as one. For example, if a company has 10 (ten) directors, then one-third of the total strength of the Board of Directors will be four for the sake of the Section 287(2) of the Act. For the purpose of counting number of directors forming the quorum, the directors who are interested should not be taken into account. Only those will form the quorum who are disinterested in the matters to be discussed at the meeting.

If the requisite quorum is not present at the meeting, it stands adjourned. It will be held on the same day, time and place in the next week unless otherwise provided in the articles of the company. If that day falls on a public holiday or Sunday, the meeting will be held on the next succeeding day which is a week day, at the scheduled time and place. If the quorum is not present throughout the conduct of the meeting any decision or resolution passed will be invalid unless there is a specific provision in the articles of the company.

Proper Quorum

To constitute a proper quorum, at least two disinterested directors or one-third of the total strength, whichever is higher must remain present throughout the meeting. However, the business transacted at a Board meeting at which the quorum was present, would be invalid where the Board itself was not validly constituted and was not legally competent to transact any business on behalf of the company. As per Companies Act, if the quorum is present and it is found that the number of directors present is below the minimum fixed by the articles, any business transacted under such conditions is held valid. Where the Board meeting cannot be held for want of quorum, any difficulty that arose out of such situation can be finally decided by the company at the general meeting. Decisions are taken by majority unless the articles otherwise provide.

Chairman of the Meeting

Every meeting must have a chairman to preside over it. The articles of the company may name the chairman or may give discretionary powers to the directors to elect the chairman under the Regulation 76 of Table 'A'. When the directors elect the chairman, they also fix-up the period for which the elected chairman is required to hold the office. He is required to be present at the scheduled time and if he is not present within five minutes after the time fixed for holding meeting, the directors are entitled to elect anyone of them present as the chairman of the meeting.

General Powers of the Board

The Board of Directors can do all such acts and things and can also exercise all such powers as the company is authorised to do so. Whatever powers exercised or acts done should be wholly in the interests of the company. Section 291 of the Act states that any action or power to be done or exercised respectively by the company in general meeting under the provisions of the memorandum or the articles of the company cannot be done by the Board. No regulation made by the company in a general meeting shall invalidate any prior act of the Board which would have been valid if that regulation had not been made.

Powers to be exercised by the Board

Section 292 of the Act empowers the Board of Directors to exercise the following powers on behalf of the company by means of resolutions passed at the meeting of the Board :

(a) The power to make calls on shareholders in respect of money unpaid on their shares.

(b) The power to issue debentures.

(c) The power to borrow money otherwise than on debentures.

(d) The power to invest the funds of the company.

(e) The power to make loans.

By passing a resolution at a meeting the Board of Directors can, under Section 292 of the Act, delegate the above powers mentioned under clauses (c), (d) and (e) to any committee of directors, the managing director, the managing agent, secretaries and treasurers or the manager of the company. In the case of a banking company the above powers can be delegated to a manager or other principal officer or branch officer of the company. While delegating the powers, all details such as (a) the purpose for which the money is to be borrowed, (b) the extent to which they are authorised to borrow etc., must be specifically mentioned in the resolution to be passed to this effect. Every resolution delegating the power, must specify the total amount up to which the fund may be invested, the nature of the investments which may be made and the limit up to which money may be borrowed by the delegate.

Under Section 292(5) of the Act, a company in general meeting can impose certain restrictions and conditions on the powers of the Board in respect of powers given to the Board.

Matters to be passed by the Board

(1) Board's sanction should be given by a resolution passed at a meeting of the Board to such contracts in which any directors or their relatives of firms are interested.

(2) A director who is interested in any contract to be entered with by the company should disclose his interest at the board's meeting. This must be passed by the board by passing the necessary resolution (Section 209).

(3) Disclosure by directors of their shareholding should be given in writing at a meeting of the board for its approval (Section 308).

(4) A person who is already a managing director or manager of another company can be appointed as managing director of a company provided such an appointment is made by a unanimous resolution passed by the directors at a meeting of the Board of Directors (Section 313).

(5) Investment in shares and debentures of companies under the same management can be made by the directors provided it is passed by a unanimous resolution at the meeting of the Board of Directors (Section 372).

(6) A person who is already a manager or managing director of another company can be appointed as manager if such appointment is passed by a unanimous resolution passed at the meeting of the Board of Directors.

Restrictions on the Powers of the Board (Section 293)

(a) Can not sell, lease or otherwise dispose of the whole or substantially the whole of the undertaking of the company;

(b) Can not remit or give time for repayment of a debt due by a director;

(c) Can not invest otherwise than in trust securities, the sale proceeds, resulting from acquisition without the consent of the company, of any property undertaking of the company;

(d) Can not borrow in excess of the aggregate paid-up capital of the company plus its free reserves;

(e) Can not contribute to charities, etc., in excess of Rs. 25,000 or 5 per cent of average net profits in the course of any financial year. Every company must disclose in its Profit and Loss Account any amount contributed by it to any political party or for any political purpose. This applies also to private companies.

However, acceptance of deposits by banking companies will not be deemed to be borrowing by them. The appointment of sole selling agents made by the Board of Directors must be approved by the shareholders in the next general meeting after the appointment, otherwise the appointment will be void. The Board will have no discretionary powers to appoint sole selling agents.

Legal Position of the Director

As the directors are special agents of the company they are expected to exercise such powers as are vested in them by the memorandum and articles of association. As trustees they are expected to display the utmost good faith in their dealings with the company. They are not supposed to use any information, money or property of the company for their own benefit at the cost of the company. If they do so and any damage or loss is caused to the company, they are liable to make it good.

Voting at General Meeting

A director can exercise his voting right both as a shareholder and a director at a general meeting. As a shareholder, he looks after his own interest while exercising his right to vote. But when he votes in the capacity of director as a special agent or trustee, he has to consider the best interest of the company. Normally he is not expected to vote at a general meeting against his own voting at Board meeting.

Position of Individual Directors

A director cannot act on behalf of the company as an individual director. Being one of the Board of directors he has to act jointly and not severally *i.e.*, alone. But he is expected to exercise only those powers which are delegated to him by the Board or articles. He should take reasonable care and precaution in the consideration of every matter while exercising any power given to him. He cannot relieve himself of his duties so long as he acts as a director. No full-fledged director can be a dummy director or a nominal director to keep watch over the proceedings of the Board meetings. Under fiduciary powers, they can issue shares at par even when market value of such shares is at premium. Such discretionary powers should be exercised strictly in good faith. Whatever discretion that they are exercising should not oblige a section of the shareholders. A director is not bound to give continuous attention to the affairs of the company unless he is a whole-time director. Where some officials are appointed to perform important duties under provisions of articles, a director is justified in reposing faith such officials entrusted with duties to perform them honestly. Though all books of account are open to free inspection by a director, he is not expected to go through each and every entry in the books. However, he is supposed to make good any damage or loss caused to the company through his gross negligence.

Delegation of Duties

Unless the articles authorise them to do so any duties entrusted to directors cannot be delegated to others. Any powers given to them by shareholders in general meeting cannot be transferred to any other person howsoever competent he may be. Where any power is either irregularly or excessively exercised by any body for the Board, the Board is empowered to ratify the same.

Procedure at Board's Meeting

Having seen that the quorum is full and getting himself fully satisfied that the meeting can be deemed to be properly constituted, the chairman will request the secretary to read the notice of the meeting and the minutes of the last meeting. After the minutes are read before the board, the chairman will ask the other member directors of the meeting as to the correctness of the minutes. If there is any omission or any wrong statement and if such errors or omissions are pointed out by any of the directors, they will be rectified accordingly. After having done so, the chairman will once again ask the directors whether the minutes as read out can be taken as finally correct. Now if no objection is raised by directors as to the drafting of the minutes, the minutes will be confirmed by the chairman as correct. The chairman is required to sign the minutes which implies the confirmation or he can sign the same with some additional words running as "the minutes of the board meeting held on the 30th December, 2001, were read and signed as a correct record".

Date.................... ....

Chairman

The chairman should put his initials whenever corrections are made in the minutes as pointed out by member directors.

Thereafter, the chairman will take up the items for discussion as per the agenda. But if he finds it convenient to change the order of the items given in the agenda, he is at liberty to do so in the interest of the company. Under this discretionary power, he may take any items for discussion as the conditions may permit him to do so. However, the usual practice is not to disturb the order of items appearing on the agenda. The chairman will see that the routine matters are first disposed of thereby providing more room for discussion on important items.

During the conduct of the meeting the chairman will ensure that sufficient discussion on every item of the agenda has taken place. He shall also see that every member director who likes to take part in the discussion is given an equal opportunity to express his opinion on the subject-matter. After having seen that the matter has been discussed at length, the chairman will put the motion to vote by show of hands for taking the final decision. The majority will decide the fate and then resolution to this effect will be passed according to the decision of the majority. Where there is a *"tie", i.e.,* equal votes, on both the sides, the chairman can arrive at the final decision by exercising his. *'casting vote'*. The chairman should see that a director interested in the matter on which the resolution is to be passed is not allowed to cast his vote 'on that particular resolution. This fact should be incorporated in the minutes pertaining to this matter.

The discretionary powers are vested in the chairman of a meeting in respect of writing out the minutes. If in the opinion of the chairman, there is any matter which may be regarded as defamatory of any person, such matter may not be incorporated in the minutes. Similarly, matters that are irrelevant or immaterial to the proceedings or that are harmful to the interest of the company may not be included in the minutes by order of the chairman (Section 193).

Resolution by Circulation

Under Section 289 of the Act, to pass a valid resolution it must be circulated in draft together with the necessary papers to all the directors or to all the members of the committee then in India. But, it should not be sent to less in number than the quorum fixed for a meeting. The resolution circulated in draft should have been approved by such of the directors as are then in India or by a majority of such of them as are entitled to vote on the resolution.

Validity of Directors

Under Section 290 of the Act, all acts done by a person in the capacity of a director are valid even if his appointment was invalid on account of any defect or disqualification as per provisions of the Act or the articles of the company. But any act done by him will not be valid if his appointment can be proved to be invalid.

Director's Committees

If permitted by articles, directors may appoint sub-committees for specific purposes. While appointing such committees the Board will fix terms and conditions under which these committees are expected to function. Whatever provisions are applicable to Board Meeting under the Companies Act, 1956 also applicable to Meetings of Director's Committees.

Reg. 73 to 81 of Table 'A' of Schedule 1 of the Act provide provisions regarding proceeding of meetings of the Board of directors. The Board of directors may meet for the dispatch of business. It is empowered to adjourn or regulate its meetings in the manner it thinks fit. On the requisition of another director, a director of the company can call a meeting of the Board. All questions arising at the meeting of the Board shall be decided by a majority of votes unless otherwise expressly stated in the Act. The chairman will have a second or casting vote when votes cast in favour of and against the motion are equal. The Board will elect the chairman and determine the period for which the elected chairman is to hold office. Where a chairman is not elected or the elected chairman is absent for five minutes after the time fixed for holding the meeting, the directors present may choose some one out of them to be the chairman of the meeting. The Board is further empowered to delegate any of its powers to committees consisting of members of its body as it thinks fit. This committee will have to discharge duties as per terms and conditions imposed by the Board. The meeting may be adjourned if such an act is seemed proper by the Directors present. All acts done by any meeting of the Board or committee thereof or by any person acting as a director shall be as valid as if every such person had been duly appointed, although it may be discovered later on that there was some defect in the appointment of such directors or of any person acting as Director. A resolution in writing, signed by the members of the Board or a committee shall be valid and effectual unless it is otherwise expressly provided in the Act.

MEETINGS OF THE SHAREHOLDERS

There are four types of meetings of shareholder :

(1) Statutory Meeting

(2) Annual General Meeting

(3) Extraordinary General Meeting

(4) Class Meetings

STATUTORY MEETING

Holding of the Meeting

A "statutory meeting", is the meeting of the shareholders. At this first meeting convened by the directors a complete report, regarding the working of the company and the progress made since its registration is placed before the shareholders by the directors. This report is called a "statutory report". Thus, the statutory meeting is called to give idea about the general affairs of the company to the shareholders. Although the shareholders have got right to discuss the statutory report at large, they are not empowered to pass a resolution pertaining to any matter about which no notice has been given.

Legal Provisions

The proceedings of the statutory meeting are governed by Section

165 of the Companies Act, 1956 by which it is obligatory to every company limited by guarantee and having a share capital to hold a statutory meeting *within a period of not less than one month and not more than six months* from the date at which the company is entitled to commence its business. A private company need not hold this meeting.

Notice of Meeting

As soon as the board of directors takes the decision to hold the statutory meeting it sends a notice of the meeting to all shareholders entitled to attend the meeting. Such a notice is given at least 21 days before the date of the meeting specifying therein that it is a notice of the statutory meeting.

Statutory Report

From the contents of the notice, it is clear that a copy of the statutory report must be forwarded at least 21 days before the meeting. However, if all members entitled to attend and vote at the meeting agree to receive the same within a shorter period than 21 days, it may be forwarded later than is required and it shall be deemed to have been duly forwarded as required by this Section.

The board of directors is responsible to forward copies of "Statutory report" to every member of the company at least 21 (twenty-one) days before the day on which the meeting is to be held.

Particulars of Statutory Report

As per Section 165(3) of the Companies Act, 1965 the statutory report shall set out the following particulars pertaining to the general affairs of the company :

(1) The total number of shares allotted, distinguishing shares allotted as fully or partly paid-up otherwise than in cash.

(2) In the case of partly paid-up shares, the extent to which they are so paid-up and the consideration for which they are allotted.

(3) The total amount of cash received by the company in respect of all the shares allotted, distinguished as aforesaid.

(4) The abstract of the receipts of the company and of the payments made upon the date within seven days of the date of the report. The receipts of the company from the shares, debentures and other sources must be shown separately in the abstract.

(5) All particulars concerning the balance remaining in hand and on account or estimate of the preliminary expenses of the company.

(6) The names, addresses and occupations of the directors of the company and of its auditors, and also, if these be any, of its manager and secretary; and the changes, if any, which have occurred in such names, addresses and occupations, since the date of the incorporation of the company.

(7) All particulars of any contracts (with proposed modification) which are to be submitted to the meeting for its approval.

(8) Any underwriting contract that has not been carried out and the reasons to that effect.

(9) The arrears, if any, due on calls from every director, managing agent or firm in which the managing agent is a partner.

(10) The particulars of any commission or brokerage paid or to be paid in connection with the issue or sales of shares of debentures to any director, or to the managing agent or to any partner of the managing agent.

Certification of the Statutory Report

The statutory report shall be certified as correct by not less than two directors of the company. If there is a managing director for the purpose of certifying the report, then he should be one out of two directors. Besides, it should also be certified by the auditor of the company in respect of the following :

(a) Matters relating to shares allotted by the company;

(b) The cash received in respect of such shares and

(c) The receipt and payments of the company on capital account.

Filing of Statutory Report

Now, the board is required to send a copy of the statutory report certified by two directors and auditor of the company, to the Registrar for registration forthwith after it has been sent to the members of the company.

Procedure of the Meeting

The chairman of the meeting starts the proceeding by requesting the secretary to read the notice of the meeting. The board should prepare a list showing the names, occupations and addresses of the members of the company and the number of shares held by them. This list is to be produced at the commencement of the statutory meeting. The Board should ensure that this list is kept open and accessible to any member of the company during the continuance of the meeting. Having seen that the notice is read the chairman of the meeting may commence the business according to the items of the agenda.

The chairman brings to the notice of the members present that the list of members is open for inspection. Thereafter, he says that the statutory report already circulated may be taken as read. Now, the progress made by the company since its incorporation is explained by the chairman to the members present at the meeting. He welcomes the discussion and views of different members on the matters pertaining to the statutory report and whenever it is necessary, he gives replies so as to satisfy the members. Thus, all matters appearing on the agenda are taken up in a serial order and the necessary decisions are taken by passing requisite resolutions. However, a resolution cannot be passed if no notice to that effect is given in accordance with the articles. Under such circumstances, the members present at the meeting are at liberty to discuss any matter relating to the formation of the company or arising out of the statutory report. The meeting is dispersed after the vote of thanks to the chairman.

After the meeting is over, the secretary prepares the minutes which are signed and confirmed at the next meeting. Unless the minutes are signed by the chairman, they are not deemed to be the correct official record of the proceeding of the meeting.

Adjournment of the Meeting

Under sub-section (8) of Section 165 of the Act the meeting may be adjourned from time-to-time and at any adjourned meeting, any resolution can be passed of which notice has been given in accordance with provisions of this Act, before or after the former meeting. The adjourned meeting shall have the same powers as the original meeting.

Penalty for Default

If default is made in complying with the provisions of Section 165 of the Act, *i.e.,* if the meeting is not held or the statutory report is not filed, the court may ask the company to wind-up its operations. Every director or other officer of the company who is in default will be punishable with a fine which may extend to five hundred rupees for every day during which the default continues. The above provisions are not applicable to a private company.

Duties of the Secretary

(1) He should give adequate notice to all members bringing to their notice the date, time, venue, etc.

(2) He should prepare statutory report in the prescribed form and get it approved at the Board of Director's meeting.

(3) He should print that report and send the same to all members so as to reach them at least 21 days before the meeting.

(4) He should file a certified copy of the statutory report with the Registrar of the Companies.

(5) He should prepare an Agenda of the meeting in consultation with the Chairman and a detailed list of members.

(6) He should see that all necessary arrangements are made for holding the meeting smoothly.

(7) He should help the Chairman in determining the quorum and also to read out the notice of the meeting.

(8) He should read the statutory report if he has been asked by the Chairman.

(9) He should help the Chairman in the smooth conduct of the meeting.

(10) He should note down the proceedings of the meeting.

(11) He should prepare minutes and get them approved and signed by the Chairman of the same meeting within 30 days of the meeting held.

ANNUAL GENERAL MEETING (AGM)

Called shareholder's meeting, this type of meeting is very important from the practical point of view, as it gives an opportunity to all shareholders to take part in the discussions pertaining to the important aspects of the company affairs such as appointment of directors, passing of dividends and approving of annual accounts, etc. The annual general meeting is usually held once a year within six months after the closing of the financial year of the company.

Penalty for Default

If default is made in holding a meeting, every officer of the company who is in default shall be punishable with fine which may extend to five thousand rupees and in case of continuing default with a further fine which may extend to Rs. 250 for every day till the default continues.

Holding of the AGM (Section 166)

1. Provisions. The first annual general meeting of the company should be held within eighteen months of incorporation. Subsequent annual general meeting should be held within fifteen (15) months of the preceding annual general meeting. It should also be held within six months after the closing of the financial year of the company. Except in the case of first annual general meeting the Registrar of Companies, on application, can extend the time for holding the meeting. So application for extension of time may be made to the Registrar, who can extend the time up to not more than three months for any special reason. He has no power to extend the time of the first annual general meeting. The interval between the two general meetings should not be more than fifteen months.

2. Place. No annual general meeting can be held on a public holiday. It should be held only in the town, city or any other place where the registered office of the company is situated.

3. Statutory Requirement. The annual general meeting must be called as per Section 166 of the Act whether the annual accounts are ready or not for consideration at the meeting. If the accounts are not ready, the A.G. meeting, called within the prescribed period be adjourned for the purpose of considering the accounts. Even after the expiry of the prescribed period, the meeting can be held with the permission of the Registrar. No meeting can be called, even within the prescribed period without passing a resolution to this effect by the Board of Directors. In the absence of required resolution, the Board should ratify the effect before such meeting is held.

If the company has not called the meeting within the specified period, any member may bring the fact to the notice of the Company Law Board which can call the meeting of the company or issue orders specifying therein the terms and conditions for calling and conducting the annual general meeting. It has also got the right to order that even person present in the person or proxy shall constitute a meeting and such a meeting shall constitute of annual general meeting of the company.

Notice of the AGM

1. The notice of 21 (twenty-one) days must be given to all members who are entitled to attend and vote at the meeting. It should also be sent to every person entitled to a share in consequence of death or insolvency of a member; and lastly, to the auditor or auditors of the company.
2. The notice of the meeting should contain the following particulars :
   (i) where it relates to an annual general meeting, a statement to the effect that it is the notice of the annual general meeting;
   (ii) the place at which the meeting will be held; this should be either the registered office of the company or a place within the town or village where the registered office of the company is situated. It can be held at these places only if all the members give their consent to this effect. Private companies may hold their meeting at any place.
3. The date on which the meeting will be held; this day should not be a public holiday.
4. The hour at which the meeting will be held, the meeting should be conducted only during business hours unless the articles of the company prescribe otherwise.
5. A statement of business to be transacted at the meeting *i.e.,*
   (i) consideration of directors' reports and accounts;
   (ii) declaration of dividend;
   (iii) election of directors in place of those retiring and
   (iv) election of auditors in place of those retiring will be considered as ordinary business; any other business will be deemed to be a special business.
6. In the case of special business the notice should contain all particulars concerning each item of special business.
7. In regard to all special business, the notice should give an idea as to the nature and extend of the interest of the directors,

managing agents, secretaries and treasurers, or manager in such business; it should also give information regarding the extent of shareholding interest in the company of every such person. The notice should also contain a statement where anyone of the above-mentioned officials holds more than 20 per cent of the company's paid-up capital.

8. Where the business of the meeting includes approval of any document, the place and time where it can be inspected should be given in the notice in the form of a separate statement.
9. It should be specifically mentioned in the statement of the notice that in the case of companies having a share capital, a member entitled to vote is also entitled to appoint one more proxy whether he or they are members of the company or not.
10. The Profit and Loss Account and Balance Sheet for the period ill review for which the annual meeting is called must be attached to the notice of the meeting.

Admission Card

Where the meeting is exclusively meant for the members, only the members entitled to attend and vote at the meeting may be allowed to attend meeting. Admission cards are given to each member who is required to sign the card and hand it over at the entrance. This card is duly checked by the secretarial staff with the register of members. If the member forgets to bring this card, he can attend the meeting by signing the attendance book.

Proxy

Any provision allowing the member to lodge a proxy with the company more than forty-eight hours before the meeting is void. A proxy need not necessarily be a member. A non-member can be appointed as proxy. More than one proxy can be appointed in public companies while in private companies only one can be appointed unless the articles provide otherwise. Members other than those who are, appointed proxies are entitled to inspect the proxies lodged with the company. The inspection of proxy is allowed by any member of the company provided he does so before one hour of the time fixed for the commencement of the meeting and ending of the proceedings of the meeting.

EXTRAORDINARY GENERAL MEETING (EGM)

Clause 47 of Table A (Schedule I) provides that all general meetings other than the annual general meeting shall be called as extraordinary general meetings.

An EGM is convened for transacting some special or urgent business that may arise in between two AGMs; *for instance,* change in the objects or shift of registered office or alteration of capital or removal of a director(s)/auditor(s).

Business to be transacted. All business transacted at such meeting is called special business. Therefore, every item on the agenda must be accompanied by an 'Explanatory Statement' in terms of section 173.

Who may call. An EGM may be called :

(i) By the Board of Directors of its own accord; (clause 48 of Table A to the Act);

(ii) By the Directors on requisition;

(iii) By the requisitionists themselves;

(iv) By the Company Law Board.

(i) *By the Directors :* The Board of directors may call a general meeting of the members at any time by giving not less than 21 days' notice [Section 171(1)]. A shorter notice may, however, be held valid if consent is accorded thereto by members of the company holding 95 per cent or more of the voting rights [Section 171(2) (ii)].

In exceptional cases of urgency any director (in the absence from India of requisite number of directors to form quorum in the Board meeting) or any two members of the company may convene an EGM.

(ii) *By the Directors on requisition [Section 169] :* The board of directors must convene a general meeting upon request or requisition if the following conditions are satisfied:

(a) The requisitionists must be such number of members who, at the date of the deposit of the requisition, are the holders of 1/10th of total voting power. Thus, in case of a company having share capital they should hold at least 1/10th of such of the paid-up capital that carries right to vote in regard to that matter [Section 169(4)(i)]. Preference shareholders have voting right only as regards matters relating to the preference shareholders. They have no general voting right and, therefore, no right to requisition in respect of other matters. If the company does not have a share capital, they should at least hold 1/10th of the total voting power of the company in regard to that matter [Section 169(4)(b)].

(b) The requisition must state the objects of the meeting, *i.e.*, it must set out the matters for the consideration of which the meetings is to be called [Section 169(2)].

(c) Requisition must have been deposited at the registered office of the company [Section 169(3)].

(d) Requisition must be signed by the requisitionists [Section 169(2)].

In case all the aforesaid conditions are satisfied, *i.e.*, a valid requisition has been received, the Board of directors must within 21 days of the receipt of the requisition call the meeting giving at least 21 days' notice fixing the meeting within 45 days of the receipt of the requisition [Section 169(6)].

(e) Where two or more distinct matters are specified in the requisition, the validity of each such matters shall be determined independent of each other before convening the meeting.

Where the resolution proposed is a special resolution, requirements of section 189(2) must be complied with, *viz.*, it should be so described and explanatory statement be annexed.

(iii) *By the requisitionists themselves [Section 169(60)]* : If the Board of directors does not or fails to call the meetings as aforesaid (*i.e.*, within 21 days fixing the date of the meeting within 45 days of the deposit of a valid requisition, the meeting may be called :

(a) by the requisitionists themselves.

(b) In case of a company having share capital, by one or more requisitionists as represent :

- a majority in value of the paid-up share capital held by all the requisitionists; or
- at least 1/10th of the paid-up share capital carrying voting rights in respect of that matter,

which ever is less.

(c) In case of a company not having share capital, by one or more requisitionists who represent at least 1/10th of total voting power of the company in regard to the matter of the requisition.

(d) Meeting must be held within 3 months of the date of the deposit of the requisition [Section 169(7)].

(e) Where two or more persons hold any shares or interest in a company jointly, a requisition, or a notice calling a meeting, signed by one or some of them shall, for the purposes of this section, have the same force and effect as if it had been signed by all of them [Section 169(8)].

An institutional shareholder, has the same rights as every other shareholder to requisition an extraordinary general meeting.

Whether preference shareholders can attend a meeting in which no business affecting them is to be conducted and what are their rights in such a meeting — Under section 172(2)(i), notice of every meeting of the company is required to be given to every member of the company. From this it may be inferred that although there is no express provision to that effect, every member of a company is entitled to attend every general meeting. However, it is clear from section 87(2)(a) that the holders of preference shares do not have any right to vote on resolutions placed before the company, which do not directly affected the rights attached to the preference shares. Further, in respect of resolutions in regard to which preference shareholders have no right to vote, they have also no right to take part in the discussion, even though they have the implied right by virtue of section 172(2)(i) to attend the meeting.

Any reasonable expenses incurred by the requisitionists by reason of the failure of the Board to call a meeting shall be repaid to the requisitionists by the company. Any sum so repaid shall be retained by the company out of any sums due or to become due from the company by way of fees or other remuneration for their services to such of the directors as were in default [Section 169(9)].

According to the Explanation contained in section 169, a meeting convened by the requisitionists (because of failure of the Board to convene) commenced on a day within three months from the date of the deposit of the requisition can be adjourned to a day after the expiry of the aforesaid three months.

Sections 193 and 195 are not applicable to the minutes of the requisitioned meeting and minutes are to be proved as a matter of fact.

(iv) *By the Company Law Board [Section 186].* If for any reason it is impracticable to call a meeting of the company, other than an annual general meeting, the Company Law Board may direct the calling of the meeting :

(a) on its own motion, or

(b) on an application of the director,

(c) on an application of any member entitled to vote at that meeting.

For the aforesaid meeting, the Company Law Board may give directions in respect of the place, date and manner in which the meeting be held and conducted. It may also give such ancillary or consequential directions as it thinks expedient, including a direction that one member present in person or proxy shall be deemed to constitute a meeting.

Types of Resolutions

Following three types of resolutions may be moved at the general meeting :

(1) Ordinary Resolution of Shareholders,

(2) Special Resolution of Shareholders,

(3) Resolution with Special Notice.

However, now there can be no extraordinary resolutions. In case of ordinary resolution a single majority is needed to pass it. In the case of special resolution, the intention to propose it as a special resolution should be given in the notice of the meeting. It should be passed by 3/4th majority, *i.e.*, the number of votes cast in favour of the resolution should three times the number cast against it.

The following requirements must be fulfilled in the case of resolutions with special notice :

(a) Persons intending to move such a resolution with special notice should give fourteen days' notice of their intention to the company.

(b) On receipt of this the company is required to give a notice of the proposed resolution to its members.

1. Ordinary Resolution. An ordinary resolution is one which requires a simple majority, that is, the votes in favour should exceed the votes against the resolution. Section 189(1) states that a resolution shall be an ordinary resolution when the votes at a general meeting cast by members in its favour are more than the votes cast against it. The votes may be cast on a show of hands or on a poll in general meeting of which due notice as required by the Act has been given. Those remaining neutral will not be counted either way. All matters which are not required by the Companies Act or the company's articles to be done by a special resolution, are done by means of an ordinary resolution.

Business transacted by ordinary resolutions. The following business may be transacted by an ordinary resolution :

(a) Issue of shares at a discount (Section 79).

(b) Adoption of statutory report (Section 165).

(c) Adoption of annual accounts (Section 210).

(d) Appointment of auditors and fixing their remuneration (Section 224). However, where 25 per cent or more of the subscribed capital of a company is held jointly or singly by a public financial institution, a Government company, a nationalised bank or an insurance company carrying on general insurance business, the appointment of an auditor shall be by a special resolution of the annual general meeting (Section 224A).

(e) Appointment of directors at the annual general meeting unless the articles contain contrary provisions (Section 255).

(f) Variation in the number of directions of the company within the limits fixed by the articles (Section 258).

(g) Declaration of dividends.

(h) Issue of bonus shares in accordance with the provisions of the articles.

(i) Authorising voluntary winding up under specified circumstances (Section 484).

(j) Appointing and fixing remuneration of liquidators in members' voluntary winding up (Section 490).

2. Special Resolution. A resolution shall be a special resolution when (a) the intention to propose it as a special resolution has been specifically mentioned in the notice calling the general meeting; (b) the notice required under this Act for convening the general meeting has been duly given; and (c) the number of votes cast in favour of the resolution is three times the number cast against it [Section 189(2)].

Thus, a special resolution is one which is passed at a general meeting of a company by a majority of three-fourths of the members present and entitled to vote.

The idea of a special resolution is to ensure that every important matter is decided after due deliberation and with the consent of a large number of shareholders present at the meeting, in person or by proxy.

Business transacted by special resolution. The business of a general meeting must be transacted by means of a special resolution when so required by the Act or by the articles. The following are the matters which require special resolution under the Act :

(a) Alteration of the memorandum in the matter of shifting of registered office from one State to another and also alteration of the objects clause subject to confirmation of the Company Law Board (Section 17).

(b) Alteration of the name of the company with the approval of the Central Government (Section 21).

(c) Alteration of the articles of association (Section 31).

(d) Authorising the offer of right shares to non-members (Section 81).

(e) Creation of reserve capital (Section 99).

(f) Reduction of capital (Section 100).

(g) Variation in the rights of holders of any class of shares (Section 106).

(h) Removal of registered office outside the local limits of the city, town or village in which it is situated (Section 146).

(i) Authorising payment of interest out of share capital (Section 208).

(j) Declaration of investigation into the affairs of the company (Section 237).

(k) Authorising voluntary winding up of the company (Section 484).

3. Resolution requiring special notice. Where special notice of a resolution is required by the Act or the articles of a company, notice of the intention to move the resolution should be given to the company not less than fourteen days before the meeting at which it is to be moved. The company on receipt of such special notice will give the notice of the resolution to the members at least seven days before the meeting in the same manner in which notice for a meeting is given. Where that is not practicable, it may be given by advertisement in a newspaper having an appropriate circulation or in any other mode allowed by the articles (Section 190).

Special notice is required by the Act in the following cases :

(i) for a resolution for appointment as auditor of a person other than a retiring auditor (Section 255);

(ii) for a resolution at an annual general meeting providing expressly that a retiring auditor shall not be reappointed (Section 225).

(iii) for a resolution for removal of a director before the expiry of his term (Section 284);

(iv) for a resolution for appointment of another person as a director in place of the director removed (Section 284); and

(v) for a resolution for the appointment as director of a person other than retiring director (Section 257).

The articles of a company may provide additional matters in respect of which special notice is required.

Registration of Certain Resolution and Agreements

A certified copy under the signatures of an officer of the company, of the following resolutions and agreements must be registered with the Registrar within 30 days after passing or making thereof :

(i) special resolutions;

(ii) resolutions which have been agreed to by all the members of a company, but which, in the absence of such an agreement, would have to be passed as special resolutions;

(iii) any resolution of the board or an agreement executed by a company relating to the appointment, reappointment or renewal of appointment of a managing director or variation of the terms of a managing director;

(iv) all resolutions or agreements binding on all members of any class of shareholders, although they have not been agreed to by all those members;

(v) resolutions passed by a company conferring power under Section 293 upon its directors to sell or dispose of the whole or any part of company's undertaking, to borrow money beyond the limits of the paid-up capital and free reserve of the company, and to contribute to charities beyond fifty thousand rupees or five per cent of the profits, whichever is greater;

(vi) any resolutions approving the appointment of sole selling agents under Section 294 or 294AA:

(vii) resolution for voluntary winding up passed under Section 484; and

(viii) copies of terms and conditions of appointment of a sole selling agent appointed under Section 294 or Section 294AA (Section 192).

Circulation of Resolution

The company should circulate the resolution among its members when some members of the company having 5 per cent of the total voting power or if one hundred members commanding a paid-up capital of Rs. 1 (one) lakh or more and also having a right to vote give notice of their intention to move a resolution at the meeting. A statement of not more than one thousand words pertaining to the resolution to be considered at the meeting should also be circulated along with the notice of the meeting. In the case of resolutions, the company is not bound to circulate if they are not deposited with the company six weeks before the meeting. In the case of statements, they should be deposited two weeks before the meeting. It is necessary for the requisitionists to deposit adequate amount so as to enable the company to meet the requisite expenses in effecting circulation (Section 188).

However, an exception to the above provision is that in the case of a banking company, if the board of directors think that the circulation of any statement as desired by the requisitionists will be detrimental to the interest of the company, such statement may not be circulated; while in any other case the board cannot refuse to circulate the resolutions [Section 188(5)].

If any trading or banking company desires that because of the defamatory nature, any resolution or statement should not be circulated, then it can apply to the court seeking its order to the effect.

Procedure at the AGM

1. First of all, the secretary of the company should see that the notice as stated above is sent to all members entitled to attend and vote at the meeting.

2. The next immediate step is of closing the registers in case the dividend is to be declared at that meeting, and of making arrangements for the printing of dividend warrants. Generally, the register of transfers is closed for 14 days from the conclusion of the meeting by giving not less than seven (7) days' notice in a newspaper.

The members will meet at the scheduled time at the place as specified in the notice.

3. Quorum. The quorum for a general meeting is at least two members personally present in the case of a private company and five members personally present in the case of public companies. The articles of a company may provide for a large number in either of cases. Any provision in the articles specifying lesser number of persons than prescribed under Section 174 of the Act is void. If the quorum is not present within half an hour from the time fixed for the meeting, the meeting shall stand dissolved in case the meeting is called upon the requisition of members. In other cases, it shall stand adjourned to the same day, place and time in the next week provided that the day does not fall on any holiday. In the case of an adjourned meeting, any number of persons even lesser than required (2 and 5) will constitute the quorum.

4. Chairman. Out of the members present, one will be elected as chairman to preside over the meeting. But the articles of a company can provide any special provision to the contrary. The chairman will proceed with the items as per agenda. Along with the notice of the meeting, the secretary will also read directors' report and thereafter the chairman will request the company auditors to read their reports. In the absence of auditors, the secretary will read that report. The directors' report is usually taken as read. However, auditors' report cannot be taken as read. Items given in the agenda will be discussed one by one and will be put to vote. It is a practice for the chairman to address the shareholders giving a broad outline of the progress made by the company.

5. Voting. Generally, all resolutions are decided by 'show of hands'. If a poll is demanded in respect of the election of the chairman or adjournment of the meeting, it must be taken at once or within forty-eight hours of the demand. However, the chairman has power to prescribe the manner in which the poll is to be taken. He should appoint two, scrutineers to scrutinise the votes. A poll may be demanded by proxy, or by members having 10 per cent of the paid-up capital or 10 per cent of the voting power. In the case of private companies, one member can demand poll when not more than seven persons are present and two members have to demand it when there are more than seven members present. Members are given option to cast their votes as they like, *i.e.*, to cast votes or not to cast their votes. A proxy will have no right to speak nor will he have a right to vote on a "*Show of Hands*". He can vote only when a poll is taken.

6. Election of Directors. One-third of the elected directors should retire at each annual general meeting. They are, however, eligible for re-election and unless it is specifically decided not to re-elect them or some others are appointed in their places, they will be deemed to be re-elected. Where a person is to be appointed in the place of a retiring director, 7 days' notice of the intention to nominate him should be given to the company. This provision is applicable to public companies only. If any associates or employees of the managing agents are to be appointed as directors, then it can be done only by passing a special resolution. A notice to this effect should be given to the company and later on the company is required to send notice of the resolution to its members. Election of every director should be made by a separate resolution. If two directors are to be elected at the meeting, they cannot be elected by passing one common resolution unless the meeting unanimously resolves otherwise. It is required to file with the company the consent of the person agreeing to act as director in case he is not one of the retiring directors and the company should file the same with the Registrar within thirty days of his election.

7. Election of Auditors. Though auditors are appointed by the board within one month from the date of registration of the company, but the subsequent appointment of auditors is to be made at each annual general meeting. The retiring auditor is reappointed unless he is disqualified or he expresses his unwillingness to be reappointed or the company has decided not to reappoint him. If, a new person is to be appointed in the place of retiring auditor, then fourteen days' notice of the intention should be given by the company and the company should send a copy of it to the retiring auditor and to give notice of the resolution to members also. The retiring auditor can make a representation to the company that the company should circulate the same among its members. If it has not been circulated, it can be read at the meeting. All auditors except the retiring auditor should be intimated within 7 days of the appointment. The auditor of the company has a right to attend and speak at the general meeting. He can speak on the matter concerning him as auditor of the company. His report must be read at the general meeting,

8. Minutes. While writing the minutes of the general meeting, the secretary should ensure that they contain all important questions put in the meeting and a good summary of the proceedings of such a meeting. No minutes will be circulated among the members under the provisions of the Act, but if a member requests for a copy of minutes, the same can be supplied to him on payment of Re. 1 (one) or such charges that are reasonable and fixed by the company. The secretary should ensure that within thirty (30) days of the conclusion of the meeting, the minutes are duly entered in the minutes book. Every page of the minutes should be initialled while the last page should be dated and signed. Minutes should not be pasted on the minutes book. If any director is authorised by the board to sign the minutes of the general meetings, he can do so; otherwise they should be signed by the chairman of the general meeting within 14 days after the meeting.

After Conclusion of the Meeting

Within forty-two days of the AGM, three copies of the Balance Sheet and the Profit and Loss Account signed by the managing director, managing agent, secretaries and treasurers, manager or secretary or a director must be filed with the Registrar of Companies. This provision is also applicable to private companies. Where the Balance Sheet etc., has not been adopted at the meeting, a statement giving reasons of non-adoption should be attached to the Balance Sheet and filed with the Registrar. If a dividend is declared at the AGM then it must be paid to the registered shareholders or dividend warrants should be posted to them within 42 days of the meeting. The minutes of the AGM should be written within 30 days in the minute book kept for purpose and signed and dated by the chairman of the said meeting.

Provisions under the Amendment Act (Section 181)

(1) Every company shall hold all annual general meeting each year.

(2) Meeting should be held at interval not exceeding fifteen months.

(3) The first annual general meeting may be held within 18 (eighteen) months from the date of incorporation. If a meeting is so held, it need not be held in the year of incorporation or the next year.

(4) Notice convening the meeting must specify the meeting as the annual general meeting.

(5) A public company may fix the time of such meeting in the articles or by resolution in preceding annual general meeting. Private companies may also fix AGM in the same manner.

(6) Meetings must be held either at the registered office of the company or at some other place within the city, town or village in which the registered office of the company is situated.

(7) The Central Government has been empowered to exempt any class of companies from the provisions pertaining to time and place of annual general meeting.

(8) The chairman, if any, of the Board, shall preside as chairman at every general meeting of the company.

(9) If the chairman is not present within fifteen (15) minutes after the time fixed for holding the meeting or is unwilling to act as chairman, then the directors present shall elect one of them to be the chairman of the meeting.

(10) In case no director is willing to act as chairman, members present shall choose one among themselves as the chairman of the meeting.

(11) No business shall be transacted at any adjourned meeting other than the business left unfinished at the meeting from which the adjournment took place.

(12) If the meeting is adjourned for thirty days or more, notice of the adjourned meeting should be given as in the case of an original meeting.

(13) Any business other than that upon which a poll has been demanded may be proceeded with, pending the taking of the poll.

(14) The Registrar can extend the time up to three (3) months. He cannot exercise this power in the case of the first meeting.

(15) In addition to the fine upto Rs. 50,000 for default in complying with the above provisions, a further fine upto Rs. 2,500 for everyday is imposed, under the Amendment Act till such default continues.

QUESTIONS

1. What are different kinds of meetings of the shareholders of a company? When and how are these meetings held?
2. What is a statutory meeting? What is statutory report and what are its contents?
3. What are the statutory provisions regarding the holding of an annual general meeting? What business is transacted at such a meeting?
4. "The general meeting alone is the company's primary organ and the directors are merely the company's agents or servants at all time subservient to the general meeting." Comment.
5. What are the provisions of the Companies Act, 1956 which particularly relate to the convening and holding of a general meeting of a company on requisition?
6. Can the directors of a company postpone the holding of its annual general meeting beyond the statutory time limit on the ground that the annual accounts are not ready?
7. What do you understand by a quorum? Must a quorum be present throughout a meeting? What is the procedure if a quorum is never formed?
8. What are the requisites of a valid meeting?
9. What do you understand by a proxy? What are the statutory provisions regarding proxies?

10. What are the provisions of the Companies Act, 1956 as to the length of notice required for calling general meetings of a company? In what circumstances may a general meeting be validly held when the notice given is shorter than that normally required by the Act?

PRACTICAL PROBLEMS

1. At a meeting of a company, only 15 shareholders were present. 9 voted for a special resolution and 2 against and 4 not vote at all. No poll was demanded and the chairman declared the resolution to be carried. Is this a valid resolution?
[**Hint.** Yes (Section 189)].
2. S, a shareholder, after appointing P as his proxy at a meeting of the company, himself attended the meeting and voted on a particular resolution. P thereafter claimed to exercise his vote. Examine his claim.
[**Hint.** His claim is invalid (Cousins *Vs.* International Brick Co. Ltd.)].
3. Default has been made in holding the annual general meeting of a company more than 18 months having elapsed since the date of the last such meeting. What can be done in the circumstances by a member who wishes that the meeting should be held?
[**Hint.** He may apply to the Company Law Board which may call or direct the calling of a general meeting of the company (Section 167)].
4. By inadvertence, the secretary of a company failed to send notice to 9 members of the company of a special resolution to be proposed at an annual general meeting. The addressograph plates containing the names and addresses of these 9 members had been removed from the file because the dividend warrants sent to those addresses had been returned or remained uncashed with the result that the company wished to verify their addresses. When the notices were sent out, these plates had not been replaced. The special resolution was passed at the meeting. Is the resolution valid?
[**Hint.** Yes (West Canadian Colieries Ltd., Re; Section 172)].
5. The shareholders of a company duly called upon the managing director to convene a meeting of the company at which they wanted to move a motion removing the managing director from his post. The managing director failed to oblige them, so the shareholders themselves met at a place other than the registered office of the company and by a resolution removed the managing director from his post. Is the resolution validly passed?
[**Hint.** Yes, provided the meeting is held within 3 months from the date of the deposit of requisition by the-requisitionists (Section 169)].

6. The Articles of Association of a company require the instrument appointing a proxy to be received by the company 75 hours before the meeting. Is it a valid requirement? If not, what are its effects?
[**Hint.** No (Section 176)].

16

WINDING UP OF A COMPANY

Meaning

Defining the term winding up Prof. Gower says, "Winding up of company is the process whereby its life is ended and is properly administered for the benefits of its creditors and members. An administrator, called liquidator, is appointed and he takes the control of the company, collects its assets, pays it debts and finally distributes any surplus among the members in accordance with their rights."

A company is an artificial person, created by law, it cannot die a natural death. Whenever the life of a company is put to an end, it must be through a legal process. It remains in existence until the process of its winding up is completed. Winding up of a company means the stage when the business of the company is dissolved, all the assets of the company are realised and the money realised is distributed among the creditors, debenture-holders and shareholders of the company. If the company does not realise the money, sufficient enough to pay off its creditors, then it asks for the money from its shareholders if there is any uncalled money on the shares.

Thus, the term winding up means the process of realization of the assets, payment of the liabilities and distribution of surplus if any, among the members of the company. It is also known as liquidation of a company.

Modes

According to Section 425 of the Indian Companies Act, 1956, a company may be wound up in any of the following three ways :

1. Compulsory winding up by court.
2. Voluntary winding up.
3. Winding up under the supervision of court.

DISSOLUTION OF A COMPANY

Meaning

Dissolution means the stage when the company ceases to exist. Its existence comes to an end. Thus dissolution of a company means the following :

1. The existence of a company ends.

2. The existence of the liquidator of the company also ends.

3, There is no more recognition of any loan of the company because the company is no more in existence.

4. No work can be carried in the name of company.

Methods

According to the provisions of Indian Companies Act, 1956, a company may be dissolved by any of the following three methods :

1. The Name of the Company is removed from the Register of Companies by the Registrar. According to Section 560 of the Indian Companies Act, 1956, the registrar of companies may remove the name of any company from its register, if the company is not doing its business for a long time or if the company is not a going concern. If the name of the company is so removed from the register of companies, it automatically goes into liquidation. However, it may apply to the court against the removal of its name from the register of companies by the registrar. If the court is satisfied with the argument, given by company that the company was a going concern at the time when its name was removed from the register of companies by registrar, the court may order the registrar to re-enter the name of company into register of companies. In this case, the removal of the name of company by the registrar will not be effective.

2. Dissolution By the Order of Court. According to Section 394 of the Indian Companies Act, 1956 a court may order for the dissolution of a company, on its re-organization or reconstruction or on the amalgamation of two companies. On such order of the court, the company is dissolved.

3. Dissolution by Liquidation. When the liquidator of the company has completed all the formalities of the winding up of the company, the company is taken to be dissolved.

LIQUIDATION *Vs.* DISSOLUTION

Basis of Difference	*Winding up*	*Dissolution*
1	2	3
1. Existence of Company	The company remains in existence, until the process of winding up is completed.	The existence of a company ends with the dissolution.
2. Verification of loans	Creditors of the company have to verify their claim.	Verification is not required because the company is not in existence.
3. Reasons	Reasons are given in sections 633, 502 and 484.	Reasons arc given in sections 509, 497 and 481.

(Contd.)

1	2	3
4. Liquidator	The whole process is completed by its liquidator.	No question arises of liquidator because the existence of' company has already ended.
5. Sale of Assets and payment of Debt	The liquidator realizes all the assets of the company and makes the payment of debt of the company.	The company is dissolved after having done all these works.
6. Scope	It is a method of dissolution of a company.	It incorporates the winding up and no company can be dissolved without winding up.

METHODS OF WINDING UP OF A COMPANY

According to Section 425 of the Indian Companies Act, 1956 a company may be wound up in the following three methods :

I. Compulsory winding up by court.

II. Voluntary winding up.

III. Winding up under the supervision of court.

I. COMPULSORY WINDING UP BY COURT

According to Section 433 and 434 of the Indian Companies Act, 1956 the court may order for the winding up of a company. This is known as the compulsory winding up of the company. This may be done in the following circumstances :

1. Special Resolution of the Company. If the company has resolved by passing a special resolution that the company may be wound up by the court, the court may order for it. However, if the court is of the opinion that the winding up of the company will be against public interests, it may decide not to wind up the company, even if the resolution to that effect has been passed by the company. This is not a popular method because whenever the members of company decide for the winding up of the company, they decide for voluntary winding up, because in that case, the interference of the court will be least.

2. Default in holding the Statutory Meeting or in submitting the Statutory Report to the Registrar. A public company is under the obligation to call a statutory meeting within a period of 6 months of obtaining the certificate of commencement of business and to submit a statutory report with the registrar of companies at least 21 days before the date of statutory meeting. If the company fails in holding the statutory meeting or in submitting the statutory report with the registrar, the court may order for the winding up of the company. However, the court may extend the time for doing so. The court is not bound to order for the winding up in this case also.

The petition for the winding up of the company on this ground may be moved by the registrar of companies or by a contributory of the company, on or after the expiry of 14 days after the last date on which the statutory meeting must have been held.

3. If the Business is not commenced within One Year of Incorporation or if the Business is suspended for One Full Year. A company must start its business within one year from its incorporation. If a company does not commence its business within this period or the business of the company is suspended for one full year, the court may order for the winding up of the company. Here again the court may or may not exercise this power. If the court is satisfied with the reasons, furnished by the company for not commencing the business or for the suspension of business, it may decide not to order for the winding up of the company.

4. If the Number of Members goes below the Minimum Number. Under the provisions of the Indian Companies Act, a private company must have minimum 2 members and a public company must have minimum 7 members. If the number of members of a company goes below it, the court may order for the winding up of the company. In this case the court is bound to order for the winding up of the company.

5. If the Company is Unable to Pay its Debts. The court may order for the compulsory winding up of the company if a Company is deemed to be unable to pay its debts in the following cases :

(i) If the company is unable to pay a creditor a loan of Rs. 500 or more, within 3 weeks of the demand of the loan.

(ii) If the company fails to pay any creditor in whose favour, a decree has been passed by the company.

(iii) If the company is unable to pay its debts this way, the court may order for the winding up of the company, if the applicant proves that the company is commercially insolvent.

6. Just and Equitable. The court may order for the winding up of a company if it is of the opinion that it will be just and equitable to do so. On the basis of judgment of the court, following are the examples, when the court may order for the winding up of a company on this ground :

(i) If the company is suffering a continuous loss for a long time and the court is of the opinion that the business cannot be carried on except at loss.

(ii) If the company was established to carry out an illegal or fraudulent business or if the business, being carried out by the company, becomes illegal.

(iii) If there is a complete deadlock in the management of the company.

(iv) If the entire capital of the company is almost wasted and when it is a mere 'bubble'.

(v) If the majority of the shareholders have adopted a policy of oppression and mismanagement towards the minority shareholders of the company.

(vi) If there is a material dispute among the members of the company and the court is of the opinion that such dispute may cause an injury to the company.

(vii) If the main object of the company has failed.

(viii) If the company is being managed and directed in a fraudulent manner.

(ix) If the court considers any other reason to be a just and equitable ground for the winding up of the company.

Petitioners for the Winding Up

According to Section 439 of the Indian Companies Act, a petition to the court for the compulsory winding up of the company may be made by the following persons :

1. By the Company. A company may itself make a petition to the court for its winding up in the following cases :

(i) If the company has passed a special resolution to this effect, or

(ii) If the directors of the company are of the opinion that the circumstances of the company are leading it to be insolvent. In this case, the directors are not required to be authorised for making such petition by any resolution of the shareholders.

2. By the Creditors. If the company is unable to pay its debts, petition may be filed to the court for the compulsory winding up of the company, by any creditor or creditors of the company. A petition can be made by a prospective creditor also on this ground, with tire prior permission of the court.

3. By Contributories. The term contributories means the members and the past members of the company who ceased to be the members within one year before the commencement of winding up. These are liable to contribute to the assets of the company, in the event of its winding up. They can also move an application to the court for the winding up of the company on any grounds mentioned earlier except No. 1 & No. 5.

A list of contributories is made out in two parts, A and B. List A includes the names of present members of the company whose names appear on the register of members on the commencement of winding up of the company. List B includes the names of past members of the company who have ceased to be members within a year preceding the winding up.

The liability of a present member (List A contributory) is as follows :

(i) in case of a company limited by shares, no contribution shall be required from him exceeding the amount remaining unpaid on the shares held by him [Section 426(1)(d)].

(ii) in case of a company limited by guarantee, no contribution shall be required from him exceeding the amount undertaken to be contributed by him to the assets of the company in the event of its being wound up [Section 426(1)(e)] and

(iii) in the event of the winding up of a company limited by guarantee which has a share capital every member of the company shall be liable to contribute to the extent that he guaranteed plus any sums unpaid on the shares held by him as if the company were a company limited by shares [Section 426(2)].

The liability of a past member is as follows :

(i) a past member shall not be liable to contribute if he has ceased to be a member for one year or upwards before the commencement of the winding up [Section 426(1)(2)].

(ii) a past member shall not be liable to contribute in respect of any debt or liability of the company contracted after he ceased to be a member [Section 426(1)(b)] and

(iii) no past member shall be liable to contribute unless it appears to the court that the present members are unable to satisfy the contributions required to be made by them [Section 426(1)(c)].

The extent of liability of a past member is the same as that of present members discussed above.

Obligations of directors and managers whose liability is unlimited. Section 322 states that by virtue of the provisions of the memorandum of association of a company, the liability of any of its directors or manager may be made unlimited though the liability of members is limited. It is further provided in Section 427 that any of such directors or manager shall be liable, in the event of winding up of the company, in addition to his liability as a shareholder, to make further contribution as if he were a member of an unlimited company. Both present and past officers of the company shall be liable under the above provisions. But a past director or manager is not liable :

(i) if he has ceased to hold officer for a year or upwards before the commencement of the winding up;

(ii) if the debt or liability was incurred after he ceased to hold office; and

(iii) if the court does not deem it necessary to require further contribution (Section 427).

Legal representative in case of member's death. If a contributory dies, his legal representatives shall be liable to contribute to the assets of the company in discharge of his liability, and shall be contributories accordingly (Section 430).

The liability of the legal representatives of a deceased contributory is limited to the value of estate coming into his hands.

Official assignee or receiver in case of a member's insolvency. If a contributory is adjudged insolvent, his assignees in insolvency shall represent him for all the purposes of the winding up and shall be contributories accordingly (Section 431).

Liquidator of a body corporate which is a member. If a body corporate, which is a contributory is ordered to be wound up, its liquidator shall be the contributory (Section 432).

Any other person whom the court may so direct in case of fraudulent conduct of business. If in a winding up it appears that any business of the company has been carried on with intent to defraud creditors of the company or any persons or for any fraudulent purpose, the court may declare that any persons who were knowingly parties to such business shall be personally liable for all or any of the debts of the company. The application may be made by the Official Liquidator, the liquidator, or any creditor or contributory the company (Section 542).

Nature of the Contributory's Liability

Section 429 specifies the nature of the liability of a contributory. The liability of a contributory is in the nature of a debt but it does not become payable until a call is made. Thus the liability of a contributory, though commencing at the date of winding up, is only contingent, until a call is made. This section gives to the liquidator a new cause of action which a company itself might not have. For example, if the claim of the company for the realisation of any call from a member is barred by limitation, such a member becomes liable to pay all that has remained unpaid on his shares including the unpaid call when the company goes into liquidation.

The liability of the contributory does not arise by virtue of his contract to take shares from the company. Rather it arises by reason of the fact that his name appears on the register of members of the company. The liability of the contributory is a statutory liability arising after winding up has started. It was held that it is no answer to a liquidator's clam against any person whose name appears on the register as member, that there was an agreement with the directors to exclude this statutory liability.

Similarly, after a winding up order is made it is not open to a person whose names appears on the register of members to object to his name being placed on the list of contributories on the ground that allotment to him was void.

At the same time, a shareholder who has purchased shares from the company on the basis of a false and misleading prospectus can avoid his liability before the company has gone into liquidation. He cannot avoid his liability if the company goes into liquidation because upon the commencement of liquidation, the rescission of the contract and repayment of money to the subscriber would injure the creditors by decreasing the assets available for payment of their debts.

Section 71 lays down that an irregular allotment shall be voidable at the option of the allottee within two months of the statutory meeting or within two months of the allotment where no statutory meeting is to be held. Such an allotment is voidable even if the company is in the course of winding up within the time specified. This means that a contributory can avoid his liability if he acts within the prescribed time even if company is in the course of winding up.

If the shares of a person have been forfeited for non-payment of calls more than a year before the commencement of the winding up, he shall be liable for the call amount with interest as a debtor of the company for which the company can file a suit. But he cannot be placed on the list of contributories.

Contributory's right to set-off. The court may make an order on any contributory to pay any money due to the company from him. The sum payable must be exclusive of any money payable by the contributory as a shareholder [Section 469(1)].

In an unlimited company, the court may allow to the contributory, by way of set off, any money due to him on an independent dealing or contract with the company. But no set off will be allowed for any money due to him as a member of the company in respect of any dividend or profit [Section 469(2)(a)].

In the case of limited company, the court may give the above allowance to any director or manager or manager whose liability is unlimited [Section 469(2)(b)].

In the case of any company, whether limited or unlimited, when all the creditors have been paid in full, any money due on any account to a contributory from the company may be allowed to him by way of set-off against any subsequent call [Section 469(3)].

4. By any Two or All of the Parties together, mentioned above. The company, its creditors, contributories, may also present a petition for the compulsory winding up of the company jointly.

5. By Registrar. The registrar of the companies may be empowered for making such petition on the following grounds :

(i) If the company makes any fault in holding the statutory meeting or in submitting the statutory report to him.

(ii) If the company does not commence its business within a year after the date of its incorporation, or the business of the company remains suspended for one full year.

(iii) If the number of members of a company goes below the minimum number of members by law.

(iv) If the company is unable to pay its debts as disclosed by its account, or from the report of a special auditor or from the report of an inspector.

(v) When the registrar is of the opinion that it will be just and equitable to wind up the company.

6. By the Central Government. The Central Government may also file a petition for the winding up of a company. It may also authorise any person to make such a petition. Such a petition is made if it appears to the government, from the report of the investigating inspector, that the company is being managed in a fraudulent or illegal manner or in a manner against the interest of its creditors or members or any other person.

Procedure

(1) Commencement of the Winding up by the Court (Section 441). The process of winding up by the court commences on the day on which a petition of this intention is filed to the court. However, if the company has already passed a resolution for the winding up of the company, the date of passing such a resolution by the company, will be deemed to be the date of the commencement of the process of winding up. If a winding up order is made by the court, based on more than one petitions, the process of winding up is deemed to have commenced from the date of the earliest petition filed to the court. The date of commencement of winding up is very important for various matters, such as, 'avoidance of petitioner volunteer' and for ascertaining the liability of the past members.

(II) Powers of the Court on Filing the Petition. At the filing of a petition compulsory winding up of a company, the court gets the following powers :

1. To stay Proceedings against Company (Section 442). The court empowered to pass stay order of any suit or proceedings, pending against the company in any other court, on such terms as it thinks fit. The court may pass such stay order on the application made to it by the company, or any creditor or any contributory. If the suit against the company is pending in the Supreme Court or in any other High Court, the application for the stay order must be made to the court concerned, which may order for the stay.

2. Hearing Petition (Section 443). After receiving the petition for winding up of a company, the court fixes a date for the bearing of petition. It issues a notice to the company, at least 14 days before the date of hearing, to appear before the court and state its case for the winding up. The notice will also be notified to all the creditors and contributories of the company, so that they may present their objections, if any.

On the date of hearing, the court may act in any of the following manners, after hearing all concerned parties :

(i) Dismiss the petition.

(ii) Adjourn the hearing.

(iii) Make any interim order.

(iv) Make an order for the winding up of the company.

(III) Consequences of the Winding up Order (Section 444). If the court makes an order for the winding up of a company, it will result in the following consequences :

1. The court will fix the powers, duties and remuneration of the official liquidator.
2. The court will inform the official liquidator and the registrar of companies about the winding up of the company.
3. Section 445(1). states that the petitioner and the company must file a certified copy of the order of the court with the Registrar of Companies, within one month of the order of the court. The Registrar will notify such an order in the official gazette.
4. Section 445(3) states that the order of the court for the winding up of a company shall also be deemed to be a notice.
5. The powers of the board of directors are terminated. These powers will be exercised by the official receiver.
6. Section 449 states that the official liquidator shall become the liquidator of the company by virtue of his office.
7. Any debts payable at any time become immediately payable on the order of winding up.
8. The order of winding up shall operate in favour of all the concerned parties.
9. Section 446 states that after the order of winding up has been made, no suit or legal proceeding can be commenced against the company, without permission of the court. If a suit is pending against the company at the time of its winding up, it shall not be proceeded with, except with the permission of court.
10. Section 446 states that the court, ordering the winding up of the company, shall have full powers to entertain or dispose of any new or pending suit or legal proceeding against the company, any suit or legal proceeding pending in other court at the time of order of winding up shall have be transferred to the court which has ordered for the winding up of the company.

(IV) Dissolution of the Company. When all the formalities of the winding up of a company are completed, the company is deemed to be dissolved. A copy of the dissolution of the company must be filed with the Registrar of Companies within 30 days.

II. VOLUNTARY WINDING UP OF A COMPANY

According to Section 484 Indian Companies Act, 1956 when the members or creditors of a company agree to settle their affairs and disputes with the mutual consent, it is called voluntary winding up of the company. In this type of winding up, there is no interference by the court. The company, its members, and its creditors are free to settle their affairs, without going to a court.

Conditions of Voluntary Winding Up

Under Section 484 of the Indian Companies Act of 1956, the voluntary winding up of a company may take place in the following circumstances :

1. On the Expiry of Period. If a company, by its articles of association, is established for a certain time, it may be liquidated voluntarily by passing an ordinary resolution on the expiry of the said period.

2. On the Happening of Certain Event. If the company, by its articles of association, is established for the purpose of a particular work, it may be voluntarily wound up on the happening of that event.

3. By Passing a Special Resolution. Section 485 of the Indian Companies Act states that a company may be wound up, at any time without assigning any reason, by passing a special resolution for the purpose.

This section further states that the resolution for the voluntary winding up of the company, whether it is an ordinary resolution or a special resolution, must be advertised within 14 days of passing the resolution in the official Gazette and also in any leading News Paper, being circulated in the district where the registered office of the company is situated. If the company or any officer of the company does not comply with this provision, they may be punished with a fine which may be extended upto Rs. 50 per day for the period during which the default continues.

Commencement

According to Section 486 of the Companies Act the voluntary winding up of the company shall be deemed to be commenced from the date on which a resolution to that effect is passed by the company.

Consequences

1. Closure of the Business. According to Section 487 of the Indian Companies Act, the company ceases to carry on its business, from the date of commencement of voluntary winding up. However, the company may be allowed to carry on its business till some certain period, if it is required for the beneficial winding up of the company.

2. Powers of Liquidator. According to Section 487, the possession of the asset of the company is transferred to its liquidator who realizes the assets and distributes them among the creditors of the company.

3. Discharge of the Employees. A resolution passed by a company for its voluntary winding up serves as the notice of discharge to all the employees of the company. However, the employees continue if the business of the company is continued for the beneficial winding up of the company, or when the liquidation of the company is done only with a view of its reconstruction. No compensation will be payable by the company to its employees for such transfer. But if an employee was appointed on contract basis and the term of contract has not expired on the date of winding up, the company will be liable to pay the damages for the breach of contract.

4. Powers of Board of Directors. All powers of the Board of Directors, managing director and manager will be automatically delegated to the liquidator, on his appointment. However, the following powers remain with Board of Directors :

(i) The power to give notice to the registrar about any vacancy arising in the office of liquidator and the name of newly appointed liquidator, if any.

(ii) The powers will, of course, continue with them, if the company in its general meeting, or the liquidator, or the committee of inspection, or creditors in the case of voluntary winding up by creditor, authorise the board of directors to continue their power.

5. Transfer of Shares. Section 537 of the Indian Companies Act provides that any transfer of shares or alteration in the status of members can not be allowed after the commencement of the winding up of the company, unless it is made with the prior permission of the liquidator.

Types of Voluntary Winding up

(I) Voluntary Winding up by Members

A company may be voluntary wound by its members only when it is capable of paying its debts. Such voluntarily winding up requires that :

(i) The company must make a declaration of solvency and

(it) The company must also pass a special resolution for its voluntary winding up within a period of 5 weeks from the date of declaration of solvency.

Legal Procedure of Voluntary Winding up by Members

1. Declaration of Solvency. Every company which is to be voluntarily wound up by its members, must make a declaration of solvency made by a majority or all of the directors. When there are only two directors, at a meeting of the board of directors, the declaration must be verified by an affidavit, declaring that the company has no debt to pay, or that the company will be able to pay its debt in full within a period of 3 years from the date of commencement of winding up.

This declaration must be made within 5 weeks from the date of passing of the resolution for the voluntary winding up of the company. It must be delivered to the registrar of companies before the said date. It should be accompanied with a copy of the report of auditors of the company.

The declaration of solvency must be duly verified by the directors of the company. It must contain the following facts :

(i) That they are making this declaration only after proper verification.

(ii) That they believe that the company has no debt to pay, or that the company will be able to pay its debt, if any, within a period of maximum 3 years, from the date of commencement of winding up of the company.

If the directors are found liable for making a false declaration of solvency, they may be punished with an imprisonment for a period of six months or with a fine which may extend up to Rs. 1000 or with both under section 488 of the Indian Companies Act.

2. Passing a Special Resolution. The members of the company must pass a special resolution for the voluntary winding up of the company within a period of 5 weeks of making the statutory declaration. The resolution, once passed, must be published in News Paper of the district of the registered office of the company, within 14 days of its passing.

3. Commencement of the Winding up. Section 490 of the Indian Companies Act provides that after making declaration of solvency and passing the special resolution for the winding up of the company at its general meeting, the same meeting of the company must appoint one or more liquidators for the winding up of the company. The remuneration of such liquidator is also to be decided by the same meeting. Normally, the secretary of the company is appointed as liquidator. The remuneration so fixed can not be increased under any circumstances.

4. Rights of Board of Directors. According to Section 491 of the Indian Companies Act once the liquidator is appointed by the company, all the powers of the board of directors, managing director, etc., are delegated to the liquidator. However, if any vacancy arises in the office of liquidator, he is empowered to inform the registrar of such a vacancy.

5. Filling of the Vacancy of Liquidator. According to Section 492 of the Companies Act, if the liquidator resigns from his post or there occurs a vacancy by death, or otherwise, the company may fill up such vacancy by passing a resolution to this effect in its general meeting. Such a meeting is called in accordance with the provisions of the articles of association of the company or in accordance with the directions issued by the court. If more than one liquidators are appointed by the company, the other liquidators can not work until new liquidator is appointed to fill up the vacancy so caused,

6. Notice of the Appointment of Liquidator to the Registrar. Section 493 of the Companies Act provides that the company is under an obligation to inform the registrar about the appointment of liquidator. If any change takes place in the office of liquidator because of a casual vacancy, it must also be informed to the registrar. If the company or any officer of the company does not comply with this provision, they may be punished with a fine which may extend upto Rs.100 per day. The liquidator is also required to inform the Registrar of Companies about his appointment within 30 days.

7. Restrictions on the Power of Liquidator to accept Shares etc. Under Section 494 the liquidator can not accept any shares or any other like interest of another company, in consideration of transfer or sale of the business or property of the company going into liquidation, with the purpose of distributing such shares amount to the members of the liquidating company. However, they can do so, if the company permits by passing a special resolution.

8. Duty of Liquidator to call a Meeting of Creditors. Section 494 of the Indian Companies Act states that if the liquidator feels that the company will not be able to pay this debt in full within the required period or that the company, has not paid in full and the required period has expired, then he must call a meeting of the creditors of the company, immediately. A statement of assets and liabilities of the company must be laid before this meeting by the liquidator. In this context thereafter, winding up shall be deemed as the winding up of creditors.

9. Duty of Liquidator to call General Meeting. Under Section 496 of the Indian Companies Act, if the winding tip process of a company continues for more than one year, the liquidator must call a meeting of the members of the company every year. A statement of his acts and dealings and a report of the progress of the winding up process during the year must be laid by him before the meeting.

10. Final Meeting and Dissolution. When the process of winding up is completed, the liquidator will call a final general meeting of the members of the company. Detailed accounts of the winding tip of the company will be laid by him before the members.

For such meeting, an advertisement must be published in the Official Gazette and also in one of the Local News Papers specifying the time, place and object of meeting.

11. Submission of the Particulars of the Meeting with the Registrar. The liquidator must send a copy of the Official Gazette and a copy of the advertisement to the registrar for filing. A copy of the final account of winding up and a return of the meeting must also be filed with the registrar within a period of 5 weeks after the date of meeting. If the liquidator does not comply with this provision, he may be punished with a fine which may extend upto Rs. 500.

12. Report to the Court by the Official Liquidator. Official liquidator will scrutinise the accounts and minutes of the meeting and also the books and papers of the company and will report the results of his scrutiny to the court.

13. Dissolution of the Company. If the report of the official liquidator is clear, the company is deemed to be dissolved, from the date of submission of the report to the court. But if the report of the liquidator is unsatisfactory, the court shall direct the official liquidator to make further investigation of the affairs of the company. The official liquidator will again report to the court on such further investigation. The court may make an order for the dissolution of the company with effect from the date specified in the order, or may make any other order, as per the circumstances of the case.

(II) Voluntary Winding up by Creditors

When a company is unable to pay its debts and in making a declaration of solvency, it may be voluntarily wound up only by its creditors. Section 488(5) of the Indian Companies Act states hear if the creditors of the company pass a resolution for such voluntary winding up, it is called "creditors voluntary winding up". This method of winding up is adopted, by the insolvent company. In this case, the creditors get the controlling powers over the proceedings of winding up of the company.

The following procedure should be followed by a company for creditors' voluntary winding up :

1. Meeting of the Members and Creditors (Section 500). For the creditors' voluntary winding up of the company, the board of directors must convene two separate meetings for passing the resolution for voluntary winding up of the company — one of the members of the company and the other of the creditors of the company. 'The meetings may be held on the same day, one after the others, or on two consecutive days.

2. The Statement of Affairs to be presented before the Meeting of Creditors Section 500(3)1. The board of directors must present a statement of the position of company and a list of the creditors of company and estimated amount of their claims before the meeting of creditors over which one of the directors will preside.

3. Information of the Resolution to the Registrar (Section 501). The company must file a copy of the resolution passed for the voluntary winding up of the company at the meeting of creditors, to the Registrar of Companies within 10 days of passing the resolution. If this information is not filed with the registrar within the specified time, the company and every officer of the company liable for the mistake, shall be punishable with a fine which may extend upto Rs. 500 per day, till such information is filed with the registrar.

4. Appointment of Liquidator (Section 502). The members and creditors of the company will appoint a liquidator or liquidators at their meetings. If the liquidators appointed at such meetings are the same person or persons, no problem arises. But if the liquidators appointed at such meetings are different, the liquidator or liquidators appointed by the meeting of creditors shall perform the duties of the winding up of the company. If the creditors do not appoint any liquidator at their meeting, liquidator appointed by meeting of members shall be treated as final. The information of appointment of liquidator or liquidators must be filed by the members and creditors of the company to the court. If no liquidator is appointed at any of the meetings, the person may be nominated by the court also.

5. Committee of Inspection (Section 503). The creditors are empowered to appoint a committee of inspection, consisting of not more than 5 members, at the same or subsequent meeting. It such a committee is appointed, the members of the company may also appoint 5 members for this committee, at a subsequent general meeting. If the creditors of the company object to the appointment by the members, the matter will go to the court and the decision of the court shall be final. The powers of such committee will remain the same as those of a committee appointed in case of compulsory winding up, under the order of the court.

6. Remuneration of Liquidators (Section 504). The remuneration of liquidators will be decided by the creditors of the company. It they do not do so, it shall be decided by the court. The remuneration once fixed can not be increased in any circumstances, whatsoever.

7. Powers of the Board of Directors (Section 505). The powers of the board of directors, or managing director, or manager of the company shall cease on the appointment of liquidator. If, however, the committee of inspection decides to continue their powers, these will continue. If there is no committee of inspection, the creditors of the company may allow their powers to continue.

8. Vacancy in the Office of Liquidator (Section 506). If any vacancy arises in the office of liquidator by death, resignation, or otherwise, the creditors in general meeting, may fill up such vacancy.

9. Restrictions on the Power of Liquidator to accept Shares (Section 507). The liquidator can not accept shares or any other interest of another company, in consideration for the transfer or sale of business or property of the company, going into liquidation with an object to distribute them among the creditors of the company. However, the liquidator may do so with the permission of court or of the committee of inspection.

10. Meeting of Members and Creditors (Section 508). If the process of winding up of a company continues for more than one year, the liquidator of the company must call the meetings of the members and the creditors of the company every year in which he must present the progress of the process of winding up. If he does not call the meeting as required, he may be punished with a fine which may extend upto one thousand rupees.

11. Final Meeting [Section 509]. When the process of winding up of the company completes the liquidator must call the meetings of members and creditors of the company. The accounts and final statement about the position of the company is to be presented by him before such meetings. A notice of such meeting must be published in official gazette and also in the local newspaper so that the members and creditors of the company may come to know about the date and place of the meeting. If the liquidator does not call this meeting, he may be fined upto Rs. 5000.

12. To File a Copy of the Account of Winding up to the Official Liquidator and Registrar. The liquidator of the company must file a copy of the final account of the winding up of the company to the official liquidator and the Registrar of Companies.

13. Scrutiny by Official Liquidator. On receiving such accounts the official liquidator scrutinizes them and reports to the court about his scrutiny.

14. Winding up of the Company. If the report of the official liquidator is favourable, the court may order for the winding tip of the company. But if the report of the official is unfavourable, the court may order the official liquidator to further investigate into the affairs of the company. The official liquidator will again submit his report to the court on his investigation. On receiving such report the court may pass the necessary order.

WINDING UP BY MEMBERS *Vs.* BY CREDITORS

Basis of Difference	*Voluntary Winding up by Members*	*Voluntary Winding up by Creditors*
1. Solvency	Wound up when the company is in the position to pay its debts.	Would up when the company is not in a position to pay its debts.
2. Declaration of Solvency	The directors have to make a declaration of solvency.	There is no need making declaration of solvency.

(*Contd.*)

Basis of Difference	Voluntary Winding up by Members	Voluntary Winding up by Creditors
3. Meetings	A meeting of only members of the company is called.	The company is to call two meetings : one of the members and another of the creditors of the company.
4. Appointment of liquidator	The liquidator is appointed by the meeting of members of the company.	The meeting of members as well as the meeting of creditors appoint the liquidators.
5. Remuneration	The remuneration of liquidators is fixed by the general meeting of the members.	The remuneration of liquidators is to be fixed by the meeting of creditors or by committee of inspectors. In alternative, the remuneration of liquidators will be fixed by the court.
6. Appointment of the Committee of Inspectors	There is no question of the appointment of any committee of inspectors.	A committee of inspectors may be appointed.
7. Filling of the Vacancy in the office of Liquidator	If any vacancy arises in the office of liquidators it may be filled by the members of the company.	The vacancy so caused is filled by the creditors of the company.
8. Continuation of the Rights of Directors	The general meeting of the members may allow the continuation of the powers of directors.	The continuation of powers of directors may be allowed by the meeting of creditors or by the committee of inspectors.
9. To accept Shares in consideration of Sale of Assets	The liquidators may accept the shares in consideration of sale of assets, if they are allowed to do so by the company by virtue of a special resolution.	The prior permission of court or the committee of inspector is required to do so.
10. To call the Final Meeting	A final meeting is called only of the members of the company.	Two final meetings are called — one of the members and the other of the creditors.

III. WINDING UP UNDER THE SUPERVISION OF COURT

According to Section 522 of the Indian Companies Act, 1956, when a company is wound up voluntarily and the process of winding up is completed under the supervision of a court, it is called the winding up of the company under the supervision of court. When the winding up of a company is in progress, any creditors or any contributories or the liquidator the company may apply to the court, requesting the court to supervise the process of winding up of the company. Such application may be made to the court on any or all of the following grounds :

1. If the liquidator is negligent in realizing the assets, or

2. The rules regarding the winding up are not being duly observed, or the majority shareholders are working in a fraudulent manner, against the interest of minority shareholders.

Legal Provisions

1. Application for the Winding up under the Supervision of Court (Section 523). The members or creditors must submit an application to the court for the winding up of the company under its supervision. On such application, the court will enjoy the same rights as enjoyed by court on the application for the compulsory winding up by the court.

2. Appointment of Liquidator [Section 524(1). When the court received an application for the winding up of a company under its supervision it may make an order that the voluntary winding up of the company be continued under its supervision and on the terms and conditions specified by the court, while making such order. Court may also appoint one or more liquidators for carrying on the process of winding up of the company. Only such liquidators will be authorised to carry on the work of the winding up of the company.

3. To remove the Liquidator and to fill up the Vacancy [Section 524(2)]. The court is empowered to remove any liquidator. If any vacancy arises in the office of liquidator, by any reason, the court is empowered to fill up such vacancy.

4. Appointment of Official Liquidator [Section 524(3)]. The court may appoint an official liquidator for the purpose of winding up of the company in both the above circumstances.

5. Appointment or Removal of Liquidator on the Application of Registrar [Section 524(4)]. The court may appoint a liquidator for a company if the registrar of the companies applied to the court for such an appointment.

6. Rights and Duties of the Liquidators Appointed by the Court (Section 525). The liquidators appointed by the court will enjoy the same powers and duties as the liquidators appointed by the members or creditors of the company.

7. Dissolution of the Company (Section 526). When a company is wound up under the supervision of the court, the liquidator may exercise his rights, subject to the restrictions imposed by the court in the same manner, as if the company was being wound up voluntarily.

Advantages

1. Protection of Interest of Creditors and Members. The court may fix the terms and conditions, required for the protection of interest of the shareholders and creditors of the company.

2. Control over Liquidator. The liquidator has to perform his duties in accordance with the orders issued by the court for the purpose. The court may impose certain restrictions on the appointment of liquidator.

3. Attachment Against the Company becomes Ineffective. All the attachments against the company become void and are not binding upon the company.

4. Postponement of Legal Actions. All the suits filed against the company are suspended and no fresh suit can be filed against the company.

5. Rights of the Compulsory Winding up. The court enjoys all the rights and powers as in the case of compulsory winding up by the court.

COMPULSORY *VS.* VOLUNTARY WINDING UP

Compulsory winding up of a company by the court and the voluntary winding up under the supervision of court may be distinguished on the following basis :

1. Regulation. Compulsory winding up of a company is regulated according to the provision of Sections 433 and 434 of the Indian Companies Act while Voluntary winding up under the supervision of court is regulated under section 522 of the Act.

2. Reasons of Winding up. Compulsory winding up of a company is ordered for the reasons like — default in holding the statutory meeting, default in submitting the statutory report, if the number of members goes below the minimum, if the company does not pay its debts, if, the company does not commence its business within one year of obtaining the certificate of commencement of business. On the other hand, winding up under the supervision of court is the result of the decision of the members or creditors of the company to do so.

3. Provision of Imprisonment. There is provision for imprisonment in the compulsory winding up by the court. In the voluntary winding up under the supervision of court on the other hand, there is no provision of imprisonment.

4. Commencement of the Process. Under the compulsory winding up the process of winding up of the company is commenced by the court. On the other hand, winding up under the supervision of the court or basically a voluntary winding up and the process of this winding up is commenced by the creditors or members of the company.

OFFICIAL LIQUIDATOR

Official liquidator means a person or persons who help the court to complete of the compulsory winding up of a company. When a company goes into compulsory winding up under the order of the court, a person or persons are appointed by the court to perform the duties relating to the winding up of the company. Such person or persons are called official liquidators. Official liquidator realizes the assets of the company and distributes them among the creditors and contributories. The surplus, if any, is distributed among the members. Only the official liquidator can function as liquidator in the case of compulsory winding up of a company. The court has no power to appoint private persons or liquidators.

After receiving the winding up petition and before passing the winding up order, the court may appoint the official liquidator as a provisional liquidator who has same powers as a liquidator. As soon as the order of winding up of the company is passed by the court, the provisional liquidator shall automatically become the liquidator of the company.

Powers of the Official Liquidator

Section 456 of the Indian Companies Act describes the powers of the official liquidators as follows :

(1) Powers to be exercised with the Sanction of the Court. These are exercised by the official liquidator only with the sanction of court :

1. To carry on the Business of the Company. He may carry on the business of the company for its beneficial winding up. All the liabilities incurred by the official liquidator while carrying on the business of the company shall be liabilities of the company because the official liquidator works on behalf of and in the interests of the company.

2. To sell the Properties. He may sell all the movable and immovable properties of the company, through auction or under the personal contracts. He may transfer these properties also.

3. To distribute the Money. He may do all other things as may be necessary for winding up of the company. He may distribute the money so realized in the manner, he thinks fit.

4. To charge the Assets. He may take loan by creating charge on all or any of the assets of the company.

5. To carry on the Legal Proceedings. He may institute or defend any legal proceedings, civil or criminal, in the name and on behalf of the company.

6. To appoint Advocate. He may appoint an advocate to assist him in the performance of his duties.

7. To disclaim any Property. If he feels that any particular property is burdensome and has ceased to be an asset and has become a liability, he disclaims such property.

8. To compromise. He may make a compromise for the calls, debts and other liabilities with the contributories or debtors of the company. He may also take any security in discharge of any such claim and give a complete discharge in respect thereof.

9. To pay the Creditors. He may make the payment in full to any class of creditors. He may also make any compromise or arrangement with the creditors.

(II) Powers to be exercised without Sanction of the Court. An official liquidator enjoys following powers which he can exercise on his own for exercising which he need not get any sanction of the court.

1. To inspect the Records. He may inspect any record of the company without paying any fee.

2. To use the Seal of the Company. He may use the common seal and the documents of the company.

3. To deal with the Negotiable Instruments. He can deal with the negotiable instruments for and on behalf of company. He can write, accept and endorse the bills of exchange, cheques, promissory notes, etc.

4. To collect the Money. He can collect any such money which a contributor was to contribute to the company. He may take all the necessary steps for collecting such money.

5. To sue. If he feels necessary he may sue the contributories for realising the money due from them.

6. To appoint Agent. If he feels that he is unable to do any particular work on his own, he appoints the agent for doing such act.

Duties of the Official Liquidator

The official liquidator discharging the functions for the winding up of a company has to perform following duties :

1. To conduct the Winding up Process (Section 451). It is the duty of the liquidator to complete the process of compulsory winding up of a company. He must perform all such duties as the court may impose upon him. He is to realise the assets of the company, to make the payment to the creditors of the company and to divide the surplus, if any, among the members of the company.

2. To submit the Preliminary Report to the Court (Section 455). The directors, manager and secretary of the company shall submit a statement of affairs to the official liquidator in the prescribed form and verified by an affidavit, within 21 days from the date of order of winding up or from the date of appointment of a provisional liquidator, whichever is earlier. This statement of affairs must disclose the following particulars :

(i) Assets of the company.

(ii) Debts and liabilities of the company.

(iii) Names, addresses and occupations of all the creditors of the company, mentioning separately the amount of secured and unsecured debts due to them.

(iv) Particulars of the security in the case of secured debts.

(v) The names, addresses and occupations of the debtors of the company.

(vi) Airy other information required by official liquidator.

On receiving the above statement the official liquidators submits preliminary report to the court within 6 months from the date of winding up.

3. Custody of the Properties of the Company (Section 456). The official liquidator must take all the books, documents and assets of the company into his custody. He is only a custodian of the properties of the company.

4. To follow the Directions Given by the Committee of Inspection [Section 460(4)]. The official liquidator must give due to the directions given to him by the resolution of the creditors or contributories at the general meeting of the company or by the committee of inspection. If the directions given by the committee of creditors or contributories and the directions given by the committee of inspection differ on any point, the former shall be final.

5. To call the Meetings of Creditors and Contributories [Section 460(3)]. If the amount is at least 1/10th in value of the creditors or contributories, by passing a resolution direct or request in writing to the official liquidator to call their meeting, it is his duty to call the meetings of the creditors and contributories. In addition, he may call general meeting of the creditors or contributories of the company.

6. To maintain Proper Books (Section 461). The official liquidator must maintain proper books in the prescribed form, so that the entries of the proceedings of the meeting may be entered and any other matter may be recorded. Any creditor or contributor of the company may inspect any such books, subject to the control of court.

7. To present an Account to the Court (Section 462). The (official liquidator must present air account of his receipts and payments in the prescribed form, in duplicate, to the court at least two times a year. The court gets the account audited. One of the copies of the account is delivered by the court to the registrar and other copy is kept in its record. Such copy shall be open to the inspection of the creditor or contributor or any other interested person.

Thus, the official liquidator must perform his duties in accordance with the provisions of Indian Companies Act and directions of the court using his own discretion whenever necessary.

COMMITTEE OF INSPECTION

According to Section 464 of Indian Company Act, 1956 the court may order for the appointment of a Committee of Inspection to help the liquidator. Such order may be given by the court at the time of making order for the winding up of a company or at any time thereafter. The liquidator should call a meeting of creditors of the company within a period of 2 months from the date of order of the court. The members of the committee will be decided at such meeting. The liquidator should call a meeting of the contributories of the company, within 14 days of the date of meeting of creditors, for the decision of the creditors regarding the membership of the committee of inspection. If the contributories make any change in the committee of inspection as appointed by the creditors, the liquidator shall apply to the court for taking the direction from the court.

Section 465 of the Indian Companies Act, 1956 lays down the following legal provisions regarding the committee of inspection :

1. Number of Members. A committee of inspection can not have more than 12 members who are appointed either by the creditors or by the contributories or by the court.

2. Inspection. Committee of inspection may inspect any document or any book of the company.

3. Meeting. Any member of the committee of inspection or the liquidator may call the meeting fixed by the committee.

4. Quorum of a Committee. Quorum of the committee will be 1/4th of the total number of members of the committee. The committee shall take all its decisions by majority. The committee cannot do any work in the absence of quorum.

5. Resignation of a Member. Any member of the committee may resign at any time by giving an information in writing to the liquidator.

6. Vacation of the Office of a Member. If any member of the committee is declared insolvent or if he remains absent for the 5 consecutive meetings of the committee, his office is deemed to be vacated.

7. Removal of a Member. Any member of the committee may be removed by passing an ordinary resolution to that effect. For this, a notice of at least days must be given to the concerned member.

8. Filling of the Vacancy. If any vacancy arises in the office of committee of inspection, it may be filled by the creditors of the company or contributories of the company. But if the company is about to be dissolved, the vacancy should not be fulfilled.

9. Functions of the Committee. The most important function of the committee of inspection is to inspect the records of the liquidator.

QUESTIONS

1. Define winding up of a company and explain the various methods

of dissolution? Distinguish between winding up and dissolution of a company?

2. Describe the different methods of winding up of a company.
3. Explain the different modes of winding up of a company. What are the provisions of the Indian Companies Act, 1956 regarding the compulsory winding up of a public company.
4. Discuss provisions of company law regarding the compulsory winding up of a public company.
5. What are the circumstances under which a company may be winding up voluntarily? Explain the types of voluntarily liquidation. State the legal procedure regarding declaration of solvency.
6. Describe the voluntary winding up of a company members. How does it differ from the voluntary winding up by creditors?
7. "It is in general just and equitable that a company should be wound up when its substratum is shown to have gone." Discuss the tests to be applied in this regard before a winding up order is passed under the 'just and equitable' clause.
8. In what cases may a company be wound up by the Court? Under what circumstances may the Court give an alternative remedy to winding up? Who may apply to the Court to exercise this power in this connection?
9. Once a defunct company removed from the Register, who can apply and within what period of time, for its restoration?
10. "The power of the Registrar of Companies to strike off the name of a company is meant to be used in cases where a company is not legally dissolved when it should be so dissolved."

    Briefly discuss the legal provisions regarding striking off the name of a defunct company in the light of the above statement.

PRACTICAL PROBLEMS

1. S, a builder, wrote to a hotel company offering to take 300 shares in the company, if a contract for the renovation of the hotel was given to him. His offer was accepted, 300 shares were allotted to him and the directors passed a resolution that S should have the contract. S paid his deposit on shares and attended 2 meetings of the shareholders. No such contract was made and the company went into liquidation. Is S liable as a contributory?

   [**Hint.** No (Aldborough Hotel Co., Re, Simpson's Case)].
2. A company's trade has been suspended temporarily owing to the trade depression with *bona fide* intention to continue its operations when conditions improve. A petition was made to the Court for winding up the company. Decide.

   [**Hint.** The Court will dismiss the petition as in such circumstances it does not consider it just and equitable to order winding up of the company. Sec. 433 (f) : Middlesborough Assembly Rooms Co., Re].

3. A private company has only 2 shareholders who are also the directors with equal rights of management and voting power. The company has made large profits, but there is a complete deadlock in the management of the company. One of the shareholders applied for the winding up of the company. Decide.
[**Hint.** The Court will order the winding up of the company on the just and equitable ground. Section 433 (f) : Yenidje Tobacco Co. Ltd., Re].

4. There is a persistent violation of the regulations and the Statute and an appeal to the general body of shareholders is not likely to put an end to it on account of the fact that those responsible for violations are in control. The aggrieved shareholders file an application for winding up. Decide.
[**Hint.** The Court will order the winding up of the company on 'just and equitable' ground. Section 433 (f) : Sabapathi Rao *Vs.* Sabapathi Press Ltd., A.I.R. (1952) Mad. 4891.

5. A company was registered to carry on the testator's business. The managing director had a prepondering voting power in the company. The directors omitted to hold meetings, submit accounts, or recommend dividends and they had laid themselves open to the suspicion that their object in so omitting was to keep the shareholders in ignorance of the company's position and to acquire the shares at an undervalue. An application for winding up is filed. Decide.
[**Hint** The Court will order the winding up of the company on the 'just and equitable' ground Section 433(f) : Loch *Vs.* John Blackwood Ltd.].

6. A company was ordered to wound up in January, 2000 Among its liabilities the company owed Rs. 10,000 as arrears of income-tax for the assessment year 1996-97 in respect of which an assessment order was passed in November 1998. The Income-tax Department claims to be a preferential creditors under Section 530. Will the claim be upheld in the winding up proceedings?
[**Hint.** No (Section 530)].

7. A creditor of a company applied for winding up of the company for its inability to pay his claim, after proper demand had been made by him and on the lapse of the 3 weeks from the date of such demand. It was proved to the satisfaction of the Court, during inquiry, that the company was commercially solvent. Will the Court order for the winding up of the company?
[**Hint.** The Court may order for the winding up of the company, Sections 433 (e) and 434].

8. An application was made by a father as guardian of his minor

daughter for shares and the company registered the shares in the name of the daughter describing her as a minor. The company went into liquidation and the father of the minor was placed on the list of contributories. The father resists this. Decide.
[**Hint.** The father cannot be placed on the list of contributories (Palaniappa Mudaliar *Vs.* Official Liquidator Pasupathi Bank Ltd.)].

9. Ever since its incorporation in 1970 and for 30 years thereafter, a company never met either in a shareholders' or in a directors' meeting, did not file for more than 10 years any summaries or list of shareholders, treated the company's properties as though they were properties belonging to the individual members, and sales, transfers and various dealings with these properties took place for all over those 30 years as though the individual members were the owners thereof. Will the Registrar be justified in striking off the name of the company from the Register?
[**Hint.** Yes (Rai Sahib *Vs.* N. Mandal's Estates Ltd., Re)].

10. Pending a suit filed by P, a petitioner, for recovery of certain dues from a private limited company, the Registrar of Companies on being informed by its directors that it was not operation and had ceased to exist, struck the name of the company off the Register. The petitioner obtained a decree in that suit and applied to the Court for an order directing restoration of the company to the Register.
Can the company be restored to the Register on the application of the petitioner?
[**Hint.** Yes (Section 560)].

17

Majority Rule and Prevention of Oppression and Mismanagement

MAJORITY RULE AND MINORITY PROTECTION

Rule of Majority : Foss *Vs.* Harbottle

The principle of rule by majority has been made applicable to the management of the affairs of companies. The members pass resolutions on various subjects either by simple majority or by three-fourth majority. Once a resolution is passed by the requisite majority then it is binding on all the members of the company. As a resultant corollary, the court will not ordinarily intervene to protect the minority interests affected by the resolution, as on becoming a member, each person impliedly consents to submit to the will of the majority of the members.

An action was brought by two shareholders, 'F' and 'T', of a company, on behalf of themselves and all other shareholders against the directors and solicitor of the company, alleging that by concerted and illegal transactions they had caused the company's property to be lost. It was alleged that the directors were acting in concert and effecting various fraudulent and illegal transactions whereby the property of the company was misapplied was wasted. It was prayed that the defendant might be decreed to make good to the company the losses. The question was as to the maintainability of the suit (Foss v Harbottle).

The Court held that the action could not be brought by the minority shareholders. The wrong done to the company was one which could be ratified by the majority of members. The company was the proper plaintiff for wrongs done to the company, and the company can act only through its majority shareholders. The majority of the members should be left to decide whether to commence proceedings against the directors.

Exceptions to 'the rule in Foss *Vs.* Harbottle'

In the following cases the rule in Foss *Vs.* Harbottle does not apply, *i.e.*, the minority shareholders may bring an action to protect their interest :

1. *Ultra vires and illegal acts :* 'The rule in Foss *Vs.* Harbottle' does not apply where the act complained of is *ultra vires* the company.

2. *Breach of fiduciary duties :* A derivative action may be brought against directors and promoters who have been guilty of a breach of their fiduciary duties to the company, if they are able to prevent the company from suing them in its own name because they control a majority of the votes at a general meeting, or because they are otherwise able to prevent a general meeting from resolving that the company shall sue them.

When a director is in breach of fiduciary duty, every shareholder may be regarded an authorised organ to bring the action.

3. *Fraud or oppression against minority :* Where the majority of a company's members use their power to defraud or oppress the minority, their conduct is liable to be impeached even by a single shareholder.

4. Inadequate notice of a resolution passed at a meeting of members.

5. When the Act or articles require a special majority for passing a resolution.

6. Statutory exceptions :

(a) *Section 106.* In case of different class of shares, rights attached to the shares of any class if varied, can be challenged in court by not less than 10% of issued shares of that class who had not assented to the variation.

(b) In case of reconstruction and amalgamation of a company which is being wound up shall be sanctioned by the Court provided it has not been conducted in a manner prejudicial to the interest of its member or to public interest (Section 394).

(c) If offer to take over bids is assented by 90% shareholders, the dissenting shareholders can apply to Court for not acquiring their shares.

(d) In case of oppression and mismanagement.

A company is an artificial person created by law. Its shareholders enjoy the overall powers of controlling its administration and management through passing the resolution at their meetings, annual general meeting and extraordinary general meeting. The decisions at the meetings of shareholders are taken, either by a simple majority (*i.e.* 50 per cent majority) or by special majority (*i.e.*, 75 per cent majority), depending upon the provision of Indian Companies Act or the articles of association of the company. Therefore, under this arrangement, the decision taking, in all the matters of a company, is the wish of the majority shareholders who dominate the management of a company. By making a group the shareholders in majority may make a scheme which may be against the interests of the minority shareholders.

A separate chapter has been inserted in the Companies Act to confer certain rights on the minority shareholders to protect their interest. Both the court and the Central Government have been given powers to prevent any oppression of minorities as well as mismanagement of companies.

Meaning of Oppression

As there is no mention of the exact meaning the word "oppression" in the Companies Act. It has been left to the courts to decide whether there is any oppression or not. Normally it is felt that the oppression exists where "the conduct of the majority shareholders may be treated as oppressive if it involves a visible departure from the standards of fair violation of the conditions of fair play on which every shareholder who entrusts money to the company is entitled to rely". Thus, in oppression the conduct must be unjust, burdensome, harsh and wrongful.

Characteristics of Oppression

1. Oppression must be of Continuing Nature. Oppression should be of such a nature that it will have a continuous impact on minorities and must exist at the date of the petition. It should, therefore, occurs before any relief can be granted. The court is not empowered to grant any concession merely on anticipation of oppression.

2. Oppression as a Member. No complaint can be made about oppression except by a member of the company. It is imperative for the member to prove that he is suffering from oppression in the capacity of a member.

3. Facts must justify a Winding-up Order. The facts alleged in the petition must be such as to justify a winding up order under the "just and equitable" clause of Section 433.

Who can Apply to Court?

Under Sections 397, 399 and 401, the following parties are entitled to apply :

(a) Any members of a company who complain that the affairs of the company are being conducted in a manner oppressive to any members may apply to the court for an order, provided such members have a right to so apply by virtue of Section 399.

(b) In the case of a company having a share capital, not less than one hundred members of the company or not less than one-tenth of the total number of its members, whichever is less or any member or members holding not less than one-tenth of the issued share capital of the company, provided that the applicant or applicants have paid all calls and other sums due on their shares.

(c) In the case of company not having a share capital, not less than one-fifth of the total number of its members. Where any share or shares are held by two or more persons jointly they shall be counted only as one member.

(d) Under Section 401, the Central Government may itself apply to the court for an order under Section 397 or 398 or cause an application to be made to the court for such an order by person authorised by it in this behalf.

When Minority Interest is Protected?

Supremacy of the majority of shareholders over minority shareholders is set aside and minority is fully protected under the following circumstances :

(1) Where the act done is *ultra vires* the company or illegal. Majority of shareholders cannot ratify an act which is illegal.

(2) Where the act is passed by an ordinary resolution when it is required to be passed by a special resolution.

(3) Where the majority of members commit fraud on, the minority and such members are in control of the company. The majority members are supposed to exercise their powers in the best interest of the company as a whole and in *a bona fide* manner.

(4) Where the rights of any individual shareholder have been infringed. For example, his name is illegally removed from the Register of members or he has been prohibited to attend and vote at general meeting when he is not in any way disqualified under the Act.

Powers of the Court

Under Section 397 or 398, without prejudice to the generality of the powers of the court, it can issue orders for :

(1) The regulation of the conduct of the company's affairs in future.

(2) The purchase of shares or interests of any members of the company by other members thereof or by the company.

(3) In the case of a purchase of its shares by the company as aforesaid, the consequent reduction of its share capital.

(4) The termination, setting aside or modification of any agreement arrived at between the company and any of the following persons : (i) the managing director, (ii) other director, (iii) the manager and (iv) the secretaries and treasurers.

(5) Any other matter for which in the opinion of the court is just and equitable that provision should be made.

(6) The setting aside of any transfer, delivery of goods, payment, or any other act done by or against the company within three months before the date of application, against an individual which would be deemed in his insolvency to be a fraudulent preference (Section 402).

(7) Under Section 403, the court may, on the application of any party to the proceeding, make any interim order for regulating the conduct of the company's affairs.

(8) Section 407 provides that where under Section 397 or 398, the order of a court terminates, sets aside or modifies an agreement with any managerial personnel, it will not give rise to any claim either for damages or for compensation for loss of office against the company.

(9) Section 407(1-b) states that no managerial personnel whose agreement is so terminated shall be re-appointed or, act in any managerial capacity (managing or other director or manager, etc.) without the leave of the court for a period of five years from the date of the order.

(10) No court shall grant leave unless notice of the intention to apply for leave has been served on the Central Government and that Government has been given all opportunity of being beard in the matter.

Powers of Central Government

Section 408 empowers the Central Government to prevent oppression or mismanagement and the powers are as follows :

(1) On receipt of an application from not less than two hundred members of the company or from members holding not less than one-tenth of the total voting power, it may appoint not more than two persons, being members of the company, to hold office as directors for not more than three years on any one occasion.

(2) This power is exercised only if it is satisfied after such inquiry as it deems fit to make for preventing, any oppression or mismanagement.

(3) It may further pass an order that until the new directors are appointed, not more than two members of the company recommended by the Central Government shall hold office as additional directors of the company.

(4) It should be noted here that for the purpose of counting two-thirds of the total number of directors, any director appointed by the Central Government will not be taken into account.

(5) Section 409 provides that where a complaint is made to the Central Government by any managerial personnel of a company that as a result of a change which has taken place or is likely to take place in the ownership of any shares held in the company, a change in the Board of directors is likely to take place which (if allowed) would affect prejudicially the affairs of the company, the Central Government may, by order, direct that no resolution passed or action taken to effect a change in the Board of directors after the date of the complaint shall have effect unless confirmed by the Central Government. The Central Government can make an interim order before completing the inquiry. These provisions shall not apply to a private company.

PROVISIONS OF THE INDIAN COMPANIES ACT TO PREVENT OPPRESSION AND MISMANAGEMENT

Prior to the enactment of the Indian Companies Act, 1956, there were the provisions for the prevention of oppression and mismanagement of a company. After the enactment of this Act, the minority shareholders have many legal provisions in their favour. If they feel that the oppression and mismanagement is taking place in the company, they may take the protection of the provisions of Indian Companies Act to prevent it. The following are the provisions of the Companies Act in this regard :

1. Provision of Special Audit (Section 233A). If the company is not being managed in a proper manner, the special audit of the accounts of company may be ordered so that the irregularity in the accounts may be checked and prevented.

2. Elimination of the Post of Managing Agents (Section 324). The post of managing agent is eliminated since 3rd April, 1970, no company can appoint managing agents.

3. Registration of the Company (Section 20). No company can be registered with a name which may confuse the general public in any respect.

4. Appointment of Inspector (Section 237). If the company is doing anything against a public policy or if it is expected that the company may cheat anyone, the Central Government may appoint inspection to look into the affairs of the company.

5. Protection of Employees. Under the provisions of Indian Companies Act, no company can terminate any of its employees, unless and until the charges against the employee are proved.

6. Protection of Creditors. The creditors may go to the court for appropriate action, if they feel that the management of company is not going in accordance with the provisions of Indian Companies Act or the articles of association of the company.

7. Restriction on the Transfer of Shares (Section 250). If the transfer of shares is likely to make changes in the board of directors of the company, such transfer may not be allowed for a period of 3 years.

Thus, the provisions of Indian Companies Act, 1956, are sufficient for the prevention of oppression and mismanagement of a company. The interests of the minority shareholders of the company are also duly protected by these provisions.

Areas of Court Interference

Under following circumstances an individual shareholder may appeal to the court for the prevention of oppression and mismanagement of the company :

1. Where the Act done is Illegal or Ultra Vires the Company. The rule of supremacy of majority cannot apply, if the act done by majority shareholders is illegal or *ultra vires* the company. Any shareholder of a company may file a suit of injunction to prevent the company from doing such acts.

2. Where the Act done is based on a Resolution Passed by an Insufficient Majority. Different resolutions are to be passed by shareholders of the company by different majority. While some can be passed only by a simple majority, other resolutions require the majority of 3/4th of the shareholders of the company. If any resolution is passed by an insufficient majority, the acts of the company based on it will be fully void and any shareholder of the company may file a suit of injunction to restrain the company from doing any act based on such resolution passed by an insufficient majority.

3. Where the Act Constitute a Fraud on the Minority. The rule of supremacy of majority is based on the assumption that the majority shareholders stand in a fiduciary position and they must exercise their powers in a *bona fide* manner which must be in the interest of the company and not against the interest of minority shareholders for their own benefit at the cost of minority shareholders. In this case, any shareholder of the company can prevent it from doing any act based on any such resolution. Therefore, if the majority shareholders use their powers for the fraud against the minority shareholders, the rule of supremacy of majority shareholders will not apply. A resolution shall be valid if it is passed in a *bona fide* manner and for the benefits for the company, even though, it may be against the interest of any individual shareholder or minority shareholders.

4. If the Rights of Any Member are infringed. The majority shareholders cannot pass any resolution, by any majority, to deprive any shareholder from the rights conferred upon him as a member, either by the Indian Companies Act or by the articles of the company. Therefore, if any resolution is passed by the majority shareholders with any such intention, any shareholder of the company can, in his own name, bring an action, against such resolutions.

5. If Sections 397 and 398 of the Indian Companies Act apply. Sections 397 and 398 of the Indian Companies Act, 1956 state that a certain number of members of a company may bring an action against the company and request the court to prevent the oppression and mismanagement of the company.

REMEDIAL ACTIONS BY THE CENTRAL GOVERNMENT

Section 408 of the Indian Companies Act, 1956 empowers the central government to prevent the oppression and mismanagement of a company. The application to the Central Government must be filed by the persons discussed above. The Central Government may take the following actions for the prevention of oppression and mismanagement of a company :

1. Appointment of Directors. Section 408(1) provides that if the Central Government is satisfied that the affairs of the company are being conducted in the manner of oppression and mismanagement, or against the interest of company, it may appoint such number of persons as it may consider necessary as the directors for the company, to protect the interests of company itself or its shareholders or the public interest. Such directors can be appointed for such period of time, as it thinks fit, not exceeding 3 years at a time. Prior to the Companies (Amendment) Act, 1974, the Central Government was empowered to appoint only two directors in this manner. This Amendment Act has empowered the government to appoint any number of directors.

2. Special Provisions Regarding the Directors so Appointed. The directors, appointed by the Central Government in the manner discussed above, enjoy following special privileges :

(i) It is not necessary for them to be a member of the company.

(ii) It is also not necessary for them to acquire the qualifications shares of the company.

(iii) They are not liable to retire by rotation.

(iv) They are not counted with the other directors of the company.

(v) They are empowered to issue such direction to the company as they consider necessary for the management of the company.

(vi) The Central Government may also require them to report to it from time to time with regard to the affairs of the company.

3. Appointment of Directors on the Basis of Proportionate Representation. If the Central Government is of the opinion that the directors in the company have not been appointed on the basis of proportionate representation, it may issue an order to the company to appoint its directors on such base.

4. Appointment of Additional Directors. If, by any reason, the directors are not appointed on the basis of proportionate representation, the Central Government may order for the appointment of additional directors.

5. Any Change in the Board of Directors. Section 409 provides that the Central Government is empowered to order that change should be made in the board of directors of the company, if in the interests of the company. The company cannot make any change in its board of directors, till the directors or additional directors appointed by the central Government, are in the board of directors of the company.

6. To terminate the Managerial Personnel. The Central Government may apply to the High Court for the removal of managerial personnel if they are discharging their duties in a fraudulent manner.

QUESTIONS

1. Give the provisions of Indian Companies Act, 1956 for the prevention of oppression and mismanagement in a company. State the powers of the Court and Government.

2. What are the provisions of the Indian Companies Act with regard to the protection of minority shareholders against oppression and mismanagement by majority shareholders? Indicate the powers of the Court and also of the Central Government in this regard.
3. What powers may be used by the Central Government to prevent oppression and mismanagement of a company?
4. "The will of majority must prevail," is the principle of company management. Are there any exceptions to this rule?
5. "A proper balance of the rights of the majority and minority shareholders is essential for the smooth functioning of a company. Why?
6. What are the provisions of the Companies Act, 1956 for the prevention of oppression of the minority shareholders and mismanagement of a company?
7. What remedies are available to the minority shareholders of a company against oppression or mismanagement?
8. Majority will have its way but the minority must be allowed to have its say. Discuss this proposition with reference to prevention of oppression and mismanagement in a company.
9. What are the powers given to the Company Law Board and the Central Government by the Companies Act, 1956 for the prevention of oppression and mismanagement in a company?
10. State the Rule in "Foss *Vs.* Harbottle" and exceptions to this rule.

PRACTICAL PROBLEMS

1. Three directors of a company entered into a contract in their own name but they used their position to obtain the contract. By virtue of their shareholding (3/4ths of the issued share capital) they caused the company in general meeting to declare that it had no interest in the contract. A minority shareholder brought action. Will he succeed?
   [**Hint.** Yes (Cook *Vs.* Deeks)].
2. A takes proceedings against the directors of a company of which he is a member to compel them to make good the losses sustained by the company owing to their fraud. Will he Succeed?
   [**Hint.** No. The company can itself take the proceedings if it thinks fit to do so (Foss *Vs.* Harbottle)].
3. The Articles of a company empowered the chairman, with the consent of a meeting, to adjourn the meeting and also provided for taking a poll if demanded by 5 shareholders. The adjournment was moved, and declared by the chairman to be carried; a poll was then demanded but the chairman refused it. A shareholder brought an action for declaration that the chairman's conduct was illegal. Will this action succeed?

[**Hint.** No. If the chairman was wrong, the company alone could sue (MacDougall *Vs.* Gardiner)].

4. A, B and C own respectively 50 per cent, 30 per cent and 20 per cent of the issued share capital of a company and A and B are its directors. The company has made good profits but the directors refuse to recommend the declaration of dividend and A and B, as majority shareholders, pass a resolution at a general meeting to the effect that their remuneration as directors shall be 90 per cent of the profits. To wind up the company would in this case, unfairly prejudice the minority shareholders. What alternative remedy is available to C and how may it be applied?

   [**Hint.** C can file a petition to the Company Law Board for an order under Section 3971.

18

Company Investigation

DEFINITION OF INVESTIGATION

Used with regard to a company the term investigation means the intensive or comprehensive checking of the books of accounts of company. Though the auditor checks and verifies the books of accounts, but if there is some fraud or mistake suspected, even after the audit, there arises a need of investigation. Under investigation, the accounts of a company are checked very strictly so that the real financial position of the company may be disclosed.

Defining the word investigation Spicer and Pegler said, "Term Investigation implies an examination of accounts and records for special purpose."

REASONS OF INVESTIGATION

The Central Government may appoint one or more competent persons and inspectors to investigate and report on the affairs of any company in such a manner as it may direct. It may order for the investigation either on request or on its own initiative, in the following circumstances :

1. At the Dissatisfaction of the Shareholder (Section 235). The shareholder may apply to the Central Government for the investigation of company. But the shareholders, making such request, must be :

(i) **Section 235A.** At least 200 members or the members holding 1/10th of the total voting power, if the company is having share capital.

(ii) **Section 235B.** At least 1/5th of the total number of members, if the company does not have share capital.

At the request of the above number of shareholders, the central government may order investigation of the affairs of a company of the matters, as requested by the shareholders.

(iii) **Section 236.** If the members of a company apply to the central government for the investigation of the company, their applications must be submitted by the evidences to prove that there exist good reasons for the investigation. The central government may ask the persons, requesting for the investigation, to furnish a security of an amount, not exceeding Rs. 2,500, for the payment of the costs of investigation.

2. At the Dissatisfaction of the Registrar. The registrar of companies may also apply to the Central Government for the investigation of the affairs of a company in the following circumstances :

(i) **Section 234(6).** If the information or explanation required by the registrar, is not furnished within the certain time, or if the documents submitted by the company disclose any unsatisfactory state of affairs, or if the document does not disclose a full and fair statement of the matters to which it relates.

(ii) If it is represented to the registrar of companies by any person or persons dealing with the company or by the creditors of the company that the business of the company is being carried on in a fraudulent manner or for unlawful purpose and the registrar agrees with the representation.

The Central Government may order for the investigation of the affairs of a company, if it is satisfied with the reason for investigation, furnished by the registrar.

3. At the Self Desire of the Central Government. The Central Government may order for the investigation of the affairs of a company on its own, if it is of the opinion :

(i) That the business of the company is being conducted with an intention to defraud its creditors or members or any other persons or otherwise for a fraudulent or unlawful purpose or in a manner oppressive of any of its members, or

(ii) That the company was established for any fraudulent purpose, or

(iii) That the persons concerned with the formation of the company or with the management of the company have been guilty of fraud or misfeasance or other misconduct towards the company or any of its members, or

(iv) That the company has failed to give its members, all the information, which the members are entitled to receive from the company.

In all the above conditions, the Central Government may take steps to order for the investigation of the affairs of a company, without any request from any corner.

4. If a Special Resolution is passed by the Company [Section 237(A)]. If the company itself passes a special resolution for investigation, the Central Government may order for the required investigation.

5. On the Order of the Court [Section 237(A)]. The Central Government may order for the investigation of a company, if the court declares that the affairs of the company must be investigated.

When ordering for the investigation of the affairs of a company, they appoint one or more competent persons as the Inspectors. It is to note in this context that a firm or body corporate or an association of persons may not be appointed as the Inspectors.

POWERS OF THE CENTRAL GOVERNMENT

The remedy to prevent mismanagement or exploitation of members of creditors, has been defined under the head 'Investigation' in the Indian Companies Act under Sections 235 and 251.

Investigation is an enquiry about the profit and loss, goodwill, investment and other assets and liabilities of a company, needed for the protection of interest of the investors. Investigation of the company's affairs, ownership and shares and debentures is done under Section 235, 246, 247, 248, and 250.

1. Section 235. A member of a company or the Registrar may ask the Central Government for investigation of the affairs of a company. The Central Government may appoint inspectors to investigate and to report thereon. The following parties may apply for investigation.

(i) **Section 235(a).** In the case of a Company having share capital, 200 members or members holding not less than 1/10th of the total voting rights.

(ii) **Section 235(b).** In the case of a company not having share capital, 1/5th of the total members of the company.

2. Section 234. On a report by the Registrar of companies if the information required has not been furnished within time or it does not disclose the full state of affairs and in his opinion the business of company is being carried on for fraudulent activities.

3. Section 237(2). The company passes the special resolution.

4. Section 237(2)(a). The court orders to declare to investigate the affairs of the company.

5. Section 237(2)(b). The Central Government itself may take initiative for investigation in the following circumstances :

(i) That the company's business is being conducted with intent to defraud its creditors, members or any other persons or otherwise for a fraudulent or unlawful purpose, or in a manner oppressive of any part of its members; or

(ii) That the company was formed for any fraudulent or unlawful purpose; or

(iii) That the persons concerned in the formation or the management of the company have been found guilty of fraud, misfeasance or misconduct towards the company or its members; or

(iv) That the members have not been given all the information which they are entitled to receive.

6. Section 236. When an application is made by the members to the Central Government it must contain some sound reasons for investigation and a security not exceeding Rs. 1000 for expenses must be deposited.

INSPECTORS

Under Section 238, if the Central Government thinks proper it may appoint an inspector, but the inspector so appointed may be only an individual, not firm, body corporate or other association. To perform his duties, the Inspector enjoys the following powers :

1. Section 239(2). He has the power to investigate the affairs of another body corporate which is or has been at any time the subsidiary or holding company of it or the company managed by the managing agent or secretaries and treasurers or their associates of that time or managed by any of the director or managing director. In some of the classes he must obtain prior approval of the Central Government before using such power.

2. Section 239 (1-A). With the previous approval of the Central Government he requires any body-corporate to furnish information or all the books and papers of company which are relevant and necessary for the purpose of his investigation.

It is the duty of all the officers of the company to help him in this connection.

3. Section 240(2). The Inspector may examine on oath any of the officer, employee or agent of the company. He may call any other person personally with the previous approval of the Central Government.

4. Section 240 (I-B). The Inspector may keep in his custody the books and papers produced to him for the period of six months only.

5. Section 240(3). If any person makes any default to produce any book or paper or any information which is necessary for investigation or refuses to present himself personally, before the inspector, he shall be punishable with imprisonment for a term which may extend to six months or with fine up to Rs. 20,000 or with both and with a further fine of Rs. 2000 for every day of default after such refusal.

6. Section 240-A. The Inspector is empowered to seize books and papers of the company, where he has reasonable ground to believe that certain books and papers which are likely to be destroyed, mutilated, altered, falsified or secreted. But this he can do only after the permission of the First Class Magistrate is obtained. The documents must be returned after investigation to the person from whose custody they were seized.

Inspector's Report

1. Section 241(1). The Government may also require the interim report from the Inspector who at the end of the investigation makes his final report to Central Government. The report may be written or printed as the Government directs.

2. Section 235. A copy of the report must be filed at the registered office of the company and also to any body corporate dealt within the report. If the inspectors are appointed at the request of members a copy of the report must be furnished to them.

3. Section 241. Where inspectors are appointed under Section 237 in pursuance of an order of the court, a copy of the report must be furnished to the court by the Central Government. The Central Government on receipt of prescribed fee may furnish the copy of the report to any interested person. The Government is empowered to publish the report.

EXPENSES OF INVESTIGATION

The expenses incurred for investigation are to be defrayed by the Central Government itself in the first instance and after this they are reimbursed as may be specified by the court :

(i) By any person who is convicted on a prosecution or who is ordered to pay damages.

(ii) By any company in whose name proceedings are brought.

(iii) By any managerial personnel dealt with by the report.

(iv) By the applicants if appointment of Inspector was made on their applications.

1. Section 247 and 248. Investigation of Ownership of Company [Section 247(1)]. When it is difficult to know the actual benefited shareholders because of vesting their shares in the hands of trustees or nominees who control the power and use it for the benefit of the shareholders in the general meeting of the company, the Central Government is empowered to make an investigation to know the real persons who control the company, influence the policy of the company and who are financially interested in the success or failure of the company.

2. Section 235. The Government may appoint one or more Inspectors for investigation and may assign a number of powers to carry out their work.

3. Section 247. When the investigation has been completed by the Inspector he must submit his report to the Central Government. The Government is not bound to furnish the copy of the report to the company or any other person but a copy of the report must be filed with the Registrar.

4. Section 247(6). The expenses incurred for investigation by the

Central Government are recovered from the persons on whose application the investigation was made.

[248. Information regarding persons having an interest in company or in body corporate or firm acting as managing agent thereof. Omitted by the Companies (Amendment) Act, 2000 as provisions relating to managing agents, etc. had become redundant after abolition of system by Act 17 of 1969.]

[249. Investigation of associateship with managing agent, etc. Omitted by the companies (Amendment) Act, 2000 as provisions relating to managing agents, etc. had become redundant after abolition of system by Act 17 of 1969.]

Investigation of Shares and Debentures Dealing

1. Section 250(1). The Central Government is empowered to impose restrictions on the transfer of shares or debentures so as to facilitate the investigation. The following restrictions may be imposed by the Central Government on shares or debentures on the advice of the inspector but these restriction should not exceed the period for more than 3 years.

2. Section 250(2). (i) Any transfer of those shares shall be void :

(ii) Where those shares are to be issued they shall not be issued and any issue thereof or any transfer of the right to be issued therewith, shall be void.

(iii) No voting right shall be exercised in respect of those shares.

(iv) No further shares shall be issued in the light of those shares and any issue of such shares or any transfer of the right to be issued therewith, shall be void.

(v) Except in a liquidation, no payment shall be made of any sums due from the company on those shares, whether in respect of dividend capital or otherwise.

3. Section 250(3). When some transfer of shares or debentures has taken place in a company and this has affected the composition of Board of Directors, and the Central Government is of the opinion that the change taken place is prejudicial to the public interest then the Government may issue order that :

(i) The voting rights on those shares shall riot be exercisable for the period not exceeding 3 years.

(ii) No resolution passed in this connection shall effect unless confirmed by the Government.

4. Section 250(4). Where the Central Government has reasonable ground to believe that transfer of shares is going to take place whereby the composition of Board of Directors is likely to take place, the Government may order that any such transfer of shares shall be void for a period not exceeding 3 years.

5. Section 250(6). Any person aggrieved by such an order of the Central Government may apply to the court and the court after being heard by the Central Government, if it thinks fit, by order vacate any such order of the Central Government.

6. Section 250(9). Any person who contravenes the restrictions imposed by the Central Government shall be punishable with fine upto five thousand rupees or imprisonment for a term not extending to six months or both.

7. Section 250. A prosecution shall not be instituted except by or with the consent of Central Government.

8. Section 251. A legal adviser need not disclose to the Registrar or to the Central Government or to an inspector appointed by the Central Government any privileged communication made to him except the name and address of his client. A banker of any company is not bound to disclose any information as to the affairs of the customers.

QUESTIONS

1. Define Investigation. Under what circumstance, it is ordered by the Central Government?
2. In what circumstances the Central Government may order for the investigation of the affairs of a company? What are the rights of inspectors appointed as such? What are the rights of the Central Government on the basis of the report of such inspectors?
3. Explain the circumstances as well as the manner in which an investigation can be carried out into the affairs of a company.
4. When and by whom can an investigator be appointed to investigate the affairs of a company? State the powers of the inspector in relations to investigation.
5. State the circumstances in which and by whom an investigation into the affairs of a company can be ordered.
6. What are the circumstances in which the Central Government can order investigation into the affairs of a company.

19

Company Taxation

TAXATION POLICIES

In modern times, the Government of a country plays a dominant role in the shaping of financial, commercial and general policies of the business concerns and taxation policy is one of such powerful instruments of intervention. The right to tax the citizens of a country and the right to tax domestic corporations are inherent in the sovereign jurisdiction of every country and its Government. Due to constantly increasing burden of taxations the taxation of business enterprises has become a major source of revenue for the Government. The duties and functions of Government include the development of infrastructure facilities, public education, public health and provision of various social services like unemployment insurance, old age pension, etc. To acquire funds in huge quantity the government has to levy taxes on incorporated as well as unincorporated sector to cover the costs. The causes for confident reliance on corporate sector for special tax treatment arc political feasibility and administrative convenience. Business corporations do not exercise voting power in elections as individuals. Hence government, now-a-days, depend on corporate sector for additional revenues to a large extent.

IMPACT ON BUSINESS FINANCE

At a time when corporate taxation is contributing greatly to the national exchequer, the impact of taxation policies on business finance is more visible and critical. The role of taxation policies in business decisions is increasing, day by day with the increase of its burden. As a number of taxes on business may kill the incentive and hamper the expansion of production capacity, it becomes imperative to examine the major impacts of corporate taxation policies on the financial management business enterprises.

GUIDE TO MANAGEMENT DECISIONS

According to Husband and Dockery, the normal objective of management is to run a business with the least possible costs consistent with the Corporation's established operating policies. So it is commonly expected that unless there are compelling reasons for not doing so, the management will always make efforts to minimise taxes like any other cost. It is possible only when the management makes continuous efforts and tries to make optimum decisions relating to various operating and financial phenomena capital structure. They enable the concern to create its image. In maintaining its goodwill, they provide the company a cost free capital. They form the basis for a steady dividend policy. The creation of reserves increases the network of shares. Lastly, reserves increase the resources of the company which can be utilised by the management at their discretion.

ASSESSMENT OF JOINT STOCK COMPANY

1. However small amount it may be, the company is liable to pay income tax on its total income.

2. Income-tax is payable on a company's total income at a flat rate.

3. For taxation purposes, Companies have been classified as closely held companies and widely-held companies and different rates of tax are applicable to them.

4. There is no exempted capital gains in the case of companies. However small these capital gains of a company may be, they are liable to tax. The rate of income-tax applicable to short term capital gains is the same as is applicable to other income of the company. In the long term capital gains relating to land and building the rate is 50% and on capital gains relating to other assets., it is 40 per cent.

5. After 31st March 1976 newly promoted companies are entitled to a deduction from their profits equal to 7.5 per cent of the capital employed for first 5 years.

6. Under Section 104, there is a provision of additional income-tax to be imposed on the undistributed profit of a closely-held company.

7. Domestic companies are entitled to a deduction of the whole of the income by way of dividends received from a company which is formed and registered under the Indian Companies Act, 1956 after 28th Feb., 1975 and is engaged exclusively in the manufacture or production of fertilizers, pulps and newsprint, cement, pesticides and several other products mentioned in the 9th schedule to the Income Tax Act, in other cases, domestic companies are entitled to a deduction of 60 per cent of such dividend income.

8. 100 per cent deduction is allowed to Indian companies received as dividend income on the shares in a foreign company allotted to that Indian Company in consideration of any patent, invention, model, design, secret formula or process or information for production.

9. 100 per cent of deduction is allowed to Indian Companies in respect of any income by way of royalty, commission, fees, etc., earned from any foreign government or foreign enterprises in consideration for the use of any patent, invention, model, design, secret formula or

process of information concerning industrial, commercial, or scientific knowledge, experience or skill.

10. 15 per cent of interest paid by non-banking or non-financial companies on deposits received by them from the public is disallowed in computing their total income.

11. I.T.O. is authorized to disallow any expenditure income or providing any benefit or amenity to a person who has a substantial interest in the company or to a relative of the director, if in his/her opinion it is excessive or unreasonable.

12. Joint Stock Companies are entitled for general deduction admissible to other business entities in computing their total income u/s 30-37 of the Income Tax Act, 1961.

13. The amount of income-tax is increased by a surcharge at the rate of 2-1/2 of such income.

14. Under the Companies (Profits) Surtax Act 1964, a company is required to pay surtax on its chargeable profits in excess of the statutory deduction at the following rates :

(a) Where the chargeable profits do not exceed 5 per cent of the capital (as computed for this purpose) 25 per cent.

(b) On the balance, if any, of the chargeable amount, 40 per cent.

COMPANY IN WHICH PUBLIC ARE SUBSTANTIALLY INTERESTED

Section 2(18) of the Indian Income Tax Act, 1961 states that following are the companies in which it is deemed that the public are substantially interested :

1. A Company Owned by the Government or Reserve Bank. If a company is owned by the Central Government or any State Government or jointly by the Central Government and a State Government or by the Reserve Bank of India, it is deemed that the public are substantially interested in such company. A company in whose share capital, the Central Government or State Government or Reserve Bank of India or any Corporation of the Reserve Bank have 40 per cent or more shares, is also deemed to be the company in which public are substantially interested.

2. Non-Trading Company. A company which has been established under Section 25 of the Indian Companies Act, 1956 for the promotion of Arts, Science, Commerce, Religion, Culture etc., is deemed to be a company in which public are substantially interested.

3. A Company Declared So. If a company without having share capital is declared that in it public are substantially interested, it will be deemed as such.

4. A Company fulfilling Certain Conditions. A company which is not a private company and fulfils any of the following conditions, may be deemed as a company in which public are substantially interested :

(i) Equity shares of a company with a minimum of 50 per cent voting rights (In case of an Industrial Company 40 per cent) must be held by the company or by an incorporation established under any Act or by a company in which public are substantially interested or by a company which is a subsidiary of such a company.

(ii) The shares of the company are listed in any Indian recognised Stock Exchange on the last date of the previous year.

(iii) The shares were allowed to be freely transferred by the members of the company during that previous year and the management of the company was not controlled by less than 5 persons at a time.

TYPE OF COMPANIES UNDER INCOME-TAX ACT

The companies have been divided into following parts under the Indian Income-Tax Act :

1. Indian Company
2. Foreign Company
3. Trading Company
4. Industrial Company
5. Investment Company

RESIDENCE OF A COMPANY

An Indian Company may be divided into following two parts :

1. Resident Company. Section 6(3) of the Indian Income Tax Act, 1961 states that a resident company means a company which is incorporated in India and which has been managed and controlled in the previous year.

2. Non-Resident Company. A company which does not fulfil any of the above conditions of a resident company, is called non resident company.

CHARACTERISTICS OF INDIAN COMPANY TAXATION

1. Income-Tax Return. The companies in India have to submit their Income-Tax Returns within a certain time with the Income Tax Officer of their area. In this return, the company has to declare its income for the previous year.

2. Signature on the Return. The managing director of the company must sign the income tax return on behalf of company. If there is no managing director in the company, any director of the company may sign the return on behalf of company.

3. Assessment of Tax. A company has to pay the income-tax on its income as an independent assessee.

4. Compulsion to pay Income Tax. A company is liable to pay income-tax on the total income, however, small it may be.

5. Constant Rate of Income Tax. The income-tax is calculated for companies at a constant rate. It follows that the slab system of tax rate is not applicable for companies to calculate the tax.

6. Tax on Capital Gains. A company has to pay the tax on all its capital gains, whether short term capital gains or long term capital gains. The rate of income-tax applicable to short term and long term capital gains is the same as is applicable to other income of the company. Long term capital gains upto Rs. 15,000 are totally exempt. Such long term capital gain in excess of Rs. 15,000 will be dealt with as under :

(a) In respect of L.T.C.G. relating to lands or buildings or bullion or jewellery Rs. 15,000+10 per cent of the excess over Rs. 15,000 will be deducted;

(b) In respect of L.T.C.G. relating to equity shares of venture capital undertakings :

  (i) In the case of a company other than venture capital company Rs. 15,000+30 per cent of the excess over Rs. 15,000 will be deducted;

  (ii) In the case of venture capital company Rs. 15,000+60 per cent of the excess over Rs. 15,000 will be deducted;

(c) In respect of L.T.C.G. relating to other assets Rs. 15,000+30 per cent of the excess over Rs. 15,000 will be deducted.

Where the L.T.C.G. relates to all categories of capital assess referred to above (a), (b) and (c), the deduction of Rs. 15,000 shall first be allowed from L.T.C.G. relating to the assets mentioned in (a) and (b) and the balance of Rs. 15,000 if any, shall be deducted from L.T.C.G. relating to assets mentioned in (c).

This deduction shall also be made from Long term capital losses in order to compute the loss under the head 'Capital Gains'.

7. Additional Income Tax. Under Section 104, there is a provision for additional income tax on the undistributed profits of a company.

8. Deduction for Royalty, Commission, Fees. If an Indian company earns any income by way of royalty, commission, fees etc. from a foreign government of foreign company, the Indian company shall be allowed for a deduction of an amount equal to 50 per cent of such income.

QUESTIONS

1. Explain the impact of taxation policies on the financial policies of the business corporations.
2. What are the salient features of assessment of Joint Stock Companies in India?
3. In which Companies Public are substantially interested? Describe types of Companies under Income Tax Act and as per residence. Give characteristics of Indian Company Taxation.

20

COMPROMISE, ARRANGEMENT AND RECONSTRUCTION

COMPROMISE AND ARRANGEMENT

Meaning

Compromise and arrangement are used in the same sense though these two words are different. In case of compromise, the need arises of any dispute, which is reconciled under the provisions of Indian Companies Act, by way of a compromise. On the other hand, no dispute is required for arrangement.

According to Section 390B the word 'compromise' includes any settlement of a matter in dispute, between the company and its creditors or members by mutual concession. An arrangement includes a re-organisation of share capital of a company which may be in the form of consolidation of shares or in the form of division of shares or by both these methods. Arrangement also includes variation of the special or preferable rights attached to shares.

According to Section 390A, the provisions regarding compromise or for an arrangement are applicable to those companies mainly, which are liable to be wound up under the Act. These are applicable to a foreign company incorporated outside India but doing business in India and to a government company also, because the foreign companies and the government companies are liable to wound up under the Indian Companies Act. The scheme of compromise of arrangement provides a substitute for winding up and save a company from going into liquidation.

There are certain conditions when a company feels itself unable to meet its normal obligation and to pay off its liabilities, because of the heavy trade losses on account of any reason. In such conditions, the company may go into liquidation because any of the creditors of the company may apply to the court for its compulsory winding up. Sections 391 to 393 have made provisions that such a company may adopt a scheme of compromise or arrangement with its creditors or members and to get the scheme approved by the parties, certified and confirmed by the court. Thus, by adopting a scheme of compromise or arrangement, the company may be saved from going into liquidation. The scheme, if adopted, binds all the parties of compromise.

When a company adopts a scheme of compromise or arrangement with its shareholders or creditors or members, new contracts are entered into by the company with them which replace the old contracts and provide the easier terms and conditions which stabilize the financial position of the company. For example, the company which adopts a scheme of compromise or arrangement, may get its shareholders and creditors agreed to accept a reduction in the rate of interest or to surrender their rights to recover outstanding interest or to accept the shares of the company. In the same manner, the preference shares, under the scheme of compromise, may be converted into equity shares or cumulative preference shares may be converted into non-cumulative or the rate of dividend may be lowered.

Statutory Provisions

1. Order by the Court to call a Meeting for a Scheme of Compromise or Arrangement (Section 391). When a scheme of compromise or arrangement is proposed between a company and its creditors or any class of them; or between a company and its members or any class of them; the court may order to call a meeting of the creditors or any class of them as the case may be. Such meeting will be conducted in the manner directed by the court. The court may give such order on the application of any of the following persons :

(i) A company itself.

(ii) Any creditor of the company.

(iii) Any member of the company.

(iv) Liquidator of the company, if the company is to go into liquidation.

2. Binding of the Compromise or Arrangement (Section 391). The compromise or arrangement will be binding on the following :

(i) All the creditors or any class of creditors of the company.

(ii) All the members or any class of members of the company.

(iii) The company.

(iv) The liquidator and contributory of the company in case the company is being wound up.

3. Approval of the Scheme of Compromise or Arrangement. Any scheme of compromise or arrangement must be approved :

(i) By the majority in number representing three-fourth in value of creditors or members, as the case may be, present and voting in person or by proxy (if the proxies are allowed) and

(ii) the scheme must be sanctioned by the court.

4. Powers of the Court. Before sanctioning a scheme under section 391, the court must examine the following :

(i) Whether the scheme converses with the provisions of law.

(ii) Whether the scheme is fair and equitable.

(iii) Whether the majority of the creditors or the members, as the case may be, are acting *bona fide.*

(iv) Whether the scheme is workable.

The court is empowered to sanction the scheme of arrangement providing for the variation of rights of the shareholder, instead of any provision to the contrary in the terms of issue of such shares or the memorandum or the articles of association of the company. However, the court must sanction a scheme of arrangement involving reduction of share capital only if the legal procedure for reduction of capital has been duly followed by the company.

Section 391(2) states that no such order should be made by a court unless it is satisfied that all the material facts of the proposed scheme are disclosed to it by the applicant.

Section 394(A) states that the court must give a notice of every application under this section to the Central Government and if any representation is made by the Central Government, that should be considered by the court before sanctioning the scheme.

5. Information of the Scheme to the Registrar. The company must file a copy of the order of court with the Registrar of Companies. The order of court will not be effective unless such copy is filed.

6. The Copy of Order to be annexed with Memorandum. A copy of the order of court must be annexed to every copy of the memorandum of association of the company, subsequently issued. In default, the company and every officer of the company, liable for the mistake which shall be punished may extend upto Rupees 10 for each copy issued in respect of which default is made.

7. All Provisions Against the Company to be stayed. After an application has been made to the court under this section, the court may at any time state any suit or proceeding against the company on such terms and conditions as the court thinks necessary. These proceedings remain stayed until the application is finally disposed off by the court.

8. Appeal to Higher Court. Any order of the court under this section will be open to appeal in any Higher Court.

9. Powers of the Court to enforce Compromise or Arrangement (Section 392). This section provides as following :

(i) When the court makes an order sanctioning a compromise or arrangement, it can supervise the carrying out of the scheme of compromise or arrangement or the Court may give such directions or make such modifications, as it considers necessary, for the proper working of the scheme of compromise or arrangement.

(ii) If the court is satisfied that the scheme of compromise or arrangement can not be worked satisfactorily with or without modifications, it can make an order for the compulsory winding up of the company.

10. Meeting of Creditors or Members. When a company calls a meeting of its creditors or any class of creditors or its members or any class of its members for passing a scheme of compromise or arrangement under section 391, section 391 states that a statement containing the terms of scheme must be sent to the members or the creditors as the case may be, along with the notice of meeting. If the notice to call the meeting is being given by way of advertisement, the above statement should either appear in the advertisement or the advertisement should point out the place at which and the manner in which the creditors or members, as the case may be, may obtain the copy of the statement, free of charge.

If the above provisions regarding the notice and the statement are not complied with, every person liable for the mistake; shall be punishable with a fine which may extend upto Rs. 500.

11. A Scheme Can be varied Only by Court. Once a scheme of compromise or arrangement has been sanctioned by a court, it can be varied only by an order of the court. It cannot be varied by the company even if all the shareholders of the company agree to do so.

AMALGAMATION

Meaning

1. To eliminate the competition.
2. To get economies of large scale production.
3. To get the economy in management and administration.
4. To create a monopoly or domination.
5. To re-organise the unsuccessful companies.

Methods of Amalgamation

1. By Sale of Shares. In this method, all the shares of a company are sold to another company and the shares are registered in the name of purchasing company, selling company receives its consideration in cash or in shares of the acquiring company. If 90 per cent of the shareholders of a class have approved the scheme, the shares of the rest shareholders can also be acquired under section 395 of the Companies Act.

2. By Sale of Undertaking (Section 394). A company may sell the whole of its undertaking to another company, provided if the purchasing company is economically sound for this. This can be done only if it is approved by court. An application may be made to the court by any person entitled to move the court. The court receives a report from the Company Law Board, whether the affairs of the company have been conducted in a manner prejudicial to the interests of members or the public interest. The court has also to give notice of every such application to the Central Government and has to take into account the representation made by the Central Government, if any, before sanctioning the scheme. The court may, then sanction the scheme and issue the necessary orders. Such an order may make provision for any of the following :

(i) Transfer of the undertaking, property or the liabilities of one company to another.

(ii) The allotment or appropriation by the transferee company of any shares, debentures, policies or other like interests in that company.

(iii) The continuation by or against the transferred company of any legal proceedings.

(iv) The dissolution without winding up.

(v) The provision to be made for any person who dissent from the scheme.

(vi) Such incidental matters as may be necessary to secure that the amalgamation shall be fully and effectively carried out.

3. By the Order of Central Government. The Central Government may order by issuing a notification for the amalgamation of two or more companies, if the Central Government is of the opinion that such amalgamation will be in the public interest. If such a notification is issued, it will contain all the terms and conditions, duties and rights under the scheme of amalgamation is to be carried out. A copy of such notification is to be presented in the Parliament.

Powers of Central Government (Section 396)

This section states as follows :

1. Order. If the Central Government is of the opinion that the amalgamation of two companies is essential in national interest, it may order for the amalgamation of those companies, by issuing a notification in the official gazette. Such notification must contain the powers, rights, interests, authorities, privileges, liabilities under which the scheme of amalgamation is to be carried out.

2. Opportunity of Hearing to the Concerned Companies. Before making the order the Central Government must send a copy of the proposed order to every concerned company and the companies must be given an opportunity to file their objections and suggestions. On receiving the objections and suggestions, the Central Government may make such modification in the order as may be seen desirable.

3. No Change in the Interest of Creditors and Members. On such amalgamation, there will be no change in the interests of the members, debenture-holders and creditors of the amalgamating companies. They will continue to have the same interests in the new company also, as they had before amalgamation in any of the amalgamated companies. If the rights of any of them is adversely affected because of such amalgamation, lie may claim compensation for such loss, which will be settled by the authority, as prescribed by the government and the amount of compensation so decided shall be paid by the new company.

4. Order to be laid Before Parliament. The Central Government is under the obligation to lay down the copy of the order before both the houses of Parliament, at an earliest possible date.

Preservation of Books and Papers

Companies (Amendment) Act, 31 of 1965, has added a new section 396A, which relates to the preservation of books of accounts and papers of the amalgamated companies. The books and papers of a company which has been amalgamated with, or whose shares have been acquired by, another company under this Chapter shall not be disposed of without the prior permission, of the Central Government and before granting such permission, that Government may appoint a person to examine the books and papers or any of them for the purpose of ascertaining whether they contain any evidence of the commission of an offence in connection with the promotion or formation, or the management of the affairs, of the first-mentioned company or its amalgamation or the acquisition of its shares.

RE-CONSTRUCTION OF A COMPANY

Meaning

Reconstruction means the formation of a new company to take over the assets of an existing company with the idea that the persons interested and nature of business remains the same. When a new company is established on the winding up of an existing company, with a view to enlarge the area of the company or to arrange the additional capital, it is called the re-construction of a company. The nature of business remains basically the same after the reconstruction :

Purpose of Re-construction

1. To strengthen the financial position of the company.
2. To overcome the defects of over capitalization
3. To collect additional capital.
4. To enlarge the area of business activities.
5. To change the place of business.

Methods of Re-construction

1. Change of Organisation. If the company appeals to the court for the re-construction under the scheme of re-organisation, it is certified by the company that the proposed re-construction is regarding the transfer of assets and liabilities of the company to any other company. The court may order for any of the following arrangement:

(i) To transfer all or a part of the assets and liabilities of the transferrer company to the transferee company.

(ii) To close the transferrer company without winding up.

(iii) To take legal action against the transferee.

(iv) To make allotment of shares and debentures.

(v) To arrange for the settlement of dissident persons.

(vi) To approve the scheme of reconstruction.

Before approving the scheme of re-construction, the court asks the Company Law Board or the Registrar of Companies to report whether the proposed scheme of re-construction is in the interest of the members of company or not. On receiving the report from the Company Law Board or the Registrar of Companies the court will consider it and if the court is satisfied with the object of the scheme of re-construction, it may allow the company to go ahead with the scheme. The court may approve the scheme in full or in part or with such modifications as it thinks fit. The company will send a copy of the application to the Central Government also, if the Central Government issues any order on such application, that should be followed by the court. The court will satisfy itself with the following :

(i) All the legal formalities have been duly complied with.

(ii) The scheme has been sanctioned by the proper representatives.

(iii) The scheme is in the interest of company.

2. Winding up. In the case of a voluntary winding up of a company, the assets and liabilities of such company are proposed to be transferred to any other company. The liquidator of the company may, under a special resolution, distribute the shares received as consideration from another company among the shareholders of the company going into winding up. Such voluntary winding up must be approved by the court.

QUESTIONS

1. Explain the meaning of the scheme of arrangement and compromise? State the provisions of Indian Companies Act regarding arrangement and compromise.
2. Explain the meaning of amalgamation. What are different methods of amalgamation of companies? State the statutory provisions regarding amalgamation.
3. Define amalgamation. Explain the powers of the Central Government for amalgamation of the companies in the national interest.

4. State the different methods of re-construction of a company. What are the legal provisions in this regard?
5. What is meant by re-construction of a company? Describe the statutory provisions regarding re-construction.
6. What are the provisions of the Companies Act, 1956 regarding arrangement for the purposes of reconstruction or amalgamation of companies?
7. How can a company make a compromise or arrangement with its members and/or creditors without going into liquidation?
8. Set out briefly the methods by which the reconstruction of a company can be carried out?
9. How may the amalgamation of a company with another company be carried out?
10. State the powers of the Central Government to provide for the amalgamation of companies in the public interest. Also explain the term 'public interest'.

PRACTICAL PROBLEMS

1. The assets of a company which is a going concern are meagre and its liabilities are heavy. The directors, who wish to avoid liquidation, propose a scheme for the reconstruction of the company involving a fresh issue of shares. Meetings of the members and creditors are thereafter held under the direction of the Court, at which the consent of the requisite 3/4th majority is obtained in favour of the scheme. Thereafter, some of the minority creditors prove before the Court that the directors had failed to disclose material facts regarding the company's financial position. Will the Court refuse the scheme on this ground?
[**Hint.** Yes (Section 391)].
2. An offer by A Co. Ltd. to purchase the whole of the issued share capital of B Co. Ltd. has been accepted by the holders of 9/10ths of the shares. What further steps (if any) can be taken by A Co. Ltd. to acquire the holdings of the dissenting shareholders?
[**Hint.** Refer to Section 395].
3. In a meeting for the sanction of a scheme under Section 391, holders of shares of the value of Rs. 6,42,700 were present but holders of shares of the value of Rs. 4,42,700 alone voted in favour of the resolution and none voted against it. Was the statutory majority required under Section 391 obtained in the meeting?
[**Hint.** Yes (Section 391)].